The Earths[...]
in Environmen[...]
and Rural L[...]hoods

Edited by

Samantha Jones
and
Grace Carswell

London and Sterling, VA

First published by Earthscan in the UK and USA in 2004

ISBN: 1-84407-053 0   paperback
        1-84407-052 2   hardback

Typesetting by Composition and Design Services
Printed and bound in the UK by Bath Press, Bath
Cover design by Andrew Corbett

For a full list of publications please contact:

Earthscan
8–12 Camden High Street
London, NW1 0JH, UK
Tel: +44 (0)20 7387 8558
Fax: +44 (0)20 7387 8998
Email: earthinfo@earthscan.co.uk
Web: **www.earthscan.co.uk**

22883 Quicksilver Drive, Sterling, VA 20166–2012, USA

Earthscan publishes in association with WWF-UK and the International Institute for Environment and Development

A catalogue record for this book is available from the British Library

Library of Congress Cataloging-in-Publication Data

The Earthscan reader in environment, development and rural livelihoods / edited by Samantha Jones and Grace Carswell
      p. cm.
   Includes bibliographical references and index.
   ISBN 1-84407-053-0   (pbk) - ISBN 1-84407-052-2 (hbk)
     1. Sustainable development-Developing Countries. 2. Economic development-Environmental Aspects-Developing countries. 3. Rural development-Environmental aspects-Developing countries. I. Jones, Samantha, 1969- II. Carswell, Grace, 1969- III. Earthscan.

HC59.72.E5E24 2004
333.7-dc22

                             2004011585

Contents

Introduction

Section I – Environmental Problems in the Tropics: Challenging the Orthodoxies

Section II – Themes in Environment and Development

IIA – Causes of Environmental Change

IIB – *Agents and Approaches in Environment and Development*

IIC – *Property, Institutions and Community-based Management*

Section III – Analytical Approaches in Environment and Development

IIIA – *Tools for Analysis*

IIIB – *Conceptual Frameworks in Environment and Development*

List of Figures, Tables and Boxes

Figures

Tables

Boxes

About the Authors

Arun Agrawal is an Associate Professor in the Department of Political Science, McGill University, Canada. His research interests include development and environmental politics; decentralization; globalization and the politics of South Asia. He has written *Greener Pastures* (1999) and is the co-editor of *Regional Modernities* (2003); *Communities and the Environment* (2001) and *Social Nature: Resources, Representation and Rule in India* (2000).

Caroline Ashley is a Research Fellow with the Rural Policy and Environment Group of the Overseas Development Institute, London. Her research interests include rural livelihoods, community-based natural resource management, pro-poor tourism strategies, and community–private partnerships. She has worked mainly in Southern and Eastern Africa. She has numerous publications with ODI, and has co-edited a special issue of *Development Policy Review* (with Simon Maxwell) entitled 'Rethinking Rural Development' (2001).

Katrina Brown is Reader in the School of Development Studies at the University of East Anglia. She specializes in environment and development issues, including environmental policy and decision-making, conservation and development, and environmental change from an interdisciplinary perspective. She is a Research Fellow at the Centre for Social and Economic Research on the Global Environment, and is co-editor of the journal *Global Environmental Change*.

Diana Carney is a freelance development consultant, currently based in Ottawa, Canada. She was previously a Research Fellow with the Overseas Development Institute where she worked closely with DFID in the development and early implementation of livelihoods thinking.

Grace Carswell is a Leverhulme Research Fellow at the University of Sussex. Her research interests include population–environment interactions, rural livelihoods in eastern Africa and agricultural change under the influence of colonialism. She has published in journals including *Journal of Agrarian Change*, *Geographical Journal* and *Journal of International Development*.

Arturo Escobar is currently Kenan Professor of Anthropology and Director, Institute of Latin American Studies, University of North Carolina, Chapel Hill. His main interests at present are: political ecology, the anthropology of development, social movement theory, and questions of globalization, violence and displacement, and the politics of place. Over the past ten years, he has worked closely with several social movements and NGOs in the Colombian Pacific, and with the Rome-based Society for International Development (SID) on projects on globalization, culture, women and place.

James Fairhead is a Professor of Social Anthropology at the University of Sussex. His research has used anthropological and historical methods to confront analytical traditions in African environmental sciences and to expose their political, social and economic commitments. More recently, he has taken an ethnographic approach to contemporary science and policy, comparing experiences in West Africa and the Caribbean. His current research looks at the ethnography of science in relation to infant immunization in West Africa and the UK. His books include *Misreading the African Landscape* (1996) and *Science, Power and Society* (2003) (both co-authored with Melissa Leach).

John Farrington is a Research Fellow in the Rural Policy and Environment Group in the Overseas Development Institute, London. He works in particular on livelihood protection and promotion, public/private partnerships, livelihood diversification and policy processes. He has a large number of publications with ODI and his books include *Development as Process* (1998) co-edited with David Mosse and Alan Rew, and *Natural Resource Management and Institutional Change* (1998) (with Diana Carney).

Clark C Gibson is an Associate Professor of Political Science at the University of California, San Diego. He has researched extensively in the field of natural resource governance, conservation and development. He has published *The Samaritan's Dilemma* (2004); *Politicians and Poachers* (1999), and co-edited *Communities and the Environment* (2001) and *People and Forests* (2000).

Samantha Jones is a Senior Lecturer in Sustainable Development at Northumbria University. Her research interests span a range of environment, development and natural resource management issues in Africa and Asia, with a particular emphasis on the application of sociological concepts to environment and development issues. She has published in journals such as *Global Environmental Change, The Journal of Rural Studies, Annals of Tourism Research* and *World Development*. Her current research examines institutions for sustainable community forestry in protected areas of Nepal.

Melissa Leach is a Professorial Research Fellow at the Institute of Development Studies, Brighton. She is a Social Anthropologist specializing in environmental and science–society issues. Research interests include social and institutional dimensions of environmental change; gender; knowledge, power and policy processes; health technologies, citizenship and participation; and social and historical perspectives on ecology, agriculture and forestry, particularly in Africa and the Caribbean. Her books include *Rainforest Relations* (1994) and *Reframing Deforestation* (1998) (co-authored with James Fairhead).

Emma Mawdsley is a lecturer at Birkbeck College, London University. She is currently exploring environmental beliefs, values and behaviours amongst India's middle classes. She is also working on a project with colleagues in Durham, India and Ghana researching the changing relationships between development NGOs and the state. Her publications include articles in *Singapore Journal of Tropical Agriculture, Progress in Development Studies, Journal of International Development* and *The Journal of Commonwealth and Comparative Politics.*

Valentina Mazzucato is a researcher at the Department of General and Development Economics, Vrije Universiteit Amsterdam and at the Department of Geography and Planning, University of Amsterdam. She is currently heading a research programme on transnational migration between Europe and Africa. She has also worked on the socio-economic aspects of technology adoption amongst farmers in Burkina Faso as well as on the effects of national agricultural research programmes on the livelihoods of West African farmers. She has published (partly jointly with David Niemeijer) in *Development and Change, Economic Geography, Geoderma, Environment and Population, Society and Place.*

David Niemeijer is an Environmental Geographer at Wageningen University. He is currently working on environmental indicators in relation to food production as well as on land degradation and desertification issues. He is also one of the lead authors of the drylands chapter of the Millennium Ecosystem Assessment. He has carried out a joint study with Valentina Mazzucato on the dynamics of local soil and water conservation practices in eastern Burkina Faso. He has also worked on the relationship between soil suitability and land use in Benin, and the development of GIS tools to visualize the relation between forests and forest product flows in Cameroon. He has published (partly jointly with Valentina Mazzucato) in *Development and Change, Economic Geography, Geoderma, Environment, Environmental Science and Policy* and *Land Degradation and Development.*

Sergio Rosendo is Senior Research Associate at the Centre for Social and Economic Research on the Global Environment, part of the University of East Anglia's (UEA) Zucherman Institute for Connective Environmental Research. His research explores institutional challenges associated with environmental governance, adopting a multi-level, cross-scale analytical perspective. His recent work has focused on collaborative approaches to natural resources management and on integrated responses to environmental change. He is also Fellow of the Millennium Ecosystem Assessment, an international initiative aimed at understanding the consequences of ecosystem change for human well-being and options to respond to such changes. His PhD, which he received from UEA's School of Development Studies in July 2003, examined the institutional dynamics of extractive reserves in Brazilian Amazonia.

Cate Turton is a principal consultant with the IDL group (www.theidlgroup.com). Her work focuses on the development of policies, institutions and organizations which support the livelihoods of vulnerable groups in marginalized environments and situations of chronic conflict and political instability. She has a particular interest in developing approaches to promote equitable natural resources and livelihood opportunities in post-conflict environments.

Chapter Sources

Section I

Environmental Problems in the Tropics: Challenging the Orthodoxies

1   Fairhead J and Leach M (1995) 'False Forest History, Complicit Social Analysis: Rethinking Some West African Environmental Narratives', *World Development*, vol 23, no 6, pp1023–1035

2   Carswell G (2003) 'Continuities in Environmental Narratives: The Case of Kabale, Uganda, 1930–2000', *Environment and History*, vol 9, no 1, pp3–29

Section II: Themes in Environment and Development

IIA – Causes of Environmental Change

3   Mazzucato V and Niemeijer D (2002) 'Population Growth and the Environment in Africa: Local Informal Institutions, the Missing Link', *Economic Geography* vol 78, no 2, pp171–193

IIB – Agents and Approaches in Environment and Development

4   Brown K and Rosendo S (2000) 'Environmentalists, Rubber Tappers and Empowerment: The Politics and Economics of Extractive Reserves', *Development and Change*, vol 31, no 1, pp201–227

5   Mawdsley E (1998) 'After Chipko: From Environment to Region in Uttaranchal', *Journal of Peasant Studies*, vol 25, no 4, pp36–54

IIC – Property, Institutions and Community-based Management

6   Agrawal A and Gibson CC (1999) 'Enchantment and Disenchantment: The Role of Community in Natural Resource Management', *World Development*, vol 27, no 4, pp629–649

Section III: Analytical Approaches in Environment and Development

IIIA – Tools for Analysis

IIIB – Conceptual Frameworks in Environment and Development

Acknowledgements

Samantha Jones would like to thank Sandie Lowen, of University College Chichester, for her administrative assistance. Grace Carswell would like to thank the Leverhulme Trust, who supported her with the award of a Special Research Fellowship. They would both also like to thank the Geography Department and Development Studies, of the School of Social Sciences and Cultural Studies, University of Sussex, for their financial contributions towards the publication of this Reader.

List of Acronyms and Abbreviations

AFRENA	Agroforestry Research Networks for Africa
AHI	African Highlands Initiative
CBNRM	community-based natural resource management
CIAT	Centre International d'Agricole Tropical
CIDA	Canadian International Development Agency
CNS	National Council of Rubber Tappers
DAO	District Agricultural Officer
DFID	UK Department for International Development
DGSS	Dasholi Gram Swarajya Sangh
DTC	development through conservation
FAO	Food and Agriculture Organization of the United Nations
GAD	Gender and Development
GED	Gender, Environment and Development
HPI	Heifer Project International
ICRAF	International Centre for Research on Agroforestry
IDRC	International Development Research Centre
IGCP	International Gorilla Conservation Project
IUCN	The World Conservation Union
JFM	Joint Forest Management
MBIFCT	Mgahinga Bwindi Inpenetrable Forest Conservation Trust
NEMA	National Environment Management Authority
NEMA	National Environmental Management Authority
NGO	non-governmental organization
NR	natural resources
OBC	other backwards classes
OSR	Rondônia Organization of Rubber Tappers
PIPs	Policy, Institutions and Processes
PLANAFLORO	Rondônia Natural Resources Management Project
PPR	pressure of population on resources
PRA	Participatory Rural Appraisal
RRA	Rapid Rural Appraisal
SA	stakeholder analysis
SEDA	Sustainable Energy Development Authority
SL	sustainable livelihoods
SLA	Sustainable Livelihoods Approach
TLU	tropical livestock unit

UFSI	Uganda Food Security Initiative
UNDP	United Nations Development Programme
USAID	United States Agency for International Development
WED	Women, Environment and Development
WID	Women in Development
WILD	Wildlife Integration for Livelihood Diversification
WWF	World Wide Fund for Nature

Introduction

Samantha Jones and Grace Carswell

Presented in this book is a selection of key articles that have been published over the last decade or so in the field of 'environment and development'. A proliferation of research in this field has helped carve out its identity as a sub-discipline of geography, environmental studies and development studies. While a few monographs bring some coherence to the field (eg Adams' (1990, 2001), *Green Development* and Forsyth's (2003) *Critical Political Ecology*), because of the interdisciplinary nature of the subject and the range of disciplinary backgrounds from which authors write, important contributions to the field can be located in a range of journals, in subjects as diverse as environmental history, anthropology, planning and political science. Edited volumes such as *Liberation Ecologies* (Peet and Watts, 1996), *Political Ecology* (Stott and Sullivan, 2000) and *The Lie of the Land* (Leach and Mearns, 1996) have captured some of the interesting critical research that has been conducted (exploring 'post-structural political ecology' and the destabilization of environmental orthodoxies). This text though, is the first of its kind. It is an edited volume that provides a more holistic coverage of the field of 'environment and development', albeit from a largely micro-level and rural perspective.

Blaikie (1985) and Blaikie and Brookfield (1987) may be attributed with writing the first key texts to draw attention to the way in which the environment (and, to a lesser extent, society) may be better understood by exploring the socio-political context in which people use the environment. Earlier studies tended to be quite technical, focusing on the physical environment, or more anthropological, with the tendency to see communities in isolation from wider society. Since their work, studies examining human–environment interactions in poor countries have flourished. The effects of the environment on people's opportunities and livelihood strategies; the impacts of resource use on the environment; and the social relations stemming from competition for scarce resources have all been dominant themes. More recently, due in part to the increasing availability of environmental data, the diversification of research methodologies and theoretical frameworks and cross-disciplinary work, the field has been moving in new and fruitful directions. It is the purpose of this text to map out some of these avenues of research.

Outline of the Book

This book is divided into three parts. The first part is dedicated towards exploring the ways in which the environment and environmental change have been conceptualized or (mis)understood. This area of enquiry is significant, not least because it has led to some substantial revisions and advances in scientific understandings of the environment, such as ecological dynamics, and has also helped to give greater credibility to local environmental knowledges.

The second part highlights a number of defined thematic areas in the environment and development literature and is divided into three sections. The first deals with key debates over two factors primarily blamed for environmental problems – population and poverty. A considerable degree of critical reflection has taken place in recent years with respect to some widely held erroneous assumptions that have perpetuated inappropriate policy directions in these areas. The second deals with key actors (and, to a lesser extent, approaches) in the environment and development arena, ranging from the micro/project level to the macro/movement level. The final part of the section shifts the emphasis towards property relations – or the relationship between people and natural resources. Debates over the ideal type of property relations to secure sustainable and equitable management of natural resources have raged for considerable time, but interesting innovations more recently, around the approaches of co-management and 'community-based natural resource management', have generated considerable optimism in this field.

The third part of the book focuses on environment and development in practice and in theory. Thus, the first part draws together some conceptual frameworks that are frequently used as tools in the field, developed for better understanding human–environment interactions and supporting sustainable development initiatives. The second part adopts a more academic slant and highlights some of the frameworks, theories and philosophies guiding research in environment and development.

All the contributions offered here are exemplary in their critical wisdom, or form excellent examples of new ways of looking at human–environment interactions in the developing world. At the same time, it is the intention to provide contributions that together, give a broad geographical and thematic coverage of relevant literature, and discuss a diversity of environments or natural resources. The text makes no attempt to provide an overview of the 'state of the environment' in developing countries or evaluate rates of environmental change (if such a text is sought, refer to Barrow (1995) or Gupta and Asher (1998)). Such aggregate level studies are fraught with uncertainty and tend to reflect inadequately on the processes underlying change. Thus most of the contributions included have in common a micro-perspective, which yields detailed empirically informed case studies, contextualized within wider socio-economic relations. This book should prove useful to undergraduate and masters students with environment and development forming all or part of their programmes of study, and to practitioners in the field wishing to gain an overview of academic debates.

The editorial introductions aim to contextualize each of the contributions, locating them in the wider debates in the field. Clearly, there are many alternative articles that would have been invaluable inclusions to this text but could not be incorporated due to the obvious constraints of space. As such, the intention is that the editorial introductions also serve as a useful bibliographic resource, pointing the reader to further resources and enabling chosen lines of enquiry to be pursued with greater ease. Issues such as gender, that are central to this field, are not dealt with in a discrete way here but emerge as a recurrent theme throughout the text, reflecting the importance of its integration into analyses rather than being 'added on' as a separate concern. Similarly other themes may be dealt with in specific sections but re-emerge in others (such as critiques of neo-

Malthusian reasoning, historically contextualized and differentiated approaches and attention to power relations), with the intention of reiterating their significance and providing greater coherence to the text.

Environment in 'Environment and Development'

Generally 'the environment', in the context of environment and development, can be taken to refer to both 'natural resources' – particularly renewable natural resources – and 'nature' or the 'natural' environment. In the former case, the environment, as a resource is valued for the prospect of consumptive use. This will be the main aspect of the environment explored in this book, as it is so central to the livelihoods of poor people in poor countries. It has been the intention to refer to studies of a range of renewable natural resources, such as water, land, forests, fisheries, rangelands and wildlife. Other renewable natural resources such as energy and air (quality) and non-renewable natural resources, however, have been excluded because of space constraints. Energy and air quality concerns tend to be greater in urban environments, where also the relative importance of the environment as a 'sink' tends to be more pertinent than that of the environment as a 'source', which as stated above, is the focus of this text.

In the latter case, the 'natural' environment, if it is valued in its state of 'naturalness' may be regarded to have non-consumptive value. This type of value is particularly prevalent among western visitors to the protected areas (such as National Parks) in developing countries. While in this context 'nature' may be valued for its intrinsic worth, studies have pointed to the fact that these environments are thoroughly socially produced, their very 'nature' stemming from long histories of human management (see, for example, Homewood and Rodgers (1987) and Agrawal and Gibson, this volume). 'De-peopling' such environments, through the discourse of biodiversity among international conservation organizations, for instance, has legitimized power over them (and their inhabitants). Less attention in this text is given to non-consumptive use of the environment, although relations of power and control over resources are key themes running throughout.

Environmental degradation is central to many studies in the field of environment and development. There have been many 'crisis' findings in terms of the extent and rate of degradation in the developing world, and this area occupies a considerable proportion of the environment and development literature (forming the first part of this text). However, as Blaikie and Brookfield (1987) can be credited with noting, 'degradation' is a particularly relative notion – what one person experiences as degradation another might view as improvement. For example, Leach and Mearns (1996) explain that professional foresters and ecologists in Africa have conventionally valued closed canopy forest – almost defining forest in these terms – such that any conversion of this vegetation is viewed to constitute degradation. Yet such a conversion may be viewed positively by local inhabitants where bush fallow vegetation might provide a greater range of gathered products. The term 'degradation', then, is problematic and it is important to ascertain for whom degradation is occurring and why it constitutes degradation to that user group.

However, perhaps more significantly, not only does the value placed on particular environments vary among different user groups, but so too does the relative evaluation of environmental change itself. In a post-positivist era, scientific assessments are no longer accepted uncritically. A mounting body of literature considers why assessments of environmental change are fraught with uncertainty, inaccuracy and are open to multiple interpretations (see Stocking, 1987, for example, for land degradation). In some spheres this has led authors to suggest that science's reductionist methodology is inappropriate for complex ecological and environmental systems (O'Riordan, 1995). While many would not go so far as to reject science explicitly, it is increasingly commonplace to find acceptance of the view of nature and the environment as socially constructed. Neefjes (2000) for example, starts his book with the following: 'Environments are contested. Different people see them differently, have different interests in them and have different relationships with them.' (Neefjes, 2000, p1). The constructed and contested nature of environmental 'problems' is clearly illustrated in the first part of this text and is dealt with in a more theoretical and philosophical sense in the final section.

Development in 'Environment and Development'

In contrast with the environment, which can be viewed to have a substantial quality, development is 'an idea, an objective and an activity' (Kothari and Minogue, 2002, p12). Some dramatic shifts in thinking about the meanings and definitions of development and the development process have occurred over the last 50 years accompanied by various development theories. These are outlined briefly below inasmuch as they have implications for social and environmental interventions in the developing world, which are reflected upon subsequently.

Modernization theory gained ground in the 1950s and presented an optimistic view of development in the sense that economic growth and industrialization were regarded to be a desirable and achievable path for all countries. Rostow's model, which epitomized modernization theory, suggested that transfers of technology, capital and expertise from the developed world would facilitate the transformation from 'traditional society' to a society of 'high mass consumption', as the benefits of development trickled down to the masses. As it became evident in the 1960s that inequalities persisted alongside industrialization and increasing GNP, more radical perspectives emerged, emanating particularly from Latin American scholars such as Andre Gunder Frank. In what became known as dependency theory, development and underdevelopment were regarded as two sides of the same coin, as the condition of developing countries reflected their incorporation into the global capitalist system. Chains of dependent and exploitative relations between the 'core' and the 'periphery' accounted for persistent underdevelopment, rather than underdevelopment being regarded as a temporary pre-capitalist stage as it had in modernization theory. (For a more in-depth discussion of these theories, see Gardner and Lewis, 1996; Potter et al, 1999; Hettne, 1990; Webster, 1990; Schuurman, 1993.)

Development theory has conventionally been described in terms of these two opposing paradigms (Gardner and Lewis, 1996), and in postmodern terminology, they have been critiqued as excessively deterministic 'grand-narratives' (that is, overarching explanatory theoretical frameworks, see Simon, 1997). This critique is postulated to have contributed to 'the demise of development theory' or an impasse in development studies (in addition to the 1980s being the 'lost decade' in development, characterized by economic crisis, the persistent failure of development practice and a widening gap between rich and poor). In the 1990s, and conceivably in response to this, greater attention has been given to 'human agency', as social actors are viewed as knowledgeable and capable strategizing agents rather than passive recipients of development (eg Long and Long, 1992). Development practice has become increasingly eclectic with emphasis on diversity and the primacy of local experience (Gardner and Lewis, 1996). While a multiplicity of ideologies and modes of explanation co-exist (Simon, 1997), the spotlight is on the actors in the development process and not so specifically on mechanistic processes (Schuurman, 1993).

Simultaneously, neo-liberal thought has become the new orthodoxy strongly influencing development policy (Cammack, 2002). This advocates economic liberalization and a reduction in the scope of government including in the provision of services and is regarded to be a reformulation of modernization theory (Kothari and Minogue, 2002). Informing the policies of the World Bank and the International Monetary Fund in particular, the elimination of market imperfections and market inhibiting social institutions has been a key goal. However, as the withdrawal of the state has led to the increasing impoverishment of low income groups (Schuurman, 1993) 'social safety nets' have been 'added-on' to Structural Adjustment Programmes. For Nederveen Pieterse (2001) this illustrates the 'zig-zag' character of development thinking. Another example of this is the recent highly influential debate on social capital emanating from both within and outside the World Bank (stemming from the work of Putnam (1993)), that has demonstrated the centrality of the 'social fabric' (social co-ordination and cooperation, rules, networks etc) in economic growth (see IIIB).

In terms of development policy and practice, emphasis shifted from technology and capital transfer under the modernization approach, to the provision of 'basic needs' as a policy outgrowth of dependency critiques of modernization. However, as Potter et al (1999) note, the provision of basic needs was still approached with universalistic solutions, and assumptions were made about what local people wanted. To counter this trend in the 1990s, led by the Farmer First literature of Robert Chambers and the 1992 Earth Summit, and consistent with the theoretical emphasis on diversity and human agency, 'bottom-up approaches' were called for. The emerging orientation of development policy towards participation, empowerment and capacity-building has been represented as something of a 'paradigm shift' in development policy (Shepherd, 1998) although Gardner and Lewis (1996) question whether it represents a significant challenge to the dominant discourse or merely the co-option of challenges to it. A leading role for non-governmental organizations (NGOs) in the development process became part of this discourse, simultaneously filling the 'service gap' arising from the withdrawal of the state (see Section IIB).

In theoretical terms, attention to power relations, differentiated interests, negotiation and 'knowledge interfaces' has taken the bottom-up approach a stage further (eg Beyond Farmer First, Scoones and Thompson, 1994). Also there have been more radical alternatives to the 'development from below' discourse, by authors such as Escobar who make a call for autonomy, endogenous change, transfers of power and resources, alternative development paths and the support of new social movements (Potter et al, 1999). Such anti-(or post-)development theorists (Such as Sachs, 1992; Escobar, 1995; Rahnema and Bawtree, 1997) challenge the western construction of development (that is the objective of the 'post-World War II development project' to engineer particular changes in the so-called 'Third World', Matthews, 2004) and the homogenizing effects that its imposition has on local cultures. However, this perspective has been the focus of much criticism, not least for romanticizing indigenous cultures and the objectives and potential of new social movements and for limited proposal of alternatives to development (see Potter et al, 1999; Lehmann, 1997; Nederveen Pieterse, 2001, for example).

Just as indicators of development have mirrored development thinking – crudely speaking from GNP per capita (modernization), to social indicators of basic needs provision (dependency/neo-Marxist) to wellbeing, consciousness, capacity and power ('post-impasse') – so too have other areas intersecting with development. Approaches to gender have been traced (eg by Barrett, 1995, Leach et al, 1995) from those under modernization approaches which assumed that income was pooled, that all household members worked together for the same ends and therefore that women could be incorporated into development projects as unpaid family labour (see Dey, 1981 for an example of irrigation projects in the Gambia), to those targeting women specifically to meet their basic needs (labelled Women in Development or WID approaches). Recognizing that power relations must be understood for any real improvement in the position of women in society, Gender and Development (GAD) approaches emerged stressing women's empowerment and the removal of 'false consciousness'.

When the environment is brought into the equation a similar shift has been called for. Women, Environment and Development (WED) approaches have been critiqued for essentializing women as 'victims of environmental degradation' or 'efficient managers'. WED also encompasses ecofeminist perspectives where women are assumed to have a natural affinity with nature, and women's and environmental interests are seen as complementary (see Jackson, 1993; Agarwal, 1992 and Leach et al, 1995). In place of WED, Gender, Environment and Development (GED) is advocated, entailing an analysis of 'gendered micro-political economy of resource use' (Leach, 1991). Under GED, the divisions of responsibilities, rights, activities between men as well as women are studied in the context of how wider social relations of gender pattern resource use. This perspective avoids treating women as a homogenous group (for excellent examples from the Gambia, see Carney, 1993 and Schroeder, 1993, 1997). GED is also known as feminist political ecology (Rocheleau, et al 1996) and feminist environmentalism (Agarwal, 1992).

The shifts in development policy also have implications for environment and development. For example, under the neo-liberal agenda the environment has been reconceptualized as a form of capital ('natural capital') as in the Sustainable Livelihoods framework (see IIIA), which generates a perspective in which it can be readily substituted with other forms of capital (Pearce et al, 1989). In recognition of the capacity of institutions to effectively regulate resource use, there is a trend towards the control of non-privately owned resources being devolved from the state to the community, as indigenous knowledge forms a foundation for natural resource management, and may be superseding the more managerialist types of intervention (rhetorically, at least). A greater role for environmental NGOs and application of the discourse of participation and empowerment in environmental spheres is evident (see sections IIB and IIC). In line with more post-development perspectives, interest in grassroots environmental movements has flourished.

The Relationship between Environment and Development and the Notion of Sustainable Development

While Redclift (1989, p2) notes that 'the environment is frequently placed in jeopardy by development', it was not until the late 1970s that important changes in thinking regarding environment and development were causing two previously separate issues to be seen as interdependent concerns (Elliott, 1999). There was a growing recognition that the goals of environment and development were no longer regarded to be conflicting but were indeed the same (Lele, 1991; Barbier, 1987, citing Bartlemus, 1986).

The concept of *sustainable development*, emerging from the mid 1980s with the World Conservation Strategy (1980), Our Common Future (1987) and the Rio Earth Summit (1992), has become one of the best known and most frequently cited terms relating to environment and development (Adams, 2001). A vast body of literature has emerged reviewing in-depth, the origins of the concept, its meaning and application (eg Lele, 1991; Frazier, 1997; Rao, 2000; Adams, 2001). It has been approached from an economic perspective (eg Barbier, 1987 and Pezzey, 1992), and ecological perspective (eg Munn, 1989) and comparisons of the two (eg Tisdell, 1988).

While conceptually, it has been noted that sustainable development can be incorporated without effort into both 'blue' (neo-liberal) and 'red' (socialist) development models (Schuurman, 1993), in practice, sustainable development has presented a potential greenwash over 'business-as-usual' (Adams, 2001, pxvi). A growing optimism has developed that represents something of a shift from the pessimistic scenarios of the 1970s, with concerns about the 'limits to growth', emphasizing a trade-off between development (economic growth at least) and environmental quality, towards stressing a more complementary relationship between them and the potential for the 'growth of limits' (Adams, 1995, Escobar, this volume). As Adams (1995) notes, the success of mainstream sustainable development is due very largely to its compatibility with technocratic, managerial, capitalist and modernist ideology. Our Common Future is entirely consistent with the economic paradigms of the industrial north, focusing on fairly minor reforms (Adams, 1995).

Yet sustainable development is a highly contested and problematic term. For example, Adams (2001) asserts that northern environmentalists are to be credited for the infusion of environmental concerns into the development discourse and environmentalism in turn embodies a broad range of thinking (see O'Riordan, 1981; O'Riordan and Turner, 1983 and Elliott, 1999 for an account of the spectrum of environmental thinking, and Pepper, 1984; Eckersley, 1995; Hannigan, 1995 for a history of western environmental thinking). As such, the mainstream discourse of sustainable development is implicitly challenged by the radical stream of environmentalism, as discussed by Adams (1995). Furthermore, Redclift (1989) notes, adopting the terminology of Robert Chambers (1983, 1989), sustainable development is 'first' thinking (ie the enlightened rich) rather than 'last' (where the poor are concerned more directly about livelihoods). He suggests a mental leap is required along the lines of sustainable livelihoods thinking, which has now indeed, become a major approach in environment and development employed by the Department for International Development, for example (see Section IIIA). Redclift's critique is echoed by anti-development theorists who give attention to the power relations implicit in the construction of the discourse of sustainable development (see Escobar, this volume).

Notions of sustainable development, and accounts of the relationship between environment and development are implicit in a number of the contributions in this text but are not explicitly engaged with further. We find some sympathy with Frazier's (1997, p182) view that the 'the term is a source of confusion, contention and even deception' and Adams's (2001, pxvi) assertion that the 'rhetorical vagueness of that master-phrase "sustainable development" has made it far too easy for hard questions to be ignored, stifled in a quilt of smoothly crafted and well-meaning platitudes'. Furthermore, the term may now be most strongly associated with the international policy making arena, in areas of climate and energy in particular, the examination of which is beyond the scope of this text.

References

Adams, W M (1995) 'Green development theory? Environmentalism and sustainable development', in Crush J *Power of Development*, Routledge, London

Adams, W M (1990, 2001) *Green Development: Environment and Sustainability in the Third World*, Routledge, London

Agarwal, B (1992) 'The gender and environment debate: lessons from India'. *Feminist Studies* 18(1): 119–158

Barbier, E B (1987) 'The concept of sustainable economic development'. *Environmental Conservation* 14(2): 101–110

Barrett, H (1995) 'Women in Africa: The neglected dimension in development'. *Geography* 80(3): 215–224

Barrow, C J (1995) *Developing the Environment: Problems and Management*, Longman, Harlow

Blaikie, P (1985) *The Political Economy of Soil Erosion in Developing Countries*, Longman, Harlow

Blaikie, P and Brookfield, H (1987) (eds) *Land Degradation and Society*, Methuen, London

Cammack, P (2002) 'Neoliberalism, the World Bank and the new politics of development', in Kothari, U and Minogue, M (eds) *Development Theory and Practice: Critical Perspectives*, Palgrave, Hampshire, 157–178

Carney, J (1993) 'Converting the wetlands, engendering the environment: the intersection of gender with agrarian change in The Gambia'. *Economic Geography* 69(4): 329–348

Chambers, R (1983) *Rural Development: Putting the Last First*, Longman, Harlow

Chambers, R et al (1989) (eds) *Farmer First*, Intermediate Technology Publications, London

Dey, J (1981) 'Gambian women: Unequal partners in rice development projects?'. *Journal of Development Studies* 17(3): 107–122

Eckersley, R (1992) *Environmentalism and Political Theory*, UCL Press, London

Elliott, J A (1999) (2nd edition) *An Introduction to Sustainable Development*, Routledge, London

Forsyth, T (2003) *Critical Political Ecology: The Politics of Environmental Science*, Routledge, London

Frazier, J G (1997) 'Sustainable development: modern elixir or sack dress?'. *Environmental Conservation* 24(2): 182–193

Gardner, K and Lewis, D (1996) *Anthropology, Development and the Post-modern Challenge*, Pluto Press, London

Gupta, A and Asher, M G (1998) *Environment and the Developing World: Principles, Policies and Management*, Wiley, Chichester

Hannigan, J (1995) *Environmental Sociology: A Social Constructionist Perspective*, Routledge, London

Hettne, B (1990) *Development Theory and the Three Worlds*, Longman, Harlow

Homewood, K and Rodgers, W A (1987) 'Pastoralism, conservation and the overgrazing controversy', in Anderson, D M and Grove, R (eds) *Conservation in Africa: People, Policies and Practice*, Cambridge University Press, Cambridge

Jackson, C (1993) 'Doing what comes naturally? Women and environment in development'. *World Development* 21(12): 1947–1963

Kothari, U and Minogue, M (2002) (eds) *Development Theory and Practice: Critical Perspectives*, Palgrave, Hampshire

Leach, M (1991) 'Engendered environments: Understanding natural resource management in the West African Forest Zone'. *IDS Bulletin* 22(4): 17–24

Leach, M and Mearns, R (1996) *The Lie of the Land: Challenging received wisdom on the African environment*, James Currey, Oxford/Heinemann, Portsmouth

Leach, M, Joekes, S and Green C (1995) 'Gender relations and environmental change'. *IDS Bulletin* 26(1): 1–8

Lehmann, D (1997) 'An opportunity lost: Escobar's deconstruction of development'. *Journal of Development Studies* 33(4): 568–577

Lele, S M (1991) 'Sustainable development: a critical review'. *World Development* 19(6): 607–621

Long, N and Long, A (1992) (eds) *Battlefields of Knowledge*, Routledge, London

Matthews, S (2004) 'Post-development theory and the question of alternatives: A view from Africa'. *Third World Quarterly,* 25(2): 373–384

Munn, R E (1989) 'Towards sustainable development: an environmental perspective'. *Development* 2(3): 70-79

Nederveen Pieterse, J (2001) *Development Theory: Deconstructions/Reconstruction*, Sage Publication, London

Neefjes, K (2000) *Environments and Livelihoods: Strategies for Sustainability*, Oxfam, Oxford

O'Riordan, T (1981) *Environmentalism*, Pion, London

O'Riordan, T (1995) (ed) *Environmental Science for Environmental Management*, Longman, Harlow

O'Riordan, T and Turner, R K (1983) 'The nature of the environmental idea: Introductory essay', in O'Riordan, T and Turner, R K (eds) *An Annotated Reader in Environmental Management*, Pergamon, Oxford: 1–17

Pearce, D, Markandya, A and Barbier, E (1989) *Blueprint for a Green Economy*, Earthscan, London

Peet, R and Watts, M (1996) *Liberation Ecologies*, Routledge, London

Pepper, D (1984) *The Roots of Modern Environmentalism*, Routledge, London

Pezzey, J (1992) 'Sustainability: An interdisciplinary guide'. *Environmental Values* 1: 321–362

Potter, R B et al (1999) *Geographies of Development*, Longman, Harlow

Putnam, R (1993) *Making Democracy Work: Civic Traditions in Modern Italy*, Princeton University Press, Princeton

Rahnema, M and Bawtree, V (1997) *The Post-Development Reader*, Zed Books, London

Rao, P K (2000) *Sustainable Development: Economics and Policy*, Blackwell, Oxford

Redclift, M (1989) *Sustainable Development: Exploring the Contradictions*, Methuen, London

Rocheleau, D, Thomas-Slater, B and Wangari, E (1996) *Feminist Political Ecology*, Routledge, London

Sachs, W (1992) (ed) *The Development Dictionary: A Guide to Knowledge as Power*, Zed Books, London

Schroeder, R A (1993) 'Shady practice: gender and the political ecology of resource stabilization in Gambian garden/orchards'. *Economic Geography* **69**(4): 349–365

Schroeder, R A (1997) 'Reclaiming' land in The Gambia: Gendered property rights and environmental intervention'. *Annals of the Association of American Geographers* **87**(3): 487–508

Schuurman, F J (1993) 'Introduction: Development theory in the 1990s' in Schuurman F J (ed) *Beyond the Impasse: New Directions in Development Theory*, Zed Books, London

Scoones, I and Thompson, J (1994) *Beyond Farmer First*, Intermediate Technology Publications, London

Shepherd, A (1998) *Sustainable Rural Development*, Macmillan Press, Basingstoke and London

Simon, D (1997) 'Development reconsidered: New directions in development thinking'. *Geografiska Annaler* **79B**(4): 183–199

Stocking, M (1987) 'Measuring land degradation', in Blaikie, P and Brookfield, H (1987) (eds) *Land Degradation and Society*, Methuen, London

Stott, P and Sullivan, S (eds) *Political Ecology: Science, Myth and Power*, Arnold, London

Tisdell, C W (1988) 'Sustainable development: differing perspectives of ecologists and economists, and relevance to LDCs'. *World Development* **16**(3): 373–384

Webster, A (1990) *Introduction to the Sociology of Development*, 2nd Edition, Macmillan, Basingstoke

Section I

Environmental Problems in the Tropics: Challenging the Orthodoxies

Introduction – Section I:
Environmental Problems in the Tropics:
Challenging the Orthodoxies

Grace Carswell and Samantha Jones

Focusing on specific types of environment in the tropics, Part I of the book discusses some of the narratives and orthodoxies around the environment in the developing world. Recent literature on each of these environments has aimed to dispel 'myths' regarding the nature of the environment and the causes of problems in these areas, and the contributions here highlight revised understandings of these different environments drawing on detailed empirical studies. This short introductory section picks up on a number of themes that are raised in the following sections. They include the establishment and development of narratives around different types of environment; the role of human agency; changing views about people's impact on the environment; the significance of indigenous knowledge; 'new ecology' and equilibrium; and the importance of interdisciplinarity.

Narratives

A narrative is a 'story' (Roe, 1991) with a beginning, middle and end, often in the form of a cause, effect and solution. Narratives have apparently incontrovertible logic that provides scripts and justifications for development action. The power of policy narratives in environmental planning in developing countries has been recognized in recent years, and reference is being made increasingly to narratives in the development and environment literature (Roe, 1991; Whatmore and Boucher, 1993; Fairhead and Leach, 1995; Forsyth, 1996; Swift, 1996; McCann, 1997; Marcusson, 1999; Kull, 2000; Carswell, this volume). As Hoben states:

> The environmental policies promoted by colonial regimes and later by donors in Africa rest on historically grounded, culturally constructed paradigms that at once describe a problem and prescribed its solution. Many of them are rooted in a narrative that tells us how things were in an earlier time when people lived in harmony with nature, how human agency has altered that harmony, and of the calamities that will plague people and nature if dramatic action is not taken soon (Hoben, 1995, p1008).

He notes that successful programmes (in terms of mobilizing funds, etc) are those that:

depend on a set of more or less naïve, unproven, simplifying and optimistic assumptions about the problem to be addressed and the approach to be taken. Without such a cultural script for action it is difficult for donors and aid recipients to mobilize and coordinate concerted action in the face of the many uncertainties that characterize processes of economic, political and institutional change (Hoben, 1996, p187).

Received wisdoms are not necessarily new, and Leach and Mearns note that 'in many cases, the ideas that drive contemporary environmental policy in Africa can be traced back to early colonial times' (Rocheleau et al, 1995; Leach and Mearns, 1996, p9; Swift, 1996; Mackenzie, 2000; Carswell, this volume). The colonial legacy of environmental assumptions and narratives has been inherited by post-Independence governments, and donor agencies have also 'joined the state and national elites in perpetuating received thinking about environment–society relationships' (Leach and Mearns, 1996, p23; Carswell, this volume). In the case of the narrative around 'desertification' Swift has noted that this concept has 'less to do with science than with the competing claims of different political and bureaucratic constituencies' (1996, p73). Thus the origins and reproduction of conventional wisdom stem largely from colonial discourse and is perpetuated by post-colonial science, the media and the structure of development consultancy (see also Keeley and Scoones, 1999).

To take the example of fuelwood, narratives about the 'fuelwood crisis' have been termed the 'Fuelwood Orthodoxy' (Cline-Cole et al, 1990) or 'Gap Theory' (Leach and Mearns, 1988). This view holds that widespread deforestation is the result of increased fuelwood demand, radiating out from centres of habitation. A linear relationship is regarded to exist between population growth and fuelwood consumption and the projected difference between resource availability and population amounts to the fuelwood gap (see, for example, Timberlake, 1985; Harrison, 1987). Various empirical studies have critiqued this view, noting first that much deforestation stems from causes other than population growth (eg drought in Mali, Benjaminsen, 1997; incorporation of communities into the world market, Lohmann, 1993; land clearance in Nigeria, Cline-Cole et al, 1990). Second, most fuelwood harvested does not cause deforestation because it is from dead trees (eg Mali, Benjaminsen, 1997) or lopped branches (eg Nepal, Ives and Messerli, 1989). Third, the relationship between population growth and fuelwood consumption is mediated by urbanization (especially if other fuel sources are available), household size and composition (larger households do not need proportionally more fuel), population mobility, culture, ecology, market, etc. (Cline-Cole et al, 1990). Cline Cole et al's (1990) study around Kano in Northern Nigeria demonstrated tree densities were highest where population density was highest, due to planting, coppicing and protection of spontaneous seedlings. Their work is an excellent example of the way in which a deeper and thoroughly empirically-informed study can generate findings that challenge 'received wisdom' which also highlights the need to re-evaluate the role of people (see below).

Leach and Mearns have observed that 'by making 'stabilizing' assumptions to facilitate decision-making, narratives serve to standardize, package and label environmental problems so that they appear to be universally applicable and to justify equally standardized, off-the-shelf solutions' (Leach and Mearns, 1996, p8). Such 'received wisdoms' have had the effect of promoting external intervention in the control and use of natural resources, which in turn can have negative consequences for local people. It is for this reason that a focus on narratives is important, as they have a very real impact on policy (Swift, 1996; Carswell, this volume; see also Keeley and Scoones (1999) who examine how 'received wisdoms' get established in policy.) Being 'simplifications of cause–consequence relations' (Lambin et al, 2001) they have gained popular status and suggest simple technical solutions. There is a considerable literature now that highlights various narratives of environmental degradation and 'de-bunks' myths in a range of environments. Some of them are presented as examples in the following sections, while others include Scoones (1997); Batterbury et al (1997); Forsyth (1998); Lambin et al (2001) and Adger et al (2001).

Human Agency and Indigenous Knowledge

One central feature of these narratives is the negative role given to local people. The contributions which follow call into question, in environments ranging from forests to highlands, the negative view of people's impact on the environment. Leach and Fairhead (2000) refer to the 'preoccupation' with people's impact on 'pristine' and barely disturbed forest environments. There is an assumption that expanding farming populations progressively degrade forest land and resources and a widely held view that the conversion of land for agriculture is the major cause of deforestation (Fairhead and Leach, this volume). Their work, however, challenges this strongly negative view of human activity and they call for a reconsideration of people–forest relations. They identify three ways in which people have a positive impact on the forest: farming practices that modify soils, the creation of forest islands, and the planting and transplanting of trees (Fairhead and Leach, this volume).

In a very different setting Homewood and Rodgers (1987) note that the argument that pastoralists overstock, overgraze and damage their range (in contrast to wildlife which are seen to exist in harmony with their surroundings) has been used to justify the expropriation of land for wildlife conservation (see also Section IIC). This discrediting of pastoralist management dates back to the colonial period, when competition between African and European producers provided an incentive to portray pastoralist management as inefficient and damaging the environment (see also Anderson, 1984; Sandford, 1983; Behnke et al, 1993; Scoones, 1995). Similarly, Swift (1996) observes how, in both the colonial and post-colonial periods, the orthodox view of people's negative impact through 'inappropriate' agricultural practices and extensive pastoralism, have fed into the 'desertification' narrative.

The desertification narrative itself has long blamed human mismanagement. Colonial foresters and administrators noted clear signs of indigenous environmental mismanagement and subsequent desert advance (Adger et al, 2001). As a result of concern over dessication, shifting sand dunes and population increase (Swift, 1996) various measures were proposed to halt desertification, such as a 'belt of high forest', regulation of farming, prohibition of firing and protection of all forest areas. Concern about desertification was renewed in the 1970s following the Sahelian droughts. Lamprey (1975, cited by Adger et al, 2001) for example, concluded that that the Sahara had moved 90–

100km south between 1958 and 1975; Mabutt (1984, cited by Adams, 1990) argued that 4.5 billion hectares were at risk from desertification. In the 1970s a new explanation for desertification was proposed and there was a shift away from the narrative of moving dunes, dessication, loss of topsoil and wind-blown sands (Stebbing, 1937, 1939, cited by Swift, 1996), to the expansion of villages and water hole perimeters generated through overgrazing and fuelwood cutting (Ibrahim,1984, cited by Swift, 1996), although the former narrative still persists in crisis claims (eg Brown, 2001, cited by Forsyth, 2003).

This idea of human-induced desertification has been undermined by new research, which attributes the 'appearance' of desertification to drought conditions. This research recognises the variability (spatial and temporal heterogeneity in rainfall distribution in particular) and resilience (ie the return of vegetation under higher rainfall conditions) of the drylands and the need for flexibility in coping with a highly unstable environment (Adger et al, 2001). Dregne and Tucker (1988, cited by Hellden, 1991) analysed satellite imagery for the 1980–1990 period in terms of north–south oscillations and found interannual variations of 50–250km/year. What they found was 'normal phenomena that can be related to the normal variability of rainfall in the Sahel' (Hellden, 1991, p381). Furthermore, Hellden (1991) following detailed empirical research of the Sudan reports that there was no trend in the creation or possible growth of desert patches around 103 examined villages and water holes over the period 1961–1983; no major shifts in the northern cultivation limit; no major sand dune formations or Sahara desert encroachment and no major changes in vegetation cover and crop productivity which could not be explained by rainfall characteristics. Similar findings have been reported by Sullivan (2000) from Namibia and Rasmussen et al (2001) from Burkina Faso. Thus, Thomas and Middleton (1994) identify three commonly held 'myths' associated with desertification; that desertification is a voracious process which rapidly degrades productive land; that drylands are fragile ecosystems and that desertification is the primary cause of human suffering and misery in drylands. Despite this evidence to the contrary, the rhetoric of desertification continues to be espoused in the 'popular science' literature and by environmental organizations.

The 'Theory of Himalayan Environmental Degradation' is another narrative to have been challenged. The familiar neo-Malthusian explanation for Himalayan degradation is that population increase leads to land shortage, farmers expand agriculture onto steep slopes and cut down trees for agriculture and firewood, and this leads to soil erosion (Forsyth, 1996). In the more extreme versions of the narrative this causes flooding and siltation of the Ganges and Brahamaputra plains, extending the delta area and causing the formation of islands in the Bay of Bengal. Here upland shifting cultivators in particular are blamed for environmental problems such as deforestation, water shortages and sedimentation.

This narrative has been opposed since the 1980s, for example by Thompson et al (1986) and Ives and Messerli (1989). While they do not dispute that a significant problem faces the region, they argue that interventions need to be based on a much more 'accurate' understanding of the problem without which inappropriate policy initiatives are advanced (Ives and Messerli, 1989). Ives and Messerli's counter-narrative is based around both natural and human factors. The natural factors include the fact that the Himalayan region is highly active tectonically and rates of erosion are naturally very high in such landscapes and as such landslides are a common occurrence even on vegetated slopes. Additionally glacial melt causes high levels of siltation and bedrock weathers rapidly and can withstand high rates of soil loss. A range of points related to human management have also been made that challenge received wisdom. For example, rather than making the land less stable, terraces stabilize soils and reduce runoff and erosion rates (Ives and Messerli, 1989) but steepest slopes are avoided in favour of more frequent cultivation of flatter areas (Forsyth, 1996); people actually induce landsliding to bring 'new soil' (Forsyth, 1996) and increase the ease of terrace construction on unterraced slopes (Ives and Messerli, 1989) and road construction is a much more significant factor triggering landslides than local agricultural practices (Forsyth, 1996). Finally, it has been noted that the population of northeast India and Bangladesh living on the plains has grown considerably, such that people are increasingly populating areas that have always been susceptible to flooding, giving the impression of an increased frequency of flooding.

Finally, Carswell's research (this volume) explores how an environmental narrative in highland agriculture which developed during the colonial period and continues to this day, implicitly blames farmers for poor cultivation techniques and deforestation. Here the assumptions made by officials remain unquestioned and, with few exceptions, the policy rhetoric remains unaltered, again giving rise to inappropriate policy initiatives. But using historical sources Carswell shows that these assumptions, particularly around agricultural productivity and forestry, need to be questioned. There is evidence that here farmers have found ways (such as maintaining fallow periods) to successfully manage their land and maintain productivity (see also Carswell, 2002).

While these case studies clearly highlight a need to move away from the all-encompassing negative views of people–environment interactions and give greater consideration to indigenous knowledge, Forsyth (1996) warns of the dangers of romanticizing local knowledge. He cautions that while consulting indigenous knowledge helps to 'test wider assumptions about environmental degradation at a small scale, and present evidence that these assumptions may be misplaced, it is important ... not to romanticize local knowledge, as indeed it may have its own element of "mythology" as a result of being developed for specific time and space scales' (1996, p387; see also Murdoch and Clark, 1994; Sillitoe, 1998).

The importance of work such as the contributions included here lies not so much in suggesting that environmental problems have been exaggerated (and that we therefore have less cause for concern) as there is no doubt that environmental degradation is a very significant problem in some areas of the world. Rather these contributions suggest that blaming indigenous producers and small-scale farmers is often misplaced and greater attention should be given to challenging the practices of those with greater capacities to do environmental damage – that is, individuals and institutions holding greater wealth and power (see also IIA). Prioritizing western 'scientific' knowledge, itself grounded on often untested assumptions may yield counterproductive interventions, as the next section demonstrates.

'New Ecology' and Equilibrium

Many of the narratives discussed above are founded on a number of theories of environmental change, which have been challenged in recent years. Ideas about ecological equilibrium, carrying capacity and the notion of 'climax' vegetation have in particular been questioned (Behnke et al, 1993). The environment as studied by ecologists scientifically, has witnessed what almost might be considered to constitute a 'paradigm shift' in recent years (Warren, 1995). Behnke et al (1993) have argued that the mainstream view of range sciences is 'fundamentally flawed' in its application to certain rangeland ecologies (notably the drier rangelands, Scoones, 1995) and that the conventional theories need a 'thorough re-examination' (Behnke et al, 1993, p2).

This re-examination is taking place in what has been described 'new ecology' (Zimmerer, 1994). It represents a move away from the view of the environment as largely in equilibrium until disturbed by degrading practices (such as overgrazing), to the recognition of the existence of multiple equilibriums between which there may be non-linear (chaotic) fluctuations triggered by abiotic shifts (such as droughts and fire). Spatial and temporal heterogeneity characterize the dry rangelands. The volatility of the environment is stressed, over the tendency to regard nature as stable and homeostatic. Yet while 'stable equilibria are not achievable in many pastoral ecosystems ... long-term persistence is' (Ellis and Swift, 1988, p451). This persistence in a difficult environment is 'achieved through a series of stabilizing strategies which vary with the strength of the environmental stress' (Ellis and Swift, 1988, p457). Thus under the 'old' paradigm the 'ranch model' prevailed, characterized by fenced, fixed paddocks and range improvement for stability. Yet policies which reduce the area available or which confine pastoralists are 'an invitation to disaster' (Ellis and Swift, 1988, p458).

Warren (1995) contends that many indigenous pastoral strategies are carefully adapted to the characteristics of dryland ecosystems and traditional pastoralism is more productive than the ranch model (Scoones, 1995). Degradation through overgrazing is rare as production potentials of grassland and livestock are so limited by rainfall that livestock populations are kept low through the impact of drought. Vegetation recovers following higher rainfall due to adaptive characteristics of grassland species (see Scoones, 1995). Ellis and Swift (1988) conclude that pastoral ecosystems would be better supported by development policies that build on and facilitate the traditional pastoral strategies rather than constrain them. These strategies are characterized by the exploitation of environmental instability and contingent events as 'opportunistic management' (Behnke et al, 1993, p28; see also Sandford, 1983). This opportunistic grazing is known as tracking and involves the flexible mobility of herds to cope with spatial and temporal heterogeneity of grassland productivity. Roe et al (1998) argue that these new disequilibrium-based models of ecological dynamics enable us to see pastoralism as being driven not by risk aversion, but in terms of searching for reliability. While these are superficially similar, they show that there are important differences which have implications for pastoralist behaviour, and in turn for development policy.

Interdisciplinarity

Many of these studies that cast doubts on widely held narratives have reached such conclusions by taking a distinctly interdisciplinary approach (see, for example, Fairhead and Leach, 1998; Carswell, this volume). A strong case can be made that a firm understanding of historical change through the use of historical sources is essential for helping us better understand environmental change. Thus, Fairhead and Leach (1998) reached their conclusions about forest change by using historical sources such as travellers accounts and aerial photographs, (see also Tiffen et al, 1994) while Carswell (2002 and this volume) relies upon archival material to both show the persistent and little changing narrative about the area, and to question that narrative. In relation to the desertification debate, Swift notes that periods of intense discussion occur after periods of drought, raising the importance of historical relativity (1996, p86). More generally Forsyth (1998) has argued forcefully for the need to integrate natural and social sciences in order to avoid accepting environmental 'myths' uncritically, while at the same time 'providing an epistemologically realist basis to local development' (p107). Many of the contributions included in this text are characterized by use of a range of sources and combine natural and social scientific methodologies.

References

Adams, W M (1990) 'Development and Environmental Degradation', in *Green Development: Environment and Sustainability in the Third World*, Routledge, London

Adger, W N, Benjaminsen, T A, Brown, K and Svarstad, H (2001) 'Advancing a political ecology of global environmental discourses'. *Development and Change* **32**(4): 681–715

Anderson, D (1984) 'Depression, dust bowl, demography and drought: the colonial state and soil conservation in East Africa during the 1930s'. *African Affairs* **84**: 321–343

Batterbury S, Forsyth, T and Thomson, K (1997) 'Environmental transformations in developing countries: hybrid research and democratic policy'. *Geographical Journal* **163**(2): 126–132

Benjaminsen, T A (1997) 'Natural resource management, paradigm shifts and the decentralisation reform in Mali'. *Human Ecology* **25**(1): 121–143

Behnke, RH and Scoones, I (1993) 'Rethinking range ecology: implications for rangeland management in Africa' in R H Behnke, I Scoones and C Kervan (eds) *Range Ecology at Disequilibrium: New Models of Natural Variability and Pastoral Adaptation in African Savannas,* Overseas Development Institute, London

Carswell, G (2002) 'Farmers and fallowing: agricultural change in Kigezi district, Uganda'. *Geographical Journal* **168**(2): 130–140

Cline Cole, R A, Main, H A C and Nichol, J E (1990) 'On Fuelwood consumption, population dynamics and deforestation in Africa'. *World Development* **18**(4): 513–527

Dewees, P A (1989) 'The woodfuel crisis reconsidered: observations on the dynamics of abundance and scarcity'. *World Development* **17**(8): 1159–1172

Ellis, J E and Swift, D M (1988) 'Stability of African pastoral ecosystems: alternate paradigms and implications for development'. *Journal of Range Management* **41**(6): 450–459

Fairhead, J and Leach, M (1998) *Reframing Deforestation: Global Analyses and Local Realities: Studies in West Africa,* Routledge, London

Forsyth, T (1996) 'Science, myth and knowledge: testing Himalayan environmental degradation in Thailand'. *Geoforum* **27**(3): 375–392

Forsyth, T (1998) 'Mountain myths revisited: integrating natural and social environmental science'. *Mountain Research and Development* **18**(2): 107–116

Forsyth, T (2003) *Critical Political Ecology,* Routledge, London

Harrison, P (1987) *The Greening of Africa: Breaking Through in the Battle for Land and Food,* Earthscan, London

Hellden, U (1991) 'Desertification: time for an assessment'. *Ambio* **20**(8): 372–383

Hoben, A (1995) 'Paradigms and politics: the cultural construction of environmental policy in Ethiopia'. *World Development* **23**(6): 1007–1021

Hoben, A (1996) 'The cultural construction of environmental policy: paradigms and politics in Ethiopia', in M Leach and R Mearns (eds), *Lie of the Land: Challenging Received Wisdom on the African Environment,* Heinemann and James Currey, Oxford

Homewood, K and Rodgers, W A (1987) 'Pastoralism, conservation and the overgrazing controversy', in D M Anderson and R Grove (eds) *Conservation in Africa: People, Policies and Practice,* Cambridge University Press, Cambridge

Ives, J and Messerli, B (1989) *The Himalayan Dilemma: Reconciling Development and Conservation,* Routledge, London

Keeley, J and Scoones, I (1999) 'Understanding environmental policy processes: a review'. *IDS Working Paper* **89**

Kull, C A (2000) 'Deforestation, erosion, and fire: degradation myths in the environmental history of Madagascar'. *Environment and History* **6**(4): 423–450

Lambin, E F et al (2001) 'The causes of land-use and land-cover change: Moving beyond the myths'. *Global Environmental Change* **11**: 261–269

Leach, G and Mearns, R (1988) *Beyond the Fuelwood Crisis: People, Land and Trees in Africa,* Earthscan, London

Leach, M and Fairhead, J (2000) 'Challenging neo-Malthusian deforestation analyses in West Africa's dynamic forest landscapes'. *Population and Development Review* **26**(1): 17–43

Leach, M and Mearns, R (eds) (1996) *Lie of the Land: Challenging Received Wisdom on the African Environment,* Heinemann and James Currey, Oxford

Lohmann, L (1993) 'Against the myths' in M Colchester and L Lohmann (eds) *The Struggle for Land and the Fate of the Forest,* Zed Books, London

Mackenzie, F A (2000) 'Contested ground: colonial narratives and the Kenyan environment, 1920–1945'. *Journal of Southern African Studies* **26**(4): 697–718

Marcusson, H S (1999) 'Environmental paradigms, knowledge systems and policy. The case of Burkino Faso'. *Geografisk Tidsskrift* **2**: 93–103

McCann, J C (1997) 'The plow and the forest: narratives of deforestation in Ethiopia, 1840–1992'. *Environmental History* **2**(2): 138–159

Murdoch, J and Clark, J (1994) 'Sustainable knowledge'. *Geoforum* **25**: 115–132

Rasmussen, K et al (2001) 'Desertification in reverse? Observations from northern Burkino Faso'. *Global Environmental Change* **11**: 271–282

Rocheleau, D E, Steinberg, P E and Benjamin, P A (1995) 'Environment, development, crisis, and crusade: Ukambani, Kenya, 1890–1990'. *World Development* **23**(6): 1037–1051

Roe, E M (1991) 'Development narratives, or making the best of blueprint development'. *World Development* **19**(4): 287–300

Sandford, S (1983) *Management of Pastoral Development in the Third World,* John Wiley and Sons, Chichester

Scoones, I (1995) 'New directions in pastoral development' in I Scoones (ed) *Living with Uncertainty: New Directions in Pastoral Development in Africa,* IIED and IT Publications, London

Scoones, I (1997) 'The dynamics of soil fertility change: historical perspectives on environmental transformation from Zimbabwe'. *Geographical Journal* **163**(2): 161–169

Sillitoe, P (1998) 'The development of indigenous knowledge'. *Current Anthropology* **39**(2): 223–254

Sullivan, S (2000) 'Getting the science right or introducing science in the first place? – local 'facts', global discourse – "desertification" in NW Namibia', in P Scott and S Sullivan (eds) *Political Ecology: Science, Myth and Power*, Arnold, London

Swift, J (1996) 'Desertification: narratives, winners and losers', in M Leach and R Mearns (eds) 1996 *Lie of the Land: Challenging Received Wisdom on the African Environment*, Heinemann and James Currey, Oxford

Thomas, D S G and Middleton, T (1994) *Desertification: Exploding the Myth*, Wiley, Chichester

Thompson M, Warburton, M and Hatley, T (1986) *Uncertainty on a Himalayan Scale*, Ethnographica, London

Tiffen, M, Mortimore, M and Gichuki, F (1994) *More People, Less Erosion: Environmental Recovery in Kenya* Wiley, Chichester

Timberlake, L (1985) *Africa in Crisis: The Causes, the Cures of Environmental Bankruptcy,* Earthscan, London

Warren, A (1995) 'Changing understandings of African pastoralism and the nature of environmental paradigms'. *Transactions of the Institute of British Geographers* **20**(2): 193–203

Whatmore, S and Boucher, S (1993) 'Bargaining with nature: the discourse and practice of "environmental planning gain"'. *Transactions – Institute of British Geographers* **18**(2): 166–178

Zimmerer, K S (1994) 'Human geography and the "new ecology": the prospect and promise of integration'. *Annals of the Association of American Geographers* **84**(1): 108–125

1

False Forest History, Complicit Social Analysis: Rethinking Some West African Environmental Narratives

James Fairhead and Melissa Leach[1]

Summary

Social science analysis has helped to explain the rapid and recent deforestation supposed to have occurred in Guinea, West Africa. A narrative concerning population growth and the breakdown of past authority and community organization which once maintained 'original' forest vegetation guides policy. In two cases, vegetation history sharply contradicts the deforestation analysis and thus exposes the assumptions in its supporting social narrative; assumptions stabilized within regional narratives based more on western imagination than African realities. For each case and then at the regional level, more appropriate assumptions are forwarded which better explain demonstrable vegetation change and provide more appropriate policy guidelines.

Introduction

This paper examines social science analyses that are being used to explain environmental degradation and inform policy responses to it. We focus on two cases pertinent for exploring the production of applied social science knowledge about people–environment relations. They exemplify the type of social analysis often brought to bear to explain environmental degradation in Africa, yet it can be demonstrated that what they explain so successfully has not actually taken place.

Our examples clearly expose a spectrum of assumptions on which social science analyses – whether or not carried out by social scientists as such – tend to draw. These assumptions have strength and credibility in large part because they are linked together, diffused and stabilized within 'narratives' (Roe, 1991), that is, stories of apparently

Reprinted from *World Development*, vol 23, Fairhead, J and Leach, M, 'False Forest History, Complicit Social Analysis: Rethinking Some West African Environmental Narratives', pp1023–1035, copyright © (1995) with permission from Elsevier.

incontrovertible logic which provide scripts and justifications for development action. But once dissected from the reality they seek to construct, these explanations reveal instead how the applied social sciences can be used to lend weight to popular western perceptions about African society and environment – a mythical reality which development interventions are acting to recreate in vain. By stripping away the explained from explanations of it, our cases pave the way for rethinking people–environment relationships in this region. We do this by forwarding alternative sets of assumptions stabilized within narratives which better fit the facts.

The specific cases considered here concern Guinea's forest margin zone. They articulate, in different ways, the position that local community institutions were once better capable of controlling environmental resources than they are today, and thus of maintaining a forested environment and resisting pressure towards its degradation. This articulation enables supposed forest loss to be explained in terms of 'institutional breakdown.' An armoury of purported factors is called to account for such social rupture whose results seem so evident in a degraded landscape. These include socioeconomic change and commercialization, increasing mobility, the weakening of traditional authority, more individuated farming, the new economic and cultural aspirations of the young, new social cleavages, the alienation of local resource control to state structures, and the emergence of 'anarchic' charcoal, fuelwood and timber businesses to supply the urban market. The impact of migration is added to these arguments: Eco-ethnic integration once associated with 'forest people' with supposedly forest-benign lifestyles has been disrupted by the immigration or influence of 'savanna peoples'. Overlaying all is the spectre of population growth, as viewed through a Malthusian lens. Foreign observers today tend to date such socioenvironmental disruption to the notorious regime of Guinea's first republic (1958–1984) under Sékou Touré, imaging the colonial period as environmentally friendly, while nationals tend to took to the precolonial period to find 'good' society and environment. As if to make the point, one scholar forced the social–environmental Eden back to that period documented by the 13th century Arab geographers, ie a period where his personal moral sympathies lay (Zerouki, 1993).

Social sciences have no monopoly over these social–environmental visions in which a forest past has become a moral past. They are shared by many local administrators and school teachers, as much as external consultants and university academics. The production of history serves many ends. What will become clear is that social scientists have been complicit in producing a view of history as one of increasing tension from a harmonious past. Treating this past as a model and set of objectives for the resolution of today's tensions, they have been forging links between social and environmental conditions in a way that assists in relieving those subjected to their study of what little resource control they have.

Case 1: Forest Islands of Kissidougou

The deforestation narrative

Kissidougou looks degraded. The landscape is largely savanna, especially open in the dry season when fires burn off the grasses and defoliate the few savannah trees. Nonetheless, rising out of the savannah and surrounding and hiding each of the prefecture's villages, are patches of immense semi-deciduous humid forest. Scientists and policy-makers consider these forest 'islands' and the strips of streamside gallery forest to be relics of an original, formerly much more extensive, dense humid forest cover. Inhabitants have, they suppose, progressively converted forest into 'derived' savannah by their shifting cultivation and fire-setting practices, preserving only the belt of forest around their villages to protect their settlements from fire and wind, to give necessary shade to tree crops, to assist fortifications and hiding, and to provide seclusion for secret ritual activities. They argue that today's climate would support general forest cover, and infer from the presence of 'relic' forest islands that it once did:

> At origin, the forest between Kissidougou and Kankan was ... a dense, humid, semi-deciduous forest. The trigger of degradation is ... the farming system and the fragility of climate and soils in tropical regions. Some primary formations still exist, however, in the form of peri-village forest islands and gallery forests on the banks of water courses. These forest islands show the existence of a dense forest, which is today replaced in large part by degraded secondary forest. All the stages of degradation are represented: wooded savanna, bush savanna and grass savanna (Kan II, *Plan d'Operation*, 1992, pp6–7).[2]

Deforestation is considered to provoke problems at several levels, rendering it an urgent policy concern. At the local level it leads to soil degradation and renders farming less productive and sustainable. At the regional level – the upper watershed of the Niger river – deforestation is thought to have caused irregularities in downstream river flow and in rainfall. In addition, it is contributing to global warming. Something must be done.

Social analysis has always been instrumental in explaining this problem and its recent acceleration. In the early part of this century, the celebrated French colonial botanist, Auguste Chevalier, considered greater movement and trade during the post-occupation period to be responsible for an increase in fire-setting from a previous, less forest-harmful level (Chevalier, 1909). He considered that inhabitants conserved the forest islands for cultural reasons, presumably in a sea of otherwise degraded profanity (Chevalier, 1933). In 1948, Adam published the view prevalent in earlier archives that the Mandinka were a 'savanna' people who had migrated southward into the forest zone, and created savannah there (Adam, 1948). In doing so, they reportedly forced the original 'forest people', more benign to that resource, south and further into the forest zone.

More recently, professional social scientists have focused on environmental issues in Kissidougou, usually in the pay of international or bilaterally funded environmental programmes. One team, responsible for structuring the European Community-funded Niger river protection programme, illustrate this focus thus:

> Our questions sought to explain the deterioration of the environment, viz: erosion and soil impoverishment, the drying up of water sources, the origin and nature of forest destruction, the origin of perverse use of bush fire ... Parallel to the physical causes of soil erosion, there are others of a social, political and religious nature. We can suppose a strong relationship between soil erosion, environmental degradation and the break-up and impoverishment of socio-economic structures and relations. Environmental management is strongly linked to the state of socio-cultural structures ...The more a community is in equilibrium at

the level of social organisation, the healthier is the nature of its relations with the environment. There is a dialectical relationship between social, political and religious institutions and ecological equilibrium…In these communities,…the existence of the living is above all justified by a more or less good management of what the ancestors have left to them. This management is inscribed in the collection of laws, concrete and abstract, rational and irrational, which, once disturbed from the exterior, can be the cause of a deterioration which manifests itself as much at the level of social, religious, political and economic institutions, as at the level of the environment (Programme d'Amenagement des Hautes Bassins du Fleuve Niger, n.d., pp4–7).

In a second study, devoted to local fire-setting, the author aimed to give an inventory of cultural traits which function around the practice of fire. 'We have tried to retrace the transition from a traditional practice to "modern" practice. Our hypothesis was that the "fire social system" instituted itself as such, in destroying its host "system", the traditional one' (Zerouki, 1993, p1). In short, the author argues that 'modernity' is responsible for disrupting the once successful integration of fire control within diffuse sets of intra- and intervillage social, cultural and political relationships. He finds that 'degradation seems to be recent' and that 'it accelerates with the development of an urban network … and population growth'. The study proposed 'solutions to social dysfunctioning' (Zerouki, 1993). A co-researcher on this same study expands on the causes of such 'dysfunctioning':

> According to inquiry on the one hand from elders…and on the other by IFAN in 1968, the whole region was covered with forest about 99 years ago, corresponding to the Samorian period. War chiefs used fire for better visibility and for encampments. The introduction of the locomotive during the colonial period had a serious impact on the vegetation. Since independence, there has been demystification of sacred forests and of islands considered once as cult places, the installation of wood mills, and brick-making. Nomadic farming and herding, uncontrolled bush fire, forest fire, and runaway demography, aggravate the process of vegetation degradation already begun (Fofana et al, 1993, p49).

Other recent expert views have drawn on conventional social analysis to assert once again that the Kuranko people (who speak a Mandinka dialect) are a savannah people and brought bush fire practices with them when they pushed the Kissi further south. 'As forest people, the Kissi are not as careless as savanna people with regard to fire' (Green, 1991, p20). In a typically racialist way, agency for degradation is diffused into the ambiguity between culture and origin.

A study of an area just over the eastern border of Kissidougou, while somewhat cynical of the crisis mould of environmental analysis, nevertheless claims that:

> The degradation of forests – always qualified as 'explosive' – has continued in an accelerating fashion … Peasant exploitation is correctly identified as the principal factor of destruction, but in general, the measures taken [since colonial times] have only treated the symptoms. The social reasons for fire setting in hunting are … closely linked to growing tendencies of commercialisation and monetarization in the rural milieu. This underlines the loss in importance of traditional organisations of hunters which, to date, are marked by an anti-commercial character. [Pasture will be threatened by] growing immigration of herders into the region, a consequence of the degradation of pastures in the traditional herding

regions (eg Fouta Djallon). Traditional structures which regulate the exploitation of natural resources, most often of pre-Islamic origin, incorporate a series of conservation aspects. Some still operate … but a change is beginning to show itself: a process of social change which implies a dissolution of traditional regulative structures which are not easily reconcilable with the commercialisation trends which are more and more marked in the region (Stieglitz, 1990, pp54, 70, 77).

The author, who considers Islam to have disrupted this 'pre-Islamic' tradition, incorporates more agro-demographic explanations into her explanatory mix:

The period of cultivation being too prolonged or the fallow period too short, there is too great a loss in the nutritive materials leading finally to an irrevocable degradation of the soils. The fallow period is limited to 5–10 years. A tendency for land shortage can be seen (Stieglitz, 1990, p71).

This is the position on demographic change held by most analysts. Ponsart-Dureau, for example, an agronomy student advising a nearby project, considers that:

around 1945, the forest, according to the elders, reached a limit 30 km north of Kissidougou town. Today, its northern limit is found at the level of Gueckedou-Macenta, thus having retreated about 100 km… Demographic growth forces the villagers to exploit their land completely, and to practice deforestation which disequilibriates the natural milieu (Ponsart-Dureau, 1986, pp9–10 and 60).

Thus in different ways, each of these analyses contributes to a narrative now as prominent in Kissidougou's education and administrative circles as it is in social science analyses. Once Kissidougou had an extensive forest cover, maintained under low population densities and by a functional social order whose regulations controlled and limited people's inherently degrading land and vegetation use. The breakdown of such organized resource management under internal and external pressures, combined with population growth, has led to the deforestation apparently so evident in the landscape today. Observers invariably consider degradation as a recent, ongoing and aggravating problem. The social and economic changes are, like 'runaway demography', always seen to be accelerating out from a 'zero point' (the archetype 'tradition' so dear to Malinowskian social anthropologists and the object of description in old ethnographies). A host of indicators is drawn upon to support ideas concerning recent and ongoing degradation, such as rainfall decline since the mid-1950s, the drying-up of certain water sources, and more.

Policy implications have followed logically from the assumptions contained and stabilized within this narrative, and have changed little since its first elaboration in the early colonial period. The first policy emphasis is on the reduction of upland farming – seen as inherently forest and soil degrading and becoming more so under greater individualization and population growth – in favour of swamp farming. What upland use must remain needs to be rationalized and intensified (eg through 'model' agroforestry systems, reorganization of tenure and fallow systems). Second, policies have focused on bush-fire control through externally imposed prohibitions, regulations and practices (eg early-burning). Third, policies have attempted to control deforestation both through prohibitions on the felling of a list of protected tree species (largely those forest species commercially valuable for timber and most representative of the 'original' forest cover) and through the reservation of certain forest patches. Fourth, there are attempts at forest reconstitution through tree planting in village territories. Uniting these policies is their recourse to technology 'packages' well established in the region such as inland valley swamp development and tree planting from nurseries. Uniting them, too, is their attempt to establish or reestablish control and organization in resource management; although with changes in development philosophy, there have been changes in the levels deemed appropriate. Thus in Guinea's colonial and first republic periods, the degradation narrative justified removing the villagers' (dysfunctional, incapable) 'control' over resources in favour of the state. In bush fire, upland use, timber-felling and forest reservation policies, government administrations took over resource tenure and regulated local use through permits, fines and at times military repression. More recently, emphasis has shifted somewhat towards patching-up, reconstituting or replacing broken community control over resources: *gestion de terroir villageois* approaches provide a context for village-level planning of bush fire, upland and forest use, 'participatory' tree planting, and reservation of forest islands in favour of 'the community'.

The counternarrative

Examining how vegetation has actually changed in Kissidougou is a necessary first step in evaluating these social science analyses. Fortunately, a number of historical data sources make this possible – sources ignored or deemed unnecessary by social analysts convinced of the degradation they were explaining.[3] Aerial photographs exist for Kissidougou which clearly show the state of the vegetation in 1952–1953. These provide incontrovertible evidence that during this recent, supposedly most degrading period, the vegetation pattern and area of forest and savannah have in fact remained relatively stable. Changes which have occurred do not involve forest loss; rather there are large areas where forest cover has increased, and where savannahs have become more, not less, woody. Forest islands have formed and enlarged, and in many areas, savannahs evident in the 1950s have ceded to secondary forest vegetation.

To examine vegetation change further back, we reviewed descriptions and maps of Kissidougou's landscape made during the early French military occupation (roughly the 1890s to 1910), as well as indicators of past vegetation that emerge from oral history and accounts of everyday life in the youth of today's elderly people. These sources make clear that what was true for 1952–1994 is equally true for 1893–1952. Moreover, villagers suggest, quite contrary to policy interpretations, that they established forest islands around their settlements, and that it is their work which encourages the formation of secondary forest thicket in savannah. In 27 of the 38 villages we investigated, elders recounted how their ancestors had founded settlements in savannah and gradually encouraged the growth of forest around them.

Earlier documentary sources from the 1780s–1860s do not suggest extensive forest cover; indeed they suggest the opposite. Both Harrison, travelling to Kissi areas (~1780, see Hair, 1962), and, as we shall see in the next case, Seymour (1859/60) in Toma country southeast of Kissi, describe short grass savannahs and an absolute scarcity of trees in places which now support extensive dense humid forest. Sims (1859/60), speaking of the area just to the southeast (between Beyla and Kerouane) writes that: 'There are no trees; the whole country is prairie; for firewood the people have to substitute cow dung, and a kind of moss which grows abundantly in that country.' This picture of less, not more, forest cover in the 19th century is supported by several sets of early oral history data. All the above villages claiming foundation in savannah were established during or before the 19th century. Several village foundation stories in the south refer to conflicts triggered by the scarcity of construction wood, seemingly bizarre given the present forest and thicket vegetation, and in certain areas savannah grasses are said to have changed from those associated with drier climates to those associated with wetter ones.

It appears, therefore, that social science analyses in Kissidougou have been providing explanations for forest loss which has not actually been taking place. In doing so, they have supported a vegetation-change narrative quite at odds with – even the reverse of – more demonstrable environmental 'facts'. This casts into question the relationships between society, demography and environment valorized in these analyses. As we suggest now, there are other ways of conceiving of these relationships – counter narratives, if you will – which better fit and explain vegetation history as demonstrated.[4]

The first reconception involves recognizing that local land use can be vegetation-enriching as well as degrading. It can (and often does) serve to increase the proportion of useful vegetation forms and species in the landscape according to prevailing local values and productivity criteria. This has often meant increasing the prevalence of forest forms in a once more savannah landscape. Thus, for example, villagers have encouraged the formation of forest islands around their villages for protection, convenient shelter for tree crops and sources of gathering products, and the concealment of ritual activities. They have achieved this both through everyday use of village margin land (for instance, in the thatch and fence-grass collection and cattle-tethering which reduce flammable grasses, and in the household waste deposition which fertilizes the forest successions beginning to develop), as well as through deliberately applied techniques (such as planting forest-initiating trees and cultivating the margins to create soil conditions suitable for tree establishment). In addition, on the slopes and plateaux between forest islands, local farming and fire use practices tend to maintain existing woody cover, and upgrade soils and vegetation from savannah to forest conditions. Much farming is concentrated on land that farmers have improved, whether by long-term alterations to edaphic quality through habitation, gardening and gardening-like cultivation; or by shorter-term fallow improvement through intensive cattle-grazing, seed-source protection, the multiplication of savannah trees from suckers, or distributing forest-initiating creepers. These forms of knowledge and practice are found among all of Kissidougou's ethno-linguistic groups. There seems little basis for distinguishing between 'forest' and 'savanna' people.

A related reconception concerns the character of natural resource management 'organization'. Environmental management in this region seems to depend – and always depended – less on community-level authorities and socio-cultural organizations (which might be 'threatened' by social change), than on the sum of a much more diffuse set of relations; a constellation more than a structure. Indeed, the maintenance of long-term productivity is in many cases built into short-term production patterns; whether carried out for oneself, one's household or one's compound, these improvements frequently interact with others – spatially or temporally – so that the combined effect on resource enrichment is greater than the sum of their parts. Thus, the fires set in the early and mid-dry season by hunters to clear small hunting grounds, and by others to protect property and fallows, create barriers to more devastating later fires; and the small tree crop plantations which people make and protect behind their kitchen gardens add to the creation of the village forest island. For much 'resource management' there is no need for village or higher level management structures to 'regulate degrading pressures'. Nevertheless, village authorities do intervene in certain vegetation-influencing activities – eg in managing early-burning around the village, in protecting palm trees, in imposing cattle-tethering dates, and in coordinating the fallow rotations of farmers' contiguous plots in some Kissi areas. Village and higher level organizations also exert control over external factors which influence the agricultural environment, such as in negotiating with prospective Fula (Peuhl) pastoralist settlers or representatives of the forest service.

In this context, socio-economic change has been articulated in shifts in landscape enrichment priorities and in the composition of a continued resource management constellation. Villagers have, for example, adapted forest island quality to suit changing socio-economic conditions and commercial signals – managing them as fortresses during precolonial warfare, extending them for coffee planting when this became profitable, and abandoning coffee in favour of fruit tree and gathering-product enrichment as prices fell again. Urban employment opportunities, youth emigration and more individual economic opportunities have contributed to changes in farming organization, but today's smaller farm-households use and improve fallows as large compound ones did earlier, and modern women's individualized, commercial food cropping is concentrated in the forms of upland gardening that upgrade soils and vegetation (Leach and Fairhead, 1995). Village-level authorities have played a continuing, though shifting role within this historically flexible and diverse management constellation. There have been many social and economic changes, and there are many new social and economic problems, but these changes are rendered visible in the landscape largely through changing land use and management priorities, not through organizational 'breakdown' and vegetation degradation.

Explaining demonstrable vegetation change also suggests relationships between demographic and environmental change very different from the 'rapid population growth-deforestation' relationship upheld by the policy narrative. Despite the problems of reconstructing precolonial populations, evidence certainly does not support the idea of dramatic population growth or even steady one-way increase. Comparing census data suggests that Kissidougou's rural population has increased by only 70 per cent since 1917. Growth pockets have been concentrated around Kissidougou town and major road axes, and in many areas population has remained almost stagnant. Precolonial evidence suggests that certain areas had early 19th century rural populations significantly higher than today, and suffered radical depopulation during late 19th century wars. Indeed oral accounts, explorers' reports, early 16th–18th century documents which mention the region, and broader regional history and archaeology combine to suggest that Kissidougou had relatively high farming populations from the 16th century and long before. There is clearly as little evidence for dramatic population increase in the present century from a low precolonial baseline as there is for dramatic forest loss.

In this context, Kissidougou's forest increase trends might be supposed to relate to population stagnation or decline. This reversed argument, however, still depends on the assumption that local land use tends to convert forest and forest fallows to savannah, and thus that more people means more forest loss. A counternarrative better fits evidence of local land-use practices and vegetation history: from an earlier situation of greater savannah extent, there has been a broadly positive relationship between the peopling of this region and its forest cover. First, as settlements are associated with the formation of forest islands, more villages mean more forest islands. This relationship has been modified by changes in population distribution and settlement patterns, with greater multiplication of settlements and forest islands during the 19th century when dispersed settlement was a survival strategy, than in the 20th when much population growth has been accommodated through the expansion of existing settlements, and indeed some consolidation linked to depopulation. Still, new settlements and forest formation have more recently been associated with the movement of village sites. Second, greater population density assists the control of fire, both by providing the necessary labour and by creating the demand, filling the landscape with more places (upgraded fallows, plantations, settlement sites) which people need to protect. In certain cases, the density of such protected sites of denser vegetation easily enables the entire exclusion of fire from the territory. The districts where upland savannahs have recently ceded to dense forest fallow vegetation correlate broadly with the areas where population has grown. By contrast, low population densities make fire prevention impossible, and are a major factor in the persistence of running fire in the north and of the particular 'living with fire' management strategies used there.

Viewing people–environment relations in terms of landscape enrichment-through-use by a diverse resource management constellation responding to changing incentives thus better explains (provides a counternarrative which better fits) demonstrable vegetation and population history. Policies conceived within the degradation narrative have sometimes undermined these relations, as well as created more general problems for villagers. In removing local control over resources, they have sometimes interfered with local management of them. In the north, for example, external fire control and prohibition prevented villagers operating their sequenced management-through-use strategies,[5] forcing clandestine coping strategies and rendering village and plantation protection more difficult. Removal of local resource tenure has reduced villagers' abilities to profit from past enrichment activities (eg in selling their forest island trees for timber) and their incentives for further landscape enrichment. The implementation of repressive environmental policies has in effect taxed rural populations for supposedly harmful activities which were, in fact, benign or beneficial. More recent approaches, which focus on decentralizing resource control by establishing village-level organization and management plans, actually risk undermining the existing flexible, diverse constellation of resource management relations. When initiated by state agencies with considerable foreign support and presence and predefined ideas about environmental dynamics, real decentralization can be undermined. Finally, but by no means least, the investment in 'redressing' Kissidougou's supposed environmental degradation, an investment reaching unprecedented levels amid current aid donor concerns, carries heavy opportunity costs in terms of other more pressing rural development problems left unaddressed.

Vegetation history and its counternarrative of landscape enrichment entail different policy implications, emphasizing support to proven local practices and determinants of change. There are clearly many techniques and land uses that serve to increase forest cover, and which could provide an effective basis for external support. In working with the local ecology of fire, soils, vegetation successions and animal dynamics, these 'integrated vegetation management' practices are more locally appropriate, integrated with the social matrix and thus more cost-effective in terms of labour than are the forestry 'packages' generally proposed by outside agencies. Given that farming in the region is not inevitably degrading, environmental policy may look to support as well as to 'rationalize and regulate' agriculture, specifically to support those upland farming practices which improve soils and fallow vegetation rather than concentrate technical effort exclusively on swamps. Fundamentally, rather than increase external intervention in the organization of resource management within villages, the more important priority is to create the enabling policy and socio-economic conditions in which local resource management constellations can act effectively. This implies a shift on the part of environmental agencies away from direction (through repression or organizational restructuring as in assisted "community control") towards recognizing and supporting the diverse institutions which are actually engaged in resource management, and towards a more responsive role in providing requested services at the village level.

Case 2: The Ziama Forest Reserve

The deforestation narrative

Travelling south from Kissidougou, one enters the Upper Guinean forest region. Within Guinea this region is populous, and there are only two significant intact forest blocks, the northern-most of which is Ziama.[6] Covering an area of about 120,000 hectares, Ziama was designated a colonial forest reserve in 1932, made an international biosphere reserve within the 'Man and the Biosphere' programme in 1980, and is now the subject of a major World Bank financed conservation project. Policy narratives concerning Ziama reproduce those of Kissidougou to a significant extent, with one major scale exception: changes in the status of a major forest block are at stake, and the conservation concern is partly global.

The Ziama forest is considered to be under considerable threat as an important relic of a once much greater forest cover. As Table 1, drawn from an IUCN report on Ziama, indicates, forest cover in this part of Guinea is now only 20 per cent of what it was 'at origin', and the report emphasizes that the forest is regressing rapidly. Apart from the loss of biodiversity (of considerable international concern) this reduction is said to be causing a drying-out of the local and regional climate, evident in drier water sources and courses, thereby increasing forest loss in a vicious cycle that threatens regional agriculture.

Regional studies and administrative perceptions are based on social analysis of this deforestation and encroachment on the remaining Ziama reserve. The most detailed and explicit version of the 'analysis' is found in a socio-economic study commissioned by a conservation project (Baum and Weimer, 1992). The assumptions it forwards are

Table 1.1 *Area of Humid Forest in Forest Guinea at Different Times*

Period	Area (hectares)
At origin	1,930,000
c. 1958	1,300,000
c. 1980	1,075,000
1986	397,000

Source: République de Guinée (1990)

stabilized within a narrative not dissimilar to Kissidougou's, involving growing popula-tions of immigrant and indigenous farmers who have lost 'traditional' values and organizational forms, and who are seeking and de-wooding forested land.

As in Kissidougou, a strong contrast is drawn between a forest people, the indige-nous Toma (Loma), and a savannah people, in this case the Konianke (Mandinka), whose immigration and savannah ways threaten the forest. Thus we read of the Toma that they are 'largely fixed in their customary conceptions and habitual mode of life' (Baum and Weimer, 1992). The authors explain that the Toma 'historical and social evolution as a people in a forest environment ... favours a tendency to contemplation and sobriety'. These attitudes supported a lifestyle and traditional society which existed in harmony with the forest. The peripheral geographical situation of the Toma in terms of communication, and the largely uncommercialized nature of past economy, sup-ported these tendencies, so the argument goes.

Nevertheless, it is maintained that the Toma have lost their forest ways: "the forest has largely lost its customary importance, in favour of an essentially agricultural use of space. This evidences, without doubt, profound changes in economic orientation, espe-cially among the Toma, ancient hunters and gatherers" (Baum and Weimer, 1992). The authors are surprised to find that women manage the principal crop, rice, and this serves to reinforce the idea that the Toma have only just learned to farm; it 'reflects, without doubt the historical agricultural experience of a migratory farming, on small areas, only partially cleared'. This view builds on colonial perceptions that Toma had 'a very primitive agriculture, quite anarchic, centred on pluvial rice based on forest clear-ings...Those of the north have practically destroyed the cover of trees, those of the south, in the valleys and peneplanes, are still crushed by the forest' (Portères, 1965, pp688 and 726).

Changes in the Toma agricultural economy are linked to the opening-up of the area to commerce and markets and to the need to feed growing populations. Both these trends are linked to the immigration and influence of Mandinka people from the north – immigration which is also central in explaining the area's demographic evolution. The authors present a picture of a long-term, very gradual peopling of the Ziama region through the immigration of Toma people and then brusque changes as Mand-inka began to immigrate, now represented by second or third generation migrants. It is said that there were two villages present in the reserve when it was designated in 1932, Boo and Kpanya, having 542 and 370 persons at that time. Boo, which now has a pop-ulation of some 1600 is said to have had a population of 500 when it was founded, giving the impression that while the forest might have been lightly inhabited for long periods by forest people, it is only since the mid-19th century that it has been under a threat which is ever increasing. Immigration into the region is reported to have risen by four to sevenfold in 60 years. This rapid population growth is seen to have created severe land pressure in the areas neighbouring the reserve. Assumptions about carrying capacity under shifting cultivation are used to argue that population: land ratios are now 'fully saturated', and this largely accounts for farmers encroaching on the reserved land for farming.

This narrative – concerning a last remaining block of 'pristine' natural forest, threatened by recent socio-economic change and population pressure – provides a powerful justification for conservation. It also entails guidelines for conservation policy. 'Original' forest is easily defined as a global or regional heritage, and its conservation by global and regional guardians a moral imperative. The narrative enables reserve administrations to list deforestation problems concerning climate and water as if they had never happened before, and to justify the urgency of conservation using arguments about their irreversibility. Within earlier, colonially derived approaches, the reservation of such forest, often as part of the state's domain, was acceptably justified with minimal regard for local interests in using reserved land and resources. In Ziama as elsewhere, 'policing and patrolling' approaches characterized early forest conservation. More recently, emphasis has been placed on the need to gain the participation, acceptance and support of local populations if conservation is to be sustainable. Since local resistance to and failure to respect the reserve are seen in terms of land shortage and economic pressure, the presumed policy needs are for socio-economic development and agricultural intensification in the marginal area around the forest, accompanied by restricting of land tenure as necessary, to reduce current and future pressures on the reserve.

The counternarrative

Once again, examination of historical data showing how vegetation, population and society have changed in this region reveal the extent to which the assumptions stabilized within this narrative are ill-founded. In the Ziama case, detailed descriptions come from the published writings of several highly educated Americo-Liberians who visited what is today the forest reserve in the mid-19th century (Seymour, 1859/60; Anderson, 1870; Starr, 1912). What they saw and described in no way conformed to the enduring image of sparse Toma hunter-gatherer populations living in harmony with an isolated high forest. The two 'enclave' villages, now situated within the forests covering the wide Diani river plain, then lay in savannahs. The Ziama mountain massif, now considered the heart of the primary forest, was either bare rock or covered 'with cane grass and scarcely any tree but the palm' (Seymour, 1859/60). From the top of the massif, Seymour describes the plain as 'covered with small bushes and grass, and it gives the country the appearance of an old farm, with palms standing scattered all over it'. The ascription of 19th century identity as 'forest people', however dubious in itself, seems highly inappropriate for these savannah-dwelling Toma of Ziama.

The region had large populations, by all accounts significantly larger, not smaller than today. Thus taking the enclave villages as an example, Anderson (in 1874) considered Kpanya as 'very large' (when his account described 2500 people as small) and Seymour (in 1859/60) estimated Boo to have 3600 inhabitants. In addition, as the elders of the villages describe, these large villages had many smaller dependent settlements which no longer exist. The region was evidently highly agricultural. Seymour and Anderson describe large savannah farms of rice, maize and cassava stretching as far as the eye could see, and the short fallows necessary to sustain large populations. It was also commercially prosperous. Seymour noted 50 looms and 5 blacksmiths in Boo, and found some women wearing jewellery worth US$20–30 at that time. A little further north, at Kuankan, people walked several miles from the mountains to the plain to sell firewood. As Seymour noted, 'Firewood is scarce about this large city, but they have a good market, and it would do a person good to see the activity of the little boys, who are the principal traders in this line'. Both enclave settlements had daily and weekly markets, as did all the major towns, distant some eight to 10 kilometres one from another, and these traded in foodstuffs, livestock, cash crops (such as cotton and kola), and artisanal goods of every description. The region was not economically or geographically marginal, but central to busy and long-established forest-savannah trade routes.

Thus in the mid-19th century the Ziama area clearly did not fit the images which today's policy narratives construct for it. Unsurprisingly, then, its subsequent history also overturns the conventional narrative's image of unilineal population increase and forest destruction. The story which explains how this region became a 'primary forest' reserve within only 130 years of being heavily populated savannah turns, instead, on the wars which affected the area during 1870–1910 (Fairhead and Leach, 1994). Sustained military conflict first with Mandinka groups and then with the colonizing French caused major depopulation and economic devastation. It is this, not the extension of persistently low precolonial population densities, which explains the region's sparse populations at the turn of the century. On the abandoned settlements, fields and fallows, forest grew. By 1932 the French colonial administration recognized secondary forest worthy of reservation. That the forest grew so fast suggests that earlier intensive farming and savannah maintenance did not cause irreversible damage to forest vegetation potential; indeed it may indicate the positive legacy of previous local management practices, as in Kissidougou. By the early 1980s, conservationists were failing to distinguish Ziama's forest regrowth from primary forest. Populations since 1932 have not grown by the 400–700 per cent suggested in the socio-economic study. Using the study's own statistics, in the 41 villages in the vicinity of the reserve populations have increased by only 80 per cent since 1932, or 120 per cent if recent influxes of Liberian and Sierra Leonean refugees are taken into account.

It is clear that the stabilized assumptions which social science researchers are using to understand the nature and change of people–environment interactions in Ziama are completely at odds with a more demonstrable counternarrative centring on warfare, depopulation, forest regeneration and land alienation. The latter narrative better encompasses the experience and attitudes of today's Toma inhabitants, whose prominent display on village houses of portraits of ancestors who were killed or who fled during the wars testifies that these past events are not forgotten. It is largely this mismatch of narratives which underlies the failure of the reserve administration to build any constructive relationship with local inhabitants. Instead, their relationships are tense and have at times erupted into violence. Development activities around the reserve have seemed inadequate to calm this conflict and prevent 'encroachment' on land within it.

Achieving sustainable conservation, let alone of a participatory nature, remains a distant and unlikely goal, and much investment has been wasted in the effort.

When today's inhabitants 'encroach' they are attempting both to reclaim ancestral lands, and to re-establish control over a once peopled and prosperous, now ex-social domain politically alienated from them. Recognizing this suggests alternative, potentially more fruitful guidelines for policy. If policy-makers are to engage sensitively and productively with local communities, then local inhabitants' historical experiences need to be incorporated into policy dialogues and negotiations. Moreover, historically grounded claims to land and political authority need to be recognized and seriously addressed through conservation arrangements which, for example, cede tenurial control to local landholders, within the context of leasing or management agreements which fully recognize the value their lands now have for others.

The Regional Narrative and its Alternative

The specific narratives, concerning vegetation change and its social causes used to support policy in Kissidougou and Ziama, are examples of a broader narrative. This broader narrative contains and stabilizes assumptions which have been applied in the specific cases, but which are also written into national, regional and international policy documents.

Thus it was lamented in work incorporated into Guinea's agricultural development policy strategy that: 'The north of forest Guinea (Beyla, Kissidougou and Gueckedou) is no longer a pre-forest region, but an "ex-forest" or "post forest" region!' Stating the narrative in its perhaps most succinct and pure form, it was asserted that:

> This degradation of the natural environment…is the result of an evolution of rural societies little adapted to the rapid structural, demographic and economic changes this century, and above all, these last years…The problem today is the recession of traditional control of the orderly exploitation of space and its resources, which has not managed to follow or adapt to the recent and very rapid change in the rural world. This management becomes insufficient given a brutal increase in population [and] a progressive loss in the power of traditional control, due to the destructuration of rural society, the new amplitude of migration and the push towards agrarian individualism and the monetization of the local economy (République de Guinée, 1989, p8).

This narrative is the script of international donors, and one could fill shelves with its versions across Africa and beyond. Focusing on the population component, a recent World Bank policy review argues that:

> …traditional farming and livestock husbandry practices, traditional dependency on wood for energy and for building material, traditional land tenure arrangements and traditional burdens on rural women worked well when population densities were low and population grew slowly. With the shock of extremely rapid population growth … these practices could not evolve fast enough. Thus they became the major source of forest destruction and degradation of the rural environment (Cleaver, 1992, p67).

This, it is argued, leads to vicious spirals of shortening fallows, land depletion, yield declines, and subsequent migration to marginal lands and forests. Environmental crisis results less from the overall effect of population pressure on resource availability, as a classic Malthusian position would have it, than from the multiple effects of population pressure on the institutions seeking to control resource access and use.

In exemplifying how inapplicable current regional narratives can be to local situations, the Kissidougou and Ziama cases invite a more fundamental examination of the origins and purposes of the regional narrative itself. More than empirical evidence, such narratives depend on – and expose – the field of western imagination concerning African society; in particular, they show that stereotypes born of the colonial era are alive and well in the applied social sciences. Whether they are used to justify policies of external repression, or policies of social reorganization and 'participatory' development, the narratives justify and make imperative a role for the outsider in the control of rural resources. The broader assumptions which the regional narratives contain can be summarized as follows:

1   that African vegetation was once 'original', consisting of a climax vegetation, ie the ultimate stage of plant succession which can exist under given ecological conditions. Prevailing ecological conditions are unchanging, so that what could exist today (eg humid forest in the forest and preforest region) did recently exist. Against this most natural vegetation one can judge levels of 'degradation';

2   that African society can be seen, at origin, in terms of a traditional 'functional order'. Such order was once harmoniously integrated with 'natural' vegetation (eg as epitomized in the idea of a 'forest people' and a 'savanna people'). African farming, land and resource-use practices degrade or are at best benign to the original vegetation. Degradation is thus limited only by functional social organization (regulation and authority). From environmental degradation one can diagnose the social ills of organizational dysfunction;

3   that African rural populations only increase, and do so fast. Population increase is as such environmentally and socially damaging;

4   that African society is essentially sedentary and subsistence oriented with an anticommercial sentiment (eg in the popular imagery of 'anti-commercial' traditional hunters). Money, mobility and trade are modern and lead to socio-environmental dysfunction. African history consisted of the continuous reproduction of tradition until it began to become 'modern', whether with markets and mobility, colonial intervention, or (in some work) the arrival of Islam.

The romantic links forged between these assumptions mean that vegetation change carries very profound moral messages. 'Original climax vegetation' and 'traditional functional society' provide fundamental baselines, so that whether the concern is about society or the environment, it is possible to judge that something is wrong and assess the extent of damage. From such a vantage point, the imperative is to intervene.

These assumptions, stabilized and sometimes hidden within social science analysis, are destructive and ultimately have no policy relevance. 'The hard fact' as Sayer (1992) puts it, 'is that most aid projects, and especially those in forestry fail'. As the Kissidougou and Ziama cases exemplify, misleading narratives are fundamental to this failure. Moreover, just as for these cases there are counternarratives which better fit the facts of vegetation history, so at a more general level we follow the spirit of the articles in this special section to suggest other assumptions and a stabilizing narrative which better reflect realities surrounding African environments. The parameters of this counternarrative accord with recent developments in ecological and social theory and, significantly, they do not perpetuate the imperative for outside intervention in local resource control.

While the old narratives held within them a view of ecology which had to explain the disappearance of a natural climax vegetation, newer strands of ecological theory reject the idea of a single environmental maximum. When climate historians suggest that Africa has experienced both long-period, deep climatic fluctuations and changes in climatic variability, the history of vegetation begins to be seen as a history of continual transition, rather than of divergence from a single, once-extant climax. Recent theory suggests that such repeated transitions are likely to be between particular 'stable' vegetation states, each determined by a multi-factor complex, rather than by trends in any particular variable. If the transition-causing factor reverts to its pre-transition level, vegetation may move to another state, but need not return to its initial one (Sprugel, 1991; Scoones, 1994). Given the multiplicity of interacting factors influencing each state, shifts between them can be triggered by a particular, possibly unique, historical conjuncture of ecological factors. From this viewpoint, there is no basis for identifying a region's fundamental, archetypal vegetation. Vegetation is in continual transition, and its trajectory is determined by the legacy of past vegetation paths and present ecological conditions.

Ideas of environmental optima dovetailed neatly with ideas of static social maxima – of tradition and structure – typical of, but persisting beyond, colonial anthropology. But notions of society with a given social structure and order, maintained by functional adaptation and/or by rules and regulation, are challenged by more recent social theories giving weight to social action, processes and their capacity to shape and determine rules. Such continual structuration, over time and through social change, challenges the notion of a baseline 'traditional' societal state. That African social forms have been in constant transition dovetails with the view of vegetation as in continual transition. There is no baseline in terms of how society values vegetation (and therefore no basis for the moral argument that indigenous values once preserved a more 'natural' ideal). Vegetation values are shifting in accordance with social, economic and political changes, often of quite a conjunctural nature. The values placed on different vegetation types, conditioned by prevailing social conditions, are also socially differentiated; the high forest and wildlife priorities of today's global conservation planners are very different from the agricultural bush fallow priorities of today's Toma inhabitants.

In the West African context, these social and economic transitions have taken place within a long historical context of movement and migration, agriculture and commerce, and political and religious turbulence. The relationship between social and environmental change does not turn on the dramatic increase in any of these, but rather on people's responses to changing signals within this broader, dynamic continuity. Thus Kissidougou villagers have adapted forest island form to meet changing needs for fortification and different cash crops. Demographic change, rather than consisting always of unilinear population increase, involves periods of stability and decline, of shocks as well as secular trends. Depending on prevailing ecological and economic conditions, the effects of population growth periods can be positive as well as negative.

In the West African forest margin zones, climatic transition appears to have involved rehumidification since the mid-19th century, following a long relatively dry phase (Nicholson, 1979). Where the combination of ecological factors makes conditions marginal for forest, creating a precarious balance between forest vegetation and fire-maintained savannah, people's activities can make the difference, allowing forest vegetation to develop in grassland. Where people have socio-economic or political reasons to create forest they do so, in small patches, triggering transitions in small parts of the landscape, as has happened, for example, in Kissidougou. In open savannah and with low population densities, fire is harder to control, but as populations increase and transitions to forest are provoked in more places, fire is reduced and may eventually be eliminated. Agricultural priorities may mean large areas are maintained as bush fallow rather than allowed to develop into high forest. As populations increase further, fallow periods may need to be shortened and some resavannization can occur. But if population is removed at that point, and given the legacy of people's previous land use practices, the area may develop into high forest, as happened early this century in Ziama.

This regional counternarrative provides different, and more appropriate, guidelines for policy. In presenting socio-environmental change in a way which better fits local experience, it provides a more effective basis for dialogue and participatory development work with local populations. In removing the baseline link between social and vegetation form, it removes the justification for external intervention in the organization of resource management to reestablish a lost social order, whether by replacement with external control or by the externally promoted 'community reorganization' of recent more decentralized approaches. It suggests that more important priorities are to create the enabling policy and economic conditions in which local resource management constellations can act effectively, to support the diverse existing local institutional forms, and to build on the beneficial environmental implications of broader rural development and pricing policies – an approach which now finds support in some regional policy institutions (eg ENDA, 1992). Finally, as McNeely argues, 'because chance factors, human influence and small climatic variation can cause very substantial changes in vegetation, [the biodiversity for] any given landscape will vary substantially over any significant time period – and no one variant is necessarily more "natural" than the others' (McNeely, 1993). From this perspective, environmental policy can call on no moral high ground in recreating the natural (or the social that went with it). It becomes very clearly a question of social or political choice about what vegetation forms are desirable at any given time in social history, and about ensuring that conflicting perspectives on this – such as between local, global and intergenerational interests – are adequately articulated and addressed.

References

Adam, J G (1948) 'Les reliques boisées et les essences des savanes dans le zone préforestière en Guinee fancaise'. *Bulletin de la Société Botanique Francaise* **98**: 22–26

Anderson, B (1870) *Narrative of a Journey to Musardu: Capital of the Western Mandigoes,* S. W. Green, New York

Baum, G A and H-J Weimer (1992), 'Participation et développement socio-économique comme conditions préalables indispensables d'une implication active des poulations riveraines dans la conservation de la forêt clasée de Ziama,' Report Deutsche Forst-Consult/Neu-Isenburg, RFA/KfW, Conakry, Republique de Guinee

Chevalier, A (1933) 'Les bois sacrés des Noirs de l'Afrique tropicale comme sanctuaries de la nature'. *Revue de la Société de Biogéographie,* 37–42

Chevalier (1909) 'Rapport sur les nouvelles recherches sur les les plantes a caouchouc de la Guinee francaise' IG276, Archives du Senegal, Dakar

Cleaver, K (1992) 'Deforestation in the western and central African forest: the agricultural and demographic causes, and some solutions', in K Cleaver, M Munashighe, M Dyson, N Egli, A Peuker and F Wencélins (eds) *Conservation of West and Central Africa's Rainforests.* Environment Paper No. 1, World Bank, Washington, DC, pp65–78

Dupré G (1991) 'Les arbres, le fourré et le jardin: les plantes dans la société de Aribinda, Burkina Faso', in G Dupré (ed) *Savoirs Paysans et Développement* Karthala-ORSTOM, Paris, pp181–194

ENDA (1992) *Avenir des Terroirs: la ressource humaine* ENDA/GRAF, Dakar

Fairhead, J and Leach, M, *Reversing Landscape History: Power, Policy and Socialised Ecology in West Africa's Forest – Savanna Mosaic,* (forthcoming)

Fairhead, J and Leach, M (1994) 'Contested forests: modern conservation and historical land use of Guinea's Ziama reserve'. *African Affairs* 93: 481–512.

Fofana, S, Camara, Y, Barry, M and Sylla, A (1993) 'Etude relative au feu aprés des populations des bassins versants types du Haut Niger: monographies des Bassins Kan I, Kan II, Kiss II'. Report, Programme d'Aménagement des Bassins Versants Haut-Niger, Conakry, République de Guinée

Green, W (1991) 'Lutte contre les feux de brousse', Report, Projet DERIK, Dévéloppement Rural Intégré de Kissidougou, Conakry, République de Guinée

Hair, P E H (1962) 'An account of the Liberian Hinterland c. 1780'. *Sierra Leone Studies.* NS 16: 218–226

Holling, C S (1973) 'Resilience and stability of ecological systems'. *Annual Review of Ecology and Systematics* 4: 1–23

Leach, M and Fairhead, J (1994) 'The forest islands of Kissidougou: social dynamics of environmental change in West Africa's forest-savanna mosaic'. Report to ESCOR of the Overseas Development Administration, July

Leach, M and Fairhead, J (1995) 'Ruined settlements and new gardens: gender and soil-ripening among Kuranko farmers in the forest–savanna transition zone'. *IDS Bulletin* 26(1): 24–32

McNeely, J A (1993) 'Lessons from the past: forests and biodiversity'. IUCN, Gland, Switzerland

Nicholson, S E (1979) 'The methodology of historical climate reconstruction and its application to Africa'. *Journal of African History* 20(1): 31–49

Ponsart-Dureau, M-C (1986) 'Le pays Kissi de Guinée forestière: contribution a la connaissance du milieu; problematique de développement'. Memoire, Ecole Superieure d'Agronomic Tropicale, Montpellier

Portères, R (1965) 'Les noms des riz en Guinée: VI – Les noms des variétés de riz chez les Toma'. *Journal d'Agriculture Tropicale et de Botanique Appliquée* 12: 687–728

Programme d'Aménagement des Bassins Versants Haute Guinée (Projet Kan II) (1992) 'Plan d'Opération'. Report, Programme d'Aménagement des Hauts Bassins du Fleuve Niger, Conakry, République de Guinée

Programme d'Aménagement des Hauts Bassins du Fleuve Niger (undated), 'Etude sociologique'. Report, Programme d'Aménagement des Hauts Bassins du Fleuve Niger, Conakry, République de Guinée

République de Guinée (1989) 'La gestion des ressources naturelles'. Contribution to the lettre politique de dévéloppement agricole, Minstère d'Agriculture et des Ressources Animales, Conakry, République de Guinée, November

République de Guinée and IUCN (1990) 'Guinea forestry biodiversity study – Ziama and Diecke Reserves'. Report, IUCN for République de Guinée, Gland, Switzerland, September

Roe, E (1991), 'Development narratives, or making the best of blueprint development'. *World Development* **19**(4)

Roe, E and Fortmann, L (1982) *Season and Strategy*, Special Series on Resource Management, Rural Development Committee, Centre for International Studies. Cornel University, Ithaca, NY

Sayer, J A (1992) 'Development assistance strategies to conserve Africa's rainforests', in K Cleaver, M Munashighe, M Dyson, N Egli, A Peuker and F Wencélìns (eds) *Conservation of West and Central Africa's Rainforests,* Environment Paper No. 1, World Bank, Washington, DC, pp3–17

Scoones, I (ed) (1994) *Living with Uncertainty: New Directions for Pastoral Development in Africa,* IT Publications, London

Seymour, G L (1859–1860) 'The journal of the journey of George L Seymour to the interior of Liberia: 1858'. *New York Colonization Journal,* **IX**(12) **X**(6) and (8)

Sims, J L (1859–1860) 'The journal of a journey in the interior of Liberia by James L Sims, of Monrovia. Scenes in the interior of Liberia: being a tour through the countries of the Dey, Goulah, Pessah Barlain, Kpellay, Suloang, and the King Boatswain's tribes, in 1858'. *New York Colonization Journal* **IX**(12) **X**(6) and (8)

Sprugel, D G (1991) 'Disturbance, equilibrium, and environmental variability: what is "natural" vegetation in a changing environment?'. *Biological Conservation* **58**: 1–18

Starr, F (ed) (1912) *Narrative of the Expedition Despatched to Musahdu by the Liberian Government under Benjamin K Anderson Esq in 1874,* College of West Africa Press, Monrovia

Stieglitz, F V (1990) 'Exploitation forestière rurale et réhabilitation des forêts: premièrs résultats d'un projet de recherche interdisciplinaire en Haute-Guinée (Janv–Mai 1990, République de Guinée)'. Mimeo, Berlin

Zerouki, B (1993) 'Etude relative au feu auprès des populations des bassins versants types du Haut Niger'. Report, Programme d'Aménagement des Bassins Versants Types du Haut Niger, Conakry, République de Guinée

Notes

1   This article is the result of our joint and equal co-authorship. It is based on research funded by ESCOR of the Overseas Development Administration, whom we gratefully thank. Opinions represented here are, however, the authors' own, not those of the ODA. Many thanks are also due to our Guinean co-researchers Dominique Millimouno and Marie Kamano, to Jean-Louis Hellié for field assistance around Ziama, to the villagers we worked with in both case studies, and to our collaborating institutions: the Ministère de l'Enseignment Superieur, the Direction National des Forêts et de la Chasse, and Projet DERIK, Kissidougou.

2   This, like all subsequent quotations, have been translated from the original French by the authors.

3   More details of the following historical vegetation analysis are given in Leach and Fairhead (1994).

4   Such alternative social science analysis and its considerable evidence is documented fully elsewhere (Fairhead and Leach, forthcoming; Leach and Fairhead, 1995).

5   For more on the management-use continuum (i.e. the way people use a resource in the way they manage it), see Roe and Fortmann (1982).

6   Further details concerning this case are given in Fairhead and Leach (1994).

2

Continuities in Environmental Narratives: The Case of Kabale, Uganda, 1930–2000[1]

Grace Carswell

Summary

This article looks at continuities and change around the issue of agricultural sustainability in colonial and post-colonial Kabale. It argues that a series of environmental narratives developed during the colonial period, which have been largely unquestioned since then. It shows how the perception of the district being threatened with environmental degradation has continued from the earliest colonial period up to the present day. Many of the assumptions made by colonial officials remain unquestioned, and with few exceptions the policy rhetoric remains unaltered in the post-colonial period. It argues that recent evidence suggests that these assumptions need to be seriously questioned.

Introduction

Kabale, in the southwestern corner of Uganda, is an area of intensive agricultural production with a dense population that has, for decades, been perceived to be at risk from serious environmental degradation. From the time the British first arrived in Kabale (or Kigezi as it was then called), agriculturalists and environmentalists have written extensively about the potential for environmental disaster in the region, perpetuating fears that population pressure on the land will lead to severe environmental degradation.[2] Such concerns continue to inform contemporary policy. Uganda's *State of the Environment Report* for 1998 states that in Kabale

> The high population pressure has pushed people to farm on very steep fragile hillsides, destroying contour bunds and to practise continuous cultivation with very short fallow.

Reprinted from *Environment and History*, vol 9, Carswell, G, 'Continuities in environmental narratives: The Case of Kabale, Uganda, 1930–2000', pp3–29, copyright © (2003) with permission from White Horse Press.

As a result, soil fertility has significantly declined, yields are very low, there is a lot of soil erosion and land slides ... people are becoming poorer and suffering from chronic food insecurity.[3]

The view that Kabale is on the edge of disaster is firmly entrenched in the minds of outside observers, district officials and local residents, and frequent reference is made to these environmental problems. Despite being described in apocalyptic terms for over 50 years, however, this densely populated area of Uganda has not succumbed to serious environmental catastrophe, and the extent of environmental degradation in the district remains highly debatable.[4]

As a result of environmental concerns policy-makers (colonial officials prior to independence in 1962, and government agencies and NGOs since then) have focused a good deal of attention on the district. During the colonial period a number of policies were implemented including soil conservation measures, a resettlement scheme and swamp reclamation. Since independence, while comparable strategies have been discussed (with a particular focus on soil conservation), the extent to which the government has been able to implement its decisions has been significantly weaker. Civil unrest and insecurity as well as budgetary constraints have meant that Government's capacity to implement development strategies has been much weaker than it was in the colonial period. NGOs, however, have implemented a range of policies (particularly agricultural research and agroforestry), and there has been an increased focus on participation and emphasis on decentralization, as well as some strategic shifts (notably from land-reclamation to the protection of wetlands). Nevertheless, as this paper will show, the assumptions that underlie contemporary policy bear a remarkable similarity to those informing colonial programmes.

Conceptual Issues

The power of policy narratives in environmental planning in developing countries has been highlighted by a number of scholars in recent years.[5] Roe has explored how 'development narratives' persist through time, often in spite of evidence to the contrary.[6] Like a story, these narratives each have 'a beginning, a middle and end ... they tell scenarios not so much about what should happen as about what will happen ... if the events or positions are carried out as described.' They are 'more programmatic than myths and have the objective of getting their hearers to believe or do something'.[7] Hoben has stated:

> The environmental policies promoted by colonial regimes and later by donors in Africa rest on historically grounded, culturally constructed paradigms that at once describe a problem and prescribe its solution. Many of them are rooted in a narrative that tells us how things were in an earlier time when people lived in harmony with nature, how human agency has altered that harmony, and of the calamities that will plague people and nature if dramatic action is not taken soon.[8]

He notes that successful programmes (in terms of mobilizing funds) are those that 'depend on a set of more or less naïve, unproven, simplifying and optimistic assumptions about the problem to be addressed and the approach to be taken'. Such a 'cultural script for action' helps donors and aid recipients mobilize and coordinate action in the face of many uncertainties.[9] Adams and Hulme note that such narratives are disseminated by aid donors and media campaigns, and community leaders 'learn what to say to access external resources'. Thus the narratives become 'culturally, institutionally and politically embedded, their influence and longevity related less to their actual economic, social or environmental achievements than to the interests of a complex web of politicians, policy-makers, bureaucrats, donors, technical specialists and private sector operators whose needs they serve'.[10] Narratives are replaced only by 'counter-narratives' that tell 'a better story'. [11]

Why have such narratives proved to be so long lasting and resilient? Hoben has identified the conditions under which the power of a development narrative is enhanced, which include donor experts being strongly attached to them, there being only a weak data base on the problem, the recipient country relying heavily on expatriate experts for advice and being dependent on foreign assistance, and the government being weak and/or authoritarian.[12] All these apply (or have applied at some time in the period under review) in the case under analysis. In the case of population–environment relations, the simplicity of the neo-Malthusian narrative certainly adds to its appeal, but it is more than this. Leach and Mearns have observed that 'by making "stabilising" assumptions to facilitate decision-making, narratives serve to standardise, package and label environmental problems so that they appear to be universally applicable and to justify equally standardised, off-the-shelf solutions'.[13] Such 'received wisdoms' have had the effect of promoting external intervention in the control and use of natural resources. For some organizations the existence of such a narrative helps to justify their own existence.[14] Roe has noted that crisis narratives are a way for development experts and the institutions for which they work to 'claim rights to stewardship over land and resources they do not own. By generating and appealing to crisis narratives, technical experts and managers assert rights as "stakeholders" in the land and resources they say are under crisis ... the more crisis narratives generated by an expert elite, the more the elite appears to have established a claim to the resources it says are subject to crisis.'[15] The power of the narrative to help claim rights of stewardship over resources may in part explain the resilience of the narrative in both the colonial and postcolonial eras. Furthermore, in some parts of the colonial world (eg Kenya, Zimbabwe and South Africa) one of the reasons for the use of this narrative was to legitimate the alienation of land from Africans into the hands of whites. As the settlement of whites in Uganda had long been ruled out this did not apply in the Kigezi case. But although this essentially political ingredient was missing in the case of Kigezi this did not prevent the narrative from taking hold.

These received wisdoms are not necessarily modern constructs, and Leach and Mearns note that 'in many cases, the ideas that drive contemporary environmental policy in Africa can be traced back to early colonial times'. [16] This article will do just that, tracing how the idea of Kabale on the edge of crisis developed from the earliest colonial encounters with the district in the 1920s and 1930s.[17] The colonial legacy of environmental assumptions and narratives has been inherited by the post-Independence government, and donor agencies have also 'joined the state and national elites in perpetuating received thinking about environment-society relationships'.[18] Kabale is thus an example of an area where there has been 'remarkable historical continuity in received wisdom about environmental change'.[19]

Background to the Area

Kabale District covers an area of approximately 1800km², and lies at an altitude of between 1200m and 2347m above sea level. The mean annual rainfall is 1000mm, it is bimodal and precipitation is usually gentle and evenly distributed. Temperatures range between 9°C and 23°C. The district is made up of undulating hills with steep slopes. Many of the valley bottoms were once papyrus swamps, although most have been drained during the last 50 years, and are now cultivated or used for pasture.[20]

The area has experienced an extremely long history of human settlement and is densely populated with the most recent census giving a land density of 246 people/km².[21] This high population density is the result of both in-migration over a sustained period and high natural increase. Whilst statistics produced by early censuses must be treated with some caution (being unreliable extrapolations of very small surveys) they do suggest substantial increases in population. Between 1921 and 1959 it more than doubled.[22] As a result of population density, relatively small acreages of land are available for farming, and the system of inheritance has resulted in the fragmentation of land holdings and widely scattered plots. It was estimated that by the mid-1940s the average acreage under cultivation was less than three acres per taxpayer, or half an acre per resident person.[23]

British administration of Kigezi District was introduced relatively late in comparison with the rest of the Uganda Protectorate. It was not until after the Anglo-German-Belgian Boundary Commission of 1911 had settled the different colonial claims to the area, that civil administration was implemented.[24] The imposition of colonial rule in Kigezi was effected in part through, for example, the collection of tax. Cash to meet these new fiscal demands was earned through the sale of crops and livestock (mainly small stock) and wage labour. The main crops grown were sorghum, peas, beans and sweet potato, and peas and beans in particular were traded. Kigezi was central to a food production system and market that straddled international boundaries and encompassed Rwanda and Ankole. Attempts to introduce a variety of non-food 'cash crops' were unsuccessful as the British consistently failed to appreciate the vitality of the food crop sector in the district.[25]

Colonial Myths and Narratives

From the arrival of the first colonial officials in Kabale in the 1920s the 'dangers' that the densely populated district faced have been continually reiterated. The earliest concerns expressed were about land shortage and over-population. In 1921, it was observed that land in Kabale was intensively cultivated and 'barely suffices for present needs'. Such concerns were repeated throughout the 1920s.[26]

By the mid-1930s the problems focused more specifically on the threat of soil exhaustion and the problem of reduced fallow. Shifting concerns need to be seen in the context of a growing obsession with soil erosion, and the threat of land degradation resulting from high population growth, that was emerging throughout colonial Africa at this time. The process by which policies of agrarian reform, and in particular those related to soil conservation, emerged and evolved during the 1930s have been examined by Anderson.[27] The experiences of the Dust Bowl in the USA in the 1930s demonstrated the dangers of soil erosion, while the realization that East Africa's population was growing rapidly, and the threat of drought and famine, added to these concerns. The policies that evolved in response to this situation were broadly similar across East Africa, and much of the following discussion occurred on a regional basis. There are a number of case studies from other parts of Eastern and Southern Africa showing how concerns about the environment influenced the formulation of agricultural policy.[28]

In London the question of soil erosion was considered by the Council for Agriculture and Animal Health in February 1930, which felt that the issue was of 'considerable importance' and 'should be viewed as an East African problem'[29] and meetings were held to discuss the issue of soil erosion in the region throughout the 1930s.[30] Meanwhile, in East Africa, annual conferences were held for Directors of Agriculture from British colonies at which policy to coordinate agricultural research (including soil erosion), and the findings of such research were discussed.[31] Information gathered in one colony was disseminated at the conferences,[32] and ideas were also gathered from further afield.[33]

In Uganda the major areas of concern were cash cropping areas. According to a 1935 memo by Tothill, the Director of Agriculture, rising populations, and changing patterns of cultivation and stock rearing were putting increasing strain on the environment in these areas, and the need was identified to modify traditional forms of cultivation.[34] As cotton producing regions, Eastern Province and Buganda were the most important income generating areas for the Ugandan administration. Up to the early 1940s Kabale, not being a cash crop producing area, was rarely mentioned and it is clear from this emphasis that concerns about cash crops were crucial. Prior to this, initiatives at a national level (such as the Agricultural Survey Committee) appear to have been prompted as much by concerns over cotton yields as by concerns over soil erosion; though it suited the administration to present these initiatives as measures aimed at combating soil erosion.

Although Kabale rarely entered the discussion at a national level, concerns were being expressed within the district itself. In 1935 the District Agricultural Officer (DAO), Wickham, observed that crop yields were falling because of soil exhaustion in a ten mile radius of Kabale. He observed that it was:

> probable, though not yet determined, that all crops in this area are … deteriorating in yield, or quality… The reason for this state of affairs is clearly over-population and soil exhaustion. There is not enough land available for the essential item in the rotation – fallow – to be included at the proper intervals.[35]

Wickham saw the problem as having two related aspects – soil erosion and soil exhaustion, due to cultivation of steep hillsides, and lack of fallow respectively.[36] He warned that 'the position will inevitably and steadily become worse' and the area might cease to be self-supporting in food.[37] Similar warnings were made by subsequent DAOs. Masefield expressed anxiety over the effect falling yields were having on the ability to collect sufficient famine reserves in some areas of Ndorwa. He observed that 'the exhaustion of soil fertility is already becoming a problem in certain overcrowded areas of Kigezi'.[38] As a result of these concerns a number of policies were put into practice at the initiative of local officials. Soil conservation measures included contour planting and elephant grass strips along the contour, which were in fact modifications to indigenous practices.[39]

Although district officials kept Entebbe-based administrators up to date with progress in relation to soil conservation measures these reports made little impact and it was not until the Deputy Director of Agriculture toured the region in July 1941 that the extent to which anti-erosion measures were being carried out in Kigezi was fully appreciated by senior officials. Furthermore, adverse weather conditions in 1943 brought Kigezi's agricultural system under closer colonial scrutiny.[40] These had resulted in food shortages across much of Uganda. Marketing regulations were tightened up, the purchase of African foodstuffs for resale or export was prohibited and migration from Rwanda into Kigezi was banned. 'Famine' conditions were declared to be prevalent in the district. There was an increased awareness of the importance of food production in the area around Kabale town, as well as concern that the district itself might be vulnerable to famine. After a visit to Kigezi in early 1944, the Director of Agriculture spoke in strong language about the 'devastated area around Kabale' and emphasized the need for soil conservation measures.[41] Thus the lack of attention given to Kigezi changed abruptly in the early 1940s. Shortly afterwards Kigezi's soil conservation measures were being held up as an example to the rest of Uganda, indeed to the colonial world.

The crisis in the early 1940s coincided with Purseglove's arrival in Kigezi as DAO. Purseglove was to exert greater influence over the district than perhaps any other colonial official. He increased attention given to the district, initiating a resettlement scheme and 'stepping up' soil conservation policies, which were 'consolidated' into a programme that became known as *Plani Ensya*, ('New Plan'). Soon after his arrival, Purseglove undertook a land use survey in southern Kigezi to assess whether the area was 'over-populated', and if so to what extent.[42] It is clear that before the study had even begun it had been decided that the area was overpopulated, and the study was carried out to provide empirical support for colonial policy. Purseglove reported that 'overcultivation has resulted in soil exhaustion and a deterioration in soil structure, with a consequent reduction in the amount of water absorbed by the soil'.[43] Quoting from Jacks and Whyte's *The Rape of the Earth*, he stated that 'although serious erosion is not yet a problem we cannot afford to be complacent and wait for it to become so'. He concluded that the area around Kabale town could not continue to support an increasing population and that it would be 'most unwise to continue under the present conditions in the hope that further soil deterioration and erosion will not take place'.[44] These findings confirmed earlier fears that serious environmental degradation was likely to occur in the area unless dramatic steps were taken. Although Purseglove played a crucial role in bringing Kigezi to centre stage, his findings were in fact not particularly innovative. On the contrary, many previous officials had discussed the problems arising from high population density, soil erosion and falling yields, and Kigezi's reputation as 'over-populated' was firmly entrenched in the colonial mind by the time Purseglove arrived.

In the case of soil conservation policies, Kabale presents a rather unusual case. In contrast to other parts of the region,[45] soil conservation measures were implemented successfully, with little resistance from the local population. The soil conservation measures included strip cropping and bunding. However, the success of anti-erosion initiatives can best be attributed to the fact that the earliest measures introduced (such as planting of elephant grass along the contour and narrow plots along the contour) were modifications of a system of contour cultivation that was traditionally practised in the area.[46] Opposition to such measures in other parts of the region arose from clashes with indigenous methods of erosion control; the additional labour input required to implement measures; the extent to which local conditions were taken into account in the formulation of these schemes; and the extent to which officials on the ground were able to adapt measures to local conditions. In Kigezi, in addition to the fact that early initiatives were essentially modifications of the Bakiga agricultural system, measures were also introduced gradually and, in comparison to similar schemes elsewhere, greater effort was put into education, propaganda, and the provision of incentives. By working directly through chiefs, placing responsibility on them, and giving them authority to both judge and punish, the administration was broadly successful in getting conservation measures carried out. Additionally, suspicion of the government's motives, fears of losing land to Europeans and the rise of nationalism were critical ingredients missing in Kigezi, which in other areas facilitated the articulation of discontent.[47] Finally and crucially, the Agriculture Department was flexible enough to drop those parts of the scheme that proved inappropriate; seemingly greater attention was given to local responses to policies than elsewhere.[48]

Resettlement was a key component of the policies introduced as a result of concerns about over-population. Throughout Purseglove's period in Kabale, the target of resettling 20,000 people, as suggested in his original report,[49] was met, and relocation initiatives were presented as a great success. But with Purseglove's departure from the district in 1952, there was some reassessment and King, the new DAO, observed that the value of the scheme was often overstated as it had not even managed to achieve the resettlement of the natural increase of population.[50] By 1953, 22,002 people had been resettled, while there had been an estimated population increase of 64,280. It was 'obvious that the problem had only been scratched'.[51] There followed some discussion as to whether resettlement should continue, and be stepped up, or whether more effort should be put into finding ways for Kigezi to support a greatly increased population.[52] In the event, resettlement continued but without the commitment displayed to it during Purseglove's time. An emphasis on soil conservation was also maintained, which according to one DC had become 'the end all and be all of effort in Kigezi'.[53]

As the 1950s progressed there was an increased emphasis on a 'more rounded' approach. Shifting attitudes towards African land tenure – notably in the years following the publication of the 1955 East African Royal Commission Report – were exerting a growing influence on agricultural policy.[54] Thus, by the latter part of the colonial period, although beliefs about the threats faced by the district were largely unchanged, different policies were put forward as a solution to the problem. The shift in the emphasis of colonial policy towards individual land tenure arose partly from the conviction that concerns about sustainability could be dealt with by giving individual farmers absolute control over their land through the granting of titles. In Kigezi, land was highly fragmented, and titles could only be granted after consolidation. By the late 1950s this had become the main priority for the District's Department of Agriculture. For example, King, the DAO between 1952–1958, stressed that 'the first essential step towards increased agricultural productivity in Kigezi is to secure consolidation of fragmented holdings'.[55] However, with inadequate administrative and financial support the success of these land reform policies (which also included land enclosure, a land titling scheme and the promotion of farm planning) was more mixed than had been the case with soil conservation policies.[56]

The other major late-colonial policy arising from concern about over-population was that of swamp reclamation. This was already occurring on a small scale, being carried out by individual farmers without logistical support from the district office. However, in the latter part of the colonial era reclamation was intensified at the initiation, and with the advice and technical assistance of the administration. Reclamation of swamps was seen as a relatively cheap and easy way of increasing land for cultivation. Before the mid-1950s reclamation occurred in a somewhat piecemeal fashion. Colonial officials disagreed as to the best way forward and at this time reclamation work was characterized by serious technical difficulties. However, in 1956 a report on water resources in Uganda recommended the drainage and development of over 80 per cent of the swamp in the district,[57] and official policy shifted in favour of large-scale reclamation. Reclamation progressed apace in the late-colonial and early post-colonial period until all swamp suitable for drainage and cultivation had been reclaimed.[58]

Thus a number of policies (soil conservation, resettlement, swamp reclamation and land consolidation) developed out of colonial concerns about the threat of over-population and associated environmental degradation, and were implemented with varying degrees of success. Behind the environmental narratives that informed these policies lay an assumption that indigenous methods of cultivation were inadequate to cope with change and the increasing pressure on local resources. With only one or two exceptions there was little recognition or credit given to the ability of the agricultural system, and the people within it, to maintain the natural resource base. As Hoben has argued in the case of Ethiopia 'the neo-Malthusian narrative's denigration of indigenous agriculture … led experts and planners to overlook and filter out much information about the strengths of indigenous resource management practices'.[59] This is perhaps unsurprising in the colonial context, when prejudices about 'primitive' agricultural systems were common currency. But how did this change with the coming of Independence?

Post-colonial Narratives and Policy Rhetoric

The reputation gained by Kigezi in the colonial period is one that it has never been able to shake off. Rather, it has been continually reiterated and elaborated upon and the environmental degradation narrative remains little changed. It is striking how little the claims made about the district have changed over the past decades: statements made about Kigezi's problems today could be almost verbatim quotes from colonial reports written 50 or 60 years earlier. In recent years the familiar fears about over-population and soil erosion have been summed up by the phrase 'environmental sustainability'. The assumptions and fears behind this phrase, and the language used to convey these, have remained constant.

In the immediate post-Independence period influential writers such as William Allan, author of the pathbreaking *The African Husbandman,* commented on the 'very serious congestion' in Kabale, observing how 'all the usual symptoms of over-population' were evident, including 'almost continuous cultivation and consequent soil degradation, subdivision and excessive fragmentation of land'.[60] Studies conducted by Makerere University staff continually reiterated these familiar concerns. Kagambirwe observed soil deterioration in the area, referring to 'an assumption that there is considerable population pressure on the land'.[61] Without questioning this assumption he goes on to adopt the environmental degradation narrative, bemoaning the 'exhausted' hillslopes and 'the cry for land for cultivation'. Langlands, another Makerere researcher, observed that population pressure in some parts of the district was such that 'it is improbable that further increases could take place under existing technological practices'.[62] Kateete complained of the limited fallow resulting from population pressure on the land.[63] Meanwhile, a number of other studies addressed problems associated with land fragmentation.[64]

After a lull in the 1980s, research and publication began again towards the end of the decade. Once again the picture presented is remarkably similar to that of the 1940s and 1950s. Aspects of the neo-Malthusian environmental narrative repeatedly invoked include the assertion that over-population has led to severe land shortage, which in turn has led to reductions in fallow, increasing soil erosion and declining fertility, while deforestation is also frequently cited as a problem. Thus it is noted that erosion is 'particularly severe' in Kabale 'where high altitude mountain slopes have been greatly deforested'.[65] The 'failings' of local people are often implicit in the statements made. Joy Tukahirwa has written that in the highlands of Uganda high population growth has led to heavy pressures on the highland environment, and points in particular to 'indiscriminate cutting and burning of vegetation, overcultivation and overgrazing, and... lack of attention of soil erosion control measures ... soils are overcultivated with very little fallow'.[66] These observations, however, are not based on any scientific data and no source is cited. Similarly, the 1994 *State of the Environment Report* for Uganda, claims that the major causes of soil erosion and degradation were 'poor farming practices and high population pressure'. The Report notes that in the Rukiga county of Kabale 'soil erosion and degradation has reached alarming proportions on steep slopes due to poor cultivation techniques'.[67] According to such expert counsel, it is, quite simply, the farmers' fault.

Donor agencies have also adopted these beliefs about environmental degradation. CARE International has been involved in work with farmers living in the vicinity of the two National Parks in southwest Uganda attempting to find ways to improve local agricultural techniques.[68] A 1992 CARE report noted that 'with serious soil degradation from continuous cultivation and soil erosion, crop production is now declining in most areas... Traditional fallowing practices could conserve soil and restore fertility but fallowing has largely been abandoned because of increasing land pressure.'[69] African Highlands Initiative (AHI), a research organization working in the area, has observed that 'the highlands of south-west Uganda are in a crisis, facing severe problems of declining land productivity in a fragile, densely populated agroecosystem'.[70] A study conducted by AHI researchers concluded there was 'increased land degradation as a result of soil fertility decline, an outcome of reduced fallow [and] reduced organic matter use'.[71] The International Centre for Research on Agroforestry (ICRAF), which has a project operating in Kabale District under their Agroforestry Research Networks for Africa (AFRENA) programme, has made similar assumptions:

> Permanent cultivation, with short rotation periods, prevails [in this region] ... Soil deterioration and crop yields decline are a common consequence of such farming practices ... The sustainability ... [of the Kabale system of agriculture] is seriously threatened by the rapid decline in soil fertility... The reduction in farm size long ago resulted in the abandonment of fallowing practices and continuous cultivation is now common in the area.[72]

It is not only outside agencies who have adopted this environmental narrative. The DAO in 1996 observed that 'fields are cropped every season without a rest'.[73] According to the Kabale District Agricultural Work Plan for 1996, major problems arose from the fact that 'population pressure on land [was high], land is over cultivated with short rotation. Most soils are degraded and exhausted resulting in low productivity.'[74] In 1995, the District Environment Profile recorded that:

> The high population density and the nature of the terrain in Kabale district have led to excessive soil erosion. There is continuous cultivation of land without rest leading to soil degradation and exhaustion thus [sic] soils have low values of infiltration and soil water retention capacity. The end result of this has been highly leached soils that have consequently lost fertility. All these problems have been aggravated by land fragmentation and inadequate soil conservation measures such as terracing, mulching, contour strip planting, especially on hillslopes.[75]

Again, the negative impact of the local population is observed: 'soil erosion has also largely been accelerated by human activities. The district experiences continuous cropping of land without ample rest and … continuous cropping is carried out without appropriate soil and water conservation measures.'[76]

In the immediate post-Independence period the rhetoric surrounding environmental sustainability at national government level was little changed. Although much legislation was revised in 1964, this was more 'in form than in substance'.[77] As a consequence, there was a marked continuity in environmental policy at district level. Although organized resettlement was abandoned, the focus on soil conservation was maintained – implemented through both agricultural extension workers and local chiefs – and the policy of swamp reclamation also persisted.

In more recent years, environmental concerns have become more explicit at a national level, with, for example, the creation in 1966 of the National Environmental Management Authority (NEMA). This umbrella agency advises local and district committees on acceptable ways of managing the environment. Although these committees formulate their own natural resource policies, they are to be developed in conformity with key principles of environmental management as laid down by NEMA. The sustainable utilization of natural resources receives particular emphasis, and district environmental management plans target areas needing special assistance to ensure that resources are used sustainably.[78] Furthermore, the National Environment Statute of the 1995 Constitution established District Environment Committees, that are supposed to 'co-ordinate the work of the District Local Councils on the environment as well as ensuring that environmental concerns are integrated in all plans and projects approved by the District Local Council'.[79] But, as Mugabe and Tumushabe have noted using case studies from Southern and Eastern African 'there is a disjunction between policy pronouncements and what actually takes place on the ground'.[80] Indeed the government has had limited capacity to enforce environmental objectives throughout much of the 1980s and 1990s. However, official rhetoric continues to stress environmental sustainability as evidenced in the Environmental Action Plans.[81] There is also an increasing effort to 'mainstream' environmental issues in, for example, Uganda's poverty reduction strategy paper.[82] The emphasis on 'environmental sustainability' forms a new expression of old fears about over-population, soil erosion and land degradation. These enduring concerns continue, unquestioned, to have a major influence on policy.

While the capacity of government to implement official policy has been severely hampered by budgetary and logistical constraints in the past two decades, external agencies such as NGOs have not faced similar limitations. NGOs therefore play an important developmental role in Kabale today, with a huge number of them operational within the district[83] (see Table 2.1).

There are two main areas of NGO involvement in the district: agricultural research and agroforestry. These have arisen out of multiple, overlapping concerns, namely: low and falling agricultural productivity, deforestation, threats to food security and threats to biodiversity (both in forests, such as Bwindi and Mgahinga, and in wetlands).[84] The neo-Malthusian narrative continues to drive contemporary policy in Kabale. However, policy is also shaped by wider influences on the development process. Over the past two decades a consensus has been reached over the need for local participation in development projects.[85] Almost all development projects today adopt this rhetoric of participation, taking forms such as 'farmer participatory research' and 'community conservation'.[86]

Policy-makers involved in natural resource management, such as forests and wildlife, are also increasingly looking to decentralization (the downward transfer of responsibility from higher decision-making levels to ones more accessible to local populations) as a way forward.[87] With these broader influences in mind, the following section will examine the main areas of NGO involvement, exploring the assumptions that drive NGO interventions and their supporting evidence.

Agricultural Productivity

NGOs in Kabale today are paying much attention to ways of increasing agricultural productivity. Centre International d'Agricole Tropical, for example, has been undertaking research to try to find suitable green manures, fallow legumes and other cover crops, which can be integrated into the cropping system. CARE's goal is to protect the natural resources in and around two national parks by improving the living conditions of local people. Their work has three components: park management, local institution building and sustainable agricultural development. Project activities include the introduction of new crop varieties and improved agricultural practices and on-farm tree planting through a farmer participatory research project. Africare has four components: rural feeder road rehabilitation, soil conservation and agroforestry, agricultural productivity and post-harvest handling, and household level nutrition. They work closely with AFRENA in their natural resource management and agroforestry activities. AFRENA aims to improve agroforestry productivity systems by supporting research and extension – agroforestry is believed to assist in terrace management and help restore soil fertility and reduce soil erosion.

Behind these agricultural projects lie a number of timeworn assumptions concerning falling soil fertility and reduced fallow periods, resulting from population growth. But what is the evidence for reduced fallow? Many of the claims about the declines are made with little or no corroborative evidence. Even Were, who stated that fallows had reduced and were now too short to allow soils to regenerate, found that 77 per cent of farms had some land being rested, and provided no evidence that fallow periods had decreased.[88] Other, more recent, studies have also found high prevalence of fallow. Grisley et al conducted a survey of households in the region to examine factors affecting farmers' decisions to rest land, and found that of the farms surveyed 76 per cent had some cropland in grass fallow, with 26 per cent of the total crop-

Table 2.1 *Main NGOs Working in Kabale*

NGO	Project	Funder	Main concerns, aims, policies	Key assumptions
CARE	Development through conservation (DTC)	Danida (3rd phase) (Phase 1 & 2 by USAID)	Need to increase agricultural productivity in areas around National Parks	Agricultural productivity low and falling; need to protect biodiversity in the Parks
Africare	Uganda Food Security Initiative (UFSI)	USAID	Food security, agroforestry, tree nurseries, road construction and seed multiplication	District is food insecure; agricultural productivity low and falling
International Centre for Research on Agroforestry (ICRAF)	AFRENA	USAID	Agricultural research and extension, agroforestry, tree nurseries	Deforestation has occurred under population pressure; agricultural productivity low and falling
African Highlands Initiative (AHI)	AHI	DfID, IDRC (Canada), SDC (Switzerland), Rockefeller and others	Agricultural research and extension	Agricultural productivity low and falling
Centre International d'Agricole Tropical (CIAT)	Network on Bean Research in Africa	USAID (and others)	Agricultural research and extension	Agricultural productivity low and falling
Africa 2000	Agroforestry	UNDP	Agroforestry	Agricultural productivity low and falling
Heifer Project International (HPI)	Dairy cattle provision	USAID (and others)	Livestock and fodder	Agricultural productivity low and falling
International Gorilla Conservation Project (IGCP)	Gorilla Conservation	African Wildlife Federation, USAID	Biodiversity	Need to protect biodiversity in the Parks
Mgahinga Bwindi Impenetrable Forest Conservation Trust (MBIFCT)	Conservation and development	USAID, Netherlands	Management of national parks and development support for residents living in close proximity to the Parks	Need to protect biodiversity in the Parks

Table 2.1 *Main NGOs Working in Kabale (continued)*

NGO	Project	Funder	Main concerns, aims, policies	Key assumptions
IUCN	Uganda National Wetlands Conservation and Management Project	Netherlands	Biodiversity	Need to protect biodiversity in the wetlands

land under fallow. Their research suggested that while increasing population density resulted in a decrease in the amount of land rested, this occurred at a rate significantly lower than the corresponding increase in population density.[89]

Meanwhile, a detailed land use survey conducted in 1996 examining changes in land use patterns over a 51-year period found that the proportion of land left to fallow actually increased – from 19 per cent in 1945 to 32 per cent in 1996. Household interviews confirmed the findings, suggested that 29 per cent of land was being rested at the time of the interview. Furthermore not only has proportion of land left to fallow increased – but also the length of time that fields are rested has also increased. In 1945 just under 50 per cent of fallow land was being rested for less than six months; with just over 50 per cent being rested for more than this. By 1996 only five per cent of fallowed land was being rested for less than six months; and thus almost all the fallow land was being rested for six months or more. The average time land was left to fallow increased from 9.4 months in 1945, to 14.2 months in 1996. As would be expected these changing patterns of fallow use are not socially undifferentiated, and the evidence suggests that it is the largest landowners, and the smallest landowners, who fallow most.[90] But they do so for very different reasons: while richer households have enough land to be able to fallow as a means of soil fertility maintenance, poorer households are fallowing in part because of labour shortages.[91]

Claims about soil erosion also benefit from closer examination. The one significant published survey to which many reports refer is that by Bagoora, who surveyed four areas within one sub-county of Kabale District. Although a measure of soil erosion was calculated (number of landslide scars per km²), the hills that were investigated were purposively selected as areas where severe erosion could be visually identified. In addition, although the study area was quite small, results were generalized not only to the region of Kigezi but to all highland areas in Uganda. Despite the limitations of this study, Bagoora concluded that:

> most slopes are seriously affected by all forms of soil erosion and conservation measures are needed to prevent irreversible calamity... [T]he highlands of Kigezi are a particularly noteworthy example of the induced risk of accelerated erosion in Uganda... This form of land use [in practice in Kigezi] has done indelible damage to nature in some parts of the highlands.[92]

Bagoora's work is cited by almost every author who writes about soil erosion in southwestern Uganda, often being the only source that attempts any objective quantification of the extent of the problem. However, the small, purposively selected sample cannot be assumed to be representative of the district.[93]

In contrast to the prevailing viewpoints, a number of researchers have reported that the soils of Kabale are in fact resilient and resistant to erosion. Laboratory analysis of soil from the area by Magunda found it to be well aggregated with a stable structure and high organic matter levels. He concluded that the soil was particularly resistant to erosion.[94] Another more recent study has examined accelerated erosion using 12 natural run-off plots on which soil loss and erosion features were measured.[95] Once again, the findings contradicted conventional wisdoms, indicating that land cover rather than slope is a more important factor in determining the extent of soil erosion, and that due to low rainfall intensity and highly permeable soils, erosion is much less than would be expected. Thus, while there are few detailed studies of soil erosion, those that do exist suggest that soil erosion is actually not the problem that might be anticipated in an area with such steep slopes and continuous cultivation over many decades.[96] However, such counterintuitive studies have failed to break down the dominant discourse. Their findings tend to be ignored by most contemporary observers, who continue to agonize over supposedly high levels of erosion.[97]

Most researchers reiterate colonial perceptions connecting over-population to serious environmental degradation. Policy-makers in turn, adopt these beliefs and perpetuate the myth. The conventional wisdom has become so widely believed that it is written into reports without adequate substantiation, commencing a cycle in which such reports are then cited in subsequent documents thereby reinforcing the prevailing perceptions without valid confirmation. The strength of the narrative has ensured that this accepted 'truth' has become self-evident. The few studies that report evidence contrary to the prevailing beliefs of over-population and land degradation either fail to perceive their results as contradicting the conventional wisdom or are simply not noticed amongst the overwhelming body of opinion.

Agroforestry

For over two decades agroforestry has been promoted as a 'practical and beneficial land-use system for smallholders'[98] and a number of developmental agencies working in Kabale today have projects with an agroforestry component, including the International Centre for Research on Agroforestry/AFRENA, Africare and Africa 2000. The over-riding assumption that drives such initiatives is that deforestation has occurred in Kabale as a result of population increase, and that it is an ongoing problem. The National Soils Policy for Uganda, for example, has observed that 'erosion ... is particularly severe in ... Kabale ... where high altitude mountain slopes have been greatly deforested'.[99] An Africare survey states (without citing any evidence) that 'deforestation is widely practised'.[100] Meanwhile, the 1998 *State of the Environment Report* noted that 'expansion of agriculture on previously forested steep terrains has led to soil erosion', one of the most seriously affected districts being Kabale.[101] The District Environment Profile blames woodfuel demand: 'The high demand for woodfuel has resulted in destruction of many indigenous forests in the district. Some valuable trees such as black wattle (*Acacia mearnsii*) have been lost and besides this serious soil erosion is already being experienced. Some hills are bare and have exposed rocks.'[102] Thus, not only has deforestation occurred, but it is implicit that this has occurred as a result of relatively recent population pressure.

But what is the history of tree cover in the area? There is evidence that the area has not been deforested over the past century; rather this occurred much longer ago. Palaeoecological research undertaken in the highlands has found evidence of 'prolonged human occupation and in particular agriculture' over the past 2500 years.[103] While agriculture concomitant with more permanent settlements was probably established around 2000 years ago,[104] Taylor and Marchant note that forest clearance was highly localized and that lower altitudes were permanently cleared of forest about 1000 years ago, while higher altitudes were cleared before that.[105] As Hamilton et al have noted 'major degradation of the environment by man occurred early at this locality'.[106] By the time of the arrival of colonial officials, forests had long been cleared and hence the population increase of the past century cannot be blamed for the deforestation of the district.

A second set of assumptions connected to agroforestry posits that the planting of trees by farmers is a new practice introduced from outside. Thus researchers working for ICRAF have noted that 'except for commercial eucalyptus woodlots, very few trees are planted by farmers in Kabale district'.[107] An Africare project document notes that 'agroforestry as a land management practice [is] new to the majority of farmers in this area'.[108] It has been noted that 'little integration of tree growing in the farming system prevails in the area. Scattered woodlots of eucalyptus (*Eucalyptus* spp) and black wattle (*Acacia mearnsii*) on marginal lands and boundaries are the only common agroforestry activities.'[109] In contradiction to such beliefs, farmers have actually been growing trees for many decades. Evidence from colonial archives suggests that in the 1930s and 1940s woodlots of black wattle were common: 'coppices of wattle trees, planted on the hilltops, along the roads, and around the homestead', forming 'a marked feature of the landscape'.[110] Furthermore, tree cover more than doubled between 1945 and 1996 (from 4.1 per cent in 1945 to 9.2 per cent in 1996). Within this increase in cover there has been a change in species type: from black wattle (85 per cent of woodlots in 1945) to eucalyptus (74 per cent in 1996).[111]

Hoben has similarly observed that in the case of Ethiopia where tree cover has increased: 'the fact that trees have been integrated into highland farming systems spontaneously without government extension programmes calls into question the narrative that says peasants lack the ability or foresight to plant trees without environmental education, training and access to subsidised seedlings from nurseries.'[112] But in Kigezi, as in Ethiopia, the fact that farmers are planting trees is given only scant recognition, while the fact that tree cover has doubled over a 50-year period is rarely acknowledged.

Food Security

In the past five years reference has increasingly been made to the problem of food insecurity in Kabale district.[113] This new discourse seems to have arisen following the commencement of an Africare project in the area. Before this, the 'problem' of food insecurity was not articulated as a major concern.[114] Africare has been running the 'Uganda Food Security

Initiative' Project (UFSI) in Kabale since 1997. This project's main objectives are to enhance food security by (a) increasing the quantity of food available for home consumption, (b) protecting soils from erosion, (c) providing improved road access and (d) enhancing household utilization of food, particularly by women and children.[115] Literature produced by the project claims that 'the project started by undertaking a baseline survey in 1997 that revealed the magnitude of food insecurity in Kabale district'.[116] In fact, this survey did not measure food insecurity, nor did it measure rates of nutrition or food production.[117] Rather, the existence of food insecurity in the district was identified as an *assumption* of the survey, as well being one of its main conclusions.[118] The assumption was informed by the prevailing overpopulation/land degradation narrative. According to the baseline survey: 'due to high population density and intensive land cultivation, soil degradation has continued to threaten food security in the district.'[119] The case serves as a classic example of how data can be misused to support a priori policy decisions.

Conclusion

This paper has shown that the narratives that were established in the colonial period have continued after Independence. The colonial legacy continues to inform contemporary environmental and agricultural policy in Kabale, although this is rarely acknowledged. On occasions when reference *is* made to colonial efforts around the environment, it is done so to highlight the abandonment since independence of soil conservation measures associated with colonial rule. A 1998 NEMA report, for example, observed the 'strong element of coercion in enforcing conservation programmes in Kabale … district during the colonial era'. 'This policy', the report continued, was 'partly responsible for subsequent neglect of conservation practices after independence, because the local communities did not identify with it, leading to the removal of terrace raisers. Erosion became very intense as a result.'[120] That these measures were in fact modifications of indigenous agricultural practice, and for this reason were not rejected outright by farmers, is neglected.[121] Furthermore, in colonial Kigezi significant efforts were made with regard to education and propaganda, resulting in a high degree of local understanding of the reasons behind such policies. Nevertheless, colonial policy itself arose from a Malthusian environmental degradation narrative, which has gone on to influence local thinking. The very same phrases and explanations first employed by colonial officials, and later by their post-colonial successors, have been adopted by the local population who are now repeating them to contemporary development workers. Thus, through a process of iteration, the narrative has become deeply embedded in local thought.[122] This has major implications for policy, given the increased focus on farmer participation, as a result of which the perceptions of local people carry more weight. Meanwhile, the understandable desire to be chosen as recipients of development projects may encourage people to both say what they think development workers want to hear[123] and to stress difficulties today compared to the past. The policies of participation and decentralization therefore reinforce the reproduction of a neo-Malthusian narrative.

While there have been some changes in policy, the underlying assumptions that are made in almost all areas of policy are unchanged, and a clear neo-Malthusian environmental narrative has developed. As colonialists ignored indigenous cultivation systems that maintained soil fertility, and presented their measures as something new (and successfully introduced) so, in the post-colonial period, have agencies ignored tree planting practices. It served the colonial authorities well to ignore indigenous practices, as they could present their initiatives as successful, and fail to mention the fact that the very reason that they were successful was that they were adaptations of practices already in place. Using the same environmental degradation narrative, post-colonial agencies have implemented agroforestry programmes with little acknowledgement of the extent to which agroforestry is already practised in Kabale.

Concerns over the environment have always been explicit in Kabale. Today the term 'environmental sustainability' is used to encompass the fears and concerns about the threats associated with increasing population, soil erosion and declining soil fertility. But the assumptions and fears behind this phrase, and the language used to convey these, have changed very little. The explicit concerns with environmental issues (specifically soil erosion) date back to the 1930s. The paper has shown that development narratives have been, and indeed continue to be, externally driven: first by colonial regimes and latterly by international organizations and NGOs. The policies espoused have also changed little (although the degree to which post-Independence governments have had the capacity to put them into place has varied). Those areas of policy where there have been shifts include a reversal in policy around swamps, reflecting an increased concern (originating from outside the region) with biodiversity. The concern to increase agricultural productivity through farmer participatory research represents a shift in development method, while there has been, in NGO circles in particular, increasing focus on agroforestry as a way of increasing agricultural productivity. In Kabale, as in Ethiopia,[124] there has been little discussion of indigenous techniques of soil amelioration and the neo-Malthusian narrative rests on an essentially undynamic view of peasant behaviour. There are signs that amongst some observers this is beginning to change,[125] although this has not yet fed into the broader narratives about environmental degradation in Kabale. Thus the neo-Malthusian environmental narrative remains largely unchanged and as a result a number of assumptions are made about agricultural productivity and environmental degradation, which in turn drive policy. But there is increasing evidence, as shown by several studies presented above, that these assumptions need to be questioned, the neo-Malthusian narrative that has taken hold in Kabale needs to be reconsidered and to avoid repetition of past mistakes it is essential that a revaluation takes place.

Notes and References

1   This paper has benefited from comments from Dave Anderson, Andrew Burton, Mike Jennings and two anonymous referees. It draws on work conducted with the support of the British Academy and the British Institute of Eastern Africa. The paper examines Kabale District, which was part of the larger Kigezi District during the colonial period.
2   G Carswell, 'African farmers in colonial Kigezi, Uganda, 1930–1962: Opportunity, Constraint and Sustainability' (PhD, SOAS, 1997).

3   National Environment Management Authority (NEMA), *State of the Environment Report for Uganda 1998* (Kampala, 1999), 55.

4   K Lindblade, J K Tumahairwe, G Carswell, C Nkwiine and D Bwamiki, 'More People, More Fallow – Environmentally favorable land-use changes in southwestern Uganda' (Report prepared for the Rockefeller Foundation and CARE International, 1996). See also G Carswell, 'Farmers and fallowing: agricultural change in Kigezi district, Uganda', *Geographical Journal,* 168.2 (2002), 130–140.

5   M Leach and R Mearns (eds), *Lie of the Land: Challenging Received Wisdom on the African Environment* (London, 1996); J Fairhead and M Leach, 'False forest history, complicit social analysis: rethinking some West African environmental narratives', *World Development,* 23.6 (1995), 1023–35; J C McCann, 'The plow and the forest: narratives of deforestation in Ethiopia, 1840–1992', *Environmental History,* 2.2 (1997), 138–59; C A Kull, 'Deforestation, erosion, and fire: Degradation myths in the environmental history of Madagascar', *Environment and History,* 6.4 (2000), 423–50; H S Marcusson, 'Environmental paradigms, knowledge systems and policy. The case of Burkino Faso', *Geografisk Tidsskrift, 2* (1999), 93–103; L Mehta 'The manufacture of popular perceptions of scarcity: dams and water-related narratives in Gujarat, India', *World Development,* 29.12 (2001), 2025–411.

6   E M Roe, 'Development narratives, or making the best of blueprint development', *World Development,* 19.4 (1991), 287–300.

7   Roe, 'Development narratives', 288.

8   A Hoben, 'Paradigms and politics: the cultural construction of environmental policy in Ethiopia' *World Development,* 23.6 (1995), 1008.

9   A Hoben, 'The cultural construction of environmental policy: paradigms and politics in Ethiopia' in Leach and Mearns, *Lie of the Land,* 187.

10 For an exploration of how the narrative of 'fortress conservation' has been supplanted by the counter-narrative of 'community conservation' see W A Adams and D Hulme, 'Conservation and Community: Changing narratives, policies and practices in African conservation', in D Hulme and M Murphree, eds (2001), *African Wildlife and Livelihoods* (James Currey, Oxford).

11 Roe, 'Development Narratives', 290.

12 Hoben, 'Paradigms and polities', 1019.

13 Leach and Mearns, *Lie of the Land,* 8.

14 See J Swift. 'Desertification: Narratives, winners and losers', in Leach and Mearns, *Lie of the Land.*

15 E M Roe 'Except Africa: Postscript to a special section on development narratives', *World Development,* 23.6 (1995), 1066.

16 Leach and Mearns, *Lie of the Land,* 9.

17 See also A F D Mackenzie, 'Contested ground: colonial narratives and the Kenyan environment, 1920–1945', *Journal of Southern African Studies,* 26.4 (2000), 697–718. For a discussion of the different crises constructed in Ukambani see D E Rocheleau, P E Steinberg, P A Benjamin, 'Environment, development, crisis, and crusade: Ukambani, Kenya, 1890–1990', *World Development,* 23.6 (1995), 1037–1051.

18 Leach and Mearns, *Lie of the Land,* 23. For further examination of how 'received wisdoms' get established in policy see J Keeley and I Scoones, 'Understanding environmental policy processes: a review', *IDS Working Paper,* 89 (1999).

19 Leach and Mearns, *Lie of the Land,* 28.

20 Carswell, 'African farmers'.

21 Population and Housing Census (1991).

22 From 206,090 in 1921 to 493,444 in 1959, Kigezi District. Kabale District Archives and Uganda Government Statistical Abstracts, 1966.

23 J W Purseglove, 'Kigezi resettlement', *Uganda Journal,* 14 (1950), 139–52.

24 See W R Louis, *Ruanda-Urundi 1884–1919* (Oxford, 1963), 79–91,194–9. Also J M Coote (with postscript by H B Thomas), 'The Kivu Mission 1909-10', *Uganda Journal,* 20 (1956), 105–12. Also H B Thomas, 'Kigezi Operations 1914–17', *Uganda Journal,* 30 (1966), 165–73.

25 Carswell, 'African farmers'.

26 Letter to PCWP from J E Phillips, Acting DC, 26 Jan 1921, Kabale District Archives [KDA] District Commissioner's Office [DC] MP69 ff2. Also Note on 'Land insufficiency around Kabale', 1929, by J E Phillips, DC, KDA DC MP69 ff34. See G Carswell, 'Soil conservation policies in colonial Kigezi, Uganda: successful implementation and an absence of resistance'. Chapter in W Beinart and J McGregor, *Social History and African Environments* (Heinemann and James Currey, in press).

27 D M Anderson, 'Depression, dust bowl, demography and drought: The colonial state and soil conservation in East Africa during the 1930s', *African Affairs,* 83 (1984), 321-43. For growth of concerns in Southern Africa context see W Beinart, 'Soil erosion, conservationism and ideas about development: a southern African exploration, 1900-1960', *Journal of Southern African Studies,* 11.1 (1984), 53–83.

28 See for example A F D Mackenzie, *Land, Ecology and Resistance in Kenya, 1880–1952* (Edinburgh, 1998); J L Giblin, *The Politics of Environmental Control in Northeastern Tanzania 1840-1940* (Philadelphia, 1993); G Maddox, J L Giblin and I Kimambo (eds), *Custodians of the Land: Ecology and Culture in the History of Tanzania* (London, 1996); W Beinart and C Bundy, *Hidden Struggles in Rural South Africa: Politics and Popular Movements in Transkei and Eastern Cape* (London, 1987).

29 Minute by Stockdale, 27 Feb 1930, Public Records Office [PRO] CO 822 26/9.

30 See Carswell, 'African farmers'.

31 See for example PRO CO 822/106/5; PRO CO 822/109/10 1940; PRO CO 822/109/11; PRO CO 822/115/6.

32 Conference of Directors of Agriculture, May 1940. Memo by the Department of Agriculture Nyasaland 'The Adaptation or Modification of Existing Native Agricultural Practices Towards Better Husbandry, Memo by Department of Agriculture, Nyasaland'. Entebbe National Archives [ENA] H304 ffl.

33 For example Tothill went to India and South Africa in 1938 (See ENA H280 ffl) and Maher, from Kenya, and Hosking, from Uganda, were sent to the USA in 1938/39 to study erosion control measures. (See PRO CO 892 15/7 and KDA Department of Agriculture [DoA] 19 ff211).

34 Notes on Preservation of Soil Fertility under conditions of Native Agriculture in Uganda, by Tothill, Director of Agriculture written July 1935, ENA H175/1/II ff5. Also see ENA H218 I ffl6(1) and KDA DC AGR-MNTH ff44Enc.

35 Report for Year 1935 by Wickham, KDA DC AGR-MNTH ff53.

36 Letter to DC from Wickham, DAO, Kabale, 5 Sept 1935, KDA DoA 009exp-c ff10. Note that soil 'erosion' (eg sheet or gulley erosion) and falling soil fertility or soil exhaustion are sometimes used interchangeably.

37 Report for Year 1935 by Wickham, KDA DC AGR-MNTH ff53.

38 Letter to DC from Masefield, DAO, 23 Oct 1937, KDA DC AGR6I ff2.

39 Carswell, 'Soil conservation policies in colonial Kigezi'.

40 Despite the adverse weather conditions in this year of 'famine' it was not necessary to import food into Kigezi. Furthermore the ban on food exports to Ruanda had to be enforced through a 'strict system of frontier guards'. Western Province Annual Report [WPAR], 1946. The assertion that shortages were 'imminent' justified marketing regulations and attempts to introduce marketing controls over foodstuffs need to be seen in the light of colonial efforts to introduce a range of cash crops. See Carswell, 'African farmers'.

41 Letter from Maidment, Acting PAO to DAO 10 Feb 1944, KDA DoA 11/A/l ff9. Quoting notes made by Director of Agriculture following visit to Kigezi.

42 J W Purseglove, 'Report on the Overpopulated Areas of Kigezi', (1945). This unpublished report was not located in any archives. A copy was obtained by the author from the Purseglove family. On the Resettlement Scheme see Carswell, 'African farmers'. On its effects on the family see R E Yeld, 'The family and social change: a study among the Kiga of Kigezi, south west Uganda' (PhD, Makerere, 1969).

43 Ibid, para 13.

44 Ibid, paras 13 and 93. G V Jacks and R O Whyte, *The Rape of the Earth: A World Survey of Soil Erosion* (London, 1939).

45 See Carswell, 'Soil conservation policies in colonial Africa' for comparisons with Uluguru (Tanganyika), Central Province and Machakos (Kenya) and Carswell, 'African farmers' for further comparisons with the Usambara Land Scheme, the Sukumaland Scheme and the Pare Development Plan (Tanganyika). See also R Young and H Fosbrooke, *Smoke in the Hills: Land and Politics among the Luguru of Tanganyika* (London, 1960); P A Maack, 'We don't want terraces!' Protest and identity under the Uluguru land usage scheme', in G Maddox (ed.), *Custodians of the Land: Ecology and Culture in the History of Tanzania (London,* 1996), 159; D W Throup, *The Economic and Social Origins of Mau Mau, 1945–53* (London, 1988); D W Throup, 'The origins of the Mau Mau', *African Affairs,* 84 (1985), 399–433.

46 Indigenous farming methods include contour cultivation, ridges and mounds for root crops, trash lines, cultivation to form ridges, high use of legumes, continuous plant cover through inter- and serial-cropping. See Carswell, 'Soil conservation policies in colonial Kigezi' and W R S Critchley, C Reij and T J Willcocks, 'Indigenous soil and water conservation: a review of the state of knowledge and prospects for building on traditions', *Land Degradation and Rehabilitation* 5 (1994), 293–314.

47 In, for example, Machakos and Central Province, Kenya. See Carswell, 'Soil conservation policies in colonial Kigezi'.

48 Carswell, 'Soil conservation policies in colonial Kigezi'.

49 Purseglove, 'Report on the Overpopulated Areas of Kigezi', para 96.

50 Letter to PAD from King, DAO, 7 May 1953, KDA DoA 012-3 ff8.

51 Memo to Governor on Resettlement by Sub-Committee of Kigezi District Team (1953) KDADoAll/A/lffll5.

52 Letter to PAO from King, DAO, 7 May 1953, KDA DoA 012-3 ff8. Letter to PCWP from Fraser, DC, 3 Feb 1954, KDA DoA 1 l/A/2, ff3.

53 Letter to DC from Deputy Director of Agriculture, 26 March 1954, KDA DoA 11/A/2 ff 10.

54 East African Royal Commission, *Report of the East African Royal Commission, 1953–55* (London, Cmd 9475, 1955).

55 Letter to J King, Director of Agriculture from E W King, DAO, 9 April 1957, KDA DoA 17A-2ff214.

56 See Carswell, 'African farmers'.

57 Sir Alexander Gibb and Partners (Africa), *Water Resources Survey in Uganda 1954–55* (Entebbe, 1956). PRO CO/822/886 (57/6/014).

58 As with other colonial policies the reclamation of swamps provided opportunities for some farmers to increase their land ownership, and this has probably contributed to increased land differentiation in the area. A detailed exploration of the renegotiation of inter- and intra-household politics that was associated with Kabale's incorporation into the colonial economy is beyond the scope of this paper, but see Carswell 'Farmers and fallowing' and Carswell, 'Africa farmers'.

59 Hoben, 'The cultural construction of environmental policy', 201.

60 W Allan, *The African Husbandman,* (Edinburgh, 1965).

61 E R Kagambirwe, 'Causes and consequences of land shortage in Kigezi' (Makerere, Department of Geography, Occasional Paper 23,1973), 69 and 76.

62 B W Langlands, 'A population geography of Kigezi District' (Makerere, Department of Geography, Occasional Paper 26, 1971).

63 B M Kateete, 'Land tenure and land use in Humurwa parish, Ikumba sub-county, Rubanda County, Kigezi District', in R Tindituuza and B M Kateete, 'Essays on land fragmentation in Kigezi District' (Makerere, Department of Geography, Occasional Paper 22, 1971).

64 Such as A R Kururagire, 'Land fragmentation in Rugarama, Kigezi', *Uganda Journal,* 33 (1969), 59–64.

65 National Environment Management Authority (NEMA), *The National Soils Policy for Uganda* (Draft, Kampala, 1998).

66 J M Tukahirwa, 'Soil resources in the highlands of Uganda: Prospects and sensitivities', *Mountain Research and Development,* 8.2/3, (1988), 165–72.

67 Ministry of National Resources, National Environment Information Centre, *State of the Environment Report for Uganda* (Kampala, 1994), 26.

68 See W Adams and M Infield, 'Park outreach and gorilla conservation: Mgahinga', in D Hulme and M Murphree (eds), *African Wildlife and Livelihoods: The Promise and Performance of Community Conservation* (Oxford, 2001).

69 CARE *Development Through Conservation project proposal, 1992–1993.* A proposal to USAID. (Kabale, Uganda, 1992).

70 African Highlands Initiative (AHI), Participatory Agroecosystem Workshop, Kabale Benchmark site. Workshop held in Kabale, (March 1999), 1.

71 African Highlands Initiative (AHI) C and D Uganda Team 'Natural resource manage-ment constraints and prospects in Kabale District: A participatory rural appraisal' (Nov 1998), iii.

72 Agroforestry Research Networks for Africa Uganda National Taskforce (AFRENA). *Agroforestry Potentials for the Land-use Systems in the Bimodal Highlands of Eastern Africa: Uganda. AFRENA Report No. 4.* International Centre for Research on Agroforestry. (Nairobi, 1992).

73 Interview with Sunday Mutabazi, District Agricultural Officer, February 1996.

74 Kabale District, Department of Agriculture, 1996.

75 Uganda Government, *Kabale District Environment Profile* (National Environment Information Centre, Kampala, 1995), 43.

76 Uganda Government, *Kabale District Environment Profile* (National Environment Information Centre, Kampala, 1995), 66.

77 G W Tumushabe, 'Environmental governance, political change and constitutional development in Uganda', in H W O Okoth-Ogendo and G W Tumushabe (eds), *Governing the Environment: Political Change and Natural Resources Management in Eastern and Southern Africa* (ACTS, Nairobi, 1999), 69.

78 J Lind and J Cappon, *Realities or Rhetoric? Revisiting the Decentralization of Natural Resources Management in Uganda and Zambia* (ACTS, Nairobi, 2001).

79 Tumushabe, 'Environmental governance, political change and constitutional development in Uganda', 77.

80 J Mugabe and G W Tumushabe, 'Environmental governance: conceptual and emerging issues', in Okoth-Ogendo and Tumushabe, *Governing the Environment,* 23.

81 See also T J Bassett and K Bi Zuéli, 'Environmental discourses and Ivorian Savanna', *Annals of the Association of American Geographers,* 90.1 (2000), 67–95.

82 See S Browning and P Driver, 'Uganda's poverty eradication action plan', in 'Sustainable Livelihoods and the Environment: Sharing lessons and Approaches' *mimeo* 2001 [Background paper available on http://www.livelihoods.org].

83 R Clausen, 'A landscape approach for reviewing USAID Uganda Activities in the Southwest', *Report prepared for USAID.* (April 2001).

84 Wetlands are the one area where there has been a complete reversal of policy. While in the colonial (and early independence) period swamps were reclaimed to provide additional land, today they (now called wetlands) are being protected due to concerns about the protection of biodiversity. But such concerns are to a large degree externally driven by international conservation organisations such as IUCN which has been heavily involved in the wetlands programme. Furthermore, the expression of such concerns came too late, as by the time they were being articulated, most of the swamps had already been drained. By 1996 there was very little natural swamp land (that is swamp containing papyrus) remaining in the district. While in 1945 7.4 per cent of an area surveyed by transects was natural swamp, this figure was down to 0.05 per cent in 1996 (Lindblade et al, 'More people, more fallow'). Thus almost all the swamp land of Kigezi had been completely reclaimed for cultivation and pasture.

85 R Chambers, *Whose Reality Counts? Putting the Last First* (London, 1997). R Chambers, 'The origins and practice of participatory rural appraisal', *World Development,* 22.7 (1994), 953–69. In relation to soil conservation see C Reij, S D Turner and T Kuhlmann, *Soil and Water Conservation in Sub-Saharan Africa: Issues and Options* (IFAD: Rome, 1986). See also M Green, 'Participatory Development and the Appropriation of Agency in Southern Tanzania', *Critique of Anthropology,*

20.1 (2000), 67–89; R D Grillo and R L Stirrat (eds), *Discourses of Development: Anthropological perspectives* (Berg, Oxford, 1997).

86 Re farmer participatory research see Critchley, Reij and Willcocks, 'Indigenous soil and water conservation'; W Critchley, 'Harnessing traditional knowledge for better land husbandry in Kabale District, Uganda', *Mountain Research and Development*, 19.3 (1999), 261–72; D Miiro, W Critchley, A van der Wal and A Lwakuba, 'Innovation and impact: a preliminary assessment in Kabale, Uganda', in C Reij and A Waters-Bayer (eds), *Farmer Innovation in Africa: A Source of Inspiration for Agricultural Development* (London, 2001). Re Community conservation see Adams and Infield, 'Park outreach and gorilla conservation'.

87 See A Nsibambi, *Decentralization and Civil Society in Uganda* (Kampala, 1998); T Raussen, G Ebong and J Musiime 'More effective natural resource management through democratically elected, decentralised government structures in Uganda', *Development in Practice*, 11.4 (2001) 460–70; A Namara and X Nsabagasani, 'Decentralised Governance and the Wildlife Management Sector: Bwindi Impenetrable National Park, Uganda' *mimeo* (Centre For Basic Research, Kampala, 2001). Also J Ribot, 'Decentralisation, participation and accountability in Sahelian forestry: Legal instruments of political-administrative control', *Africa*, 69.1 (1999), 23–64. Lind and Cappon examine two assumptions associated with decentralisation: firstly, that environments *are* threatened, and secondly, that the establishment of new 'local' institutions may 'curb unwanted changes in the environment and promote more sustainable use of natural resources'. J Lind and J Cappon *Realities or Rhetoric? Revisiting the Decentralization of Natural Resources Management in Uganda and Zambia* (ACTS, Nairobi, 2001).

88 J M Were, *Population Pressure, Land Use Changes and Consequences on the Environment in Kabale District (Makeiere* University, Department of Geography, 1992). Other studies make similar claims, often without substantiation. See for example E M Tukahirwa (ed), *Environmental and Natural Resource Management Policy and Law: Issues and Options, Summary* (Makerere University Institute of the Environment, Kampala, Uganda, and Natural Resources and World Resources Institute, Washington, 1992); J Y K Zake, *Report of the Soil Fertility Survey of South Western Region Kabale and Rukungiri. South-west Regional Agricultural Rehabilitation Project* (Mbarara, Uganda, 1991); A B Cunningham, *People, Park and Plant Use: Research and Recommendations for Multiple-use Zones and Development Alternatives around Bwindi-Impenetrable National Park, Uganda* (Report prepared for CARE-International, Kabale, Uganda, 1992).

89 W Grisley and D Mwesigwa, 'Socio-economic determinants of seasonal cropland fallowing decisions: smallholders in southwestern Uganda', *Journal of Environmental Management*, 42 (1994), 81–89.

90 Lindblade et al, 'More people, more fallow'.

91 A detailed exploration into how issues of class, wealth or gender influence, and are influenced by, these changing land use patterns is beyond the scope of this paper, but see Carswell 'Farmers and fallowing'.

92 F D K Bagoora, 'Soil erosion and mass wasting risk in the highland area of Uganda', *Mountain Research and Development*, 8.2/3 (1988), 173–82.

93 For further discussion see Lindblade et al, 'More people, more fallow'.

94 M K Magunda, 'Influence of some physico-chemical properties on soil strength, stability of crusts and soil erosion' (Minnesota, PhD, 1992).

95 J M Biteete-Tukahiirwe, 'Measurement, predictions and social ecology of accelerated soil erosion in Kabale District, South-west Uganda' (Makerere, PhD 1995).

96 See also C S Farley, 'Smallholder knowledge, soil resource management and land use changes in the Highlands of southwest Uganda' (Florida, PhD, 1996).

97 Uganda Government, *Kabale District Environment Profile* (1995).

98 G L Denning, 'Realising the potential of agroforestry: integrating research and development to achieve greater impact', *Development in Practice*, 11.4 (2001), 404–16.

99 NEMA, 'The National Soils Policy for Uganda' (1998), 16.

100 Africare Baseline Survey (1997), 45.

101 NEMA, *State of the Environment Report for Uganda 1998*, 76.

102 *Kabale District Environment Profile* (1995), 34.

103 D Taylor and R Marchant, 'Human impact in the Interlacustrine region: long-term pollen records from the Rukiga Highlands' Azania, XXIX–XXX (1994–95), 293. Earlier research by Hamilton suggested that clearing of forests in the Kabale area started more that 4800 years ago with further clearing around 2200 years ago, A Hamilton et al, 'Early forest clearance and environmental degradation in South West Uganda', *Nature*, 320 (1986), 164–7. Taylor and Marchant suggest, however, that the earlier vegetation change was likely to have had a regional cause, probably a movement towards a drier or more seasonal climate (293).

104 D Taylor, 'Late quaternary pollen records from two Uganda mires: Evidence for environmental change in the Rukiga highlands of southwest Uganda', *Palaeogeography, Palaeobotany and Palynology*, 80 (1990), 283–300; D L Schoenbrun, 'The contours of vegetation change and human agency in Eastern Africa's Great Lakes region: ca 2000 BC to ca AD 1000', *History in Africa*, 21 (1994), 302. Also see P Robertshaw and D Taylor, 'Climate change and the rise of political complexity in western Uganda', *Journal of African History*, 41.1 (2000) 1–28.

105 Taylor and Marchant, 'Human impact', 294. See also D Taylor, P Robertshaw and R A Marchant 'Environmental change and political-economic upheaval in precolonial western Uganda', *The Holocene*, 10.4 (2000), 527–36.

106 Hamilton et al, 'Early forest clearance'.

107 W M Bamwerinde, S B Dickens, J Musiime, and T Raussen, 'Sharing local knowledge: farmers from Kabale (Uganda) study tree pruning systems and agroforestry in Embu (Kenya)' (Kabale, 1999), 4.

108 Africare, 'The Status of UFSI', *mimeo* (2000), 2.

109 D Miiro et al, 'Participatory Rural Appraisal Report, Bubaale Sub-county, Kabale District', Indigenous Soil and Water Conservation Project (Kabale, 1998), iii.

110 WPAR, 1932.

111 Lindblade et al, 'More people, more fallow'.

112 Hoben, 'The cultural construction of environmental policy', 200.

113 Interviews with government and NGO policy makers in 1995–96 made little reference to food security. This was in stark contrast to 2000 and 2002, when food security issues were raised on a number of occasions.

114 Although food security was not a major part of the narrative of the colonial period, concerns were periodically expressed about the threat of famine, and food exports were banned for periods throughout the 1940s and 1950s. This, however, needs to be seen in relation to colonial efforts to encourage a number of non-food cash crops. See Carswell 'African farmers'.

115 Africare, 'The Status of UFSI', *mimeo* (2000), 2.

116 Africare, 'The Status of UFSI', *mimeo* (2000), 1.

117 Africare Baseline Survey (1997), 45. The baseline survey also did not measure – or attempt to assess – changes to forest cover, despite concluding that deforestation 'widely practiced'.

118 Africare Baseline Survey (1997), 3 and 45.

119 Africare Baseline Survey (1997), 4.

120 NEMA, 'The draft National Soils Policy for Uganda' (1998), 13. See also NEMA, *State of the Environment Report for Uganda 1998*.

121 Carswell, 'Soil conservation policies in colonial Kigezi'.

122 For a discussion of the 'power and persistence of simple explanatory narratives' in the context of PRA see J Pottier, 'Towards an ethnography of participatory appraisal and research', in Grillo and Stirrat, *Discourses of Development*.

123 See also E Crewe and E Harrison, *Whose Development?: An Ethnography of Aid* (Zed Books, London, 1998).

124 Hoben, 'The cultural construction of environmental policy', 201.

125 See for example Critchley, Reij and Willcocks, 'Indigenous soil and water conservation' and Miiro, Critchley, van der Wal and Lwakuba, 'Innovation and impact'. S R Briggs, J Ellis-Jones and S J Twomlow, 'Modern methods from traditional soil and water conservation technologies', Proceedings of a DfID Land management workshop, Kabale, January 1998 (Silsoe, 1998).

Section II

Themes in Environment and Development

Introduction – Section IIA:
Causes of Environmental Change

Grace Carswell and Samantha Jones

Various 'themes' can be identified in the environment and development literature. Some offer an explanation of environmental degradation from a particular lens or theoretical perspective, other areas relate key development issues to the environment. This section of the book is in three parts, each one covering a major theme. First, we explore issues related to population and poverty and the linkages between them and the environment. The second part focuses on agents of change, exploring the role of NGOs and popular movements, while the third part looks in more detail at property, institutions and the management of resources.

Population

Neo-Malthusian explanations for environmental degradation have dominated the development literature historically and present a particularly pessimistic view of human–environment interactions. Malthus' central argument concerned the relationship between population (which he regarded as increasing geometrically) and food supply (which he regarded as increasing only arithmetically). Based on this information he concluded logically that demand would eventually outstrip supply when the carrying capacity is reached. Neo-Malthusians, then are taken to be those people who blame population growth for a whole host of the world's ills, including environmental problems and resource scarcity.

Malthusian thinking about population–environment relations has been dominant in the environment and development debate for many years and continues to have a major influence on policy (see for example Carswell, this volume). But there is a significant literature that calls this into question. Boserup (1965) in her seminal book *The Conditions of Agricultural Growth*, argued convincingly that population pressure can act as a stimulus for increased agricultural production. Since then a multitude of studies have confirmed that a positive relationship can exist between population growth and environmental improvement. Probably the most well known of these is Tiffen et al's (1994) widely acclaimed study of Machakos District, Kenya. They showed that while the population of Machakos rose from 250,000 in 1930 to just under 1.5 million in 1990 the area under terracing also increased: from 9 per cent in 1948 to 46 per cent in 1978 in some districts. Significant increases in output per head and output per unit of land were attained by the late 1980s and their study concluded that there were positive influences of population density on both environmental conservation and productivity (Tiffen et al, 1994). Mortimore and Tiffen note that what happened in Machakos 'grew logically from a conjunction of increasing population density, market growth and a generally supportive economic environment' (1995, p86). Elsewhere they stress that 'population increase is compatible with environmental recovery, provided that market developments make farming profitable' (Tiffen and Mortimore 1992, p359) arguing therefore that if farmers are allowed to operate freely in competitive markets they will manage their resources sustainably. While Tiffen et al (1994) recognize the role of the market in mediating environmental change, others place even more emphasis on it. Zaal and Oostendrop suggest that in the case of Machakos, Nairobi provides a market for higher value produce and this was instrumental in stimulating successful intensification. They have shown that travel time to Nairobi had a strong effect on agricultural intensification in Machakos, while the coffee boom was also important. Their work suggests that the 'improvement in infrastructure was a driving force behind the Machakos/Kitui miracle. The rise in population density and the coffee boom also played a role but their effect appears to have been weaker' (2002, p1284).

Other studies have supported Tiffen et al's argument that higher population densities can have a positive impact on the environment. For example in Kigezi, Uganda, another highland setting, Carswell (2002) has shown that increased population densities have been associated with increased length and frequency of fallowing (see also Adams and Mortimore, 1997). In relation to trees, a number of studies have found that increased population density is associated with higher woody biomass (see for example Cline-Cole et al, 1990; Holmgren et al, 1994; Fairhead and Leach, 1996, 1998; McCann, 1997). Studies have also pointed out that population decline can sometimes cause environmental deterioration, particularly where populations actively invest in 'landesque capital' such as soil and water conservation measures and lower population reduces the labour available to invest in soil conservation (see Blaikie and Brookfield, 1987, p33). Other critiques refute the fixed notion of carrying capacity upon which the argument is based, noting that this is neither fixed nor stable ecologically and can be influenced by human intervention (see Part I).

Furthermore, district level changes may hide a more complex picture and the Machakos study has been critiqued for its reliance on aggregate data (Rocheleau, 1995; Murton, 1999; Jones, 2000). It has been shown that intensification and degradation may occur simultaneously in a given area, even in fields belonging to the same household (for example, because of different returns to investment on different land types) and it is important that a differentiated analysis be adopted to fully understand the underlying processes (see Murton, 1999; Jones, 2000; Gray and Kevane, 2001). Bernstein and Woodward (2001) note that while it has been argued that environmental problems 'take different forms for different people in different places' (Leach and Mearns, 1996, p3) one needs to add that 'these problems typically take different forms for different (types of) people *in the same place(s)*' and by doing so another field of analysis is revealed, that of 'the dynamics and effects of social differentiation, not least as generated (and reconfigured) by processes of commoditization' (p296). They argue therefore that difference is not merely primarily, or exclusively, dependent on locality, but on social inequality (p296) (see Poverty section below). Murton's (1999) critique of the Machakos study reveals this very well. He found that while environmental positive changes may have occurred, when looked at a household level the story was more complex, with increased differentiation occurring. Gray and Kevane (2001) also provide evidence that the optimistic intensification counter-narrative is more complex arguing that intensification is a process with social costs and both winners and losers. They found that as 'intensification involves changing land rights, there is essentially a process through which wealthier farmers who have access to inputs strengthen rights while poorer farmers lose rights to land' (p575). Other elements need to be included such as 'changing asset distribution, expropriation and conflict in the process whereby individuals and social groups vie for land rights and invest in intensified production processes' (p575). Thus whether population pressure outcomes are positive or negative is mediated by many factors including poverty, the need for cash income, land rights, access to urban markets and government policies.

One set of resource users who have been frequently the target of a Malthusian argument are refugees, who have even been described as 'exceptional resource degraders'. Black and Sessay (1998a) critique this assumption, arguing that the livelihood strategies developed by refugees are similar in many respects to those of the local population. Their research revealed 'few specific characteristics of the refugee population and their activities which could lead them to use natural resources in a more destructive or wasteful way' (p45). They conclude therefore that 'there is little or no evidence to support the hypothesis that refugees are 'exceptional resource degraders', or that they do not respect local rules that help to manage and protect the environment' (p45).

Population and Institutions

The role of institutions in mediating the relationship between population and the environment has been explored by a large number of studies (Ostrom, 1990; Turner et al, 1993; Mosse, 1997; See Part IIC). Institutions have been defined as 'regularized patterns of behaviour that emerge...from underlying structures or sets of rules... and are maintained by people's practices, or indeed their active "investment" in those institutions' (Leach et al, 1997, p11). They may be both formal and informal, and are dynamic and subject to multiple interpretations by different actors. Given their historical context and the politics of social negotiation, institutions have power relations embedded in them. Institutions and membership of social networks are critical to peoples' access to, and control over, land and other natural resources (Berry, 1984; Downs and Reyna, 1988; Shipton and Goheen, 1992; Bassett and Crummey, 1993; Berry, 1993; Mehta et al, 1999). The establishment and reaffirmation of 'advantageous connections' within acceptable social formations and the incorporation of systems of multiple rights may enable access to resources in situations of high population pressure (Hyden, 1980; Shipton, 1988).

Much research into institutions, population and environment has focussed on one particular institution and its relationship with agricultural productivity, that of land tenure (see, for example, Downs and Reyna, 1988; Atwood, 1990; Barrows and Roth, 1990; Bassett and Crummey, 1993; Toulmin and Quan, 2000). It has been argued that indigenous land tenure is dynamic and evolves in response to factor price changes (Boserup, 1981; Turner et al, 1993). Thus population pressure, the commercialization of agriculture and integration with the market result in a move towards individualization of land tenure and the privatization of land rights (Platteau, 1996). Other research has suggested that indigenous land tenure provides insufficient security to induce farmers to invest in land (Feder et al, 1988; Barrows and Roth, 1990; Pingali, 1990). Such arguments have led to the endorsement by international agencies of the promotion of freehold tenure with title registration (Cleaver and Schreiber, 1994). Whether official land rights do in fact have a significant effect on the use of credit, input use, land improvements and yields has been tested by Place and Hazell (1993). They concluded 'with few exceptions, land rights were not found to be a significant factor in determining whether or not farmers made land-improving investments or used yield enhancing inputs' (1993, p16–19). The policy implications of such findings are explored by Bruce and Migot-Adholla (1994) and Migot-Adholla et al (1991).

Binswanger and McIntire (1987) interpret institutional arrangements as locally efficient ways of coping with risk and transaction costs under the given production conditions (see also Zaal and Oostendrop, 2002). Population growth alters those conditions (by changing factor proportions, scale effects, etc) and in turn gives rise to different risks and transaction costs which may make an alternative institutional arrangement (such as individualized land tenure) more efficient (see also Ruttan, 1978; Ruttan and Thirtle, 1989). A number of studies have examined how institutions change or evolve in this way and these confirm that access to resources through social networks, and the evolution of social institutions in response to changing factor ratios, are crucial. (See for example Patten and Nukunya, 1982; Riddell and Campbell, 1986; Snyder, 1996; Stone et al, 1990, 1995.)

It has been argued that where change is very rapid the 'rules of resource allocation' can become a constraint (Turner et al, 1993). But there is also evidence that even in situations of rapid change, for example through refugee influx, institutions can adapt. In their study of the role of institutions in mediating the impact of refugees on the environment Black and Sessay (1998b) have noted that there are a range of institutions important in regulating access to natural resources, and 'in varying ways, these institutions have adapted to the presence of refugees, providing some measure of control over environmental degradation' (p701).

The article included here by Mazzucato and Niemeijer is a case study that looks in detail at how people adjust to their rise in numbers, focusing on land tenure systems, as well as other customs and norms. Here increased human and livestock population density occurred alongside increases in yields with no evidence of land degradation. The study suggests that adaptations made to local, informal institutions have enabled environmentally sustainable land use within the context of a rising population and growing scarcity of resources (p171). They argue that it is more than changes to population density that is important, as many of the institutional changes and adaptations they highlight were stimulated by increased market integration (see also Bernstein and Woodward, 2001; Zaal and Oostendrop, 2002).

Poverty

Counter to neo-Malthusian thinking that population is the root cause of environmental problems is the neo-Marxist argument that poverty and exploitation are more important causes of environmental degradation. In 1987 the highly influential report by the World Commission on Environment and Development 'Our Common Future' drew attention to the linkages between poverty and the environment. It argued that environmental problems could only be addressed by confronting broader problems of poverty and inequality. The report stated that 'poverty is a major cause and effect of global environmental problems' and stressed these linkages referring to a 'vicious downwards spiral' whereby the poor are forced to overuse environmental resources for survival (1987, p27). In most developing countries the environment underpins the security and sustenance of the poor, who may be marginalized on to poorer quality land or dependent on 'the commons' (see Section IIC). Degraded environments may, themselves, create poverty with, for example, land degradation reducing yields, and forcing people to increase labour inputs. The poor are thus both the victims and agents of environmental degradation (WCED, 1987).

A number of counter-arguments to this view of the relationship between poverty and environment have been made. First, it has been argued that it is not *poverty* that is damaging to the environment, but *wealth*. Wealthy people consume more resources and generate more pollution. They have greater capability of damaging the environment compared with the poor, who may lack the capital equipment to damage the environment in a significant way (see, for example, Duraiappah, 1998; Wunder, 2001). Furthermore, studies from Tanzania have suggested that the poor may have to seek off-farm employment in order to satisfy immediate demands for cash. As a result their fields will benefit from fallowing or from nutrient inputs from those renting their fields (see Jones, 2000, this volume).

Poor people are reluctant to degrade the resources upon which their future depends. Duraiappah argues that when the poor do contribute to degradation, they do so because they have no choice (1998). Others go further: Ravnborg (2002) argues that there is no evidence of a causal relationship between poverty and degradation. The poorest farmers are not the main agents of land clearance for agriculture, and are not reluctant to adopt land and labour intensive methods of soil conservation compared with the non-poor. Her study suggests that poorest households do not sacrifice longer term concerns in favour of short-term gains any more than less poor households.

A number of authors have argued that poverty–environment linkages cannot be conceptualized as simple cause–effect relationships (Lele, 1991; Duraiappah, 1998; Scherr, 2000; Angelsen, 1997; Forsyth, 2003). Angelsen (1997) asserts that higher incomes are good for the environment in some cases, but the opposite is the case in other situations. Similarly Scherr argues that the relationship between poverty and the environment is 'highly variable' and the 'downward spiral is both avoidable and reversible' (2000, p495). She notes that there are key factors which condition poverty–environment interactions, and these are local endowments, the use of resource conserving technology and institutions that support the interests of the poor. Others have also highlighted that the links between poverty and the environment are mediated by a diverse set of factors that affect the decisions poor people make (Leach and Mearns, 1991). Duraiappah (1998) has argued that market or institutional failures play an important role in environmental degradation and poverty enhancement, while Reardon and Vosti (1995) contend that 'investment poverty' (in contrast to 'welfare poverty') needs to be considered when seeking to understand poverty–environment interactions.

They note that people may be 'investment poor' and thus unable to 'make minimum investments in resource improvements to maintain or enhance the quantity or quality of the resource base' (p1498). While the welfare-poor are usually also investment-poor, the converse is not necessarily true.

Finally, the wider actions of the poor themselves have also been explored. It has been argued that the poor should not be seen merely as passive victims of environmental degradation and the importance of the agency of individuals has been recognized (Giddens, 1984; see Section IIB). That the poor have 'unrecognized potential for adaptation and innovation' has been observed (Scherr, 2000, p495; see also Forsyth et al, 1998; Ravnborg, 2002; Forsyth, 2003). Forsyth et al (1998) maintain that rather than being forced to degrade their environment, the poor are able to adopt protective mechanisms through collective action, which reduce the impacts of demographic, economic and environmental change. Broad (1994) takes the argument about the role of the poor further, contesting the view of poor people as environmental degraders. He presents evidence from the Philippines of the poor becoming environmental activists and considers the factors which may lead them to become activists

References

Adams, W M and Mortimore, M J (1997) 'Agricultural intensification and flexibility in the Nigerian Sahel'. *Geographical Journal* **163**: 150–160

Atwood, DA (1990) 'Land registration in Africa: the impact on agricultural production'. *World Development* **18**(5): 659–71

Barrows, R and Roth, M (1990) 'Land tenure and investment in African agriculture: theory and evidence'. *Journal of Modern African Studies* **28**(2): 265–297

Bassett, T J and Crummey, D E (1993) *Land in African Agrarian Systems*, University of Wisconsin Press, Madison

Bernstein, H and Woodward, P (2001) 'Telling environmental change like it is? Reflections on a study in Sub-Saharan Africa'. *Journal of Agrarian Change* **1**(2): 283–324

Berry, S (1984) 'The food crisis and agrarian change in Africa'. *African Studies Review* **27**(2): 59–112

Berry, S (1989) 'Social institutions and access to resources'. *Africa* **59**(1): 41–55

Berry, S (1993) *No Condition is Permanent: The Social Dynamics of Agrarian Change in Sub-Saharan Africa*, University of Wisconsin, Madison

Binswanger, H P and McIntire, J (1987) 'Behavioral and material determinants of production relations in land-abundant tropical agriculture'. *Economic Development and Cultural Change* **361**: 73–99

Black, R and Sessay, M F (1998a) 'Forced migration, natural resource use and environmental change: the case of the Senegal River Valley'. *International Journal of Population Geography* **4**(1): 31–47

Black, R and Sessay, M F (1998b) 'Refugees and environmental change in West Africa: the role of institutions'. *Journal of International Development* **10**(6): 699–713

Blaikie, P and Brookfield, H (eds) (1987) *Land Degradation and Society*, Methuen, London

Boserup, E (1981) *Population and Technological Change: A Study of Long Term Trends*, University of Chicago Press, Chicago

Boserup, E (1965) *The Conditions of Agricultural Growth: The Economics of Agrarian change under Population pressure*, Allen Unwin, London

Broad, R (1994) 'The poor and the environment: friends or foes?' *World Development* **22**(6): 811–822

Bruce, J W and Migot-Adholla, S E (eds) (1994) *Searching for Land Tenure Security in Africa,* The World Bank, Washington

Carswell, G (2002) 'Farmers and fallowing: agricultural change in Kigezi district, Uganda'. *Geographical Journal* **168**(2): 130–140

Cleaver, K and Schreiber, G (1994) 'Reversing the spiral: the population, agriculture and environment nexus in sub Saharan Africa', *Directions in Development Series,* World Bank, Washington

Cline-Cole, R A, Main, H A C and Nichol, J E (1990) 'On fuelwood consumption, population dynamics and deforestation in Africa'. *World Development* **18**(4): 513–527

Downs, R E and Reyna, S P (eds) (1988) *Land and Society in Contemporary Africa,* University Press of New England, Hanover

Fairhead, J and Leach, M (1996) *Misreading the African Landscape: Society and Ecology in a forest–savanna mosaic,* Cambridge University Press, Cambridge

Fairhead, J and Leach, M (1998) *Reframing Deforestation: Global Analyses and Local Realities – Studies in West Africa,* Routledge, London

Feder, G et al (1988) *Land Policies and Farm Productivity in Thailand,* John Hopkins, Baltimore

Giddens, A (1984) *The Constitution of Society: An Outline of a Theory of Structuration,* Polity Press, London

Gray, L C and Kevane, M (2001) 'Evolving tenure rights and agricultural intensification in southwestern Burkina Faso'. *World Development* **29**(4): 573–587

Holmgren, P, Masakha, E J and Sjoholm, H (1994) 'Not all African land is being degraded: a recent survey of trees on farms in Kenya reveals rapidly increasing forest resources'. *Ambio* **23**: 391–395

Hyden, G (1980), *Beyond Ujamaa in Tanzania: Underdevelopment and an Uncaptured Peasantry,* Heinemann, London

Jones, S (2000) 'Intensification, degradation and soil improvement: utilising structuration theory for a differentiated analysis of population pressure outcomes in highland Tanzania'. *Singapore Journal of Tropical Geography* **21**(2) 131–148

Jones, S (1996) 'Farming systems and nutrient flows: A case of degradation'. *Geography* **81**(4) 289–300

Leach, M and Mearns, R (eds) (1996) *Lie of the Land: Challenging Received Wisdom on the African Environment,* Heinemann and James Currey, Oxford

Leach, M, Mearns, R and Scoones, I (1997) 'Challenges to community-based sustainable development: dynamics, entitlements, institutions'. *IDS Bulletin* **28**(4): 4–14

Lele, S M (1991) 'Sustainable development: a critical review'. *World Development* **19**(6): 607–621

McCann, J C (1997) 'The plow and the forest: narratives of deforestation in Ethiopia, 1840–1992'. *Environmental History* **2**: 138–159

Mehta, L et al (1999) 'Exploring understandings of institutions and uncertainty: new directions in natural resource management'. *IDS Discussion Paper* 372

Migot-Adholla, S E, Hazell, P, Blarel, B and Place, F (1991) 'Indigenous land rights systems in Sub-Saharan Africa – A constraint on development?' *World Bank Economic Review* **5**(1): 155–175

Mortimore, M and Tiffen, M (1995) 'Population and environment in time perspective: the Machakos story', in A J Binns (ed) *People and Environment in Africa,* John Wiley, Chichester

Mosse, D (1997) 'The symbolic making of a common property resource: history, ecology and locality in a tank-irrigated landscape in South India'. *Development and Change* **28**: 467–504

Murton, J (1999) 'Population growth and poverty in Machakos, Kenya'. *Geographical Journal* **165**(1): 37–46

Ostrom, E (1990) *Governing the Commons*, Cambridge University Press, Cambridge

Patten, S E and Nukunya, G K (1982) 'Organizational responses to agricultural intensification in Anloga, Ghana'. *African Studies Review* 25(2–3): 67–77

Pingali, P L (1990) 'Institutional and environmental constraints to agricultural intensification'. *Population and Development Review* 15(suppl): 243–260

Place, F and Hazell, P (1993) 'Productivity effects of indigenous land tenure systems in sub-Saharan Africa'. *American Journal of Agricultural Economics* 75:10–19

Platteau, J P (1996) 'The evolutionary theory of land rights as applied to sub-Saharan Africa: a critical assessment'. *Development and Change* 27: 29–86

Ravnborg, H M (2002) 'Poverty and Soil Management – Relationships from three Honduran watersheds'. *Society and Natural Resources* 15: 523–539

Reardon, T and Vosti, S (1995) 'Links between rural poverty and the environment in developing countries: asset categories and investment poverty'. *World Development* 23(9): 1495–1506

Riddell, J C and Campbell, D J (1986) 'Agricultural intensification and rural development: the Mandara Mountains of North Cameroon'. *African Studies Review* 29(3): 89–106

Rocheleau, D (1995) 'More on Machakos'. *Environment* 37(7): 3–5

Ruttan, V W (1978) 'Induced institutional change', in H P Binswanger and V W Ruttan (eds), *Induced Innovation: Technology, Institutions, and Development,* John Hopkins University Press, Baltimore and London, pp327–357

Ruttan, V W and Thirtle, C (1989) 'Induced technical and institutional change in African agriculture'. *Journal of International Development* 1(1): 1–45

Shipton, P (1988) 'Land and the uses of tradition among the Mbeere of Kenya'. *Canadian Journal of African Studies* 22(1): 164–166

Shipton, P and Goheen, M (1992) 'Understanding African land holding: power, wealth and meaning'. *Africa* 62: 307–326

Snyder, K A (1996) 'Agrarian change and land-use strategies among Iraqw farmers in northern Tanzania'. *Human Ecology* 24(3): 315–340

Stone, G D, Netting, R M and Stone, M P (1990) 'Seasonality, labor scheduling, and agricultural intensification in the Nigerian savanna'. *American Anthropologist* 92(1): 7–23

Stone, M P, Stone, G D and Netting, R M (1995) 'The sexual division of labor in Kofyar agriculture'. *American Ethnologist* 22(1): 165–186

Tiffen, M and Mortimore, M (1992) 'Environment, population growth and productivity in Kenya: a case study of Machakos district'. *Development Policy Review* 10(4): 359–387

Tiffen, M, Mortimore, M and Gichuki, F (1994) *More People, Less Erosion: Environmental Recovery in Kenya* Wiley, Chichester

Toulmin, C and Quan, J (eds) (2000) *Evolving Land Rights, Policy and Tenure in Africa*, DfID, London

Turner, B L, Hyden, G and Kates, R W (eds) (1993) *Population Growth and Agricultural Change in Africa*, University Press of Florida, Gainsville

WCED (1987) *Our Common Future,* OUP, Oxford

Wunder, S (2001) 'Poverty alleviation and tropical forests: what scope for Synergies?' *World Development* 29(11): 1817–1833

Zaal, F and Oostendrop, R H (2002) 'Explaining a miracle: intensification and the transition towards sustainable small-scale agriculture in dryland Machakos and Kitui districts, Kenya'. *World Development* 30(7): 1271–1287

3

Population Growth and the Environment in Africa: Local Informal Institutions, the Missing Link[1]

Valentina Mazzucato and David Niemeijer

Summary

Population and environment debates regarding Africa, whether Malthusian or Boserupian in nature, focus on population levels as the driving force behind the relationship between environment and society. This article argues, instead that *how* people adjust to their rise in numbers is more important than are population levels. It focuses on the role of local informal institutions such as land tenure systems, but also on customs, norms and networks, and their change over time in mediating the relationship between people and the environment. The article is based on fieldwork conducted between 1995 and 1998 in the Sahelian and Sudano-Sahelian zones of Africa, as well as on a review of colonial documents pertaining to the area written in the first half of the 20th century. The article concludes that adaptations made to local informal institutions within the past century have enabled an environmentally sustainable land use within the context of a rising population and growing scarcity of natural resources.

Neo-Malthusian and neo-Boserupian thinking are highly influential in shaping the current population–environment debates. They provide two divergent reasonings as to the effects of population growth on the environment: one negative and one positive. These views either do not take into consideration the role of institutions in mediating the relationship between population and the environment or assume a specific institutional development path. This article contributes to an increasing literature questioning 'received wisdom' or 'orthodoxies' concerning environmental degradation (Tiffenet et al, 1994; Fairhead and Leach, 1996, 1998; Benjaminsen, 1997) by focusing on the role of

Reprinted from *Economic Geography*, vol 18, Mazzucato, V and Niemeijer, D, 'Population Growth and the Environment in Africa: Local Informal Institutions, The Missing Link', pp171–193, copyright © (2002), with permission from Clark University Press.

institutions in affecting the relationship between population growth and the environment.

Although there have been plenty of studies on institutions in the population–environment nexus, they tend to consider only high-level formal institutions (eg governmental policies, research and extension organizations) macrotrends and structures (eg migration, poverty, factor markets), and land tenure regimes (see, for example, Hayami and Ruttan, 1985; Pingali et al, 1987; Lele and Stone, 1989; Bernstein et al, 1990; Turner et al, 1993; Cleaver and Schreiber, 1994). This study adds to the population–environment debates by focusing on the role of local informal institutions,[2] including, but going beyond, the land tenure system, by considering institutions, such as social networks[3], customs and norms. It asks the question, How do local informal institutions mediate the relationship between society and the environment, and what effects do they have? It draws on data collected between 1995 and 1998 in eastern Burkina Faso, as well as on colonial documents from the first half of the 20th century.

The second section reviews Malthus's and Boserup's theories and recent applications thereof to show how the role of institutions in affecting the relationship between population and the environment is either ignored or assumed to take on a specific form. It then argues the need to look explicitly at local informal institutions to inform population-environment debates. Moving down to the case-study region, the third section sets the context by describing population and environmental trends experienced in the region during the 20th century. The fourth section focuses on the way local institutions have been adapted to enable the production system to respond in an environmentally sustainable[4] way to the changing context within which agriculture is practiced. The article ends with three conclusions about the relationship between population and the environment.

Institutions in Population–Environment Theories

Malthus (1803) argued that population, if left unchecked, grows more rapidly than food production, which ultimately leads to death from starvation. He did not consider the possibility of institutional or technical change that would allow the relationship between population growth and food production to change. Ricardo (1817) added the possibility of people expanding onto new land and then intensifying cultivation by applying additional labour but concluded that returns to labour and capital would eventually diminish owing to the finite quantity of land available. Thus, he, too, assumed that technologies and institutions would remain largely unaltered.

Boserup (1965), on the other hand, introduced the variable of technological change, to argue that food production is able to keep up with population growth. She implicitly included institutional change because for technologies to change, institutions need to be amended. But her theory does not explain how institutions change, and, furthermore, their direction of change is assumed to move along a path towards becoming institutions of a market economy.[5] Boserup's reasoning is as follows: as food and land grow scarce owing to population growth, new technologies are developed in which more labour is used in conjunction with land-improvement technologies. Land is cultivated more intensively; more investments are made in permanent land-improvement structures, and more careful husbandry is practised. These changes in technologies take place as institutions change. Such institutional changes take the form of land tenure shifting from tribal or feudal based to private property based and transport, labour and capital markets developing along the lines of a market economy. Each step of this development occurs at certain population thresholds when the demands of a population reach a peak and force a change in technology or institutions to occur. However, how or why institutions should develop along these lines and not others is not explained. Furthermore, studies have shown that even in highly populated areas, institutions, such as land tenure systems, have taken on various forms (Downs and Reyna,1988; Berry, 1998).

Hayami and Ruttan (1985) provided an explanation of how institutions change in light of growing population through an extension of their widely used induced innovation model (Ruttan and Hayami, 1972) to institutions. They argued that institutions develop and change according to a country's factor endowments. As one of these factors becomes scarce, prices for the scarce factor will rise and this rise, in turn, will create incentives for institutions to change and adapt. In the case of population growth, land becomes the scarce resource relative to labour, and as a consequence, land tenure institutions will develop into systems that 'protect' land from becoming over-exploited. The theory relies on the existence of labour and land markets. However, these markets often do not exist or exist only partially in many parts of Africa. In such cases, local institutions, like customs, norms and networks, that guide how input factors are valued become central to determining whether environmentally sustainable land-use practices will be developed. For example, in the absence of labour markets, labour intensification depends on the customs and networks governing and providing access to labour.

Hayami and Ruttan (1985) share Boserup's (1965) optimism because the induced institutional innovation theory explains the creation of 'efficient' institutions that safeguard scarce resources and allow the use of plentiful ones. However, recent studies have cast a shadow on such optimism. Cleaver and Schreiber (1994) maintained that shifting cultivation and transhumant pastoral systems have not been adjusting to rapidly increasing populations, resulting in soil degradation and deforestation. Speirs and Olsen (1992) argued that inappropriate institutions can evolve as a consequence of population growth and that the mixed farming system evolving in many parts of the Sahel leads to overgrazing and environmental degradation. Others have contended that mixed farming systems may increase competition for resources among different ethnic groups and may not be as environmentally sustainable as is often hoped (Savadogo, 2000; Slingerland, 2000). Clay et al (1994) argued that with a tightening of the resource base because of population growth, the distribution of these resources becomes a key issue. Rental and share arrangements may evolve that take away the incentive to make long-term investments in land, again leading to land degradation. Furthermore, if population growth is not met by a concomitant growth in income, people will become poorer. Poverty has been cited as the cause of degradation because the poor are not able to make land-enhancing investments and because they cannot postpone production if their day-to-day livelihoods depend on that production (Hudson, 1991; Dasgupta, 1993; Ehrlich et al, 1993). Finally, it has been suggested that an influx of people into an area may cause people to have inappropriate knowledge of and practices for the agroclimatic conditions in the new area and to cultivate on marginal lands, and traditional land tenure arrangements may prove to be inadequate for protecting land that is not already in the farming cycle from these new groups (World Bank, 1991).

Case studies designed to test Boserup's thesis directly have also revealed a more nuanced picture. Hyden et al (1993) studied five African countries and concluded that population growth drives agricultural intensification, but whether intensification leads to increased well-being and environmentally sustainable practices is ambivalent. On the basis of six African case studies, Lele and Stone (1989) argued that public policies are fundamental in shaping the effects that higher population densities have on agricultural change. Without appropriate policies, higher population will lead to degrading trends.

At the same time, some studies have presented optimistic scenarios in which local populations have been able to counter degradation trends. Afikorah-Danquah (1997), Fairhead and Leach (1996, 1998) and Kepe (1997) documented cases in South Africa, Guinea and Ghana in which landscapes over the past century have gained in tree cover owing to local land management. Other recent studies (see, for example, Tiffen et al, 1994; Adams and Mortimore, 1997) have supported Boserup's (1965) thesis that population growth spurs a chain of developments that lead people to practice land-enhancing technologies. Taken together, these studies, showing evidence of both Malthusian doom and Boserupian optimism, highlight that rather than there being a universal relationship between population growth and environment, this relationship depends on *how* people adjust to an increase in their numbers. This adjustment depends on both external factors, such as policies, markets and official research and development organizations, and internal factors, such as migration, the diversification of livelihood, capital investments in agriculture, adoption of modern technology, and local, informal institutions that either hinder or aid people in making adjustments that lead to environmental sustainability. However, although external factors have been covered comprehensively by the literature on population and the environment, local, informal institutions, aside from land tenure, have tended to be left out of analyses of internal factors (see, for example, Hayami and Ruttan, 1985; Pingali et al, 1987; Lele and Stone, 1989; Bernstein et al, 1990; Turner et al, 1993; Cleaver and Schreiber, 1994).

We maintain that local informal institutions, in the form of customs, norms and networks, affect the way resources are valued and allocated and, as such, are the most immediate mechanisms through which people mediate their relationship with the environment. The mediation role that local informal institutions have implies that the effects of population growth on the environment can be fully understood only by taking local informal institutions into consideration. It also calls into question whether population levels are indeed the driving force behind the relationship between the environment and society.

The Context: The Population and Environment in the Research Area

The eastern region of Burkina Faso lies approximately between 0°20' West and 2°20' East and between 11° North and 13°30' North (Figure 3.1). With its largely savannah

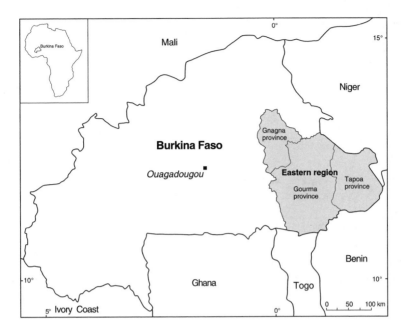

Source: Map I in Mazzucato and Niemeijer (2000b)

Figure 3.1 *Burkina Faso and the Eastern Region*

vegetation and annual rainfall averaging between 600mm in the north and 900mm in the south, the region is part of the Sahelian and Sudano-Sahelian ecological zones.

Information was collected in two villages: one in the northern Gnagna province and one in the southern Gourma province. Historical data and information were collected through aerial photographs; colonial documents from archives in France, Burkina Faso, and Niger; 25 life histories collected in both villages; various interviews with two key informants who were employed by the national extension service since the 1960s; four monographs on the region written in the 1960s and 1970s; agricultural statistics published since the 1960s; and structured interviews on vegetative and land use changes in 27 farming areas covering almost the entire territory of the two study villages.

Data and information on the livelihood and agricultural systems were collected during three years of fieldwork between 1995 and 1998. The following were conducted: a village census; a village survey; a technology survey; and an agricultural study on soils, labour input, land tenure, landraces grown, and crop sequencing for all plots cultivated by 25 married individuals and plot sizes and yields for them and their 43 children. Cultivation histories were also collected for the married individuals. In addition, structured interviews were conducted with groups of farmers in both villages to compile a list of landraces grown and how and when they were introduced in the villages. Finally, a budget study was conducted with 35 male and female married individuals from the two research villages, including those with whom the agricultural study was done.

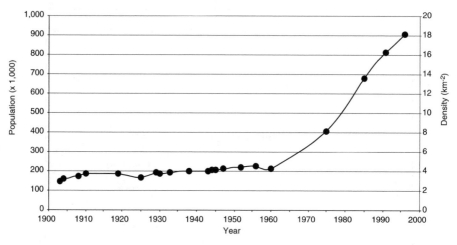

Source: Figure 4.1 in Mazzucato and Niemeijer (2000b)

Figure 3.2 *Total Population in the Eastern Region of Burkina Faso (1903–1996)*

Strong growth of human and livestock populations

The region has experienced strong population growth in the course of the 20th century, as can be seen in Figure 3.2. Although the population was remarkably stable during the colonial period, with an average annual growth of 0.5 per cent, a strong average annual growth of 4 per cent can be observed after independence in 1960.

Population densities in the region also rose steeply, from some 3 inhabitants per square kilometre in 1903 to some 18 in 1996 (Mazzucato and Niemeijer, 2000b). The 1996 population density may seem low, but it does not take into consideration the large proportion of area that is protected and/or covered by soils that cannot be cultivated and does not reflect the fact that population is not equally distributed over the area. Once these factors are taken into account (see Table 3.1), Gnagna province has a real population density of almost 47 inh. km^{-2}. Even when these factors are not taken into account, the Gnagna's rural population density of 35 inh. km^{-2} is still above the national average of 30 rural inh. km^{-2} for the Sahelian ecological zone (although not as high as some provinces on the Central Plateau, such as Yatenga, with 45 inh. km^{-2}). In contrast, Gourma province, with its rural population density of 13 inh. km^{-2}, is relatively sparsely populated, compared with the national average of 34 rural inh. km^{-2} for the Sudano-Sahelian ecological zone (Mazzucato and Niemeijer, 2000b).

The growth in rural population densities has also differed greatly between the two provinces. Figure 3.3 presents a comparison of rural population densities in 1933 and 1996 in the two provinces. It shows that while the densely populated areas were in the eastern part of Gourma province in 1933, in 1996, some of the most densely populated areas were in Gnagna province. Thus, during this period, there was a strong population growth, especially in the northwestern part of Gnagna province.

Livestock numbers, although surrounded by uncertainties (since a full count is practically impossible), have also experienced strong growth in the course of the 20th

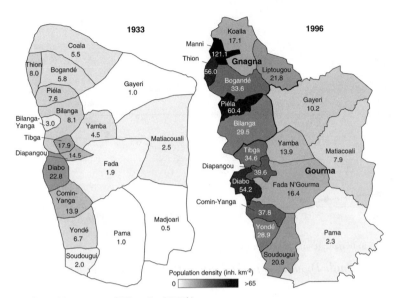

Source: Figure 4.2 in Mazzucato and Niemeijer (2000b)

Figure 3.3 *Rural Population Densities in 1933 and 1996 for the Departments of Gnagna and Gourma Province*

Table 3.1 *Population Density for the Eastern Region in 1996*

Province	Rural density	Total density	Real total popula- tion density[a]
Gnagna	34.5	35.5	46.7
Gourma	12.9	14.0	20.3

Note: a: Real total population density corrects for protected and uncultivable areas.
Source: Agricultural statistics, Table 4.1 in Mazzucato and Niemeijer (2000b)

century. Figure 3.4 shows that in 1994, cattle population in the eastern region was more than 20 times higher than in the 1920s, raising the density from less than 1 head km^{-2} in 1923 to around 14 heads km^{-2} in 1994. The number of heads per capita grew from 0.15 in the 1920s to some 0.7 to 0.9 for the period of 1969 to 1994. The growth in other types of livestock was similar to that of cattle.

Like human population densities, livestock densities vary within the region. As can be seen in Table 3.2, Gnagna province had an average tropical livestock unit (TLU) density of almost 34 km^{-2} in 1994, while Gourma province averaged 12 TLU km^{-2}. In comparison, only 4 out of 30 provinces had higher livestock densities than the Gnagna in 1994, and the national average was 19 TLU km^{-2}.

In addition to population growth, the region has also experienced a steady decline in rainfall (see Figure 3.5), amounting to a decrease of about 200mm between 1950 and the late 1990s. This pattern is similar to patterns found in the rest of the country (Mazzucato and Niemeijer, 2000b).

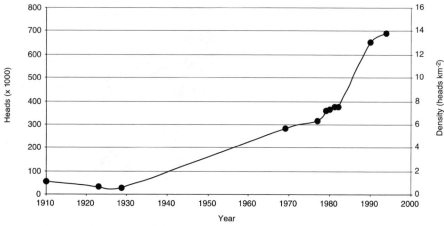

Source: Fig. 4.5 in Mazzucato and Niemeijer (2000b)

Figure 3.4 *Cattle Population in the Eastern Region of Burkina Faso (1910–1994)*

Table 3.2 *Livestock Numbers and Density in Gnagna and Gourma Provinces in 1994*

Animal	Gnagna		Gourma	
	Number of animals (heads)	Density (heads km^{-2})	Number of animals (heads)	Density (heads km^{-2})
Cattle	265,000	30.8	294,900	11.1
Sheep	241,200	28.0	289,800	10.9
Goats	426,400	49.6	367,300	13.8
Other[a]	15,208	1.8	36,410	1.4
TLU[b]	280,048	33.6	320,220	12.0

Notes: a: This category includes pigs, donkeys, horses and poultry.
b: TLU stands for tropical livestock unit and is calculated as follows: 1 dromedary = 1.1 TLU, 1 horse = 1 TLU, 1 donkey or cow = 0.8 TLU, 1 pig = 0.2 TLU, 1 sheep or goat = 0.1 TLU (Williamson and Payne, 1978).
Source: Agricultural statistics. Table 4.4 in Mazzucato and Niemeijer (2000b)

Environmental sustainability

The different trends just described could have had a degrading effect on the environment, as they are said to have had in other regions of Africa (Cleaver and Schreiber, 1994). However, on the basis of analyses of long-term agricultural statistics, aerial photos, soil fertility data, field observations and interviews, no evidence of land degradation was found in the study region. Since these analyses were discussed in detail in Mazzucato and Niemeijer (2000b), as well as in less detail in a few other publications (Mazzucato and Niemeijer, 2001; Niemeijer and Mazzucato, 2002), only the main findings are summarized here. Yields, which are often used as proxies of a degrading environment, actually rose during the past 25 years. Yields of the main staples, millet and sorghum, as well as of other important crops, such as groundnuts and maize, grew approximately by a factor of 1.5, which corresponds well with national level figures (Mazzucato and Nie-

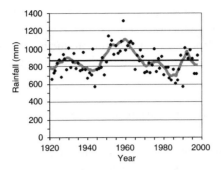

Source: Figure 5.4b in Mazzucato and Niemeijer (2000b)

Figure 3.5 *Annual Rainfall Fada N'Gourma (1920–1998)*

meijer, 2000b; Niemeijer and Mazzucato, 2002). An analysis of aerial photographs, in conjunction with interviews for the study villages, did not reveal a simple pattern of vegetation and tree cover loss but, rather, a dynamic landscape with a fluctuating land cover and species composition. This finding is supported by a number of recent remote sensing studies (Nicholson et al, 1998; Prince et al, 1998) that found no evidence of a gradual deterioration of the vegetative cover in the Sahel but, rather, fluctuations following rainfall oscillations. No evidence was observed of increased gully formation except in localized spots, nor was there any visible evidence of excessive rill or sheet erosion.

Spatial and temporal analyses of soils also did not reveal any evidence of land degradation. When recent soil samples were compared with a 1969 French soil survey, no significant difference was found in the characteristics of soil chemicals (available potassium and total carbon, nitrogen and phosphorus content). In addition, when cultivated land was compared with longtime uncultivated land, either no significant differences in chemical soil fertility were found or cultivated land was found to be more fertile as a result of land-improvement practices. Similarly, Prudencio (1993), who compared cultivated with uncultivated soils in the central part of Burkina Faso, found cultivated soils to be at least as fertile as old fallows.

Agronomic and biological land-improvement practices, such as manuring, crop rotation, and mulching, as well as mechanical practices, such as stone lines and grass strips, play an important role in maintaining and improving field fertility.[6] While the large majority of these practices were known and used even before colonial times, the frequency with which they are used and the surface covered has increased in recent times (Mazzucato and Niemeijer, 2000b). New technologies introduced within the past 50 years are the donkey-drawn plow and new crop and landrace varieties brought to the village through various formal and informal channels.

These findings suggest that the production system has been able to remain environmentally sustainable with the increasing scarcity of natural resources (land and rainfall). Furthermore, the main technological changes that took place were in the form of using and adapting existing technologies more frequently, applying them to different areas in reaction to changing environmental conditions, and the introduction of the plow and new crop and landrace varieties. These technological changes could take place only within the framework of changing and adapting informal institutions because they require greater access to productive resources. In the next section, we look at the most important changes or adaptations made to the production system within the past century, with a specific focus on how institutions have enabled these adjustments.

Institutional Changes as Adjustment Processes

There are four domains in which institutions have been modified or changed to enable the production system to adjust in an environmentally sustainable way to a context of growing natural resource scarcity: spatial organization, labour access, diversification of livelihoods and use of technology.

Spatial organization

Two important institutional changes regarding the spatial organization of production have occurred within the past century in reaction to the changes discussed in the previous section: an increase in bush camps and the rise of land-borrowing agreements. We argue that these institutional changes have allowed the population to deal with the increased scarcity of natural resources in an environmentally sustainable way.

Bush camps (*kuadabili*) consist of a single, but most often several, bush compounds (*kuadiegu*) that are inhabited during the 6- to 7-month agricultural season. Bush camps increased in the course of the 20th century initially as a reaction to colonial policy and later as a way to adjust to changing population densities, the variability in rainfall, and increased market integration. At the turn of the 20th century, wars between different kingdoms made it necessary for all villagers to stay close together for security. However, relative peace brought by colonialism, and repressive colonial policies of recruitment and taxation encouraged people to spread out in the hinterland so as not to be found by colonial authorities. This spreading out of homesteads resulted in an increase in bush compounds. As early as 1936 and 1937, censuses report 22 bush compounds for Bilam-Perga (an agglomeration of villages, including the northern study village) and 12 bush compounds for the southern research village (Mazzucato and Niemeijer, 2000b).

The growing scarcity of resources in the latter half of the twentieth century, characterized by growing population and declining rainfall, made suitable land close to the village centre scarce. Cultivating far from the inhabited centre, however, has high labour demands in travel time to and from one's fields. In a context of production units decreasing in size and therefore labour being a scarce resource, bush camps provided an institutional solution to the problem of the growing scarcity of resources by making it possible to cultivate land farther from the village centre (see Figure 3.6) while minimizing travel between home and field.

Bush compounds also allow people to deal with the increased spatial variation in rainfall that accompanies a decline in rainfall (Sivakumar, 1991). Through bush camps, households from one village compound can spread out to different locations so as to minimize the risk of all being in an area in which there is a shortage of rainfall in any given year.

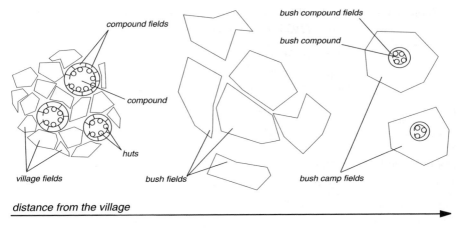

Source: Figure 4.3 in Mazzucato and Niemeijer (2000b)

Figure 3.6 *Schematic Map of the Spatial Organization
of the Most Important Types of Fields*

Finally, increased market integration, which was stimulated by colonization and further spurred starting in the 1970s by greater contact with development projects and a globalized world economy (Mazzucato and Niemeijer, 2000b), created advantages to an individualized accumulation of surplus production. Bush compounds seem to be a socially acceptable way for household heads to separate their production from the communal compound-based production of the past because a household head's desire to be independent of a compound head can be camouflaged by the need for space and for insurance against a shortage of rainfall. A village survey revealed that in 1996 there were 25 and 39 bush compounds in the northern and southern villages, respectively, amounting to 31 per cent and 39 per cent, respectively, of the total inhabitants who lived in bush camps for part of the year.

Borrowing land has also been on the increase, given the rise in population density. Borrowing land is part of the customary land tenure system. Within this system, cultivation rights are obtained by clearing a piece of land that has never been cultivated before. Within a bush-fallow rotation system, in which people cultivate land until it needs to be left fallow, land is progressively cleared and therefore 'claimed', while fallows are allowed to regenerate. This system means that early settlers of a village will have cleared and claimed more land than recently settled villagers. As more people inhabit an area, borrowing fallow land from people who have 'claimed' lots of land increasingly becomes an option for people who have 'claimed' less land (such as latecomers or newcomers). Borrowing has also facilitated the greater use of bush camps. Land far from village centres that is appropriate for establishing bush camps may be located in areas of previous settlement or cultivation or on another village's territory. Thus, cultivation rights to that land have already been 'claimed' or are under the jurisdiction of another village. To cultivate in these locations, it is therefore necessary to borrow land from those who have rights to that land.

How have these changes in the spatial organization of production affected the environment? First, both bush compounds and land-borrowing agreements have made the

Table 3.3 *Changing Land Use Patterns in Northern (1955–1994) and Southern (1955–1987) Research Villages*

Landforms	Northern Research Village			Southern Research Village		
	Total Area (Territory %)	Cultivated Area (Landform %)		Total Area (Territory %)	Cultivated Area[a] (Landform %)	
		1955	1994		1955	1987
High or sloping land	26.9	17.4	16.3	45.2	2.1	4.8
Low or flat land	73.1	23.1	67.9	54.8	1.6	10.7
Total	100.0	21.6	54.0	100.0	1.8	8.0

Notes: a: Cultivated area includes recent fallows that cannot be distinguished from cultivated fields on the aerial photographs.
Source: Aerial photo interpretation. Table 6.6 in Mazzucato and Niemeijer (2000b)

crop cultivation system mobile, even with the increasing scarcity of land. This mobility has given people access to land fit for cultivation while enabling them to leave land fallow where it needs to be left to regenerate, despite less land being available. These institutions have thus allowed the bush-fallow rotation system, a key soil conservation technology used in the area, to continue to exist even under rising population densities.[7]

A further environmental consequence of field mobility has been the fact that people have been able to exploit different land forms according to the change in climate. As a result of the dryer climate since the wet 1950s, there has been a shift from high, sloping lands towards low, flatter lands.[8] A comparison of aerial photographs taken in 1955 with those taken in 1987 and 1994 for the southern and northern research villages, respectively, shows these trends (see Table 3.3). An illustration comes from cultivation histories conducted with case study individuals in the southern village: during the wet 1950s, lower bottomlands were too wet to be able to cultivate even the local rice varieties, whereas in the dryer 1990s, they became ideal lands for rice cultivation.

Second, members of the same village compound access different farming locations through bush compounds and borrowing land and thus insure themselves against the risk of a production shortfall because of localized rainfall shortages. Rainfall can vary greatly between different farming areas, even those located within the same village territory. In the study villages, for example, rainfall recorded in 1996 and 1997 varied as much as 30 to 40 per cent between farming areas located in the same village territory. These differences can be crucial for the growth of crops, given the low rainfall levels in the area. One way to avoid being in an unlucky area in a given year is for people from the same compound or household to cultivate in different areas contemporaneously. Both bush camps and borrowing land allow them to do so. Being in an unlucky area in a given year without also having a harvest from a more lucky area would mean incurring a production shortfall that could easily plunge a household into a vicious cycle of debt and debt repayment that constitutes the poverty trap, claimed to be one of the primary causes of degrading practices (Hudson, 1991; Ehrlich et al, 1993). Studies (see, for example, Dasgupta, 1993) have found that the poor need to focus on their immediate consumption and cannot afford to postpone production to make land-enhancing investments. In southern Mali, for example, people were found to mine the soil of its nutrients to maximize their present consumption (van del Pol, 1992).

Finally, although borrowing entails temporary rights to cultivate land, farmers do not perceive it as insecure. Six in-depth cultivation histories, conducted with some of the case study individuals in the two research villages, revealed no relationship between form of tenure (borrowed or ancestral land) and use rights (individual or household field), on the one hand, and agricultural decisions and cultivation practices, on the other hand. For example, in all cases, it was found that farmers applied soil and water conservation practices to adjust to the changing qualities of the soil that were due to cultivation. That is, the farmers often increased the amount of soil and water conservation activities towards the end of the cultivation period in response to a decrease in production in certain parts of the field (Mazzucato and Niemeijer, 2000b). The fact that such a field would soon be left fallow or be used by someone else was never mentioned as a concern and is exemplified by the following comment made by a farmer: 'If you know that you can use a piece of land that you borrowed from someone for more than two or three years, it is worth maintaining the land well (*ki kibi ki tinga*) by making stone lines, wood barriers, or planting grass strips. If someone lends you a piece of land, you are going to maintain it as if it were your own'.

Labour access

Changes in the constitution of production units have made these units experience an increased need for temporary labour. This section discusses three institutional adaptations that have allowed production units to meet their new labour needs. We argue that this access puts production units in a position to practice environmentally sustainable agriculture.

Colonial rule and market integration have both led to a reduction in the size of production units (for details regarding this process, see Mazzucato and Niemeijer, 2000b). Smaller production units are at a greater risk of a labour shortfall because any event that takes members out of production, such as illness, death or birth, means that a larger proportion of total family labour is unavailable for agricultural work than when production units were larger. Thus, although the population is increasing, labour is becoming a scarce resource at the level of the production unit. Consequently, small production units are in greater need of temporary labour. Three changes to networks and customs guiding access to labour have occurred within the 20th century to enable production units to access additional labour: the use of work parties, composition of networks to access labour, and customs guiding women's role in agriculture.

Work parties

Work parties, in which people are invited to work on a person's field in exchange for a meal and/or drinks, have two functions. The production function is evident: through the work party, a person is able to catch up on important tasks, such as harvesting, that if not done in time, can make the difference between having a harvest and not having one at all. Richards (1986) even found that the major factor distinguishing farms with high and low yields in Sierra Leone was their access to work parties. However, there is also a social function to work parties in that the caller of the party exhibits and reinforces his social standing by having many people show up at his work party and offering lots of food, local beer (*dolo*), and tam-tam music to make it a festive occasion. Remy (1967) who studied Gourmantché villages to the southeast of the research area, pointed out that work parties were not always beneficial from an economic point of view: the offerings cost much more than the benefits of the work produced, which was done in a hurried manner and was thus of bad quality. Such large work parties had the effect of reinforcing the host's prestige and status within the community and thus had a political, more than a production, purpose.

Today work parties tend to be smaller and to be for production purposes, rather than for prestige. This change can be inferred by the high percentage of small work parties recorded for the case study individuals during the agricultural season and by the respondents' recollections. Furthermore, a village survey revealed that work parties are pervasive, since, on average, 1.6 and 1.4 agricultural work parties are called annually per household in the northern and southern villages, respectively. Table 3.4 shows that work parties called by case study individuals were relatively small averaging 16 participants per party, which is considerably smaller than the marriage-related work parties that have a definite prestige component and range from 25 to 100 participants. These figures are similar to those of a village survey, which revealed an average of 18 and 21 participants per work party in the northern and southern villages, respectively. In addition, expenditures per individual present do not follow a clear pattern with the wealth of the person hosting the work party (thus no clear political–social significance). Indicative of the production orientation of labour parties is the fact that 8 of the 13 work parties were called by poor to middle-wealth families and that all but one of the people who called these different work parties were running behind in their cultivation tasks.

The respondents further confirmed this trend. Three men aged 40 to 60 who were interviewed independently on this topic concluded that work parties today, compared with 30 or 40 years ago, consist of fewer people, are more frequently called, and are less festive in that tam-tams are much less frequently played.

Composition of networks

A second change that has affected access to labour is the composition of networks used to access labour. Paid agricultural labour is virtually non-existent in the area, so labour shortfalls are met by asking kin relations for their labour for short periods. The spreading out of cultivation farther and farther from the village centre and ultimately into bush camps has meant that field neighbours have become an important source of temporary labour. Kin located in other bush camps or in the village would take too much time to reach the field, and because everyone has cultivation tasks that need to be done, spending one's time in travelling is not feasible. Since bush camp neighbours include non-kin relations, the new spatial organization of production has required networks from which one can access labour to extend beyond one's own kin.

The importance of bush camp neighbours, as well as the kind of composition of networks that bush camps entail, can be seen in the number of bush camp neighbours who participated in the work parties called by case study individuals (see Table 3.4) in the study villages over a one-year period. The only people who did not have any bush camp neighbours participate were those who did not cultivate on a bush camp (Possi and Noaga) or the one person who had a marriage-related work party in which people

Table 3.4 *Agricultural Work Parties of Case Study Individuals, December 1996 to November 1997*

Person[a]	Activity	Crop	Field type	Total pps[b] (no)	Bush neigh-bours (%)	Kin[c] %	Area pp^{-1} (ha)	Costs pp^{-1} (fcfa)
Bandia[d]	Land clearing	Sorghum	Bush	22	9	95	0.109	186
Bandia	Weeding	Sorghum	Compound	10	30	100	0.035	280
Bandia	Cutting stalks	Millet	Compound	3	67	100	0.216	300
Piampo	Weeding	Millet	Bush	50	0	0	0.069	217
Possi	Weeding	Millet	Village	2.5	na[e]	100	0.182	120
Possi	Weeding	Rice	Bush	20	75	100	0.019	160
Djoulmani	Weeding	Rice	Bush	8	50	50	0.222	250
Djoulmani	Weeding	Rice	Bush	22	68	100	0.081	314
Djoulmani	Cutting heads	Rice	Bush	17	29	71	0.105	353
Marhi	Weeding	Sorghum	Bush	15	60	27	0.030	213
Marhi	Cutting heads	Rice	Bush	9	67	22	0.104	222
Sambo	Hoeing	Sorghum and millet	Bush	16	63	25	0.201	219
Noaga	Second weeding	Millet	Village	15	na	100	0.208	133
Average					16		0.122	228

Notes: a: Original names have been changed for privacy.

b: pp = participant.

c: Bush neighbours and kin are not mutually exclusive.

d: The same person and crop do not mean it is the same field.

e: na = not applicable and applies to cases in which the person calling the work party did not have a bush field.

Source: Agricultural study. Table 8.1 in Mazzucato and Niemeijer (2000b).

from the suitor's village came to work (Piampo). In the case of the brothers Marhi and Sambo who live in the same village compound during the dry season but cultivate in two different bush camps during the agricultural season, many of their neighbours who participated were not related by kin. They have a relatively small network of kin relations, so building networks with field neighbours seems to be all the more important. In fact, Marhi was difficult to locate during the rainy season because he was often working at his neighbours' work parties.

Role of women

A third change is women's new role in agriculture. The increased need for the labour of small production units has necessitated women's involvement in the production process. While at the turn of the century women cultivated some sauce ingredients on the borders of the compound fields, they now dedicate much of their labour during the agricultural season to helping with agricultural tasks on their families' grain fields that are managed by their husbands. They also cultivate their own fields of millet or sorghum and groundnuts. The production from a woman's own fields can contribute to the production unit's food needs in case the family field does not suffice or can be sold to pay for things that are customarily a woman's responsibility, like clothes, kitchen utensils and sauce ingredients. Women also contribute to the new demands of a modernizing society, such as school fees and hospital and medicinal bills.

The transition to women's active role in agriculture has been eased by an adaptation of customs that guide what women are and are not allowed to do, as well as the use of women's natal networks for agricultural purposes. Half a century ago, women in the northern village could grow Bambara groundnuts and okra only if one of their children had died. Only elderly women could cultivate tobacco because all other women would become blind if they did so. Gradually, customs changed so that women had to wait some time after their marriage before they could cultivate their own fields. For example, in the north, a newly married woman could sow neither sorghum nor cotton because she needed to have a grown-up son who could sow these crops for her. In the south, a woman could not cultivate millet if she did not have a child. She could have a personal field only if she had a child who was old enough to help her husband on the family's grain field. Later, a woman had to wait until the third year after her marriage before she could begin to cultivate a personal field. Progressively, the time that women had to wait to cultivate their own fields diminished so that today, both in the north and in the south, customs restricting when or what married women can grow are virtually nonexistent. In fact, today children, including girls, begin at around eight years of age to cultivate their own groundnut fields and later also have millet or sorghum fields.

Women's ties with their natal families have also been used to provide them with starter seed for the first cohort of women who began cultivating their own grain and groundnuts. Interviews conducted with women aged 30 to 60 both in the north and in the south, indicated that they began cultivating their own fields with seed obtained from their natal families.

These changes to institutions that have allowed today's smaller production units to meet their new labour needs have important consequences for people's ability to manage the environment in a sustainable way. First, access to enough labour allows production units to move to new fields when the land they are cultivating needs to be left fallow because clearing previously uncultivated or fallow land is a highly labour-intensive task. A small production unit with new workers and many consumers cannot clear enough land on its own to feed itself and, without the additional labour, would be forced to remain on the same piece of land and ultimately overcultivate it.

Second, by completing agricultural tasks with work parties, time is freed for applying the largely labour-intensive conservation measures that farmers were found to use (Mazzucato and Niemeijer, 2000a, 2000b). The additional time they gain allows farmers to use their knowledge of cultivation practices, their soils and landraces on which these measures are based, to capacity. Thus, as a result of having enough labour available, farmers have been able to invest in land-enhancing measures, rather than have to cultivate more land per person to feed their families. In fact, area cultivated per person for the main staple crops during the period 1970 to 1996 remained virtually the same at 0.3ha capita^{-1} in the eastern region (Mazzucato and Niemeijer, 2000b).

Access to labour allows small production units to compensate for the dramatic shifts in household labour so as not to jeopardize production. As we argued earlier, reducing the risk of production shortfalls helps avoid the poverty trap that induces people to degrade the land. Finally, the increasing role of women in agriculture, enabled through a change in customs and new uses of women's natal networks, has given today's small production unit the labour base needed to perform agricultural tasks on time and in a sustainable way.

Diversification of livelihoods

Livelihoods are diversifying in the study region, as has been found for other parts of Africa (Mortimore and Adams, 1999; Birch-Thomsen et al, 2001). Social networks are an important institutional form that has enabled people to take advantage of new livelihood opportunities brought on by increased market integration. In this section, we discuss three ways in which social networks allow people to diversify their livelihoods in the study region and, in certain cases, how these networks have changed in their form and use to provide access to these new forms of livelihood. We argue that new livelihood opportunities give people the room to manoeuvre in an increasingly resource-tight system in order to avoid degrading the environment.

One reason for accessing other people's labour is, as discussed above, to be able to free one's time to engage simultaneously in various income-earning activities. The example of a case study individual illustrates this point. Since his teenage years, Bandia had been involved in commercial activities, first by having his own petty commerce stand in the local market, then by importing goods from Togo and selling them in local markets, and most recently by trading in millet and livestock. In 1996 Bandia was at a difficult point in his life cycle when he had four children who were too young to be agriculturally active; one wife; a father who had just died, whose burial and funeral he had to organize and pay for; and a mother to care for. He also needed to move to a new field and leave the one he had been cultivating fallow. This could have been one of those years that can throw a person into a poverty trap. Field clearing is highly labour intensive. Not having access to temporary labour to clear a new field would have forced Bandia to stay on his old fields and overcultivate them, which would eventually have led to soil mining. Not having any additional hands to help him with agricultural tasks would have meant that he would have had to dedicate all of his own labour to these tasks and thus would have had no time for his commercial activities. Consequently, he would have earned less income, had to borrow money or food to make ends meet, and fallen into debt without any additional sources of revenue from which to pay back his debts: the poverty trap. Bandia, however, left his old fields fallow and set up a bush compound on borrowed land close to Piampo's bush compound. Piampo had three wives and various agriculturally active children. Piampo's daughter was often to be found in Bandia's compound helping with the household chores, thus freeing Bandia's only wife to work on Bandia's and her fields. The fact that his wife worked on the fields meant that Bandia could absent himself every once in a while to conduct his commercial activities. It was advantageous for him to engage in his trading activities during the agricultural season when selling prices were high.

The example of Bandia illustrates how accessing temporary labour allows people simultaneously to conduct various income-earning activities and how the resulting diversification of sources of livelihood may help people avoid the poverty trap, even in years when their life cycles make them most vulnerable.

A second way in which networks provide access to new income-earning opportunities is the new ties forged between Gourmantché farmers and Fulbe, semi-sedentary, livestock herders. Greater market integration has made cattle a desirable form of savings among Gourmantché because it has a high market value; the demand for livestock is such that it is virtually always possible to find buyers in the region; and cattle reproduce, thus augmenting one's savings. There are, of course, risks involved in cattle rearing, such as epidemics that wipe out one's stock. However, given that when people have money, they usually invest in cattle, the rewards of cattle rearing are perceived to be greater than the risks it entails.

Gourmantché are able to engage in cattle rearing while maintaining their focus on crop cultivation because they entrust their cattle to Fulbe herders, as is commonly done in other parts of West Africa (see, for example, de Haan et al, 1990; McIntire et al, 1992; Breusers et al, 1998). This system allows Gourmantché to keep their family labour for crop-cultivation tasks and have their cattle far from farming areas during the agricultural season so as to limit crop damage.

In areas where historical ties existed between the two groups, such as in the northern research village, farmers have relied on these relationships to initiate and maintain herding agreements. In areas where no historical ties exist between the two group, such as in the southern village, villagers have developed a system of monetary loans through which they establish relationships of trust between members of the two groups. Market integration has made it so that almost everyone is either a potential lender or a creditor. Gourmantché have taken advantage on their relatively better-off situation with respect to Fulbe by giving loans of money or grains to Fulbe. First, small loans are made, and if the creditor repays his debt, the following loan will be a bit larger. In this way, a series of loan transactions are initiated that culminate with the Gourmantché entrusting his cattle to the Fulbe. Thus, in areas where social networks did not historically include Fulbe, these networks have been broadened to include Fulbe so as to engage in livestock rearing, and new ways have been developed (through monetary loans) to establish such networks.

A third way in which networks have adapted is by gaining access to cash for new cash needs created by market integration. Now ceremonies, such as funerals, require cash and can be costly. Furthermore, the availability of modern medicine can create a large and unpredictable need for cash. Forms of networking have emerged to deal with these new cash necessities in the form of self-help groups. Cash self-help groups function like *tontines*, which have been documented in other areas of West Africa (Lelart, 1990; van den Brink and Chavas, 1991; Webster and Fidler, 1996). Life histories reveal that these forms of cash self-help groups have emerged within the past 20 to 30 years. By providing access to cash, self-help groups have the same effect as an income-earning activity in diversifying one's livelihood.

Access to income-earning opportunities outside crop production through social networks allows people not to degrade their environment despite the increased scarcity of natural resources. The possibility of making one's living from more than just crop production means that there is less pressure on people to have to eke out everything they can from the land to ensure their livelihoods, as is characteristic of the poor (Dasgupta, 1993).

Second, market incentives to engage in livestock activities could have easily led to land degradation at the village or watershed level because of overgrazing. However, the particular herding agreements developed with Fulbe and enabled through the creation of social networks between Fulbe and Gourmantché have avoided such a situation, since most cattle are grazed on transhumance routes.

Finally, networks allow people to take risks associated with an environmentally sustainable form of agriculture. For example, moving to a new piece of land involves some unknowns: one knows how one's own field produces, but one can never know exactly how a new field will produce. Furthermore, in the first couple of years, a newly cleared field produces less than its full potential because cultivating and mixing organic matter into the soil initially improves soil structure (Mazzucato and Niemeijer, 2000b). Accessing income outside crop production allows one to take these risks that are necessary to practise sustainable land husbandry.

Use of technology

With market integration and the development of research and development organizations, more technologies are available to farmers. In this section, we discuss the use of the plow and landraces, which are new to the region, to illustrate how farmers have adapted their use of networks to access these new technologies. Furthermore, we argue that these technologies enable people to practice an environmentally sustainable form of agriculture.

Networks are increasingly being used to access equipment for agricultural purposes. According to a national survey, only 3 per cent of the agricultural population in Gnagna and Gourma provinces owns a plough (MARA 1996). However, this wide-scale survey, as well as smaller-scale studies on animal traction in the area (Barrett et al, 1982), focused on the ownership of ploughs and draft animals, ignoring the possibility of borrowing them. Such an omission can lead to conclusions that underestimate the actual use of technologies in rural African agricultural practices. In following farming practices in the study region, we noted, as did Hesse (1997) and Panin (1988) in northern Ghana, the frequent practice of lending and borrowing equipment, such as ploughs, draft animals and carts, from one's network. Such borrowing does not involve explicit payment agreements. However, it is common for a borrower to offer a gift of appreciation to the lender. Both what is given and when are highly variable and dependent on the borrower's means. The respondents explained that receiving loans to purchase a donkey-drawn plough from the local extension office was not appealing, particularly because of the obligation that they would have to repay the loan within a predefined period and the high risk of events happening that would make them unable to meet their repayments. Borrowing equipment from one's network thus provided an institutional solution to gaining access to equipment.

A technology survey conducted with 47 married individuals illustrates this phenomenon. Ownership of plough and draft animals was virtually nil for women and 39

Table 3.5 *Use of Agricultural Equipment in the Research Villages, 1996*

Type of equipment	Owns (%)	Borrows (%)	Total users (%)
		Women (N = 46)	
Plough	2	59	61
Draft animal	4	30	35
Cart	0	15	15
		Men (N = 28)	
Plough	39	32	71
Draft animal	50	25	75
Cart	14	32	46

Source: Technology survey. Table 8.2 in Mazzucato and Niemeijer (2000b)

Table 3.6 *Provenance of Recently Introduced Landraces (c. 1950–1998)*

	Northern research village	Southern research village
Provenance of recently introduced landraces		
Governmental agencies	9	11
Markets	7	1
Relationships with people		
Missionary	0	9
Villagers migrating out	8	1
Migrants coming to village	0	7
Family and friends	3	2
Do not know	0	5
Total introduced within the past 50 years	27	37
Total number of landraces currently grown	85	84

Source: Structured interviews on landraces. Table 8.3 in Mazzucato and Niemeijer (2000b)

per cent and 50 per cent, respectively, for men (see Table 3.5). However, if one looks at the borrowing of ploughs, another picture emerges.

If one considers ownership and borrowing of ploughs together, then Table 3.5 shows that women use ploughs almost as much as men do (61 per cent versus 71 per cent, respectively). In general, the borrowing of equipment and draft animals is common-place.[9]

Farmers also gain access to landraces of crops, such as sorghum, millet, groundnuts and rice, and knowledge about them through networks. Table 3.6 shows that between 40 per cent and 50 per cent of recent landraces were introduced through relationships with people, such as a local missionary, villagers who migrate for some time and then return to the village with new landraces, migrants who come to the village usually to set-tle there and bring landraces with them, or family members or friends who live in other areas. Although both governmental agencies and markets also involve relationships between people, we make the distinction between the various categories because most extension work is done through official organizations or markets, whereas these results show how important informal contact between people can be for the propagation of technologies.

Borrowing equipment and accessing new landraces have made technologies available to facilitate a process of technological change and intensification to deal with the increasing scarcity of natural resources. Farmers' limited incomes have been repeatedly identified as a major impediment to the use of farm capital and therefore the productivity and environmental sustainability of African agricultural systems (de Graaff, 1996; Reardon, 1998). However, through networks, even those who cannot afford to buy equipment are able to use it. Networks allow people to access equipment without making a capital outlay and to pay for it through resources that they do have, such as labour and political allegiance. Thus, networks allow people to overcome the income constraint to practicing environmentally sustainable agriculture.

Another effect of accessing technologies on environmental sustainability is that adapting landraces to a changing climate and qualities of a soil is a form of soil and water conservation that was found to be widely practiced in the area (Mazzucato and Niemeijer, 2000b). Farmers select the most appropriate landrace for soil and rainfall conditions at a particular point in time. As soil conditions change because of continued crop cultivation, farmers plant a different landrace to make more effective use of available soil moisture and to reduce the depletion of nutrients. If rainfall is late during a particular season and farmers need to resow, they change to a faster-maturing landrace. These landraces have also been fundamental to farmers adjusting to the decline in rainfall experienced since the wet 1950s (Mazzucato and Niemeijer, 2000b). By giving farmers access to different landraces, networks contribute to the environmentally sustainable practices used in the region.

Conclusion

This article contributes to a growing body of case studies (Tiffen et al, 1994; Fairhead and Leach, 1996, 1998; Benjaminsen, 1997) that have questioned 'received wisdom' or 'orthodoxies' about environmental degradation. It explains an optimistic case in which rapid population growth has not produced any evidence of trends in land degradation, by focusing on the role of changing informal institutions in mediating the relationship between the environment and society. However, there are important differences between this study's findings and how institutions are treated in the optimistic theories of Boserup (1965) and Hayami and Ruttan (1985).

First, the case presented here indicates that people respond to more than just population densities in adjusting their interactions with the environment. Boserup's (1965) theory of technological change and subsequent applications thereof (for example, Turner et al, 1993; Tiffen et al, 1994) grant primacy to population densities as the driving force behind the relationship between society and the environment. However, many of the institutional changes and adaptations discussed in this article were stimulated, by increased market integration (see also Zaal and Oostendorp, 2002 for a similar finding in Machakos, Kenya). Market integration did not only evolve as a consequence of higher population densities leading to reduced costs of communication, as stipulated by Boserup, but was also the outcome of colonial policies and increased contact with developed countries through trade, business and development projects (Mazzucato and Niemeijer, 2000b). Furthermore, changes in the spatial organization of production and in the use of technology have also been a reaction to a decline in rainfall experienced within the past 50 years. These various sources of change suggest, differently from Boserup's theory of population thresholds, that adjustment processes do not occur only at certain crisis points in which population levels have reached an unmanageable threshold, but continuously and in reaction to a multiplicity of factors.

Second, the effects of external changes, including population growth, on the environment depend on *how* people adjust. Thus, contrary to Boserup's (1965) theory, in which institutions are implicitly assumed to develop towards those of a market economy, and contrary to Hayami's and Ruttan's (1985) theory, in which factor markets are assumed to exist, this article has focused on how informal institutions change and how they affect the relationship between the environment and society. Changes in how production is spatially organized, labour is mobilized, different livelihoods are pursued, and technologies are accessed entail institutional adjustments that mediate the relationship between people and the environment. Land tenure arrangements are now being used more than in the past to allow people to cultivate in areas farther from the village centre; customs have been modified to allow production units to split and to ease women into agriculture; and social networks have changed in their uses and composition to enable people to pursue their production goals, access technologies and engage in a diversity of livelihood activities. All of these changes have allowed people to adapt to a changing context within which agriculture is practised, while not degrading their environment. This article has thus highlighted the need to include the 'missing link' of informal institutions in population environment debates to understand the diversity of institutional responses to the multiplicity of factors that influence people's relationship with the environment.

New solutions will need to be sought as the availability of natural resources and social and economic contexts change. However, the fact that substantial institutional adjustments will be made until now makes it reasonable to expect that further adjustments will be made to face new and changing contexts within which agriculture is practised.

Finally, the emphasis of this article on adjustment processes makes us conclude, similarly to, but through a different analysis from, Cuffano (1997), that as far as population is concerned, the *rate* of population growth is more important than absolute figures of population densities. At fast rates of population growth, institutional adjustments may be difficult to make. For example, in a context of war or rampant levels of AIDS that can quickly decrease the number of people in a location and overwhelm local institutions, people may find it hard to adjust their local institutions to manage their natural resources under new conditions. However, our case study shows that even at relatively high rates of population growth in a fragile ecosystem, there can be processes of adjustment taking place through local institutions that positively affect the environment.

References

Adams, W M and Mortimore, M J (1997) 'Agricultural intensification and flexibility in the Nigerian Sahel'. *Geographical Journal* **163**: 150–160

Afikorah-Danquah, S (1997) 'Local resource management in the forest–savanna transition zone: the case of Wenchi District, Ghana'. *IDS Bulletin* **28**(4): 36–46

Barrett, V, Lassiter, G, Wilcock, D, Baker, D and Crawford, E (1982) *Animal traction in Eastern Upper Volta: A Technical, Economic and Institutional Analysis*, Michigan State University, East Lansing

Benjaminsen, T A (1997) 'Is there a fuelwood crisis in rural Mali?' *GeoJournal* **43**: 163–174

Bernstein, H, Crow, B and Martin, C (eds) (1990) *The Food Question: Profit Versus People?* Earthscan, London

Berry, S (1988) 'Concentration without privatization? Some consequences of changing patterns of rural land control in Africa', R E Downs and S P Reyna (eds), In *Land and Society in Contemporary Africa*, University Press of New England, Hanover, pp53–75

Birch-Thomsen, T, Frederiksen, P and Sano, H O (2001) 'A livelihood perspective on natural resource management and environmental change in semiarid Tanzania'. *Economic Geography* **77**: 41–66

Boserup, F, (1965) *The Conditions of Agricultural Growth: The Economics of Agrarian Change Under Population Pressure*, Allen and Unwin, London

Breusers, M, Nederlof, S and van Rheenen, T (1998) 'Conflict or symbiosis? Disentangling farmer-herdsman relations: the Mossi and Fulbe of the Central Plateau, Burkina Faso'. *Journal of Modern African Studies* **36**: 357–380

Clay, D, Guizlo, M and Wallace, S (1994) *Population and Land Degradation*, Michigan State University, East Lansing

Cleaver, K M and Schreiber, G A (1994) *Reversing the Spiral. The Population, Agriculture, and Environment Nexus in Sub-Saharan Africa*, World Bank, Washington DC

Cuffano, N (1997) 'Population growth and agriculture in poor countries: A review of theoretical issues and empirical evidence'. *World Development* **25**: 1151–1163

Dasgupta, P (1993) *An Inquiry into Well-being and Destitution*, Clarendon Press, Oxford

de Graaff, J (1996) *The Price of Soil Erosion: An Economic Evaluation of Soil Conservation and Watershed Development*, Wageningen Agricultural University, The Netherlands

de Haan, L, van Driel, A and Kruithof, A (1990) 'From symbiosis to polarization? Peasants and pastoralists in northern Benin'. *Indian Geographical Journal* **65**(1): 51–65

Downs, R E and Reyna, S P (1988) *Land and Society in Contemporary Africa*, University Press of New England, Hanover

Ehrlich, P R, Ehrlich, A H and Daily, G C (1993) 'Food security, population, and environment'. *Population and Development Review* **19**(1): 1–32

Fairhead, J and Leach, M (1996) *Misreading the African Landscape. Society and Ecology in a Forest-Savanna Mosaic*. Cambridge University Press, Cambridge

Fairhead, J and Leach, M (1998) *Reframing Deforestation: Global Analysis and Local Realities. Studies in West Africa*, Routledge, London

Hayami, Y and Ruttan, V (1985) *Agricultural Development: An International Perspective*. Johns Hopkins University Press, Baltimore

Hesse, J H (1997) 'Is bullock traction a sustainable technology? A longitudinal case study in northern Ghana'. PhD thesis, Georg-August University, Götingen, Sweden

Hudson, N (1991) *A Study of the Reasons for Success or Failure of Soil Conservation Projects*. Food and Agriculture Organization, Rome

Hyden, G, Kates, R W and Turner, B L H (1993) 'Beyond intensification'. In B L Turner, H G Hyden and R W Kates (eds) *Population Growth and Agricultural Change in Africa,* 401–439. Gainesville: University Press of Florida

Kepe, T (1997) 'Communities, entitlements and nature reserves: the case of the Wild Coast, South Africa. *IDS Bulletin* 28(4): 47–58

Lelart, M (1990) *La Tontine: Pratique Informelle d'épargne et de Credit dans les Pays en Voie de Dévéloppement,* John Libbey Eurotext, London

Lele, U and Stone, S W (1989) *Population Pressure the Environment and Agricultural Intensification: Variations on the Boserup Hypothesis,* World Bank, Washington DC

Malthus, T R, (1803) *An Essay on Population,* J M Dent, London

MARA (1996) 'Enquête nationale de statistiques agricoles ENSA (1993) rapport général. Direction des Statistiques Agro-Pastorales'. Ministére De l'Agriculture et des Ressources Animales, Ouagadougou

Mazzucato, V and Niemeijer, D (2000a) 'The cultural economy of soil and water conservation: market principles and social networks in eastern Burkina Faso'. *Development and Change* 31: 83l–1155

Mazzucato, V and Niemeijer, D (2000b) 'Rethinking soil and water conservation in a changing society: a case study in eastern Burkina Faso'. Doctoral dissertation, Wageningen University, The Netherlands

Mazzucato, V and Niemeijer, D (2001) 'Overestimating land degradation, underestimating farmers in the Sahel'. Issue Paper No 101, IIED, London

McIntire, J, Bourzat, D and Pingali, P (1992) *Crop-livestock Interaction in Sub-Saharan Africa.* World Bank, Washington DC

Mortimore, M J and Adams, W M (1999) *Working the Sahel Environment and Society in Northern Nigeria,* Routledge, London

Nicholson, S E Tucker, C J and Ba, M B (1998) 'Desertification, drought, and surface vegetation: an example from the West African Sahel'. *Bulletin of the American Meteorological Society* 79: 815–829.

Niemeijer, D and Mazzucato, V (2002) 'Soil degradation in the West African Sahel'. *Environment* 44(2): 20–31

Panin, A (1988) *Hoe and Bullock Farming Systems in Northern Ghana,* Nyankpala Agricultural Experiment Station Crops Research Institute, Tamale, Ghana

Pingali, P, Bigot, Y and Binswanger, H P (1987) *Agricultural Mechanization and the Evolution of Farming Systems in Sub-Saharan Africa,* Johns Hopkins University Press, Baltimore

Prince, S D, Brown de Colstoun, E and Kravitz, L L (1998) 'Evidence from rain-use efficiencies does not indicate extensive Sahelian desertification'. *Global Change Biology* 4(4): 359–374

Prudencio, C Y (1993) 'Ring management of soils and crops in the West African semi-arid tropics: the case of the Mossi farming system in Burkina Faso'. *Agriculture, Ecosystems and Environment* 47: 237–264

Reardon, T (1998) 'African agriculture: productivity and sustainability issues'. In C K Eicher and J M Staatz, (ed) *International Agricultural Development,* 3rd edn, Johns Hopkins University Press, Baltimore, pp444–457

Remy, G (1967) *Yobri: Étude Géographique du Terroir d'un Village Gourmantché de Haute-Volta,* Mouton, Paris

Ricardo, D (1817) *The Principles of Political Economy and Taxation,* Cambridge University Press, Cambridge

Richards, P (1986) *Coping with Hunger: Hazard and Experiment in a West African Rice-farming System,* Allen and Unwin, London

Reijntjes, C, Haverkort, B and Waters-Bayer, A (1992) *Farming for the Future: An Introduction to Low-external-input and Sustainable Agriculture,* Macmillan, London

Ruttan, V and Hayami, Y (1972) 'Strategies for agricultural development: Food Research Institute studies in agricultural economics', *Trade and Development* 9: 129–148

Savadogo, M (2000) *Crop Residue Management in Relation to Sustainable Land Use*, Wageningen University, The Netherlands

Sivakumar, M V K (1991) *Drought Spells and Drought Frequencies in West Africa*, International Crops Research Institute for the Semi-Arid Tropics, Patancheru, India

Slingerland, M (2000) *Mixed Farming: Scope and Constraints in West African Savanna*, Wageningen University, The Netherlands

Speirs, M and Olsen, O (1992) *Indigenous Integrated Farming Systems in the Sahel*, World Bank, Washington DC

Swanson, R A (1979) *Gourmantché Agriculture Part 2: Cultivated Plant Resources and Field Management*, ORD de l'Est, Fada N'Gourma

Tiffen, M, Mortimore, M and Gichuki, F (1994) *More People, Less Erosion: Environmental Recovery of Kenya*, John Wiley, Chichester, UK

Turner B L, Hyden G and Kates, R W, (eds) (1993) *Population Growth and Agricultural Change in Africa.* University Press of Florida, Gainesville

van den Brink R and Chavas J P (1991) *The Microeconomics of an Indigenous African Institution: The Rotating Saving and Credit Association*, Cornell Food and Nutrition Policy Program, Washington DC

van der Pol, F (1992) *Soil Mining: An Unseen Contributor to Farm Income in Southern Mali*, Royal Tropical Institute, Amsterdam

Vierich, H I D and Stoop, W A (1990) 'Changes in West African savanna agriculture in response to growing population and continuing low rainfall'. *Agriculture, Ecosystems and Environment* 31: 115–132

Webster L and Fidler P (1996) *The Informal Sector and Microfinance Institutions in West Africa*, World Bank, Washington DC

Williamson G and Payne W J A (1978) *An Introduction to Animal Husbandry in the Tropics*, Longman, London

World Bank (1991) *The Population, Agriculture and Environment Nexus in Sub-Saharan Africa*, World Bank, Washington DC

Zaal, F and Oostendorp, R H (2002) 'Explaining a miracle: intensification and the transition towards sustainable small-scale agriculture in dryland Machakos and Kitui districts', Kenya. *World Development* 30(7) (Forthcoming)

Notes

1 We thank Niels Röling and Leo Stroosnijder of Wageningen University, the Netherlands, for their comments and suggestions on previous material from which this article is drawn. We also thank Kees Burger for comments on a previous version of this article. We acknowledge the financial and logistical assistance of the Antenne Sahélienne and the Erosion and Soil and Water Conservation Group of Wageningen University that made the fieldwork for this study possible.

2 *Informal institution* refers to social norms; customary laws and codes of conduct; and their enforcement mechanisms, such as social networks that together guide people's behaviour within a society.

3 *Social network* refers to relationships between people that facilitate cooperation and coordination among members.

4 An *environmentally sustainable production system* 'is the successful management of resources for agriculture to satisfy changing human needs while maintaining or enhancing the quality of the environment and conserving natural resources' (TAC/CGIAR in Reijntjes et al, 1988, 1992, p2).

5 A *market economy* is characterized by private ownership of land and other goods, in which production and consumption are determined primarily by prices set through free competition.

6 For a full list of land improvement and conservation practices, see Mazzucato and Niemeijer (2000a, 2000b).

7 As population rises even more, these institutional solutions to redistribute land will no longer suffice, and other solutions will need to be developed. However, the fact that these adjustments have taken place thus far given us good reason to believe that further institutional adjustments can and will be made to face future changes in the context within which agriculture is practised.

8 This process was also noted by Swanson (1979) in this region and by Vierich and Stoop (1990) in other areas of Burkina Faso.

9 It is important to note, however, that borrowing ploughs usually entails accessing them late because the owner of a plough will first use it on his fields. Also, although borrowing equipment does not usually entail an explicit agreement for repayment, it does put the borrower under an informal obligation towards the lender. Finally, looking at the number of people who borrow says nothing about the amount of land that is ploughed. It may well be that the amount of land ploughed with a borrowed plough is less than that ploughed with an owned plough, given that borrowed ploughs are accessed late. This would make an interesting research question for an agricultural survey to address.

Introduction – Section IIB: Agents and Approaches in Environment and Development

Samantha Jones and Grace Carswell

Participation, Empowerment and Environmental Projects

Development activity that has an environmental focus is often equated with 'projects' – environmental rehabilitation projects, agricultural development projects, social forestry projects, for example. Projects led by a modernization agenda have tended to be funded and designed by 'expert' outsiders according to their identification of environmental problems and their technical solution. Sharpe notes that while conservation requires a long-term perspective, 'the activities of projects themselves are mostly narrowly instrumental... and planned over short-term tranches governed by the project cycle of donor agencies' and as such 'a climate of mistrust' often exists between projects and local people (1998, p26). It is against this backdrop that processes such as participation and empowerment are instituted. Thus, participatory development is conventionally represented as emerging out of the recognition of the shortcomings of top-down, donor-driven, outsider-led development (Cooke and Kothari, 2001) and became a key notion in development planning from the late 1980s. The rationale for participation is clear: it is 'only when the supposed beneficiaries of intervention participate in the planning and implementation of projects which are intended to benefit them will they have any interest in making development projects succeed' (Gardner and Lewis, 1996, p112). Drijver (1992) emphasizes the importance of a participatory approach to the success of environmental (conservation) projects, particularly through the use of local knowledge to develop locally appropriate solutions (Carr and Halvorsen, 2001).

Stiefel and Wolfe (1994) define participation as people achieving a greater capacity to advance their own interests and control their own livelihoods and becoming a voice in the shaping of 'development'. However, there have been diverse interpretations of participation, to the extent that various typologies of participation have been devised. Biggs (1989), to use an early example, identifies four levels of participation with respect to agricultural development and research. The first is 'contract participation' which is merely where farmers' land or services are hired or borrowed. The second is 'consultative', where researchers consult farmers, diagnose their problems and try to find solutions for them. These are both illustrative of how the radical connotations of participation have been lost as the rhetoric of participation may be used where the reality has been the token involvement of local people to legitimize decisions that have already been taken by powerful outsiders (eg Gardner and Lewis, 1994). The other two categories; 'collaborative' – where researchers and farmers are partners in the research process sustaining their interaction in diagnosis and evaluation and 'collegiate' where attempts are made to actively strengthen farmers' informal research, have more in common with Stiefel and Wolfe's (1994) definition above.

In terms of participation in environmental projects, Drijver (1992) compares four projects, one of which she describes as participatory, one as centralistic and the other two combining both types of approach. While the centralistic approach involved some 'consultative' participation, in the participatory approach the local community 'had a decisive say in the objectives, design and implementation' of the project (1992, p133). Where local involvement is token or consultative and used to legitimize projects and/or increase their efficiency, the emphasis is on participation as a *means* to achieve successful (pre-determined) outcomes. This is also the case in Twyman's study (1998), as it follows a planner-centred process, rather than being people centred. Where participation is an *end* in itself, the outcomes are less significant than the process. NGOs and donors may, under such circumstances, have to relinquish more conventional measures of project success. This, of course, may be very challenging for the donors, or indeed inappropriate, if the goal is conservation and conservation is not congruent with the interests or priorities of the local population. Even when participation is seen as an end in itself, it important to appreciate that it can serve many different interests. White (1996) argues that participation must be seen as a political process as there are always tensions regarding who is involved, how and on whose terms. Recognizing this, Sharpe (1998) explores the relevance of concepts such as participation to local development processes and forest conservation in Cameroon. His analysis focuses on the problems for 'participation' emanating from a diverse community with 'contested forest futures' and notes that 'the notion of some single indigenous community voice in participatory management is naïve' (1998, p40).

White (1996) argues that while participation has the potential to challenge patterns of dominance, it may also be the means through which existing power relations are reproduced. Cooke and Kothari (2001) similarly argue that acts and processes of participation both conceal and reinforce oppressions and injustices and suggest that as articulations of power are embedded in social and cultural practices they are less visible. They also note that 'by supposedly focusing on the personal and the local as the sites of empowerment and knowledge, participatory approaches minimize the importance of other places where power and knowledge are located, for example with "us" the western development community and with the state' (Cooke and Kothari, 2001). Carmen's (1996) criticism of the 'participation in development approach', is that as people are drawn into participating only in the design and execution of projects it distracts people away from any form of genuine (political) participation. It is important though, not to regard project 'recipients' as passive beneficiaries as they can opt out or actively sabotage a project, employing covert resistance strategies and 'weapons of the weak' (White, 1996; Twyman, 1998; see also section below).

A second and related concept to guide development interventions from the late 1980s is empowerment, which may be regarded as being at the radical end of the spectrum of participation. Indeed in a participatory typology by White (1996), the final category, 'transformative participation', captures the essence of empowerment very well. It refers to the situation whereby consciousness is raised and confidence increased to enhance people's capacity to take collective action to fight injustice (White, 1996). Empowerment has been described as 'the creation of an environment of enquiry in which people question and resist the structural reasons for their poverty through learning and action' (Cromwell and Wiggins, quoted by Okali et al, 1994). It involves critical reflection, analysis and assessment of what has hitherto been taken for granted so as to uncover the socially constructed basis of apparently individual problems (Kabeer, 1994). More explicit attention tends to be given to countering unequal power relations in the empowerment approach. Power consists not only of 'power over' (the ability to persuade, organize, command, etc) but also the ability to bring others to a certain way of thinking or enrol them in their 'projects' (Latour, 1986, cited by Villarreal, 1992). Power relations help to shape not only whose interests prevail, but also how different groups perceive their interests (Kabeer, 1994). When subordinate groups are able to view their lives from different vantage points, the effects of social conditioning may become more obvious.

Paulo Friere (1972) advocated a direct approach to political empowerment – 'raising consciousness' though popular education and organization (which he termed 'conscientization'). Conscientization enables the poor to mobilize the resources they do have: their capacity to resist and transform through their collective strength (Kabeer, 1994). The notion has been applied particularly in the sphere of gender relations. Consideration needs to be given though to the rights of outsiders to disrupt the *status quo* of another culture, particularly when it may encourage violent confrontations between vulnerable and more powerful groups (such as powerful elites backed by the state) (Gardner and Lewis, 1996).

Empowerment is little discussed in the environment and development literature, but is tackled by some authors. Schevyns (1998) and Brown and Rosendo (this volume) explore the dimensions of empowerment, the former in terms of an empowerment framework for ecotourism and the latter through the creation of 'extractive reserves' in the Amazon. Both these articles include economic empowerment as an element of empowerment, which really relates to financial gain and income improvement. Whilst these might be important criteria in their own right, arguably if regarded as an aspect of empowerment they may lead to a watering down of the concept. Brown and Rosendo (this volume) provide a useful discussion on the extent to which one group can bestow power upon another. They critically assess the use empowerment as a rhetorical devise to impose the agenda of environmental NGOs.

NGOs and Their Role in Environmental Management

NGOs may be classified as non-institutionalized, but formal groups (having adopted rules of conduct or constitutions and defining organizational goals). As organizations, according to Potter and Taylor (1996), they have at least full time staff, some sort of hierarchy, a budget and an 'office'. There has been a proliferation of development NGOs during the last couple of decades, which can be accounted for by the privatization and liberalization agendas in the developing world that have reduced the role of the state in the delivery of services (Gardner and Lewis, 1996) and because donor agencies are directing more of their budgets to NGOs (Thomas-Slater, 1992). Brehm (2000) explains that with the continued erosion of the state, NGOs have emerged as new actors which are able to form 'vertical linkages' between the state and the grassroots and 'horizontal linkages' with coalitions and networks. Their influence lies in their linking local to international level politics. In addition, Hudock (1995) notes that NGOs' assumed organizational characteristics of flexibility, innovative ability, participatory approaches and cost-effectiveness account for NGOs perceived comparative advantage over donor agencies, national governments and private firms in addressing the needs of people who are poor.

There is a diversity of (non-profit) organizations which may be legitimately grouped under the heading of NGOs (Thomas-Slater, 1992; Hudock, 1995), varying in size, skills, structure, ideology, purpose, membership, scale of operation and cultural origin (Bryant and Bailey, 1997). Their functions range from straightforward service provision, to empowerment and consciousness raising, and campaigning, lobbying and advocacy work to change the wider policy environment. Such diversity accounts in part for the debate over the role that NGOs may be able to play in the development process. While they may be in a better position to operationalize many of the more radical concepts and ideas in development, such as facilitating participation and empowerment, they may be constrained by their tendency to work within the dominant structures of the state (some may be funded by governments, while others engage with government to advocate changes in policy). Some authors have argued that NGOs may merely serve as extensions of the state, helping to maintain existing power relations and legitimize the political system (Potter et al, 1999, citing Botes, 1996).

Following the proliferation of NGOs in the developing world there has been a burgeoning academic and grey literature on the subject. It is not within the scope of this text to review this literature, but see Riley (2002), Edwards and Hulme (1992, 1996), Farrington and Bebbington (1993), Farrington and Lewis (1993), Wellard and Copestake (1993), Fisher (1997), Hulme and Edwards (1997), Dicklitch (1998), Tvedt (1998), Hudock (1999), Eade and Pierce (2000), Lewis and Wallace (2000), Barrow and Jennings (2001), Eade (2001), Edwards and Fowler (2002) and Hilhorst (2003) for general texts and edited volumes on NGOs in development.

Of greater interest here is the striking rise of environmental NGOs worldwide which has mirrored the soaring number of development NGOs more generally. One reason proposed to account for the rise in environmental NGOs is serious trends in ecosystem decline (Princen and Finger, 1994) and the growth of environmental problems worldwide (Bryant and Bailey, 1997). However, it may reflect the rise of northern NGOs in the environmental concerns of developing countries and there are suggestions that Third World environmental NGOs may reflect the interests of the middle classes and/or are tools for First World interests (Bryant and Bailey, 1997). While northern and international NGOs may pursue their own (conservation-oriented) agendas, Bryant and Bailey (1997) note that the grassroots Third World-based environmental NGOs (and grassroots environmental movements) tend to be more concerned with pursuing social justice and equity objectives for poor marginalized groups via the mechanism of environmental conservation (ie maintaining access to local environmental resources to sustain livelihoods) rather than environmental conservation *per se*. However, unlike many other political actors, such as the state and businesses, they are unwilling to sacrifice environmental quality for the often ephemeral benefits of economic growth (Bryant and Bailey, 1997).

Another reason suggested for the rise in environmental NGOs is the growing power and assertiveness of 'civil society' vis-à-vis the state in most Third World countries since the late 1970s (Bryant and Bailey, 1997). Brown and Rosendo (this volume) note that NGOs can support grassroots activity by lobbying and pressuring governments, organizing networks of support and creating 'strategic alliances'. However, significant political obstacles to the effectiveness of environmental NGOs remain. In Indonesia, Malaysia and Vietnam, Eccleston and Potter (1996) explain how environmental NGOs are confronted by powerful government and business organizations buttressed by global economic, ideological and political structures of power.

The literature on the environment and NGOs in the developing world is quite diverse. Research has examined the advocacy work of NGOs. Papers in Potter and Taylor's (1996) edited volume of the *Journal of Commonwealth and Comparative Politics*, for example, broadly address the political work of NGOs trying to influence environmental policies. They note that some political contexts and target organizations are more favourable to NGO advocacy work than others. However, Potter (1996) compares the activity (numbers and influence) of NGOs trying to influence forest policy in relatively democratic India compared with less democratic Indonesia. Although he notes that his conclusions are only suggestive and provisional, he reports that their influence may have relatively little to do with the domestic political context, which may be explained, in part, by the linkages with influential northern NGOs operating in more democratic political contexts. This supports Brehms (2000) point above about the importance of creating linkages in NGO work. The relationship more broadly between democracy, NGOs and environmental advocacy has been explored by Bryant and Bailey (1997) and Eccleston and Potter (1996). Thomas et al (2000) also present an edited volume that examines the conditions under which NGOs may exert influence on policies to conserve and use sustainably natural resources in sub-Saharan Africa.

NGO activity at a project level has been addressed by Vivian (1994). Based on her study of NGOs in Zimbabwe, she reports that while promoting themselves as instigating participatory development, NGOs rarely reflect the concerns and wishes of grassroots actors. Similarly, Sundberg (1998) questions the effectiveness of NGOs involved in the implementation of the Maya Biosphere Reserve in Guatamala. She suggests that while overall goals may coincide, the NGOs involved have unique agendas and conflicting interests (displaying a type of territorialism) and that their lack of inter-organizational coordination may be reducing their effectiveness. Furthermore, activities tended to be announced to, rather than negotiated with, local communities. Thus, many of the concerns noted about participation and empowerment in the previous section may be applied to NGO work at this level. In Brown and Rosendo's case study in contrast (this volume), strategic alliances that were developed between grassroots and organizations and environmental NGOs contributed to the attainment of both conservation and development objectives and the empowerment of grassroots organizations.

While a key concern in the literature on environmental NGOs concerns the interests of northern environmental organizations, Bryant (2002) addresses broader concerns of legitimacy and accountability. He suggests that there is a 'dark underbelly' to the NGO world, noting that politically and/or economically powerful individuals may establish 'mutant' NGOs to advance their self-serving agendas. He provides an example from the Philippines where elites who made fortunes through logging, stepped forward to be agents of forest renewal as funds became available from donors.

New Social Movements and Resistance: Livelihoods and the Environment

Unequal relations of power and resource access, under increasing scarcity, leads to struggles between groups. Outcomes reflect power relations but are not determined by them. Giddens (1984) argues that those who are subordinate have the opportunity to influence the activities of their 'superiors'. He recognizes the centrality of human agency to human behaviour, that is, the capability of people to intervene in the world and the course of events in wider social environment that is both constraining and enabling. Historically, most attention has been given to more visible and measurable forms of human agency in the form of overt resistance (Escobar and Alvarez, 1992). Examples include the well-known case of tree hugging among the Chipko movement, and more recently, resistance to damming the Narmada river in India, through sacrificial drowning, hunger strikes and road blockades (Dwivedi, 1998). Agarwal (1994), however, notes the importance of taking into account many of the covert forms of resistance, particularly in gender struggles, and provides a number of examples of women's covert resistance in India.

Scott's (1985) work has been recognized for giving greater attention to the more subtle forms of resistance, noting that the subordinate classes have rarely been afforded the luxury of open, organized political activity – this has been the preserve of the middle classes and intelligentsia. Rather they are more likely to engage in what he calls 'everyday forms of resistance', which he describes as 'the ordinary weapons of relatively powerless groups: foot dragging, dissimulation, false compliance, pilfering, feigned ignorance, slander, arson, 'sabotage, and so forth' (Scott, 1985, p29). With reference to collective resistance to colonial forest regulations in Thana district of India, Saldanha (1998) provides examples of such everyday forms of resistance, including: 'encroachments onto forest lands, thefts of timber and firewood, bribing forest guards to overlook these offences and above all, firing the forest to "manufacture dead wood"' (Saldhanha, 1998, p709). Gupta (2001), however, reflects critically upon Scott's work, suggesting that his account is founded in exaggerated claims of such acts by the rich and powerful to justify the routine repression of the poor. Furthermore, Gupta (2001) suggests that Scott overestimates the political significance of individual acts questioning whether they have the potential to make an 'utter shambles of policy' as Scott suggests.

A spectrum of forms of human agency may be recognized then, captured well by Biot et al's (1993) four categories of forms of agency. 'Confrontation' is a form of overt resistance and has been a familiar response to coercive measures. It involves direct conflict and struggle, not necessarily violent, but represents a conscious attempt to resist. It aims to directly challenge power relations and the consequence may be a transformation of social structures. 'Compliance' is effectively the opposite response and serves as a reinforcing mechanism of social norms. It reproduces social structures and maintains the status quo. 'Adaptation' occurs where agents comply with constraints by restructuring or recombining their objectives, resulting in a change of behaviour, which can also result in reflexive changes in the structures of which agents are a part. Finally 'Evasion' is where demands made (by norms/customs/regulations/coercion) fail to elicit compliance but also do not elicit struggle and confrontation. Action may satisfy the formal or ritual aspect of the demand, without fulfilling its objective. Saldanha (1998) and Jones (1995) examine resistance to colonial forestry and soil conservation projects with reference to some or all of the above types of human agency.

Social movements may be conceptualized as a collective form of resistance and generally challenge dominant ideas and a given constellation of power. In contrast to NGOs they tend to be characterized by informal and participatory modes of organization; commitment to an open and ultra-democratic system; attachment to changing societal values and willingness to engage in direct action to stop outcomes they regard as harmful (Princen and Finger, 1994). Some authors though include NGOs in the definition of new social movements (Dwivedi, 1998).

New social movements (NSMs) represent a significant voice of disquiet. Their activity is necessitated by the failure of formal political channels to effectively represent people's interests or protect the environment (Hall, 1999; Lundy, 1999). Compared with 'old' social movements (eg labour movements), their existence cannot be explained solely in terms of class struggle but more broadly in terms of both material struggles and identity politics, struggles over meaning and defence of culture, ideology and way of life (Escobar, 1996; Peet and Watts, 1996; Dwivedi, 1998). Thus new social movements may straddle class boundaries (Dwivedi, 1998) and key players may be from middle-class and educated sectors of society (see Lundy, 1999 for a case study from Jamaica). Often though new social movements consist of individuals whose livelihoods are directly threatened by 'development' (Lundy, 1999; Dwivedi, 2001; Hirsch, 2001) as local groups are mobilizing to take initiative in resisting the destructive processes that underpin their livelihoods (Hall, 1999). Yet while authors such as Escobar see NSMs as 'resisters to development' (citing Grillo, 1997) Schuurman contends that 'social movements (new and old) are not expressions of resistance against modernity; rather they are demands for access to it' (1993, p27). Conspicuous in its absence in this theoretical literature is detailed attention to the voices of those engaged in new social movements, which may reveal the complexity and diversity of motivations behind such movements (see though Dwivedi, 1998; Nandy, 2001; Routledge, 2003, for exceptions).

There is also disagreement over the potential and scope of these movements. In terms of environmental protection, Hall (1999) suggests that socio-environmental movements in Brazilian Amazonia, are the single most important factor in effective, sustainable, local natural resource management (which he terms 'productive conservation'). Yet it has been noted that some forms of collective resistance remain localized, ephemeral and easily repressed (Escobar and Alvarez, 1992) and that the success of campaigns of new social movements tends to reflect the extent to which multi-level networks and international support are mobilized (Dwivedi, 1998). This can mean that social movements in the south may be financially dependent on northern institutions, which 'begs the question about the possible discourse of imperialism imposed by Northern NGOs' (Schuurman, 1993, p203). Peet and Watts (1996, p36, citing Sachs 1992) argue that whatever their shortcomings 'the existence of such grassroots livelihood movements – rubber tappers in eastern Amazonia, tree huggers in north India or Indian communities fighting transnational oil companies in Ecuador – represents for the new social movements community the building blocks for an "alternative to development". Dwidevi (2001) in contrast, believes that demand for accountability, rather than 'alternatives', to be a defining feature of environmental movements.

Mawdsley (this volume) demonstrates the issue of northern influence on NSMs with respect to resistance to 'development' in the Himalaya by the Chipko movement. Assumed to be ecofeminists (ie concerned to protect nature for its own sake arising from the natural affinities between women and nature – see Agarwal (1992) and Jackson (1993) for a critique of this perspective) by western environmentalists, NGOs lent much support to the protection of forests. The tree huggers though, did not want their forests protected merely out of an inherent concern for the innate value of nature, but more as a 'functional livelihood strategy'. Ultimately, in the name of conservation, they lost access rights to the forest products upon which their livelihoods so depended.

References

Agarwal, B (1992) 'The gender and environment debate: lessons from India'. *Feminist Studies* **18**(1): 119–158

Agarwal, B (1994) 'Gender, resistance and land: interlinked struggles over resources and meanings in south Asia'. *Journal of Peasant Studies* **22**(1): 81–125

Alvarez, S E and Escobar, A (1992) 'Conclusion: theoretical and political horizons of change in contemporary Latin American social movements', in A Escobar and SE Alvarez (eds) *The Making of Social Movements in Latin America: Identity, Strategy, and Democracy*, Westview Press, Boulder, Colorado

Barrow, O and Jennings, M (eds) (2001) *The Charitable Impulse: NGOs and Development in East and North-East Africa*, James Currey, Oxford

Biggs, S D (1989) *A Multiple Source of Innovation Model of Agricultural Research and Technology Promotion*, ODI Agricultural Administration Unit, London

Biot, Y, Blaikie, P M, Jackson, C and Palmer-Jones, R (1993) *Rethinking Research on Land Degradation in Developing Countries*, Overseas Development Group, School of Developing Studies, University of East Anglia, UK

Brehm, V M (2000) 'Environment, advocacy and community participation: MOPAWI in Honduras'. *Development in Practice* **10**(1): 94–97

Bryant, R L (2002) 'False prophets? Mutant NGOs and Philippine environmentalism'. *Society and Natural Resources* **15**: 629–639

Bryant, R L and Bailey, S (1997) *Third World Political Ecology*, Routledge, London

Carmen, R (1996) *Autonomous Development: Humanising the Landscape*, Zed Books, London

Carr, D S and Halvorsen, K (2001) 'An evaluation of three democratic, community-based approaches to citizen participation: surveys, conservation with community groups, and community dinners'. *Society and Natural Resources* **14**(2): 107–126

Cooke, B and Kothari, U (2001) 'The case for participation as tyranny', in B Cooke and U Kothari (eds) *Participation: The New Tyranny?* Zed Books, London

Dicklitch, S (1998) *The Elusive Promise of NGOs in Africa: Lessons from Uganda*, Macmillan, Basingstoke

Drijver, C (1992) 'People's participation in environmental projects', in E Croll and D Parkin (eds) *Bush Base: Forest Farm*, Routledge, London

Dwivedi, R (1998) 'Resisting dams and "development": contemporary significance of the campaign against the Narmada projects in India'. *European Journal of Development* 10(2): 135–183

Dwivedi, R (2001) 'Environmental movements in the global south: issues of livelihood and beyond'. *International Sociology* 16(1): 11–31

Eade, D (ed) (2001) *Debating Development: NGOs and the Future*, Oxfam Publications, Oxford

Eccleston, B and Potter, D (1996) 'Environmental NGOs and different political contexts in Southeast Asia: Malaysia, Indonesia and Vietnam', in M J G Parnwell and R L Bryant, *Environmental Change in Southeast Asia: People, Politics and Sustainable Development*, Routledge, London

Edwards, M and Fowler, A (eds) (2002) *The Earthscan Reader on NGO Management*, Earthscan, London

Edwards, M and Hulme, D (eds) (1992) *Making a Difference: NGOs and Development in a Changing World*, Earthscan, London

Edwards, M and Hulme, D (eds) (1996) *Beyond the Magic Bullet: NGO Performance and Accountability in the Post-Cold War World*, Earthscan, London

Escobar, A (1996) 'Constructing nature: elements of a poststructural political ecology', in R Peet and M Watts (eds) *Liberation Ecologies*, Routledge, London

Escobar, A and Alvarez, S E (1992) 'Introduction: theory and protest in Latin America today', in A Escobar and SE Alvarez (eds) *The Making of Social Movements in Latin America: Identity, Strategy, and Democracy*, Westview Press, Boulder, Colorado

Farrington, J and Bebbington, A (1993) *Reluctant Partners? Non-governmental Organisations, the State and Sustainable Agricultural Development*, Routledge, London

Farrington, J and Lewis, D (1993) *Non-governmental Organisations and the State in Asia*, Routledge, London

Fisher, J (1997) *Nongovernments: NGOS and the Political Development of the Third World*, Kumarian Press, West Hartford, Connecticut

Forsyth, T (1999) 'Environmental activism and the construction of risk: implications for NGO alliances'. *Journal of International Development* 11: 687–700

Gardner, K and Lewis, D (1996) *Anthropology, Development and the Post-modern Challenge*, Pluto Press, London

Giddens, A (1984) *The Constitution of Society*, Polity Press, Cambridge

Grillo, R D (1997) 'Discourses of development: the view from anthropology', in R D Grillo and R L Stirrat (eds) *Discourses of Development: Anthropological Perspectives*, Berg, Oxford

Gupta, D (2001) 'Everyday resistance or routine repression? Exaggeration as stratagem in agrarian conflict'. *Journal of Peasant Studies* 29(1): 89–108

Hall, A (1999) 'Social movements, empowerment and productive conservation: the case of Amazonia', in J Mullen (ed) *Rural Poverty, Empowerment and Sustainable Livelihoods*, Ashgate, Aldershot, Hampshire

Haynes, J (1999) 'Power, politics and environmental movements in the Third World', in C Rootes (ed) *Environmental Movements: National, Local, Global*, Frank Cass and Co Ltd, London

Hilhorst, D (2003) *The Real World of NGOs: Discourse, Diversity and Development*, Zed Books, London

Hirsch, P (2001) 'Globalisation, regionalisation and local voices: the Asian Development Bank and re-scaled politics of environment in the Mekong Region'. *Singapore Journal of Tropical Geography* 23(3): 237–251

Hudock, A C (1995) 'Sustaining southern NGOs in resource-dependent environments'. *Journal of International Development* 7(4): 653–667

Hudock, A C (1999) *NGOs and Civil Society: Democracy or Proxy?*, Blackwell Publishers, Oxford

Hulme, D and Edwards, M (eds) (1997) *NGOs, States and Donors: Too Close for Comfort?*, Macmillan, Basingstoke

Jackson, C (1993) 'Women/nature or gender/history? A critique of ecofeminist "development"'. *Journal of Peasant Studies* 20(3): 389–419

Jones, S J (1995) 'Deconstructing the degradation debate: a study of land degradation in the Uluguru Mountains, Tanzania'. PhD thesis, University of East Anglia, Norwich

Josiah, S J (2001) 'Approaches to expand NGO natural resource conservation program outreach'. *Society and Natural Resources* 14: 609–618

Kabeer, N (1994) *Reversed Realities: Gender Hierarchies in Development*, Verso, London

Levine, A (2002) 'Convergence or convenience? International conservation, NGOs and development assistance in Tanzania'. *World Development* 30(6): 1043–1055

Lewis, D and Wallace, T (eds) (2000) *New Roles and Relevance: Development NGOs and the Challenge of Change*, Kumarian Press, West Hartford, CT

Lundy, P (1999) Fragmented community action or new social movement'. *International Sociology* 14(1): 83–102

Mercer, C (2002) 'NGOs, civil society and democratization: a critical review of the literature'. *Progress in Development Studies* 2(1): 5–22

Nandy, A (2001) 'Dams and dissert: India's first modern environmental activist and his critique of the DVC'. *Futures* 33: 709–731

Okali, C et al (1994) *Farmer Participatory Research*, Intermediate Technology Publications, London

Pearce, J and Eade, D (eds) (2000) *Development, NGOs, and Civil Society: Selected Essays from Development in Practice,* Oxfam, Oxford

Potter, D (1996) 'Democratisation and the environment: NGOs and deforestation policies in India (Karnataka) and Indonesia (North Sumatra)'. *Journal of Commonwealth and Comparative Politics* 34(1): 9–37

Potter, D and Taylor, A (1996) 'NGOs and environmental policies: Asia and Africa. *Journal of Commonwealth and Comparative Politics* 34(1): 1–8

Potter, R B et al (1999) *Geographies of Development,* Longman, Harlow

Putnam, R (1993) *Making Democracy Work: Civic Traditions in Modern Italy,* Princeton University Press, Princeton

Princen, T and Finger, M (1994) *Environmental NGOs in World Politics: Linking the Local and the Global,* Routledge, London

Riley, J M (2002) *Stakeholders in Rural Development: Critical Collaboration in State–NGO partnerships,* Sage Publications, London

Routledge, P (2003) 'Voices of the dammed: discursive resistance amidst erasure in the Narmada Valley, India'. *Political Geography* 22: 243–270

Saldanha, I M (1998) 'Colonial forest regulations and collective resistance: nineteenth-century Thana District', in R H Grove, V Damodaran and S Sangwan, *Nature and the Orient: Environmental History of SE Asia*, OUP, Delhi

Schevyns, R (1999) 'Ecotourism and the empowerment of local communities'. *Tourism Management* 20: 245–249

Schuurman, F J (1993) (ed) *Beyond the Impasse: New Directions in Development Theory,* Zed Books, London

Scott, J C (1985) *Weapons of the Weak: Everyday Forms of Peasant Resistance,* Yale University Press, London

Sharpe, B (1998) '"First the forest": conservation, "community" and "participation" in southwest Cameroon'. *Africa* 68(1): 25–45

Sonnenfield, D A (2002) 'Social movements and ecological modernisation: the transformation of pulp and paper manufacturing'. *Development and Change* **33**: 1–27

Stiefel, M and Wolfe, M (1994*) A Voice for the Excluded: Popular Participation in Development*, Zed Books, London

Sundberg, J (1998) 'NGO landscapes in the Maya Biosphere Reserve, Guatemala'. *Geographical Review* **88**(3): 388–412

Thomas, A, Carr, S and Humphreys, D (2000) *Environmental Policies and NGO Influence: Land Degradation and Sustainable Resource Management in Sub-Saharan Africa*, Routledge, London

Thomas-Slater, B P (1992) 'Implementing effective local management of natural resources: new roles for NGOs in Africa'. *Human Organisation* **51**(2):136–143

Tvedt, T (1998) *Angels of Mercy or Development Diplomats?: NGOs and Foreign Aid*, James Currey, Oxford

Twyman, C (1998) 'Participatory conservation? Community-based natural resource management in Botswana'. *Geographical Journal* **166**(4): 323–335

Villarreal, M (1992) 'The poverty of practice', in N Long and A Long *Battlefields of Knowledge*, Routledge, London

Vivian, J (1994) 'NGOs and sustainable development in Zimbabwe: no magic bullets'. *Development and Change* **25**:167–193

Wellard, K and Copestake, J G (eds) (1993) *Non-governmental Organisations and the State in Africa*, Routledge, London

White, S C (1996) 'Depoliticising development: the uses and abuses of participation'. *Development in Practice* **6**(1): 6–15

4

Environmentalists, Rubber Tappers and Empowerment: The Politics and Economics of Extractive Reserves

Katrina Brown and Sérgio Rosendo

Summary

Extractive reserves are important initiatives in tropical forest zones which seek to integrate conservation of natural resources with development and human welfare objectives. Increasingly in such initiatives empowerment of local communities is seen as both a means of achieving this integration and as an end in itself. This article presents a theoretically informed analysis of the interactions between rubber tappers and environmental organizations in the establishment and implementation of extractive reserves in Rondônia, Brazil. It distinguishes two dimensions of empowerment – political and economic – and examines how the alliances between organizations have impacted differentially on the two dimensions. The analysis suggests that these alliances have so far been more successful in enabling political rather than economic empowerment. Advances in political empowerment are shown, in the short-term at least, not to have resulted in improvements in livelihood conditions of poor forest dwellers.

Introduction

One of the best-known examples of grassroots environmental action is the movement of rubber tappers which emerged in Brazil during the 1980s, fighting for the conservation of forests through the establishment of extractive reserves, which can be defined as 'conservation units that guarantee the rights of traditional populations to engage in harvesting forest products such as rubber and fruits' (Anderson, 1992, p67). The creation of extractive reserves has been promoted as 'among the most important strategies for forest conservation' (Hecht, 1989, p53). The designation of extractive reserves has gained support from a diverse array of actors, particularly conservation and environmental

Reprinted from *Development and Change*, vol 31, Brown, K and Rosendo, S, 'Environmentalists, Rubber Tappers and Empowerment: The Politics and Economics of Extractive Reserves', pp201–227, copyright © (2000), with permission from Blackwell Publishing.

organizations who regard it as an opportunity to put into practice an explicit linkage between conservation and development. The rubber tappers' struggle for rights to natural resources in these areas gained world-wide media attention at a time when deforestation, especially in Amazonia, was becoming a major issue for northern environmentalists.

This article examines the concept of empowerment within the context of these initiatives. It investigates the alliances formed between environmental NGOs and other agencies and rubber tappers, and looks at how far rubber tappers have been empowered as a result of the intervention of these organizations. The evidence presented in the article derives from research in the western Brazilian State of Rondônia (see Figure 4.1) and involves a case study of a project supported by one of the largest international conservation NGOs, the World Wide Fund for Nature (WWF). This project is a partnership between WWF, local rubber tappers' communities represented by the Rondônia Organization of Rubber Tappers (OSR) and its member Associations, and a regional environmental NGO (ECOPORÉ). Research involved examination of key institutions, including the OSR and other organizations located in Porto Velho, the administrative centre of Rondônia, and case studies of three selected extractive reserves (see Figure 4.1).

The article begins by discussing theoretical perspectives on empowerment, and the different dimensions of empowerment outlined in the literature on conservation and development, including the way in which empowerment has been interpreted and implemented in conservation projects. It distinguishes two dimensions of empowerment – political empowerment and economic empowerment – and examines how each of these has been affected by the alliances between rubber tappers and external agencies in the case of extractive reserves in Rondônia. Through this analysis some issues concerned with the effectiveness of extractive reserves in providing long-term livelihood security for rubber tappers and the opportunities for enhanced economic and social welfare are highlighted.

Empowerment and Conservation: Theoretical Perspectives

Empowerment can be defined as a process through which 'people, especially poorer people, are enabled to take more control over their own lives, and secure a better livelihood with ownership of productive assets as one key element' (Chambers, 1993: 11). This implies finding means to facilitate and assist the efforts of resource-poor groups to meet their needs, either through their own organizations or through pressure on the state or other groups to make them act in their interests (Johnson, 1992). Empowerment has become a popular concept in people-orientated conservation, or conservation that attempts to integrate development and environmental protection goals (Pimbert and Pretty, 1994). Ultimately, empowerment should work towards what Chambers (1993: 92) calls a 'sustainable livelihood security'. He defines livelihood as 'a level of wealth and stocks and flows of food and cash which provide for physical and social well-being'. A sustainable livelihood includes security against sickness, against early death and against the threat of poverty. It also includes assets or entitlements which can be used to meet contingencies such as sickness and accidents. This implies 'secure command over assets as well as income'.

In addition to livelihood security, the concept of empowerment places a strong emphasis on access to the political structures and formal decision-making necessary, for example, to enable people to gain control over land and resources. It is also concerned with access to markets and incomes that allow people to satisfy physical and material needs. In other words, effective empowerment should happen at both the political and socio-economic levels. The extent to which these two aspects are connected and interdependent is relatively poorly explored in the literature. There is thus little exploration of the dynamics of empowerment, although it could be argued that there is an assumption that economic empowerment results from political empowerment, and that this assumption underscores interventions such as those in the case study discussed later in this article.

In addition to the two dimensions of empowerment and their achievement, we are concerned here with the ways in which external organizations can enable empowerment. In participatory development contexts, empowerment is sometimes interpreted in the sense that some can act on others to give them power (Nelson and Wright, 1995). It has been argued that disempowered people, due to structural constraints of various kinds, are normally incapable of identifying their own interests and acting upon them. Batliwala (1994, p131), for example, states that 'the demand for change does not usually begin spontaneously from the conditions of subjugation. Rather, empowerment must be externally induced, by forces working with an altered consciousness and an awareness that the existing social order is unjust and unnatural.' Empowerment in this light is seen as something that can be planned in order to bring about a desirable outcome, very much as a service that can be delivered.

However, an approach where one group, be it an environmental organization or a development agency, can bestow power upon another is problematic, since as Rowlands (1995, p104) argues, 'any notion of empowerment being given by one group to another hides an attempt to keep control'. Indeed, in conservation practice external agencies often seek to impose their own agendas on local people, even when they use the language of participation and empowerment in their projects (Pimbert and Pretty, 1994). True empowerment has to come from within. A generic interpretation of empowerment would be a 'process by which people become aware of their own interests and how these relate to those of others, in order both to participate from a position of greater strength in decision-making and actually influence such decisions' (Rowlands, 1995, p102). Essentially, then, empowerment is a process that cannot be imposed by outsiders or planned 'from above'. This does not preclude external support which, when appropriate, can enhance and encourage empowerment. External intervention can assist in the empowerment process, but it must be local people who decide in what ways.

Empowerment is increasingly seen as both a means and an end in people-orientated conservation projects. The WWF forest conservation project with the Rondônian rubber tappers has four main objectives: supporting the institutional development of the tappers' grassroots organizations; organizing and mobilizing local communities of rubber tappers within the extractive reserves; promoting the legal establishment and demarcation of the reserves by the state government; and testing and implementing activities that improve the socio-economic well-being of reserve residents without causing environmental degradation (WWF, 1995). The concept of empowerment emerges as a strong theme in these stated objectives. The project is concerned with enabling the rubber tappers to gain access to political decision making (in issues related to the establishment of extractive reserves), and with improving their socio-economic welfare. It also includes goals such as institutional development. The following section will examine the context of Rondônian rubber tappers and their experience with the intervention of organizations such as WWF.

Rondônia in perspective

The western Brazilian state of Rondônia encompasses an area of 243,000km^2 (see Figure 4.1). Forests occupy approximately 75 per cent of the state's territory. The dominant vegetation is upland forest (*terra firme*), although savannah (*cerrado*) covers some 9 per cent of the total, and floodplain (*várzea*) another 9 per cent. The climate is hot and humid with a mean annual temperature of 26°C. The rainy season lasts from November to May with annual rainfall ranging from 1800 to 2200mm. Only 10 per cent of the area is considered suitable for annual or permanent cultivation (Browder et al, 1996).

In the late 19th century Rondônia became an important centre for the production and commercialization of rubber. Although remote, the region was then strongly connected to world markets. In fact, the rubber trade was controlled by foreign companies and the entire production was exported. Labour to exploit the region's forests came from northeast Brazil where large numbers of rural workers were recruited to tap rubber. Around 1915 the Amazonian rubber boom ceased due to competition from Asian plantation rubber and Rondônia's economy collapsed. During the Second World War a

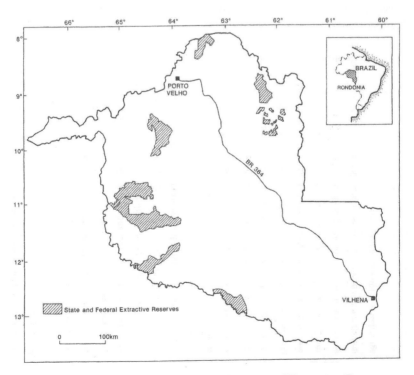

Figure 4.1 *Rondônia State and the Location of Extractive Reserve*

renewed demand for Amazonian rubber occurred when Allied countries were cut off from Asian rubber markets. After the war rubber extraction declined but never halted completely. In 1950 the region's economy still depended primarily on the production of rubber for the internal market (SEDAM, 1986).

In the 1960s Brazilian policy-makers began plans to 'develop' and 'modernize' Amazonia. Extraction of forest products had no place within the government's policies for the region. In fact, the extractive economy was seen as synonymous with backwardness and a hindrance to socio-economic progress (Homma, 1993). The building blocks of Amazonian development were considered to be agriculture, cattle ranching and mining, and in subsequent years these activities were vigorously promoted (Hecht and Cockburn, 1989). The push to develop Rondônia started in earnest in 1958 with the exploitation of cassiterite deposits. In 1968 a precarious dirt road (the BR-364) linking the region to the rest of the country was completed, making southern markets and labour more accessible. In the years that followed, small farmer settlement programmes were created bringing a significant influx of migrants to the region (Martine, 1990). A variety of subsidies was also established for the creation of cattle ranches, making forest clearing for this purpose a profitable investment (Mahar, 1989).

These policies had significant social and environmental impacts. At the social level Rondônia's population increased enormously from 70,000 in 1960 to 500,000 in 1980 (Benchimol, 1989). In the process, the social profile of Rondônia was completely altered and the traditional and indigenous populations living in the region became a minority.[1] New social groups included colonist farmers, ranchers, loggers and miners. As the variety of social actors in Rondônia increased so did the range of interests in resource use: opposing interests gave rise to conflicts which became particularly severe in the 1980s. The environmental impacts included high rates of deforestation as a result of forest conversion for agriculture and cattle pasture (Cleary, 1991).

In 1981 the government initiated POLONOROESTE, a project financed by the World Bank. The principal objective of POLONOROESTE was to asphalt the BR-364; it also included various provisions for promoting small farmer settlements, protecting the environment and supporting indigenous communities. The project encountered a series of severe problems, including a major influx of migrants beyond the handling capacity of government agencies; alarming rates of deforestation; high rates of abandonment among migrants settled in colonization projects; and invasions into conservation and indigenous areas. POLONOROESTE also gave rise to intense conflicts resulting from the indiscriminate occupation of land inhabited by forest-dependent communities by more powerful groups such as land speculators, loggers and cattle ranchers.

The chaotic social and environmental situation created under the POLONOROESTE programme gave rise to some of the most vociferous protests against any project ever financed by the World Bank. Protests came from national non-governmental environmental organizations and human rights groups and their international allies, especially North American environmentalists, and soon had international political repercussions. Under political pressure, the Bank suspended disbursements on its POLONOROESTE loans in early 1985 (Rich, 1994).

The involvement of the environmental movement in local struggles over natural resources also had an important impact on the social groups adversely affected by the development 'model' of Amazonia. It created conditions for the establishment of strategic alliances between environmentalists and forest-dependent people.

Extractivism and extractive reserves

Rubber tappers live in isolated areas deep within the forest. Their household areas, called *colocações*, are small clearings surrounded by forest and rubber trails, where one or two families live. Although their main cash income derives from the sale of rubber, the tappers, or *seringueiros*, utilize a variety of livelihood strategies to secure their subsistence, including the gathering of a wide range of forest products, shifting agriculture and small-scale animal husbandry. In the course of their long settlement in the forest, *seringueiros* have adopted methods for using resources that, for the greater part, are well adapted to the local environment, and are comparable to those of the Indians. They have developed what many view as a 'sustainable' production system, known as extractivism (Allegretti, 1990; Schwartzman, 1992).

However, rubber extraction has historically been associated with severe social and economic exploitation (Hecht and Cockburn, 1989). Rubber tappers are among the poorest and most marginalized sections of civil society in Rondônia and in the Brazilian Amazon in general. This situation results from a combination of factors: in the past, from the unequal relations of production in which extractivism was undertaken, the *aviamento* or debt peonage system;[2] more recently, from the prevalence of unfavourable marketing structures and the falling prices of extractive products in relation to the cost of living (Assies, 1997). Within this context rubber tappers have been a traditionally disempowered social group through economic relations, physical isolation, poor or no access to social services, and neglect from policy makers (Hecht and Cockburn, 1989; Melone, 1993).

During the 1980s the government's development model for the region contributed to the rubber tappers' disempowerment. This development strategy privileged cattle ranching, agriculture, and logging over other forms of land use with less ecologically adverse impacts (Hecht and Cockburn, 1989; Homma, 1993). Schmink and Wood (1987) describe the conflicts inherent in such policy, where the goals of expanded production and short-term accumulation are fundamentally at odds with environmental conservation. Despite the poverty associated with extraction of forest products, even in the 1990s this activity still provides a livelihood, however meagre, for approximately 5000 rubber tappers in Rondônia.

When information about the sustainability of extractivism and the struggles of the rubber tappers to protect the forests was disseminated in the west, environmental groups enthusiastically joined forces with this politically and economically disempowered group of Amazonians (Melone, 1993). The result of this alliance was the proposal for an innovative model for sustainable land use in Amazonia – extractive reserves. These would be 'public lands designated for the specific purpose of sustainable use of forest products such as rubber, brazil nut, and palm heart by the resident population' (Allegretti, 1990: 253). Modelled on the idea of indigenous reserves, or areas where the rights of native peoples to their traditional lands are guaranteed, extractive reserves rapidly became regarded as holding the promise of 'reconciling economic development and environmental conservation' (Anderson, 1992, p67).

However, extractivism also has its sceptics. Southgate et al (1996, p16) observe that:

> living standards among the rubber tappers of Bolivia and Brazil are miserable, compar-
> ing poorly with the meagre socio-economic norms of rural Amazon. By contrast,
> profits generated through non-timber extraction tend to lodge at the top of the market-
> ing chain. The Manaus Opera House is lasting testimony to the wealth accumulated by
> exporters during the Amazon rubber boom.

Observations such as these imply that although extractivism may be profitable for some people and in some instances, markets for extractive products need to be regulated (Assies, 1997). Furthermore, most studies of extraction look only at non-timber forest products and fail to consider the potential of sustainably harvested timber, as well as farming, hunting and fishing. Extraction may be an important element in a diversified livelihood strategy: Assies (1997), for example, describes rubber and Brazil nuts as key components of the 'agro-extractivist cycle', along with agricultural activities. However, there may be resistance on the part of conservation organizations to these activities, which are traditionally seen as conflicting with conservation goals.

Support for the establishment of extractive reserves has grown and now includes a diverse array of NGOs, researchers, financial institutions and policy-makers (Anderson, 1992). The World Bank has also endorsed the concept, especially following national and international protests against its involvement in the socially and environmentally disas-trous POLONOROESTE programme. The intense public pressure of US environmental groups supporting the rubber tappers was crucial for this shift in World Bank policy (Rich, 1994). The Bank, in turn, provided the political leverage through which pres-sure could be applied upon the Brazilian government for the establishment of extractive reserves. In effect, future World Bank loans to Brazil would be conditional upon the creation of a number of extractive reserves. In the late 1980s the World Bank announced a US$167 million loan (from a total budget of US$228.9 million) to the Rondônia Natural Resources Management Project (PLANAFLORO), aimed at repairing the dam-age caused by POLONOROESTE.

The main objective of PLANAFLORO is to promote a new approach to 'sustaina-ble development' in the state of Rondônia through a series of initiatives for the protection and management of natural resources, such as socio-economic and ecological zoning, promotion of agroforestry systems, recovery of degraded lands, environmental protec-tion, sustainable forest management, environmental education, support to indigenous communities, and creation and management of extractive reserves and other conserva-tion areas (Rondônia, 1994).

The extractive reserve movement in Rondônia has already achieved the creation of 19 extractive reserves covering an area of approximately 885 million hectares and is cur-rently pressing the state government for the creation of five more reserves totalling over 1 million hectares of tropical forest. While environmental conservation is an important function of these areas they should also be able to provide for the economic survival of the 434 families who inhabit them. PLANAFLORO has put in place some enabling conditions for the creation of extractive reserves in Rondônia. However, as will be fur-ther discussed below, these are neither a sufficient condition for their establishment nor an assurance of their effective implementation. WWF support to rubber tappers in Rondônia evolved within this context.

Recognizing the validity of the rubber tappers' aspirations, the WWF project has developed activities to enhance their incomes either directly or in association with PLANAFLORO related actions. These initiatives have the potential to empower the rubber tappers in economic terms and thus contribute to improving their 'sustainable livelihood security'. Implementation is channelled through locally established rubber tappers associations. Extractive reserves are thus seen as a means of reaching multiple objectives for conserving forest and providing a livelihood for extractivist communities. They have become a focus for external agencies, and a symbol of the struggle of marginalized people to maintain their way of life against the powerful forces of loggers and ranchers. However, they may not be viable, in economic or political terms, without outside support. The following sections of this article examine how alliances with external agencies have supported the establishment of extractive reserves, and how these have benefited rubber tappers. The political empowerment of rubber tappers through alliances to establish extractive reserves is first examined, before some of the impacts of intervention on the livelihoods and welfare of the rubber tappers and the economic dimensions of empowerment is discussed.

Political Empowerment: Actors, 'Projects' and Public Policy Advocacy

Social mobilization and organization

In Rondônia there is a long history of resistance to deforestation involving *seringueiros*, especially during the implementation of POLONOROESTE. However, in the past resistance was isolated and often resulted in unsuccessful actions. It was only in 1989 that efforts to organize the rubber tappers were given a strong impetus by the National Council of Rubber Tappers (CNS), following government plans to establish a number of reserves in the state.

In February 1989 the CNS, with support from national and international organizations,[3] promoted an important meeting of rubber tappers in the municipality of Guajará Mirim where a number of workshops and discussions concerning the problems faced by the extractivist population of the area took place. In particular, the concept of extractive reserves, their applicability to the region, and the necessary steps for their creation were extensively debated, emphasizing the need for community organization as a means to legitimize proposals for their establishment.

Similar meetings were subsequently arranged in other parts of Rondônia. As a result, several local leaders emerged who were prepared to take over the social mobilization and organization work initiated by the CNS, and to establish horizontal linkages between extractive communities, giving the rubber tappers' movement in Rondônia a context specific direction. The OSR is the result of this organizational work.

Great emphasis has been put on continuing the process of mobilization and organization of extractivists, particularly by promoting the creation of local rubber tappers'

Associations. The importance attached to social organization arises partly from the legal requirements for the creation of extractive reserves. Government rules stipulate that only representative organizations of the local inhabitants of a given forest area can formally request that area to be declared an extractive reserve. Moreover, because extractive reserves remain the property of the state and only the rights of use are transferred to rubber tappers through a community-use title, a representative organization acting on behalf of the reserve inhabitants is needed to claim that land-use title from the government.

An important part of the process of organization of rubber tappers is the 'base community work' or *trabalho de base* which happens at base community meetings *(reuniões de base)*. The creation of a local Association, for example, is normally preceded by a number of *reuniões de base* in which facilitators explain the purpose of and procedures for the creation of an extractive reserve and motivate the local inhabitants to organize themselves into an Association in order to legitimize their claims. The role of the OSR as the state-level representative of rubber tappers and that of the local Associations as its subdivisions is also explained. When the extractive areas are threatened by land grabbers, loggers or cattle ranchers, rubber tappers are encouraged to resist and organize confrontations to defend them. Community base work is thus both a consciousness-raising and an organizational activity.

Once the Association is created, base community meetings continue to be held periodically in the extractive reserves. They fulfil three important functions. First, they are the participatory channels through which local communities can express their needs and priorities as well as their views on matters that affect them, thus generating important information that feeds back into the Associations and OSR. Second, they are vehicles for the dissemination of information regarding the present and future plans of the OSR and Associations and the activities and negotiations in which they are engaged. Third, they are also arenas for discussion and decision-making on important issues of the community's general concern.

Coalition forming and empowerment

Silva (1994: 703) has argued that Latin American societies are heavily penetrated by and dependent on external actors, and that this means that a source of international support for domestic actors is often critical for the relative power of coalitions. His comparative study of pro-grassroots development coalitions in Brazil, Mexico and Peru highlights the factors which determine the make-up of coalitions as well as their effectiveness. In addition to alliances with powerful international actors, a key enabling factor in the dynamics of coalitions was found to be the initial position of key government actors and policymakers, and the institutional frameworks within which coalitions operate. In the case of Rondônia this framework was provided in the contract provisions of PLANA-FLORO which anticipate the creation and legal establishment of a number of extractive reserves in the state of Rondônia, as well as resources to promote their social and economic viability (Rondônia, 1994). In theory, therefore, when WWF initiated support for the rubber tappers in 1991 there were already some enabling conditions in place for the establishment of extractive reserves. However, during negotiations for the formulation of PLANAFLORO, several NGOs in Rondônia, with the support of national and international organizations, raised doubts about the capacity of the project to achieve its proposed objectives. Their main concern was the lack of participation of the project's intended beneficiaries – who include not only rubber tappers but also small farmers and indigenous peoples – in the formulation of the initial PLANAFLORO proposal. This was considered unacceptable in a project which, according to the World Bank, should constitute a 'model' of popular participation for subsequent Bank ventures (Millikan, 1995).

Some of these NGOs had already been working with communities of rubber tappers, small farmers and Indians and were aware of the social and economic reality of their situation. They envisaged that without effective participation, meaning a mechanism through which local people could express their needs and priorities, there was the danger that the full social and environmental potential of PLANAFLORO would not be realized, and, more seriously, that project beneficiaries would become the losers in the process. As a result of popular mobilization in Rondônia a number of representatives from NGOs and rural peoples' organizations, including the rubber tappers, were invited to a meeting with the state government and representatives of the World Bank in June 1991. The outcome of this meeting was the signing of a 'protocol of understanding' which established forms of participation by civil society in the planning, monitoring and evaluation of PLANAFLORO (Millikan, 1995).

However, true participation requires that peoples' views are effectively taken into account (Nelson and Wright, 1995). Many popular organizations do not have the voice to make their claims heard by policy-makers. In other words, although the World Bank and the government of Rondônia opened the channels for the participation of disadvantaged rural groups in PLANAFLORO this was no guarantee that their needs would be met.

Negotiations for PLANAFLORO take place within a highly technocratic environment. Generally, participation in these negotiations requires involvement in bureaucracies and in the elaboration of proposals, discussions, meetings and so forth. Many rural groups possess neither the skills or the information to take part in these institutional practices where technical or legal language is the norm, effectively excluding those who do not master such discourses. In short, for participation of rural civil society to have an impact in the planning of PLANAFLORO, rural groups are required to speak the language of policy-makers. For rubber tappers' leaders, for example, this is not easy; apart from other disempowering circumstances, they also have little formal education, which can limit the extent of their participation.

NGOs often have the knowledge and expertise that grassroots groups need to negotiate, lobby and pressure government institutions for benefits or services. In some instances they also have the means to organize large networks of support constituencies that go beyond national borders and take popular claims as far as multilateral lending institutions. This creates opportunities for strategic alliances between different sectors of civil society. Such is the case of the partnership project, in which environmental NGOs and rubber tappers work together for a common goal – the protection of the forests.

This is not to say, however, that the interest of each partner in forest conservation has the same basis. It is therefore important to understand how environmentalists and rubber tappers pursue their goals. This is where the concept of 'actor strategies' becomes useful (Long, 1992, p36; Long and van der Ploeg, 1994, p79). This refers to the way social groups use their available power resources, or their knowledge and capability, to resolve their particular problems. The rubber tappers' strategy to further their interests, in particular the establishment of extractive reserves, has been to use their image as the defenders of the forest as a tool to raise their profile and bring attention to their struggle. They have successfully enrolled other actors (ie WWF and other environmental NGOs) in their 'projects', getting them to accept particular frames of meaning, such as the sustainability of extractivism and its role in conserving the environment.

Environmental NGOs also have their own agenda, including conserving nature and ecological processes, which is translated into particular strategies. They have also discovered the strategic value of supporting the rubber tappers, where the rubber tappers become the means to achieve an end – conservation. Conkin and Graham (1995) highlight the mutual benefits of such alliances and observe how alliances between environmentalists and Amazonian indigenous groups have legitimized the involvement of First-world environmentalists in the affairs of distant nations, as well as advancing environmental causes. Assies (1997: 40–1) claims that alliances between international environmental groups and rubber tappers in Acre transformed local struggles for land rights into a global *cause célèbre,* but warns that such a strategy is in danger of fostering particular forms of patronization which impose an externally-framed, decontextualized view of forest people, creating the image of a 'mythical *seringueiro*'.

In the PLANAFLORO negotiations and in other contacts with the government this alliance has provided the means by which effective participation of the rubber tappers in the programme has been guaranteed. The rationale is simple. On the one hand, the rubber tappers have legitimate reasons for demanding the creation of extractive reserves, which incidentally are also thought to be an effective way of protecting the forest, but they lack the technical and legal resourcefulness to achieve this. Environmental NGOs, on the other hand, are interested in forest preservation and have the know-how to pressure the government into adopting environmental protection measures, but they have a fragile base for their demands. Thus, by supporting the rubber tappers, the NGOs' position is strengthened by claims that they are defending human rights and the rights of oppressed, politically disempowered people, rather than the preservation of flora and fauna. This is important since the empowerment process here is, if not reversed, at least working in both directions. In other words, this alliance empowers environmentalists as much as it empowers rubber tappers.

The participation of the rubber tappers in PLANAFLORO was a substantial achievement which might not have been possible without the the support of WWF and other NGOs. Yet, this was still not a sufficient condition in itself for the creation of extractive reserves. Demands for extractive reserves are met by strong opposition from political and economic élites, particularly those associated with cattle ranching, logging and land speculation (Hecht and Cockburn, 1989; Schwartzman, 1992), since extractive reserves contain valuable resources (wood and land) which are coveted by different actors. As shown in Table 4.1 these actors also have their particular strategies to further their interests.

The table distinguishes seven principal groups of actors and sets out their interests, scale of influence and means to achieve their aims. The groups are not exhaustive, nor necessarily exclusive, but they demonstrate the range of actors. Alliances have formed between a number of these different groups at various times, when common interests and aims are identified.

Table 4.1 Actors and Agents in Forest Management in Rondônia

Group	Position in the political economy	Scale of influence	Source of power	Interests/aims	Means to achieve aims
Rubber tappers	Integrated into the national and international economy but in disadvantaged position; marginalized and ignored by the government	Local and regional	Limited but increasing	Livelihood maintenance; secure access to forest resources through the creation of extractive reserves	Coalition formed with other social groups to increase influence beyond the "local"; use of environmental language to capture external support
Rondônia NGO Forum	Very diverse	Regional	Strategic alliances; drawing on each others' power resources	To ensure that PLANAFLORO meets its social and environmental objectives; enable the participation of disadvantaged groups in PLANAFLORO	Lobbying; networking with national and international NGOs; legal and technical advice to marginalized groups
Logging industry	Flourishing business; important source of revenue in Rondônia	Local, regional and national	Economic importance; govt. support; ability to earn foreign exchange	Profit; easy access to areas rich in high value timber often within extractive reserves	Illegal logging; lobby govt. officials; offering bribes to prevent law enforcement; buy timber illegally from some tappers
Cattle ranchers	Own large areas of land; important activity in Rondônia; links to the logging industry	Local, regional and national	Many land-owners hold important positions in local, state and national governments	Profit; expanding pasture to areas occupied by extractive reserve	Pressure the government to delay or prevent the creation of extractive reserves
State and national government	Includes politicians with direct or indirect interests in logging and ranching	Local, regional and national	Political and administrative	Mixed attitudes regarding the establishment of reserves; safeguard vested interests of élites; economic growth, national development	Votes for legal provisions for creation of reserves to satisfy conditions imposed by the World Bank; shows little political will to create reserves; creates bureaucratic barriers for the establishment of reserves
International conservation NGOs	Self appointed defenders of the world's ecological integrity	International	Financial support from individuals; business and govts.; scientific knowledge; large network of support	Conservation of biodiversity and ecological processes	Support local struggles to protect forests; financial and technical support for local groups; lobbying World Bank and national governments
World Bank	Multilateral financial institution	International	Economic; institutional	Economic development of region	Imposes conditions on the Brazilian government for the protection of environment and livelihoods

To overcome the political impediments outlined above (see also Silva, 1994), rubber tappers have built strategic alliances with different social and institutional actors. These alliances have been formalized by their participation in the NGO Forum of Rondônia. The Forum was created in 1991 following the commitment of the World Bank and the state government to allow a greater role for civil society in the PLANA-FLORO negotiations. It is composed of non-profit organizations representing small farmers, rubber tappers, indigenous communities, local rural unions, researchers, educators, environmentalists, and groups involved in the defence of human rights. The main activity of the Forum has been to monitor and coordinate the participation of its members in PLANAFLORO (Millikan, 1995).

By joining the Forum, the rubber tappers have been able to take advantage of the fact that a project funded by a multilateral financial institution is bringing a major capital influx into Rondônia. PLANAFLORO provided the political leverage through which the government could be pressured into taking notice of the rubber tappers' claims for the creation of extractive reserves. In fact, the Forum, through its large network of support, has been able to channel the *seringueiros*' claims directly to the World Bank. Since many of the contract provisions of PLANAFLORO were not being implemented by the government, the Forum submitted a request to the World Bank Inspection Panel asking for an investigation of the project. Among the contractual arrangements of PLANAFLORO was the establishment of several extractive reserves which the government had covertly tried to stall. The protests of the Forum led the World Bank to review the project and urge the Brazilian government to establish the extractive reserves without delay (Forum de ONGs, 1996).

In July 1995, after years of delay, the creation of a number of extractive reserves totalling almost 900,000 hectares was finally announced. The claims of the rubber tappers would almost certainly have gone unnoticed before the World Bank if they had not been integrated into a wider protest coming from diverse sectors of the Rondônian civil society represented by the NGO Forum. Once more, the rubber tappers were able to enrol others in their particular 'projects'. However, whether the establishment of extractive reserves has improved the livelihoods and welfare of the rubber tappers and their communities is uncertain. The following sections examine these economic dimensions of empowerment in the context of rubber tappers' livelihoods and their interactions with other NGOs in establishing extractive reserves.

Economic Empowerment and Extractivist Livelihoods

This section first outlines the main components of extractivist livelihoods; it then identifies the key factors which act as constraints to extractivism and reviews the impact of intervention, including that by WWF with the OSR.

Extractivist livelihoods

The livelihood of a rubber tapper family in Rondônia depends on a range of economic and subsistence activities that usually include harvesting forest products, hunting, fishing and farming. A similar system is described by Assies (1997) in Acre state. The main source of household income is derived from the sale of specific extractive products: rubber, brazil nuts and, to a lesser extent, copaíba oil.

The extraction of latex from the rubber tree (*Hevea brasiliensis*) is the main economic activity for rubber tapper households. A typical family produces an average of 900kg of rubber annually, although this varies according to the abundance of rubber trees in each landholding (*colocação*), the number of household members dedicated to rubber extraction, and the time allocated to other activities. The income derived from rubber sales is not constant throughout the year. In the wet season rubber harvests decline considerably since the greatest concentration of *Hevea* tend to be on flood-plains (*várzeas*); when these are flooded, rubber extraction becomes difficult or impossible.

Brazil nuts (harvested from *Bortholletia excelsa*) are another significant marketable forest product in Rondônia. Very importantly for the households' economic strategies, brazil nuts are harvested and marketed from December to February, when rubber extraction drops sharply or becomes impracticable. They are also consumed by the household and constitute an important component of its diet. However, since *Bortholletia excelsa* is only found in upland forest (*terra firme*), this source of income is not available in all reserve areas.

Copaíba oil (*Copaifera* spp.) is a forest product that rubber tappers have long used as a medicinal oil for treating wounds, influenza and coughs, or as fuel for lamps. In recent years the demand for copaíba oil as an homeopathic product has grown in Brazil, making it an alternative source of income for some extractivist communities. Copaíba grows in both flood-plain and upland but the density of trees is low. In addition, the copaíba oil can only be harvested every few months since more frequent harvests may kill the tree. Copaíba oil is thus unlikely to be a major source of income for many households.

Forest products have not only an important economic value for rubber tapper households but also a significant subsistence value. Households use a wide range of products from the forest as food, fuelwood, building and fencing materials, and medicines. Rubber tappers hunt and fish and, for many, these are their main sources of protein. When asked about the advantages of living in the forest instead of urban areas, rubber tappers often point out that in the city they are totally dependent on cash earnings for food, whereas in the forest they can usually fish, hunt and plant manioc, rice or beans. As they say, 'in the city if you do not have work you go hungry'.

Swidden agriculture is another important component of the livelihood strategies of rubber tappers. The tappers call themselves agro-extractivists rather than just extractivists. Many households farm a swidden plot (*roça*) averaging 1.4 hectares in which manioc, beans, rice or maize are cultivated. Sugar cane, pineapple, banana and papaya may also be intercropped. The harvest is for the household's own consumption but in some cases a surplus is produced and sold, therefore constituting an additional source of income. The heterogeneity of the Amazonia region means that the suitability of soils for agriculture varies from one area to another even within the same extractive reserve. While some households are self-sufficient in food crops, others can only produce a fraction of their

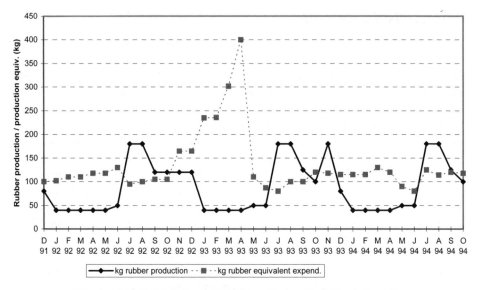

Figure 4.2 *Rubber Production Required to Buy Basic Supplies*

needs. Rubber tapper livelihoods thus have to be seen in the context of these activities, and not just rubber extraction.

Constraints on extractivism

There are important constraints on the livelihood opportunities for agro-extractivist households in Rondônia, including dependence on one or two key products; the limitations imposed on extraction by seasonality and the ecological variability of the forest; the lack of access to reliable markets; poor prices for extractive products; and lack of integration with other aspects of livelihoods. Examination of the livelihood strategies of the rubber tappers demonstrates that extractivism is the main income-generating activity in extractive reserves; at present levels, however, this income does not meet the rubber tappers' needs. While most households rely on rubber for the greatest proportion of their income, findings suggest that on a monthly basis rubber earnings are usually less than expenditure on food and other essential items. In effect, many tappers assert that income obtained from rubber sales alone can only fully meet the basic needs of a family of five during the peak months of rubber harvesting.

This is illustrated in Figure 4.2 which compares average household monthly rubber production with the quantity of rubber needed to buy a bundle of basic supplies.[4] This diagram shows that in 23 out of 24 months, households did not harvest sufficient rubber to generate income to purchase basic supplies. Rubber tappers also suffer because rubber has been supported by an indirect subsidy which has gradually been reduced, bringing rubber prices down (see also Assies, 1997). The price of food and other essential items has increased disproportionately in relation to prices obtained for rubber and other extractive products, further eroding the rubber tappers' ability to meet their basic needs.

A significant share of the profits generated by forest products is captured by intermediaries. Extractivism in Amazonia has historically been characterized by unequal relations of production. For many years rubber tappers were exploited by landowners (*seringalistas*) through the *aviamento* system. When the rubber trade became less profitable landowners gradually abandoned the rubber estates and the marketing of extractive products was taken over by middlemen (*marreteiros*). At present, *marreteiros* continue to dominate the extractivist economy in Rondônia with the consequence that producer margins remain low.

Interventions to strengthen livelihoods

Although extractive reserves are supported by a range of different actors, and are regarded by many as an important strategy for integrating conservation and development, reserve inhabitants are poor, lead isolated lives, and have inadequate access to health and education. They hope for better lives and identify higher incomes and improved access to social services as their most pressing needs. In recent years efforts have been made to improve and sustain livelihoods within extractive reserves. These initiatives include the G7 Pilot Programme for the Protection of the Brazilian Rain Forest (PP-G7),[5] and the PLANAFLORO project. WWF has also developed activities to enhance the incomes of reserve inhabitants either directly or by helping to strengthen the capability of the rubber tapper organizations to implement PLANAFLORO related actions. Direct initiatives include expanding the range of marketable forest products and improving marketing channels. These activities have the potential to empower the rubber tappers in economic terms and to contribute to 'sustainable livelihood security'.

WWF is attempting to address the first constraint highlighted above, the economic dependence of rubber tapper households on key extractive products. It has initiated efforts to diversify the range of commercially valuable products that can be sustainably extracted from the forest. Rubber tappers use a remarkably wide range of forest products, but only a small proportion are marketed and most products are harvested for their consumptive value as food, fuelwood, building and fencing materials, and medicines. An estimate in the field identified 30 different plant species regularly used by rubber tapper households in Rondônia. These represent only the most frequently harvested and the total number is thought to be significantly greater. Many studies provide evidence of a larger number of forest products used by other groups in Amazonia including colonist farmers (Muchagata, 1997).

Many of the products harvested by the rubber tappers have commercial potential and some already have established regional markets. Among the most important are the açaí fruit *(Euterpe oleracea)* and palm hearts extracted from a variety of palms including *Euterpe*. Açaí palms have the advantage that they can be easily managed on a sustainable basis for both fruits and palm hearts due to their multi-stemmed self-regenerative habit. Recently, WWF has initiated a study to analyse the economic and ecological viability of useful palm species such as *Euterpe* in the Jaci Paraná reserve. More information is necessary before appropriate measures for improving markets and income generation can be implemented.

Timber is the most valuable product from the forest. WWF is currently establishing a pilot project in two extractive reserves in Rondônia for the extraction of timber on a sustainable basis. Extractive reserves contain valuable timber resources which can be harvested sustainably to provide an additional income source for rubber tappers. The project has already generated some controversy among reserve inhabitants, in particular concerning labour inputs and distribution of benefits. Concerns have also been raised about its economic viability. The costs of implementing this kind of scheme are substantial: they include the elaboration of a management plan; adoption of harvesting methods that have a minimal impact on surrounding vegetation; and regeneration of harvested species. The economic return from timber after extraction costs are deducted is uncertain. The first stages of the project are now completed and the first timber harvests are expected to begin soon.

Given the dominance of intermediaries in the regional forest product trade WWF has helped the rubber tappers to establish alternative marketing arrangements that enable them to secure a better price for extractive products. This is the only WWF activity aimed at improving the economic welfare of rubber tappers that has been fully implemented. Its objective is to eliminate the need for marketing intermediaries in extractive reserves. However, this is not straightforward to implement. Although they exploit the rubber tappers, the middlemen form the bridge between extractive products and far-away markets. They also supply extractivist communities with staple foods and other essential goods, transporting them to the remote extractive reserves. The middlemen cannot simply be eliminated without a reliable and efficient way to supply communities with essential goods also being created. One solution is to establish community trading posts run by the local Associations *(cantinas)* in strategic locations within the extractive reserves, allowing residents to purchase basic supplies without having to travel great distances.

Setting up a marketing and supply structure requires great investment. First, a workable transportation infrastructure for both goods and extractive products is needed. Second, storage facilities have to be built in order to keep products until a sufficient amount has been gathered for selling to a large buyer. Third, there has to be initial capital to buy extractive products from producers, and to purchase goods from a wholesaler. In this case, transport and storage facilities were provided by PLANA-FLORO and the initial capital was supplied by WWF.

Problems with these new marketing structures have arisen as a result of the local Associations' lack of experience in management. The local Associations have gradually lost their initial capital and this has made the sale of extractive products through the new system difficult. Furthermore, the *cantinas* have not been able to replace their stocks. This initiative has not had a great impact on the economic well-being of the rubber tappers, some of whom continued interacting with middlemen in accordance with relationships of patronage developed over many years (see Hugh-Jones, 1992, on the complexity of these interactions).

WWF has helped to strengthen the organizational and administrative capability of the rubber tappers organizations, especially of the OSR, to implement PLANAFLORO related initiatives so that these organizations can collaborate as active participants in developing and implementing the programme. More specifically, WWF has helped the rubber tappers to establish the physical infrastructure of the OSR and local Associations (acquisition of headquarters; office equipment including computer, printer, and fax machine), and it assists with maintenance expenses such as phone and electricity.

WWF also provides financial resources to staff the rubber tapper organizations. This support has allowed the OSR and local Associations to pay a salary to the rubber tappers' leaders so that they can spend more of their time working in extractive reserve related activities. It has also enabled ECOPORÉ to appoint two technical and legal advisers to work with the OSR. In addition, the tapper organizations have been able to employ a secretary to help with administration and accountancy. WWF has thus contributed to building the capacity of the rubber tapper organizations, with the result that they are better prepared to negotiate, administer and implement PLANAFLORO initiatives. The exact contribution of this type of support to the economic welfare of extractivist communities is difficult to establish. To date, PLANAFLORO has provided substantial infrastructure support to extractive reserves with the construction of storage facilities and the acquisition of vehicles and machinery (rice peelers, sugar cane threshers, outboard engines). There are also plans to establish a factory to process rubber and a series of small processing units to shell, grade, and package brazil nuts. How rubber tappers will benefit from these PLANAFLORO initiatives depends greatly on their ability to manage and take control of them. Improving the organizational capability of grassroots organizations may be a decisive factor determining the extent to which PLANA-FLORO can generate long-term economic benefits for extractivist communities.

In summary, there are a number of ways to address the disadvantages of extractivism so as to improve the socio-economic well-being of the rubber tappers. The WWF support for the Rondônian rubber tappers has attempted to do this by providing financial and/or technical assistance for the development of several economic activities. These include the establishment of alternative marketing networks; development of income-generating activities based on new products; search for and expansion of markets for rainforest products; and local processing of extractive products. Some of these activities are still at a very early stage of development, and thus it is difficult to anticipate their impact on the economic well-being of extractivists. Where results are already visible, namely in the establishment of alternative marketing networks, significant management problems have arisen and as a consequence, objectives have not been met. This is partly because the activities supported by WWF are related more to the creation of extractive reserves than to the development of income-generating activities that improve the socio-economic well-being of reserve inhabitants. So far, the alliances with different external agencies have not resulted in the significant economic empowerment of rubber tappers.

Conclusion

This review suggests that intervention by WWF and strategic alliances with other NGOs have enhanced the empowerment of the rubber tappers in political terms, but have not been so successful in economic terms. The rubber tappers have won recognition of their rights to certain resources through the establishment of large tracts of land designated as extractive reserves. On the other hand, they continue to lead precarious and impoverished lives and struggle to generate income to meet basic needs.

The case reviewed here reveals some of the complexities and dynamics of the alliances or relationships between grassroots organizations and outside agencies and NGOs.

Where the objectives are mutually beneficial and are not in conflict then such alliances can be successful in furthering multiple interests. Such alliances may empower environmental groups, as well as grassroots organizations. Alliances may form for specific purposes – such as the legal establishment of extractive reserves – although the objectives and interests of the various groups and actors are quite different and they will be impacted upon in different ways.

This research raises questions about the viability of extractivism as a means of providing a secure livelihood for rubber tapper communities, and extractive reserves as sustainable conservation designations. Evidence presented here highlights both the extreme poverty of some rubber tapper households, and the lack of a sustainable livelihood security, and suggests that much needs to be done before extractivism can provide rubber tappers with secure incomes. Many rubber tapper families feel economically and socially disempowered. Rubber tappers perceive two development priorities: first, higher incomes in order to satisfy physical and material needs; second, access to social services such as health and education. So far, alliances with outside agencies have been unable to meet these aspirations to a significant degree. There may be reasons for this beyond the control of the current alliances, such as prices set by world markets, and structural impediments which require alliances with much more powerful groups to influence and effect change.

As yet there is the little evidence of how the successful implementation of the extractive reserves and improvements in rubber tapper livelihoods and welfare are linked. We cannot deduce whether political empowerment will lead to economic empowerment or whether assured rights of access to natural resources in the forest will lead to more secure livelihoods. Much of the available literature might lead us to expect this, although highly disadvantageous terms of trade, dependence on a few products, and unstable markets may prove too difficult to overcome, even given alliances with international organizations. Schmink and Wood (1987) have highlighted the unstable nature of extractivist economies, and a growing body of literature indicates that extractivism is unlikely to provide an adequate income for forest communities (Browder, 1992a, 1992b; Salafsky et al, 1993).

In addition to the dynamics of the different dimensions of empowerment, it is also important to recognize the dynamics of the alliances between actors and the changes in their interests, power and coalitions over time. Silva (1994) has emphasized the conditions which influence and enable the formation of alliances, and again these conditions will change over time. We have highlighted this with regard to the changing emphases of the World Bank, and with regard to the development of POLONOROESTE and PLANAFLORO, and now perhaps PP-G7, as providing alternately very conflicting and more enabling institutional and programmatic frameworks for the evolution of alliances and establishment of the extractive reserve system in Rondônia. As Conkin and Graham (1995) point out, international alliances are potentially fragile and may pose political risks domestically for grassroots organizations. This may in turn affect the sustainability of the rubber tappers' way of life if the wider political and institutional context changes drastically.

In conclusion, our study finds that strategic alliances between grassroots organizations and environmental NGOs and other agencies can empower grassroots organizations in certain circumstances, and can contribute to meeting conservation and development objectives. In the case of the Rondônian rubber tappers these interactions have helped to politically empower rubber tappers to gain legal rights to extractive reserves. These interactions have facilitated the process by which extractive reserves have become politically viable spaces in terms of being legally recognized and established; however, these areas have yet to be proven viable in terms of providing secure and sustainable livelihoods for forest dwellers like the rubber tappers.

Acknowledgements

The authors gratefully acknowledge the support of WWF International. We would also like to thank the OSR in Rondônia and many of the rubber tappers who have been generous with their time and help in the course of our research. This project has also been supported by the UK Department for International Development (DFID), which supports policies, programmes and projects to promote international development. DFID provided funds for this study as part of that objective but the views and opinions expressed are those of the authors alone. We also acknowledge the insightful comments of two anonymous reviewers. Views expressed in this paper, and any errors and omissions, remain the responsibility of the authors.

References

Allegretti, M (1990) 'Extractive reserves: An alternative for reconciling development and conservation in amazonia', in A Anderson (ed) *Alternatives to Deforestation: Steps Toward Sustainable Use of the Amazon Rain Forest*, Columbia University Press, New York, pp252–264.

Anderson, A (1992) 'Land-use strategies for successful extractive economies in Amazonia'. *Advances in Economic Botany* 9: 67–77

Assies, W (1997) *Going Nuts for the Rainforest: Non-timber Forest Products, Forest Conservation and Sustainability in Amazonia*, Thela Publishers, Amsterdam

Batliwala, S (1994) 'The meaning of women's empowerment: new concepts from action', in A Sen, A Germain, L C Chen (eds) *Population Policies Reconsidered: Health Empowerment and Rights*, Harvard University Press, Boston, MA, and New York, pp127–138

Benchimol, S (1989) *Amazonia: Planetarização e Moratória Ecologica*, Centro de Recursos Educacionais, São Paulo

Browder, J O (1992a) 'Social and economic constraints on the development of market-oriented extractive reserves in amazon rainforests'. *Advances in Economic Botany* 9: 33–41

Browder, J O (1992b) 'The Limits to Extractivism'. *Bioscience* 42: 74–181

Browder, J O, E A T Matricardi, W S Abdala (1996) 'Is sustainable production of timber financially viable? A comparative analysis of mahogany silviculture among small farmers in the Brazilian Amazon'. *Ecological Economics* 16: 147–159

Chambers, R (1993) *Challenging the Professions: Frontiers for Rural Development*, Intermediary Technology Publications, London

Cleary, D (1991) 'The greening of the Amazon', in D Goodman and M Redclift (eds) *Environment and Development in Latin America*, Manchester University Press, Manchester and New York, pp116–140

Conkin, B A and L R Graham (1995) 'The shifting middle ground: Amazonian Indians and ecopolitics'. *American Anthropologist* 97(4): 695–710

Forum de ONGs (1996) 'Um novo Planafloro'. *Notícias do Forum* 4(8): 3

Hecht, S (1989) 'Chico Mendes: chronicle of a death foretold'. *New Left Review* 173: 47–55

Hecht, S and A Cockburn (1989) *The Fate of the Forest: Developers, Destroyers and Defenders of the Amazon*. Verso, London and New York

Homma, A K O (1993) *Extrativismo Vegetal na Amazonia: Limites e Oportunidades*. EMBRAPA, Brazil

Hugh-Jones, S (1992) 'Yesterday's luxuries, tomorrow's necessities: business and barter in northwest Amazonia', in C Humphrey and S Hugh-Jones (eds) *Barter, Exchange and Value*, Cambridge University Press, Cambridge, pp42–74

IEA (Institute de Estudos Amazonicos e Ambientais) (1994) *Levantamento Socio-economico da Reserva Extractivista do Rio Ouro Preto*, IEA, Porto Velho

Johnson, H (1992) 'Rural livelihoods: action from below', in H Bernstein et al (eds) *Rural Livelihoods: Crises and Responses*, Oxford University Press, Oxford, pp274–300.

Long, N (1992) 'From paradigm lost to paradigm regained? The case for an actor-oriented sociology of development', in N Long and A Long (eds) *Battlefields of Knowledge: Interlocking Theory and Practice in Social Research and Development*, Routledge, London, pp16–43

Long, N and J D van der Ploeg (1994) 'Heterogeneity, actors and structure: towards a reconstitution of the concept of structure' in D Booth (ed) *Rethinking Social Development: Theory, Research and Practice*, Longman, Essex, pp62–89.

Mahar, D (1989) *Government Policies and Deforestation in Brazil's Amazon Region*. The World Bank, Washington DC

Martine, G (1990) 'Rondônia and the fate of small farmers', in D Goodman and A Hall (eds) *The Future of Amazonia: Destruction or Sustainable Development?*, Macmillan, London, pp23–48

Melone, M (1993) 'The struggle of the *Seringueiros:* environmental action in the Amazon', in J Friedmann and H Rangan (eds) *In Defence of Livelihood: Comparative Studies on Environmental Action,* Kumarian Press, West Hartford, CT, pp107–126.

Millikan, B H (1995) 'Pedido de investigação apresentado ao Painel de Inspeção do Banco Mundial sobre o PLANAFLORO', Forum de ONGs e Movimentos Sociais que Atuam em Rondônia/Friends of the Earth, Porto Velho

Muchagata, M (1997) *Forests and People: The Role of Forest Production in Frontier Farming Systems in Eastern Amazonia*. DEV Occasional Paper OP36, School of Development Studies, University of East Anglia, Norwich

Nelson, N and S Wright (1995) *Power and Participatory Development: Theory and Practice*. Intermediate Technology Publications, London

Pimbert, M P and J N Pretty (1994) 'Parks, people and professionals: putting participation into protected area management'. Draft discussion paper, UNRISD/IIED/WWF, Geneva

Rich, B (1994) *Mortgaging the Earth: The World Bank, Environmental Impoverishment and the Crisis of Development*, Earthscan, London

Rondônia, Governo de (1994) *Programa de trabalho PLANAFLORO: primeiro semestre de 1996,* Governo de Rondônia, Porto Velho

Rowlands, J (1995) 'Empowerment examined'. *Development in Practice* 5(2): 101–107

Salafsky, N, B L Dugelby and J W Terborgh (1993) 'Can extractive reserves save the Rainforest? An ecological and socioeconomic comparison of non-timber forest extraction in Peten, Guatemala, and West Kalimantan, Indonesia'. *Conservation Biology* 7(1): 39–52

Schmink, M and C H Wood (1987) 'The political ecology of Amazonia' in P D Little, M Horowitz and A E Nyerges (eds) *Lands at Risk in the Third World: Local Level Perspectives,* Westview Press, Boulder, CO, pp38–57

SEDAM (Secretaria do Desenvolvimento Ambiental) (1986) *Diretrizes Ambientais para Rondô-nia,* Ministerio do Desenvolvimento e Meio Ambiente, Brasilia

Shwartzman, S (1992) 'Social movements and natural resource conservation in the Brazilian Amazon', in S Counsell and T Rice (eds) *The Rainforest Harvest: Sustainable Strategies for Saving the Tropical Forests,* Friends of the Earth, London, pp207–217

Silva, E (1994) 'Thinking politically about sustainable development in the tropical forests of Latin America'. *Development and Change* 25(4): 697–721

Southgate, D, M Coles-Richie and P Salazar-Canelos (1996) 'Can Tropical Forests be saved by harvesting non-timber products?'. CSERGE Working Paper GEC 96–02, Centre for Social and Economic Research on the Global Environment, University of East Anglia and University College London, Norwich and London

WWF (1995) 'BR0087 Brazil: social and environmental support for Rondônian rubber tappers', in *WWF Latin America/Caribbean Programmes,* WWF, Gland, Switzerland, pp4230–4231

Notes

1 'Traditional peoples' refers to non-tribal social groups long established in Rondô-nia. The term as it is used here comprises two main groups: *ribeirinhos* or riverine people living in floodplain areas whose livelihoods depend primarily on a combination of permanent agriculture and fishing; and rubber tappers. Both groups are the result of a rich racial mixture of Europeans, Africans and Indians. These people are often referred to as *coboclos,* defined by Schmink and Wood (1987, p40) as 'racially mixed population that grew with the migration to the region during the rubber boom'. 'Indigenous peoples' or 'Indians' are used to refer to the native or tribal population of Amazonia.

2 Hecht and Cockburn (1989) provide a detailed account of the *aviamento* system. Hugh-Jones (1992, p69) notes the wide range of different relationships which exist between traders and describes a continuum between barter and debt-peonage which depends on the asymmetries of power between different parties.

3 These included rural workers' unions and environmental organizations such as the Institute of Amazonian Studies which played a key role in supporting the rubber tappers movement in Acre (see Melone, 1993).

4 These data derive from a survey undertaken in 1994 by the Institute of Amazonian Studies (IEA) in the Ouro Preto Extractive Reserve, Rondônia. IEA gathered data on household rubber production and incomes over time and compared it to the cost of a bundle of basic supplies needed to maintain an average family for 30 days, the components of which were identified by the rubber tappers themselves.

5 The PP-G7 supports a number of extractive reserves in Brazilian Amazonia, one of which is the Ouro Preto Extractive Reserve in Rondônia.

5

After Chipko: From Environment to Region in Uttaranchal

Emma Mawdsley

Summary

Although the Chipko movement is practically non-existent in its region of origin it remains one of the most frequently deployed examples of an environmental and/or a women's movement in the south. A small but growing number of commentators are now critiquing much neopopulist theorizing on Chipko, and this article provides an overview of these critiques. It then takes the debate further with reference to a more recent regional movement in the hills. By doing so, the author argues that it is possible to develop a more plausible account of gender, environment and the state in the Uttaranchal region, and illustrate common weaknesses in neopopulist understandings of Chipko and other social movements in the south.

Introduction

The Chipko movement of the Uttaranchal region[1] in India is one of the most frequently cited movements in the contemporary literature on social and/or environmental mobilizations in the south. Rangan and Garb (1996) suggest that it has taken on iconic status, and it is certainly seen by many as an inspiring example of local action against the alienating and destructive incursions of the modern developmental state (Redclift, 1987; Weber, 1987; Bandyopadhyay, 1992; Ekins, 1992; Escobar, 1995). However, over the last five years a small but growing number of authors have started to critique the highly popular and widely 'traded' neopopulist interpretations of the Chipko movement(s). These criticisms centre on theoretical and empirical objections to certain ecofeminist and ecocentric portrayals of the mobilizations (Jackson, 1993a), and the insufficient attention paid to the political and/or economic context of the Chipko protests (Mitra, 1993; Aryal, 1994; Rangan, 1996). Moreover, very little is left of the Chipko movement(s) in its region of origin save for its memory – a decline that is rarely analysed in these neo-

Reprinted from *Journal of Peasant Studies*, vol 25, Mawdsley, E, 'After Chipko: From environment to region in Uttaranchal', pp629–649, copyright © (1998) with permission from Frank Cass Publishers.

populist accounts, and is sometimes not even evident when 'the Chipko movement' is glibly deployed as a example of an environmental and/or women's movement in the south.

This article will provide an overview of these critiques, but will also take the arguments further through an analysis of a more recent social movement in the hill region, namely the (very recently acceded to) demand for a separate Uttaranchal State within the federal Union of India. It is my contention that, by examining the continuities and differences between the Chipko protests of the 1970s/80s (and their heavily manufactured image) and the regional mobilization of the 1990s, it is possible to illustrate certain weaknesses in much neopopulist theorizing about Chipko, and thus develop a more plausible and sensitive account of gender, environment and the state in the Uttaranchal Himalaya.

The article will start with a brief narrative overview of the Chipko protests and the regional movement before turning to one of the most prolific and widely read neopopulist writer on the Chipko movement, Vandana Shiva. Shiva's ecofeminist and 'anti-development' account of the movement will be reappraised in the light of the Uttaranchal regional movement with particular reference to the changing relationship between state and society, gender interests and environmental issues. The article will also draw on Ramachandra Guha's analysis of the Chipko movement(s), and explore whether his vision of 'peasant versus the state' can still be said to have contemporary salience in the hills. The article reflects a broader unease with certain aspects of neopopulist theorizing about social movements in the south, issues that will be taken up in more detail in the conclusions.

The Chipko Movement(s)

The forests of the Uttaranchal Himalaya have long been central to the livelihood strategies of the mountain people who live there.[2] In the past most households depended on a diverse bundle of economic activities, but traditionally the two most important elements were migration and agroforestry. This pattern is still found today, although the balance of importance appears to be shifting towards migration and other sources of paid employment (Whittaker, 1984; Bora, 1987, 1996). The steep slopes of the middle Himalaya do not offer rich agricultural pickings, and the forests provide essential inputs of fertilizer (in the form of leaf mulch), grazing, fodder, fuel and a host of other non-timber forest products, such as medicinal herbs, fibres and foodstuffs (Nand and Kumar, 1989). Given this situation, the alienating and often deeply insensitive encroachments of colonial forestry in the region were profoundly felt, and provoked significant resistance (Pant, 1922; Guha, 1989).

After Independence little appeared to change, as the State-managed Forest Department continued largely to neglect the interests and needs of the local people, despite the latter's heavy dependence on the forests. Much has been written about the ongoing erosion of villagers' rights in relation to the forests (Guha, 1989), the Forest Department's concentration on Chir Pine (*Pinus roxburghii*) at the expense of far more productive trees for the local agroforestry (Singh, 1993), and other post-colonial continuities in both forest policy and praxis (Rawat, 1993). But as well as these 'subsistence issues' there are another set of complaints which relate to the Uttaranchalis' place in the

Note: For military reasons most maps of Uttaranchal are sparsely detailed and deliberately inaccurate. The locations of the villages are estimates.

Figure 5.1 *Map of Uttaranchal*

commercial exploitation of the forests, and which tend to be less well analysed. For example, the Forest Department, and the private contractors who won the forest auctions from the Department, preferred to employ more 'biddable' Nepalis and other migrants than local men (Tucker, 1993). The Forest Department also charged small local units higher prices for raw materials than it charged large industries down on the plains (Das and Negi, 1983), and little effort was made to set up processing stages in the hills for the timber or timber products, which would otherwise have created employment and added value to the region's 'exports' (Rangan, 1996). Closely related, indeed central, to these livelihood issues, were the growing concerns over the environmental impacts of the Forest Department's increasing penetration into the hills (which was greatly expanded and accelerated after the huge strategic road building programme that followed the Indo-Chinese War of 1962), and its working practices, many of which were argued to be ecologically degrading (Mishra and Tripathi, 1978; Guha, 1989). These perceptions were strongly reinforced by a series of disastrous floods in the region in the early 1970s (Pathak, 1994).

This then was the situation in which the Dasholi Gram Swarajya Sangh (DGSS), a small industrial corporation with strong Gandhian overtones, based in Gopeshwar, was operating. Its members, under the leadership of Chandi Prasad Bhatt, ran a turpentine unit, manufactured agricultural implements, and organized demonstrations against liquor sales, Untouchability and the forest contractor system (Guha, 1989). In 1973 the DGSS clashed with the Forest Department over the provision of hundreds of trees to a large sports company from the plains, Symonds, after they had just been refused a few trees from the same forest. The DGSS decided to stop the Symonds's contractors by intervening between the axemen and the trees if they had to, thus giving rise to the movement's famous name – Chipko is Hindi for 'adhere' or 'stick to', although it is usually translated in a more 'feel-good' way as 'hug'. After successfully preventing fellings in Mandal forest, Chandi Prasad Bhatt and the others made the critical decision to alert the villagers around Phata-Rampur, some 80km away, to the fact that the forests around them were now under threat from the same company, and offered to help them defend them. Thus, by moving beyond their immediate local needs to embrace a wider spatial and temporal perspective, Chipko was born as a meaningful social movement with regional implications.

Over the next decade a whole series of Chipko protests took place, although it should be noted that the task of establishing even a simple history of the movement(s) is complicated by the differing and sometimes contradictory accounts written by major figures involved in Chipko, as well as the host of 'outside' commentators. Some postmodernists might argue that there is room for all of these accounts of the Chipko movement(s), and I would certainly concur with the idea that the recovery of an 'objective history' of Chipko is neither possible nor desirable. That said, I do believe we can privilege certain stories over others, and that such a commitment can and should be made on the basis of an ethical responsibility to our research subjects.[3] I will not go into (another) detailed account of the Chipko protests here, although more will emerge below. What I will argue is that we need to develop a more complex view of the Chipko protests than has popularly been recognized in which, at different times and in different places, both commercial and 'subsistence' issues were at stake. The Chipko protests differed according to the particular times, places and circumstances of communities and individuals in the hills. Thus, the struggle described above, in Mandal village, clearly centred on access to raw materials for small scale industrial use. Mandal is on the road, and is only a few kilometres from Gopeshwar, with the larger town of Chamoli also relatively near by, facilitating the transport and sale of goods. However, in Reni village, the site of a widely celebrated incident in 1974 in which women were especially prominent in protecting their forests from the contractors, such industrial opportunities were much more limited. Reni is a remote village close to the Indo-Tibet border and some distance off a poor quality road. Here the villagers, and particularly the women, given a gendered division of labour in which women are responsible for the vast majority of work relating the forests, were protecting a major subsistence resource. Few analysts of the Chipko movement seem willing to recognize this grassroots diversity in the movement, or the fact that as well as being spatially diverse, such interests can shift over time, as we will see below in the discussion of events at Doongri-Paintoli.

It is clear from Chipko's origins in the DGSS, and the widespread support the movement(s) received in the early/mid-1970s, that these protests spoke to a serious concern of many hill women and men; namely that the state's management of the forests offered few dividends for the local people in this already economically marginalized area, and further, that it was degrading the ecological base upon which local people depended.

These dual issues add up to a single concern with winning a livelihood through a bundle of activities, including village-based agroforestry, paid work within the hills and paid work outside of the hills in the plains. For different individuals, families and villages, the relative importance and possible combinations of these strategies varied and continue to vary according to a range of circumstances over which they have more or less control. However, in a number of the more populist accounts of 'Chipko', the economic demands of the movement(s) are downplayed (or even refuted) in favour of the movement's ecological consciousness. These accounts were highly influential, and over the late 1970s and 1980s national and international perceptions of Chipko came to be increasingly dominated by this strictly environmental perspective (see below). Shamser Singh Bist, a local activist in the hills, felt that: 'the final act of betrayal came when a potentially radical movement for self-determination and self-management of our resources turned into a purely conservationist one' (quoted in Mitra, 1993, p36).

Saxena (1992) suggests that Chipko died with the imposition of the moratorium in 1981, a 15 year ban on felling above 1000m in the region that was introduced directly as a result of the Chipko agitations.[4] But the legislation was deeply resented by many hill people because, they argued, Forest Department felling continued while local people were further excluded from the forest. Opposition to the legislation in Uttaranchal even resulted in a '*Ped Katao Andolan*' in 1988–1989 – a movement to *cut trees down* – because it was argued that it was stalling some 4500 development projects all over Garhwal and Kumaon. Significantly, many of the leaders associated with this movement were involved with a nascent regional political party seeking a separate hill state, and it is this much less well known movement to which we turn next.

The Uttaranchal Movement

Throughout India's independent history there have been demands that the Uttaranchal region should be recognized as a separate state within the federal Union of India. These demands were primarily based on the region's geographical difference from the rest of Uttar Pradesh (between the hills and the plains); its historical separation during the pre-colonial and much of the colonial period; and a post-Independence discourse of internal colonialism, primarily in relation to the forests. For most of this time these demands were largely confined to elite-urban groups, and received little support from the majority of the hill people (Bhatkoti, 1987), although by the early 1980s there is evidence that the idea was starting to receive wider support, even if it still could not be said that the issue commanded committed popular support (Mawdsley, 1997). Then, in July 1994, the separate hill State issue suddenly and unexpectedly exploded into a mass movement. Huge confrontations with the State apparatus ensued, sometimes peaceful, sometimes violent, and there followed a period of intense upheaval. The immediate cause of the agitation was the passing of a piece of Uttar Pradesh State legislation concerned with reservation (or positive discrimination) in government employment and education for what are called the Other Backward Classes (OBCs). These are the vast mass of 'middling' agricultural and artisanal castes who are estimated to make up some 52 per cent of India's population. The legislation followed the Centre's implementation of the Mandal Commission's proposals in 1989,[5] something which has had enormous ramifications for India's political landscape. In addition to the long-standing 15 per cent reservation for the Scheduled Castes (the former Untouchables) and the 7.5 per cent reservation for the Scheduled Tribes was added 27 per cent reservation for the OBCs. This brought the total reservation quota up to just under 50 per cent, the (much abused) ceiling the Supreme Court has set, leaving 50 per cent (theoretically) for open competition and the high castes.[6]

But while the all-India percentage of Brahmins and Rajputs is estimated at around 11%, in Uttaranchal, for various historical reasons, these high castes make up close to 85% of the population.[7] Thus because of the unusual caste composition of the Uttaranchal hills, the OBC reservation policy would have excluded a considerable percentage of the hill population from two important routes to economic and social mobility (education and government posts) in an already highly constrained economic environment. The State government of Uttar Pradesh took no account of this, and the legislation was widely seen as the 'final straw' in what was perceived to be decades of neglect and exploitation. In the opening weeks of the mass agitation two critical themes emerged which saw it shift from an anti-reservation struggle to the demand for a separate state (Mawdsley, 1996). These centred on the closely related issues of development and politics. While there are still claims that the region is being subjected to internal colonialism by the State of Uttar Pradesh (voiced in newspapers, at meetings and in discussions), it is generally conceded that the region has started to receive more 'development' funds from both the State and Central governments over the last couple of decades. The main grievance now being articulated is that the economic and developmental marginalisation of the hill area is due to the fact that *plains*-based planners in the distant State capital of Lucknow are unable (as well as unwilling) to understand the development needs of the *hill* population, environment and economy. In other words, the region's 'backwardness' is being increasingly interpreted not simply as the result of straight-forward exploitation and/or neglect, but as a more profound inability of the plains-based planners to 'properly' develop the hills.

The political dimension of this argument rests on the fact that the region only accounts for 4 per cent of the State's population, and is thus of negligible importance to State politics. For many, a separate hill State is the solution to this lack of a political voice – vital in a political economy which continues to be heavily dominated by a 'developmental state'. It is widely felt that a smaller, separate State would be more accountable and more responsive to the needs and demands of local people, and that it would have greater representation at the (new) State and national level. Above all, hill development would be planned and administered by people from the hills.[8]

Despite their many differences, the Chipko protests and the regional movement clearly had/have their origins in similar or overlapping issues. These include a lack of control over local resources (both in terms of 'traditional' rights of access to forest resources and in terms of modern commercial opportunities); competition over national versus local need; environmental concerns; and local critiques of development planning and administration. However, these contiguities are *not* apparent from a reading of many neopopulist accounts of the Chipko protest(s), which offer a very different set of understandings about the environment, development and often gender relations in the hills. The next section will explore this discrepancy through an analysis of Vandana Shiva's account of the Chipko protests.

From Environment to Region

Women versus men?

Vandana Shiva has written about the Chipko movement in a number of books and articles (including Shiva and Bandyopadhyay, 1986, 1987; Shiva, 1988 and 1992; Mies and Shiva, 1993). Her analysis can be firmly located within the neopopulist paradigm, but it derives its theoretical force primarily from ecofeminism. A variety of perspectives can be identified within ecofeminism (WGSG, 1997), but most proponents argue that it provides a radical development alternative which centres on diversity, nurturing, holism, and social and environmental justice (Mies and Shiva, 1993). Some ecofeminists argue that there is an essential congruity between women and nature because of women's biological capacity to bear life, and because of their shared objectification and domination by patriarchal systems of exploitation and control. Rather than resist the nature/culture, woman/man dichotomy, as 'traditional' feminists have sought to do, these ecofeminists celebrate the supposed congruence. Shiva argues that: 'Women and nature are intimately related, and their domination and liberation are similarly linked. The women's and ecology movements are therefore one, and are primarily counter-trends to a patriarchal maldevelopment' (Shiva, 1988, p47).

Shiva argues that in Uttaranchal, as elsewhere in India, indigenous forest management has traditionally been the realm of women, both in the division of labour and in the domain of knowledge. Women, she says, embody *prakriti*, or the feminine principle, which seeks to nurture and maintain the harmony and diversity of the natural forests as a life source, and which stands in sharp opposition to the masculinist sciences that dominate modern development discourses (Shiva, 1988).[9] Commercial forestry, introduced by colonialists and perpetuated by the Indian state, is analysed as a prominent example of such reductionism and violence. Local men, she argues, have also been colonized by this system – cognitively, economically and politically. It is peasant *women* who have deeply and concretely experienced forest destruction and who have, therefore, risen up to challenge the reductionist values of the factory and the market by reviving the 'ancient Indian conception of forest culture'. Here, self-sustaining forest communities are viewed as the highest expression of societal and civilizational evolution, a vision which conflicts vividly with the picture of a tainted, violent and profligate 'modern world' (Nanda, 1991). Shiva argues that: 'the women of Garhwal (the western half of Uttaranchal) started to protect their forests from commercial exploitation even at the cost of their lives, by starting the famous Chipko movement, embracing the living trees as their protectors' (Shiva, 1988, p67).

She suggests that women not only fought outside contractors and the Forest Department in their struggle to reclaim the feminine principle in forest use and management, but also resisted the commercial instincts of their own menfolk. Chipko is thus represented as an explicitly ecological *and* feminist movement through which the women of the hills sought to re-establish a 'traditional' harmonious relationship with nature. The link with the DGSS and other cooperatives, which Shiva derides as meeting largely male concerns, is described as a temporary merger early on in the movement. Soon afterwards, she suggests: 'a new separation took place between local male interests for commercial activity based on forest products, and local women's interests for sustenance activity based on forest protection' (Shiva, 1988, p71).

But there are a number of empirical objections to this account. First, although women played an absolutely central part in the Chipko protests, Sunderlal Bahuguna, Chandi Prasad Bhatt, Dhum Singh Negi and the many other men who were involved were not always or only their 'students and followers', as Shiva maintains (1988, p67). Men were genuinely committed to the various strands of the Chipko movement, and contributed significantly to their organizational and ideological force. Although the desire to redress the balance and bring to the public eye many of the otherwise un-named women who were involved in the movement is thoroughly laudable, the way Shiva does this is to mirror the technique of those whom she criticizes, and so to exclude men. Shiva also undermines the roles others played in the Chipko movement, including leftists and students, who did not fit into the picture of ecofeminist protest. For example, like many others minded to celebrate the romantic image of the Chipko movement as women hugging trees high in the Himalayan forests, she rarely mentions the town-based demonstrations, such as the critical protests disrupting the forest auctions.

Shiva's use of Hinduism in relation to gender and the environment might also be questioned. Shiva employs the concepts of *shakti* (feminine primordial energy) and *prakriti* (its manifestation in nature) as one of the principal means by which she explains specifically 'Indian' (which she surprisingly often elides with Hindu) definitions of nature and culture, and thus environmental understanding. She suggests that in 'traditional India' power and fertility at the cosmological and everyday level were attributed to women, who were venerated accordingly (Shiva, 1988), but that this was then displaced by the patriarchy of colonialism, development and science. But in Hindu tradition (especially the high Brahminical texts that Shiva draws upon) women's *shakti* is a major 'reason' for their *subordination* by men, not their veneration, and certainly not their liberation. Shakti does have a positive side, especially in its 'latent' form, but it is not context-free, and it is erroneous to see *shakti* or *prakriti* as unambiguously empowering, and then to build upon it an ideology of nature–culture/woman–man relations in the Himalayas. It is men's *fear* of *shakti* (which often translates into women's sexual energy),[10] that underlies Manu's famous dictum that: 'In childhood a woman should be under her father's control, in youth under her husband's, and when her husband is dead, under her sons' (The Laws of Manu: 5.147, Doniger and Smith, 1991).

Clearly a critique of Shiva's interpretation of the Chipko movement also crosscuts with the wider debates over ecofeminism. To differing extents, the various ecofeminist perspectives have been criticised on several fronts, notably for their essentialisation of women as a universal and biologically-determined category, and their tendency to romanticize the past (Nanda, 1991; Eckersley, 1992; Jackson, 1993b; Levin, 1994) – two criticisms which are applicable to Shiva's analysis of the Chipko movement. There is very little historical evidence for the idealized picture of 'traditional' environmental *or* gender relations that Shiva draws in her call to return to a more harmonious past (Greenberg et al, 1997). Indeed, as Kelkar and Nathan (1991) point out, mainstream

Indian civilization (which Shiva celebrates) was established precisely by clearing forests for settled cultivation, while at the same time women became increasingly subordinated to men through the development of caste society.

Shiva makes the valid observation that it is women who often bear disproportionately the personal, economic and social costs of environmental deterioration, and this is certainly the case in Uttaranchal. But as Agarwal (1992) notes, this by no means *necessarily* translates into an essentialist reading of women's environmental interests, knowledge or agency, in which the primal mutuality of women and nature is an automatically privileged relationship. If 'sound ecological practice' clashes with a hill woman's needs and responsibilities, such as in the case of a fuelwood shortage, then she is likely to prioritize the latter, particularly given the heavy burden placed upon many women by the out-migration of men. Even this argument presupposes the idea that, if they were in a position to, women always and everywhere have both the knowledge and the desire to preserve the environment. While this has been demonstrated to be true of particular women and communities all over the world, women's ecological knowledge and 'affinity' is not automatic but is historically and culturally dependent. In the Jharkhand, for example, Jewitt (1996) found that men were often the principal bearers of environmental knowledge, despite the fact that this is an *adivasi* (tribal) society where, if anything, ecofeminists would argue that women have an even more pristine relationship with the environment.

Women's decisions are constrained and enabled by a series of overlapping and sometimes competing gendered and social relations, and by the limitations and opportunities provided by the local environment as it is shaped by local factors *and* regional/national structures and events. They must make decisions and take actions on the basis of a host of conditions which differ for each woman in space and time. These can include their age, health, marital status, education, their fears and aspirations, whether they are in their natal or marital village, whether they and/or their household has access to other income sources, and endlessly on. Reducing women's decisions to a set of biologically determined characteristics devalues their agency, fails to recognize that they may also 'align' with other identities (caste and class, to name just two), and undermines the fact that they are situated in certain locales which impose and offer a specific set of constraints and opportunities, as with the differences between Mandal and Reni villages. Nowhere is this more clearly demonstrated than in Doongri-Paintoli, the site of a very famous Chipko incident in 1980, in which women defied their own menfolk as well as the Forest Department contractors in order to protect their forests. Here there was indeed a conflict of interests between the men and women of the village, as the women wanted to preserve the nearby forest (the loss of which would have spelt considerable hardship for them) while the men were more willing to accept the Forest Department's compensation (over which they would have had more control). But the women fought to prevent the complete clearance of their forest as a *functional livelihood strategy*, not because of a desire to retain or return to some pristine 'traditional' village life. This is made abundantly clear in the comments of Gayatri Devi, who had taken part in the original struggle and who is now deeply disappointed with the lack of development in the village. She said: 'We could have sacrificed more [forest] if we were assured a road to the village, a school, a proper water supply and a primary health centre' (Mitra, 1993, p50).

Mitra asked 'What did you get out of Chipko', and I will quote Gayatri Devi's full reply:

I don't know. We acted to save our trees. We never clung to any tree but when I went to Delhi, I was told that ours was a very big *andolan* [movement]. Maybe it was, but we never got anything out of it. The road to our village is yet to be constructed and water is still a problem. Our children cannot study beyond high school unless they can afford to go and stay in a town. The girls simply cannot do that. Now they tell me that because of Chipko the road cannot be built because everything has become *paryavaran* [environment] oriented nowadays. Chipko has given us nothing. We cannot even get wood to build a house because the forest guards keep us out. Our rights have been snatched away (Mitra, 1993, p51).

This issue of gender interests in the hills can be explored further with reference to the role played by women in the Uttaranchal movement. Women as a 'political community' are firmly positioned within its ideological and organizational mainstream,[11] and there are a number of women politicians and leaders who are strongly involved in the movement. Thus we might ask whether women are pursuing specifically gender-related demands through the agitation for a separate hill State *as well as* or *in opposition to* the main goals of the movement? The brief answer is that there is indeed one dimension of the mobilization that, although by no means exclusively a women's issue, has been particularly important in mobilizing the support of some women, and that is the anti-liquor protests that have accompanied the agitation. Many women in the hills suffer from the economic and personal effects of their male relatives drinking, and there is a long history of protest against selling liquor in Uttaranchal (Pathak, 1985). Within some parts of the movement this theme is an important one, and primarily a women's issue. For example, in one anti-liquor rally in Pithoragarh, a prominent *sarvodaya* worker drew on an explicitly Gandhian vision of a liquor-less Uttaranchal. 'Otherwise', she asked, 'what is the point of the separate state for women?'[12]

But the vast majority of women with whom I spoke saw the *principal* benefit of a separate State as being the creation of more jobs (or the freeing up of present ones) for their fathers, brothers, husbands and sons (and occasionally, some said, for themselves). A secure income, preferably from a government job, was perceived by both men and women to be increasingly essential to survive in the hills. A woman from Mandal village – the site of that first famous confrontation – told me that: 'Nowadays it's like this: if you have jobs you can eat. If you don't have a job you can get nothing. The wild pigs are destroying the crops in the fields; women are working hard in the fields but getting nothing.'[13]

Hyperbole aside, there is a real message here, and in many of the other statements and discussions I heard. There is evidence of growing aspirations amongst some women which centre not on the village or traditional agricultural obligations (and therefore also on forests), but on towns and employment (for themselves and, more frequently, their husbands and sons) within and outside of the region. The following statement is taken from an interview in September 1994 with Gangotri Devi, an elderly woman from Mandal village:

She [her younger companion] is BA passed, and doesn't know how to work in the fields because she is always with her books and pens. But we are always in the fields. After the creation of a separate State some boys and girls will get jobs... All the people are coming onto the streets [protesting] to get jobs – like this girl and that boy [*points*] – then they will be able to feed us as well as their children. There is nothing good in this Garhwal –

little agricultural production and no job opportunities. All the educated boys are hanging out on the streets.

This is not to deny that many women *are* deeply concerned by agro-environmental issues in the hills, but they allied this with a concern about other ways of winning a livelihood in Uttaranchal, including the commercial exploitation of the forests – something that Shiva tends not to acknowledge. Gender issues *are* central to any analysis of forests and resistance in Uttaranchal, but many women recognize that the arena of their struggles and potential opportunities extends far beyond the village and nearby forest to the region, state and even nation. In the final section, this question of scale, and of the relationship between 'peasants and the state', is picked up in a discussion of Ramachandra Guha's (1989) analysis of Chipko.

Peasant versus the state?

In 'The Unquiet Woods', Ramachandra Guha presents a sophisticated sociological analysis of continuity and change in popular movements against the pre- and post-colonial states in Uttaranchal. As well as placing Chipko in its cultural and historical context, Guha is one of the few authors who analyses the varying space–time geographies of the Chipko protests. He explores the different environmental philosophies present in the movement, the various types of protest deployed, gender relations within the hills, and Chipko's goals and outcomes. Reminiscent of E P Thompson, Guha approaches the relationship between peasants and the state in Uttaranchal through the lens of the moral economy, and suggests that villagers saw Chipko as a fight for basic subsistence denied them by the institutions and policies of the state. Although Guha's faith in peasant moral economies as a basis for contemporary forest regeneration and management is open to qualification (see Jewitt and Corbridge, 1997), he does perhaps provide the most definitive historical study of social movements in Uttaranchal to date. But, I would suggest that the model of resistance that Guha presents, that of peasant *versus* the state, does not entirely hold outside of the struggle over forests and, by the 1990s, is no longer sufficient to conceptualize even forest tensions between hill people and the state.[14] This too has a bearing on the declining mobilizing power of Chipko and the increasing interest in the idea of a separate hill State.

The mountains of Uttaranchal are a daunting environment in which to enforce the writ of law, and it was only following the expansion of the road system after 1962 that the penetration of the state and its adjuncts (administrative, developmental and disciplinary) could significantly accelerate in the hills. Accompanying this 'space–time compression' were immense and complex socio-cultural and economic changes. By the 1970s/1980s, the state had, in some form or other, penetrated many aspects of daily life, albeit highly unevenly in depth and spread. One effect has been that it has become more difficult and more risky for villagers to oppose the state outright, for example, by ignoring forest laws.

Guha argues that peasant movements like Chipko are: 'defensive, seeking to escape the tentacles of the commercial economy, and the centralizing state' (Guha, 1989, p196). But while this may have been true to an extent in the 1970s, I believe that it is too one-dimensional to encompass the full variety and depth of the relationship(s) between 'peasants' and the developmental state *or* the commercial economy in the 1990s. The Uttaranchal regional movement demonstrates that the capture and manipulation of state power, state patronage and state resources are now very much part of the interplay between domination and resistance in Uttaranchal. While the state may be presented as an agent of oppression in terms of the forests, it is also a source of opportunities. These are not limited to jobs and education, although both are increasingly important in a marginal area with a growing population in an increasingly competitive economy. Rather, as hill people have become more informed and more politicized, they have sought more power and a bigger voice in the processes of development planning and development administration, and more access to development funds – the main controller of which is of course, the state. The object of the Uttaranchal regional struggle was the *capture*, not the *rejection*, of the state and thus state power.

The growing politicization of the state and civil society in India since the mid-1960s has been recently intensified by, amongst other things, the expansion of the reservation system in 1989, and post-1991, the push towards the liberalization of the economy. Kohli (1990) argues that a highly interventionist state, in attempting to deal with a poor economy, has in the process become the object of intense political competition. These changes are reflected in a contemporary relationship between state and society in Uttaranchal that is more complex than 'peasant versus the state'. The regional movement demonstrates the growing volatility of the electorate, and an increasing willingness and capacity to organize around particular identities in order to further their demands at the state and national level. Confrontation with the state has not disappeared, as the events of 1994/1995 demonstrate, nor covert resistance, but it is now increasingly directed towards appropriating political and administrative power rather than directly opposing it. This suggests that, as many Uttaranchalis know, but which many 'post-developers' are less willing to admit, that the politics of the local continue to be reflexively engaged with, and must be understood in relation to, regional, national and other supra-local political, economic and cultural influences.

Conclusions

'Chipko' has taken on the function of a metaphor for subaltern environmental resistance in that it has acquired meanings and associations that extend far beyond, or even have little resemblance to, the specific times, places and circumstances of its mobilisation. There is much to be said for the argument that more important than 'accuracy' is the fact that 'Chipko' has served as a inspiration for activists both in India and elsewhere against social and environmental injustice.[15] But as I have argued in this paper, the ecocentric/ecofeminist representations of Chipko that came to dominate popular images of the movement played a small but not insignificant part in the movement's failure to achieve the changes that were desired by many in the hills. Chipko developed primarily as an economic struggle, with male and female activists recognizing that the survival of the forests had become an a priori condition for the possibilities of development that they sought to realize, within the geographical constraints of the mountains. Environmental concern was not lacking, but a sound environment was seen as a *func-*

tional requirement for a sound local economy. Within this, different 'subsistence strategies' were articulated at different times, in different places, and by different people, as we saw in the protests in Mandal, Reni and Doongri-Paintoli. Ironically (given their relativist sympathies), many neopopulist writers have constructed rather universalist accounts of the movement (ecological, ecofeminist and/or anti-development) which undermine or ignore Chipko's complexity, and which depend on a cultural, economic and political localism which simply does not reflect the reality of men and women's lives in Uttaranchal. We do an injustice to the vast majority of the women and men of Uttaranchal if we understand them to want to return to some idealized traditional past that is unlikely ever to have existed. This was not the message that was being articulated in the 1970s through the Chipko protests, and is certainly not true of today's regional demands.

Some of these criticisms point to a more general set of concerns about a number of common features and tendencies within much neopopulist writing on social mobilizations in the South. One such is the tendency to view 'local' communities as rather static and inward-looking (Collins, 1997). This image underpins notions of 'traditional villagers', whose livelihoods are intimately dependent on the local environment, and whose lifeworlds are constructed and given meaning only through their immediate surroundings. But this offers a very partial understanding of people's lives in the hills, and does not reflect their familiarity and engagement with a whole series of supra-local influences. The transition from the Chipko protests to the regional mobilization underlines the fact that it is misguided to rely on the sparse and reductionist accounts of 'the local' as set forward in much neopopulist theory in understanding the diverse livelihood strategies, identity formations and outlooks of the vast majority of hill men and women.

Acknowledgements

My thanks to the Economic and Social Research Council for funding this work, and to Professor Ian Simmons for reading the first draft.

References

Agarwal, B (1992) 'The gender and environment debate: lessons from India'. *Feminist Studies*, **18**(1): 119–158

Aryal, M (1994) 'Axing Chipko'. *Himal* 7(1): 8–23

Atkinson, E T (1882–1884) *The Himalayan Gazetteer*, 3 Volumes, reprinted 1989, Cosmo Publications, New Delhi

Bandyopadhyay, J (1992) 'From environmental conflicts to sustainable mountain transformation: ecological action in the Garhwal Himalaya', in D P Ghai and J M Vivian (eds) *Grassroots Environmental Action: People's Participation in Sustainable Development*, Routledge, London, pp259–280

Berreman, G D (1963) *Hindus of the Himalayas: Ethnography and Change*, Oxford University Press, New Delhi

Beteille, A (1992) *The Backward Classes in Contemporary India*, Oxford University Press, New Delhi

Bhatkoti, D N (1987) 'Elites and political change in Tehri: a study in the politics of mass movement and regional development', PhD thesis, Garhwal University

Bhatt, C P and Kunwar, S S (1982) *Hugging the Himalaya: The Chipko Experience*, DGSS, Gopeshwar

Bora, R S (1987) 'Extent and causes of migration from the hill regions of Uttar Pradesh', in V Joshi (ed) *Migrant Labour and Related Issues*, Oxford, New Delhi, pp187–210

Bora, R S (1996) Himalayan Migration: A Study of the Hill Region of Uttar Pradesh, Sage, New Delhi

Collins, J L (1997) 'Development theory and the politics of location: an example from north eastern Brazil', in V Tucker (ed) *Cultural Perspectives on Development*, Frank Cass, London and Portland, OR

Das, J C and Negi, R S (1983) 'The Chipko movement', in K S Singh (ed) *Tribal Movements in India, Volume 2*, Manohar, New Delhi, pp383–392

Doniger, W and Smith, B K (1991) *The Laws of Manu*, Penguin, New Delhi

Eckersley, R (1992) *Environmentalism and Political Theory: Towards an Ecocentric Approach*, University College London Press, New Delhi

Ekins, P (1992) *A New World Order: Grassroots Movements for Global Change*, Routledge, London and New York

Escobar, A (1995) *Encountering Development: The Making and Unmaking of the Third World*, Princeton University Press, Princeton, NJ

Galanter, M (1978) 'Who are the OBCs? An introduction to a constitutional puzzle'. *Economic and Political Weekly*, 28 October 1978, pp1812–1828

Galanter, M (1984) *Competing Equalities: Law and the Backward Classes in India*, Oxford University Press, New Delhi

Ghai, D P and Vivian, J M (eds) (1992) *Grassroots Environmental Action: People's Participation in Sustainable Development*, Routledge, London

Government of Uttar Pradesh (1991) *Draft Eighth Five-Year Plan (1992–1997) and Annual Sub-Plan (1992–1993)*, Uttaranchal Vikas Vibhag, Lucknow

Greenberg, B, Sinha, S and Gururani, S (1997) 'The "new traditionalist" discourse of Indian environmentalism'. *The Journal of Peasant Studies*, **24**(3): 65–99

Guha, R (1989) *The Unquiet Woods: Ecological Change and Peasant Resistance in the Himalayas*, Oxford University Press, New Delhi

Jackson, C (1993a) 'Environmentalisms and gender interests in the Third World'. *Development and Change*, **24**(4): 649–677

Jackson, C (1993b) 'Women/nature or gender/history: a critique of ecofeminist development'. *Journal of Peasant Studies*, **20**(3): 389–419

Jewitt, S (1996) Agro-ecological knowledges and forest management in the Jharkhand, India: tribal development or populist impasse? PhD thesis, Cambridge University

Jewitt, S and Corbridge, S E (1997) 'From forest struggles to forest citizens? Joint forest management in the unquiet woods of India's Jharkhand'. *Environment and Planning A* **29**(12): 2145–2164

Joshi, M C (1990) 'The Khasas in the history of the Uttarakhand', in M P Joshi, A C Fanger and C W Brown (eds) *Himalaya: Past and Present, Volume 3*. Shri Almora Book Depot, Almora, pp193–200

Joshi, M P (1990) *Uttaranchal Himalaya: An Essay in Historical Anthropology*, Shri Almora Book Depot, Almora

Kakar, S (1978) *The Inner World: A Psychoanalytic Study of Childhood and Society in India*, Oxford University Press, New Delhi

Kelkar, G and Nathan, D (1991) *Gender and Tribe: Women, Land and Forests*, Sage, London

Kohli, A (1990) *Democracy and Discontent: India's Growing Crisis of Governability*, Cambridge University Press, Cambridge

Kurtz, S N (1992) *All the Mothers Are One: Hindu India and the Cultural Reshaping of Psychoanalysis*, Colombia University Press, New York

Levin, M G (1994) 'A critique of ecofeminism', in L P Pojman (ed) *Environmental Ethics: Readings in Theory and Application*, Jons and Bartlett Publishers, London

Mawdsley, E E (1996) 'The Uttarakhand agitation and the other backward classes', *Economic and Political Weekly*, 27 January 1996, pp205–210

Mawdsley, E E (1997) 'Non-secessionist regionalism in India: the Uttarakhand separate state movement'. *Environment and Planning A* **29**(12): 2217–2235

Mies, M and Shiva, V (1993) *Ecofeminism*, Kali for Women, New Delhi

Mishra, A and Tripathi, S (1978) *Chipko Movement: Uttarakhand Women's Bid to Save Forest Wealth*, People's Action for Development with Justice, New Delhi

Mitra, A, 1993, 'Chipko today', *Down To Earth*, 30 April 1993

Nand, N and Kumar, K (1989) *The Holy Himalaya: A Geographical Interpretation of Garhwal*, Daya Publishing House, New Delhi

Nanda, M (1991) 'Is modern science a western patriarchal myth: a critique of populist orthodoxy', *South Asian Bulletin*, **11**(1) and (2): 32–61

Pant, G B (1922) The Forest Problem in Kumaun, Allahabad

Pathak, A (1994) *Contested Domains: The State, Peasants and Forestry in Contemporary India*, Sage, New Delhi

Pathak, S (1985) 'Intoxication as a social evil: anti-alcohol movement in Uttarakhand', *Economic and Political Weekly*, 10 August 1985, pp1360–1365

Quigley, D (1993) *The Interpretation of Caste*, Clarendon Press, New Delhi

Rangan, H (1996) 'From Chipko to Uttaranchal: development, environment and social protest in the Garhwal Himalayas, India', in R Peet and M J Watts (eds) *Liberation Ecologies: Environment, Development, Social Movements*, Routledge, London and New York, pp205–226

Rangan, H and Garb, Y (1996) 'Conflicting histories: negotiating reality and myth around the Chipko movement', Mimeo

Rawat, A S (1993) (ed) *Indian Forestry: A Perspective*, Indian Publishing Company, New Delhi

Redclift, M (1987) *Sustainable Development: Exploring the Contradictions*, Routledge, London and New York

Sachs, W (1992) (ed) *The Development Dictionary*, Zed, London

Saxena, N C (1992) 'Why did it fail?' The Hindu survey of the environment, pp35–38

Shiva, V (1988) *Staying Alive: Women, Ecology and Survival in India*, Kali for Women, New Delhi

Shiva, V (1992) 'Women's indigenous knowledge and biodiversity conservation', in G Sen (ed) *Indigenous Vision: People of India's Attitude to the Environment*, Sage, New Delhi and London, pp205–214

Shiva, V and Bandyopadhyay, J (1986) *Chipko: India's Civilizational Response to the Forest Crisis*, INTACH, New Delhi

Shiva, V and Bandyopadhyay, J (1987) 'Chipko: rekindling India's forest culture', *The Ecologist*, **17**(1), pp26–34

Singh, S P (1993) 'Controversies of Chir Pine expansion in the Central Himalaya' in A S Rawat (ed) *Indian Forestry: A Perspective*, Indian Publishing Company, New Delhi, pp307–314

Tolia, R S (1994) *British Kumaun-Garhwal: An Administrative History of a Non-Regulation Hill Province. The Gardner and Traill Years (1815 AD–1935 AD)* Shri Almora Book Depot, Almora

Tucker, R P (1993) 'Forests of the Western Himalaya and the British colonial system (1815–1914)', in A S Rawat (ed) *Indian Forestry: A Perspective*, Indian Publishing Company, New Delhi, pp163–192

Weber, T (1987) *Hugging the Trees*, Penguin, Harmondsworth

Whittaker, W (1984) 'Migration and agrarian change in Garhwal District, Uttar Pradesh', in T P Bayliss-Smith and S Wanmali (eds) *Understanding Green Revolutions: Agrarian Change and Development Planning in South Asia*, Cambridge University Press, Cambridge, pp109–135

Women and Geography Study Group (1997) *Feminist Geographies: Explorations in Difference and Diversity*, Longman, Harlow

Notes

1   The Himalayan part of the State of Uttar Pradesh (see map). The region is also known as the Uttarakhand. There are small semantic differences, but the important distinction is that the Bharatiya Janata Party (recently elected to Central Government in India) use Uttaranchal. I prefer the less politically appropriated name of Uttarakhand, but now that the BJP have declared that a new State of Uttaranchal will be created (see note 9), it seems sensible to change.

2   With the exception of some small Tibeto-Mongloid tribal groups, the vast majority of the Uttaranchal population belongs to the Hindu and Aryan majority of northern India. The Pahari language group is closely related to Hindi, which is also widely spoken in this region [Berreman, 1963].

3   This brief sketch is based on 15 months of fieldwork in Uttaranchal, and interviews with some of the key proponents of the movement, including Chandi Prasad Bhatt, Sunderlal Bahuguna, Dhum Singh Negi, Shamsher Singh Bist, women from Mandal village, and many other villagers who had (and had not) taken part in Chipko protests of the 1970s and 1980s. I also had access to local Hindi newspaper archives and other Hindi documents, as well as a large number of English accounts.

4   It also tied in with the reactionary and hotly contested ideas being mooted in the Draft Forest Act of 1981 (Fernandes and Kulkarni, 1983; Pathak, 1994).

5   The States adopted the legislation at different times. In Uttar Pradesh this followed the election of a 'middle/low caste' government in 1993.

6   Reservation is an enormously complex issue, and this is a extremely simplified outline. For details, see Galanter (1978, 1984) and Beteille (1992).

7   Various suggestions have been put forward for this highly unusual caste pattern, including Berreman (1963), MC Joshi (1990), MP Joshi (1990) and Quigley (1993).

8   The Central Government has just, in April 1998, announced that the State of Uttaranchal will be created, along with Vananchal and Chhatisgarh.

9   By referring to a 'feminine principle', as Jackson (1993b) notes, Shiva rightly tries to avoid the pitfall of biological determinism. This way she can include certain men, such as Sunderlal Bahuguna who, she says, through listening to the quiet voices of women, has retained an ability to articulate the feminine-ecological principles of Chipko. But having made the distinction between the categories of 'woman' and 'feminine principle', she goes on to collapse them repeatedly.

10   For a psychoanalytical account of male fear of the sexualized woman in India, see Kakar (1978). Digressing slightly, for a fascinating critique of Kakar, see Kurtz (1992).

11 This was more than evident when watching the marches, rallies and meetings in villages and towns, talking to men and women, reading newspaper reports, and simply observing and participating in the movement.

12 Interview, 22, December 94

13 Interview, 21, September 94

14 An important issue which there simply isn't the space to go into in this paper, is the question of how these arguments play out in relation to the federal division, in other words between State (of Uttar Pradesh) and state (central) power.

15 My thanks to Paul Routledge for pointing this out.

Introduction – Section IIC:
Property and Institutions and
Community-based Management

Samantha Jones and Grace Carswell

The Commons

Poor people in the developing world tend to have limited access to resources and may disproportionately depend upon resources such as grazing land, forests, fisheries, wildlife and water that are not privately owned by other individuals (often referred to as common property resources). Following the publication of the landmark essay *The Tragedy of the Commons* by Garrett Hardin in 1968, there has been much intervention in the management of such resources. Hardin's argument rested on the logic of a 'thought experiment' based around an imaginary village commons. He convincingly explained that each herdsman would find it profitable to graze more animals than the pasture could support. The private benefit would exceed the private cost of each additional animal as the costs of maintaining the rangeland would be shared by the group as a whole. Hardin's logic became an explanatory metaphor for the inevitability of over-exploitation of common property.

Ciriacy-Wantrup and Bishop (1975) are accredited with first drawing attention to the fact that Hardin confused common property regimes (where resources are held by an identifiable group of interdependent users able to exclude outsiders and regulate use by its members and where rights are often recognized in customary law) with open access scenarios (where there is an absence of well defined property rights, access is often unregulated, and the resource is free and open to everybody, encouraging 'free-riding'). Surprisingly little solid empirical research on common property resource management followed until the early 1990s. Since then there has been mounting evidence to confirm that a great proportion of renewable natural resources have been governed by complex norms, rules and regulations (institutions) devised by the user group (eg Jodha, 1986; Ostrom, 1990; Swift, 1991; Tang, 1992; Britt-Kapoor, 1994; Freudenberger et al, 1997; Beck and Nesmith, 2001; Thorburn, 2000). Such institutions determine how much and what aspect(s) of the resource may be used and how the benefit streams of the resource may be utilized (by whom and for what purpose). A distinction is made between informal institutions (eg cooperation, exchange, moral and spiritual controls based on indigenous belief systems) and formal institutions such as local traditional heads, organized user groups, village committees, etc (Richards, 1997). Generally a diversity of institutions exists, operating at various scales, generating overlapping and multiple resource rights (Rochealeau and Edmunds, 1997) and arbitrating contested resource claims.

It has been noted that a feature of common pool resources is that controlling access (exclusion) is difficult and joint use involves subtractability (where each user is capable of subtracting from the welfare of others) (Feeny et al, 1990). Common property regimes may thrive where the inherent productivity of the resource is too low to create the economic surplus that is needed for the transformation to private property and/or where uncertainty over resources productivity is rife (Bromley, 1992; Runge, 1992; Eggertsson, 1993; all cited by Knudsen, 1995). However, some authors have pointed out that there is nothing inherent within the resource that dictates the appropriate management regime. It is the institutional context or set of social relations that actually defines the property regime (that is the benefit stream to be derived from a resource). The property relations defining a common property regime is where 'individuals agree to limit their individual claims over a resource in the expectation that other group members will do the same' (Richards, 1997). The terms 'common property institutions' or regimes and 'common pool resources' are used to reflect the distinction between social relations and resource characteristics.

As collective action is a feature of the governance of common pool resources, there has been much interest in the reasons behind collective action. These studies have been critiqued for relying too heavily on rationality and economic incentives and ignoring symbolic, cultural, political, local and historical factors affecting collective action (see Mosse, 1997; Cleaver, 2000; Johnson, 2001 and Mehta et al, 2001 for a fuller account). One such area of research defines the conditions favourable to collective action under common property regimes, the most well known is Ostrom's set of 12 design principles that account for the robustness and endurance of successful common property institutions (Ostrom, 1990). However, as many as 35 factors have been highlighted as being critical to the organization, sustainability and adaptability of common property institutions (Agrawal, 2001). Generally, this body of work has been criticized for ignoring the influence of the external environment; focusing on single use resources; assuming economic rationality; drawing attention away from the more important understanding of processes; giving insufficient attention to ad hoc processes, unconscious acts and blurring of the rules; for being prescriptive and deterministic; and an impossibly costly and somewhat redundant research task (Campbell et al, 1992; Steins and Edwards, 1999; Cleaver, 2000; Agrawal, 2001).

Co-management and Community-based Natural Resource Management

Scholarly activity on the commons then, has shown that resource users often create institutional arrangements and management regimes that help them allocate benefits equitably (for example Thorburn, 2000, although this is contested for example by Adams et al, 1997; Mosse, 1997; Leach et al, 1997), over long periods of time with only limited efficiency losses (Richards, 1997; Agrawal 2001). Simultaneously, common property regimes are being threatened and eroded by state appropriation, market integration and population growth (although see Freudenberger et al, 1997; Richards, 1997; Campbell et al, 2001; Lam, 2001; Ballabh et al, 2002 for discussions on the erosion and resilience of institutions and their responses to change). Recognition of these facts within policy circles, combined with a number of other factors such as the liberalization agenda, the failure of states to sustainably manage natural resources (due to high transaction costs) and the recent emphasis on bottom-up development, has led to new approaches in the management of non-privately owned resources. These have largely involved the devolution of power from the state to local communities (Kellert et al, 2000) and may be labelled as co-management or community-based natural resource management (CBNRM). Co-management involves the cooperative or joint management of the resource by the user community and central government (Taylor, 1998), while CBNRM broadly enables a greater role for communities in managing resources upon which they depend.

These approaches represent a significant shift in natural resource management, illustrated by Agrawal's (2001) point that governments in over 50 countries, in forest management alone, are pursuing initiatives that devolve some control over resources to local users (citing FAO, 1999). Community-based natural resource management for wildlife management in Africa and Joint Forest Management in India are considered in more detail below (see also Western and Wright, 1994; Poffenberger and McGean, 1996; Ghimire and Pimbert, 1997; Agrawal and Gibson, 2001 and Hulme and Murphree, 2001 for general texts in this field). The approach has also filtered into the management of a wide range of other resources such as fisheries (Sen and Nielsen, 1996; Sunderlin and Gorospse, 1997; Johnson, 2001; Pomeroy et al, 2001), watersheds (Wittayapak and Dearden, 1999; Sneddon, 2002), grasslands (Kull, 2002) and is advocated by Thorburn (2000) to secure the sustainable use of marine resources.

India's Forestry Programme pre- and post-independence epitomized the problems associated with state regulation of renewable natural resources: high transaction costs of protecting resources (policing and monitoring), under-protected and consequent degradation of resources, the erosion of indigenous institutions and potentially alienating and conflicting relations between forest protection staff and communities. A national programme of social forestry was instituted, but this was deemed a failure, largely due to minimal local involvement. In 1988 a more radical shift in forest policy was prompted by a number of factors, including successful initiatives to involve communities in forest protection in West Bengal, Gugarat and Haryana states; evidence that local spontaneous self-governance had occurred in the states of W. Bengal, Orrisa and Bihar (Campbell, 1992; Krishnaswamy, 1995; Pattnaik and Dutta, 1997; Sundar, 2000); and calls for change made by 'forest intellectuals' such as Guha and Gadgil (Corbridge and Jewitt, 1997). The National Forest Policy for the first time acknowledged the need for community participation and the importance of allowing communities access to non-timber forest products (Raju, 1997). This 'Joint Forest Management' (JFM) programme represented a move away from meeting commercial and industrial requirements towards meeting the needs of rural and tribal populations (Sarin, 1995). A Government of India circular in June, 1990, specified that access to forest land and usufructory benefits would accrue to those who organized into village institutions (Arora, 1994). At least 16 states have developed their own versions of JFM orders and it is estimated that nearly 20,000 communities have formed forest protection committees, covering 2 million hectares of forest (3–5 per cent of India's total forest area) (Poffenberger, 1996). There is considerable variation across India in JFM systems, in terms of the degree of participation and protection (Sundar, 2000), particularly of women (see Agarwal, 1997), but this co-management system is largely regarded as a resounding success.

A second pioneering example of co-management is community-based wildlife management in Africa. While India experienced large-scale appropriation of forest resources by the colonial state, in Africa resource appropriation was associated with the designation of game reserves for hunting. Many of these were later reclassified as national parks, justified on the grounds that local people constituted the key threat to the environment (Dwivedi, 1996). Local people were expelled from many of these areas and their consumptive resource use prohibited. The approach has come known as 'fortress conservation' or the 'fences and fines' approach. As in the case of JFM, transaction costs were high and the state often failed to prevent poaching (the criminalized term for hunting). Simultaneously, negative consequences were felt by local people, including damage to their crops from wildlife, restrictions on the use of natural resources upon which they were often heavily dependent, and in some instances resettlement, often without adequate compensation (Ghimire, 1994; Gibson and Marks, 1995). Few incentives were in place for the sustainable use of natural resources.

Pioneered by the CAMPFIRE programme in Zimbabwe CBNRM, or community wildlife management or community conservation as it is variously known, has become the model for protected areas management throughout Africa and beyond (see Matzke and Nabane, 1996; Campbell et al, 1999 and Murombedzi, 1999, 2001; Alexander and McGregor, 2000; Wainright and Wehrmeyer, 1998 and Gibson and Marks, 1995 for Zambia for Zimbabwe; Songwar, 1999 for Tanzania; Sharpe, 1998 for Cameroon; Kepe et al, 2001 for South Africa; Peters, 1998 for Madagascar; Infield and Adams, 1999 for Uganda; Jones, 1999 for Namibia; Kellert et al, 2000 for Nepal and Kenya and Twyman, 1998, 2000, for Botswana). Adams and Hulme (2001) identify two elements to the community conservation narrative: first, the imperative to allow people in and around protected areas or with property rights there (in land or living resources) to participate in the management of conservation resources and second, linking conservation to local development needs. These objectives create 'a space within which a great variety of different kinds of conservation interventions lie' (2001, p14). Jones (1999), for instance, makes a distinction between the 'Park and Neighbour' approach, designed to minimize conflict in protected areas through compensation, revenue sharing and community development and CBNRM where sustainable use of and local proprietorship over resources is encouraged. The former may be regarded as biocentric and cannot be regarded as co-management whereas the latter is anthropocentric and embodies co-management principles. The latter is better suited to the many environments in which human use has shaped the local ecology and biodiversity value – something which has tended to be overlooked by international conservation organizations aiming to protect biodiversity (see Homewood and Rodgers, 1987; Fairhead and Leach, 1994; Agrawal and Gibson, this volume) and for which patterns of customary rights exist.

While CBNRM is widely considered a substantial improvement on the 'fences and fines' approach, significant critical reflections have been voiced. Communities have been regularly treated as homogenous with members having complementary interests, yet they are dynamic, factional and internally differentiated by gender, caste, wealth, ethnicity, age and origin for example (see Li, 1996; Leach et al, 1997; Brosius et al,

1998; Moore, 1998; Twyman, 1998; Sharpe, 1998; Belsky, 1999 and Agrawal and Gibson, this volume). This has led some to call for a greater attention to power relations, institutions and differentiated interests in CBNRM initiatives (Kull, 2000; Kepe et al, 2001; Agrawal and Gibson, this volume) as new institutional arrangements often reproduce the social relationships that marginalize certain groups, such as women (Martin and Lemon, 2001). Other critics note that the success of schemes has been limited (Gibson and Marks, 1995; Kellert et al, 2000) and that social and ecological resilience may be undermined by the imposition of formal rules (Turner, 1999; Twyman, 1998). Ultimately, the success of CBNRM may depend on the value of the resource to the community, population densities and the extent to which proprietorship or ownership is transferred to communities (Murphree, 1993; Campbell et al, 1999; Jones, 1999; Murombedzi, 1999). Adams and Hulme (2001) believe that what is needed is broad-based 'enabling' policies that promote the creation and strengthening of networks of institutions and organizations that have the flexibility to deal with contingency and complexity. 'The question is not whether state action or community action is better: both are essential, along with private sector support – the challenge is how to develop effective mixes of state, community and private action in specific contexts' (Adams and Hulme, 2001, p22).

References

Adams, W M and Hulme, D (2001) 'Conservation and community: changing narratives, policies and practices in African conservation', in D Hulme and M Murphree (eds) *African Wildlife and Livelihoods: The Promise and Performance of Community Conservation,* James Currey, Oxford

Adams, W M, Watson, E E and Mutiso, S K (1997) 'Water, rules and gender: water rights in an indigenous irrigation system, Marakwet, Kenya'. *Development and Change* 28: 707–730

Agarwal, B (1997) 'Environmental action, gender equity and women's participation'. *Development and Change* 28: 1–44

Agrawal, A (2001) 'Common property institutions and sustainable governance of resources'. *World Development* 29(10): 1649–72

Agrawal, A and Gibson, C C (eds) (2001) *Communities and the Environment: Ethnicity, Gender and the State in Community-based Conservation,* Rutgers University Press, New Jersey

Alexander, J and McGregor, J (2000) 'Wildlife and politics: CAMPFIRE in Zimbabwe'. *Development and Change* 31(3): 605–27

Arora, D (1994) 'From state regulation to people's participation, case of forest management in India'. *Economic and Political Weekly,* 19 March, 691

Ballabh, V, Balooni, K and Dave, S (2002) 'Why local resources management institutions decline: a comparative analysis of Van (Forest) Panchayats and forest protection committees in India'. *World Development* 30(12): 2153–2167

Beck, T and Nesmith, C (2001) 'Building on poor people's capacities: the case of common property resources in India and West Africa'. *World Development* 29(1): 119–133

Belsky, J M (1999) 'Misrepresenting communities: the politics of community-based rural ecotourism in Gales Point Manatee, Belize'. *Rural Sociology* 64(4): 641–666

Brit-Kapoor, C (1994) 'A tale of two committees: a villager perspective on local institutes; forest management and resource use in two central Himalayan Indian villages'. *ODI Rural Development Forestry Network Papers* 17(a)

Brosius, J P, Lowenhaupt Tsing, A and Zerner, C (1998) 'Representing communities: histories and politics of community-based natural resource management'. *Society and Natural Resources* 11: 157–168

Campbell, B, Bryon, N et al (1999) 'Moving to local control of woodland resources – can CAMPFIRE go beyond the mega-fauna?' *Society and Natural Resources* 12: 501–509

Campbell, B, Mandondo, A et al (2001) 'Challenges to proponents of common property resource systems: despairing voices from the social forests of Zimbabwe'. *World Development* 29(4): 589–600

Campbell, J Y (1992) 'Joint forest management in India'. *Social Change* 22(1): 36–54

Ciriacy-Wantrup, S V and Bishop, R C (1975) '"Common property" as a concept in natural resource policy'. *Natural Resources Journal* 15: 713 –727

Cleaver, F (2000) 'Moral ecological rationality, institutions and the management of common property resources'. *Development and Change* 31: 361–383

Corbridge, S and Jewitt, S (1997) 'From forest struggles to forest citizens? Joint forest management in the unquiet woods of India's Jharkhand'. *Environment and Planning A* 29: 2145–2164

Dwivedi, R (1996) 'Parks, people and protest: some observations on the mediating role of environmental action groups in grassroots resource conflicts'. *Institute of Social Studies Working Papers* 228, The Hague

Fairhead, J and Leach, M (1994) 'Conservation forests: modern conservation and historical land use in Guinea's Ziama Reserve'. *African Affairs* 93: 481–512

Feeny, D, Berkes, F, McCay, B J and Acheson, J M (1990) 'The tragedy of the commons: twenty-two years later'. *Human Ecology* 18(1): 1–19

Freudenburger, S M, Carney, J A and Lebbie, A R (1997) 'Resiliency and change in common property regimes in West Africa: the case of the Tongo in The Gambia, Guinea and Sierra Leone'. *Society and Natural Resources* 10: 383–402

Ghimire, K (1994) 'Parks and people: livelihood issues in national park management in Thailand and Madagascar'. *Development and Change* 25(1): 195–229

Ghimire, K B and Pimbert M (1997) *Social Change and Conservation*, Earthscan, London

Gibson, C C and Marks, S A (1995) 'Transforming rural hunters into conservationists: an assessment of community-based wildlife management programs in Africa'. *World Development* 23(6): 941–957

Hardin, G (1968) 'The tragedy of the commons'. *Science* 162: 1243 – 1248

Homewood, K and Rodgers, W A (1987) 'Pastoralism, conservation and the overgrazing controversy', in D M Anderson and R Grove (eds) *Conservation in Africa: People, Policies and Practice*, Cambridge University Press, Cambridge

Hulme, D and Murphree, M (eds) (2001) *African Wildlife and Livelihoods: The Promise and Performance of Community Conservation*, James Currey, Oxford

Infield, M and Adams, W M (1999) 'Institutional sustainability and community conservation: a case study from Uganda'. *Journal of International Development* 11(2): 305–315

Jodha, N S (1986) 'Common property resources and rural poor in dry regions of India'. *Economic and Political Weekly* 31(27): 1169–1181

Johnson, C (2001) 'Community formation and fisheries conservation in southern Thailand'. *Development and Change* 32(5): 951–74

Jones, B (1999) 'Policy lessons from the evolution of a community-based approach to wildlife management, Kunene region, Namibia'. *Journal of International Development* 11: 295–304

Kellert, S R, Mehta, J N et al (2000) 'Community natural resource management: promise, rhetoric, and reality'. *Society and Natural Resources* 13: 705 – 715

Kepe, T, Cousins, B and Turner, S (2001) 'Resource tenure and power relations in community wildlife: the case of Mkambati area, South Africa'. *Society and Natural Resources* 14: 911–925

Knudsen, A J (1995) *Living with the Commons: Local Institutions for Natural Resource Management*, Report for Chr Michelsen Institute, Bergen, Norway

Krishnaswamy, A (1995) 'Sustainable Development and Community Forest Management in Bihar, India'. *Society and Natural Resources* 8: 339–350

Kull, C A (2002) 'Empowering pyromaniacs in Madagascar: ideology and legitimacy in community-based natural resource management'. *Development and Change* 33: 57–78

Lam, W F (2001) 'Coping with change: a study of local irrigation institutions in Taiwan'. *World Development* 29(9): 1569 – 1592

Leach, M, Mearns, R and Scoones, I (1997) 'Challenges to community-based sustainable development: dynamics, entitlements, institutions'. *IDS Bulletin* 28(4): 4–14

Li, T M (1996) 'Images of community: discourse and strategy in property relations'. *Development and Change* 27: 501 – 527

Martin, A and Lemon, M (2001) 'Challenges for participatory institutions: the case of village forest committees in Karnataka, South India'. *Society and Natural Resources* 14(7): 585–597

Matzke, G E and Nabane, N (1996) 'Outcomes of a community controlled wildlife utilisation programme in a Zambezi valley community'. *Human Ecology* 24(1): 65–85

Mehta, L, Leach, M and Scoones, I (2001) 'Environmental governance in an uncertain world'. *IDS Bulletin* 32(4): 1–9

Moore, D S (1998) 'Clear waters and muddied histories: environmental history and the politics of community in Zimbabwe's Eastern Highlands'. *Journal of Southern African Studies* 24(2): 377–403

Mosse, D (1997) 'The symbolic making of a common property resource: history, ecology and locality in a tank-irrigated landscape in south India'. *Development and Change* 28(3): 467–504

Murombedzi, J C (1999) 'Devolution and stewardship in Zimbabwe's CAMPFIRE programme'. *Journal of International Development* 11(2): 287–293

Murombedzi, J C (2001) 'Committees, rights, costs and benefits: natural resource stewardship and community benefits stewardship in Zimbabwe's CAMPFIRE programme', in Hulme, D and Murphree, M (eds) *African Wildlife and Livelihoods*, James Currey, Oxford/Heinemann, Portsmouth

Murphee, M W (1993) *Communities as Resource Management Institutions*, International Institute of Environment and Development, London.

Ostrom, E (1990) *Governing the Commons*, Cambridge University Press, Cambridge

Pattnaik, B K and Dutta, S (1997) 'JFM in Southwest Bengal: a study in participatory development'. *Economic and Political Weekly*, 13 Dec 1997, 3225

Peters, J (1998) 'Sharing national park entrance fees: forging new partnerships in Madagascar'. *Society and Natural Resources* 11: 517 – 530

Poffenberger, M (1996) *Linking Government with Community Resource Management: What's Working and What's not?* A report on the 5th Asia forest network meeting, Surajkund, India, Southeast Asia Sustainable Forest Management Network, Research Network Reports No 9

Poffenberger, M and McGean, B (1996) *Village Voices, Forest Choices: Joint Forest Management in India*, Oxford University Press, Delhi

Pomeroy, R S, Katon, BM and Harkes, I (2001) 'Conditions affecting the success of fisheries co-management: lessons from Asia'. *Marine Policy* 25(3): 197–208

Raju, G (1997) *Joint Forest Management: The Dilemma of Empowerment*, Institute of Rural Management, Anand, Working Papers, **109**

Richards, M (1997) 'Common property resource institutions and forest management in Latin America'. *Development and Change* 28(1): 95–117

Rocheleau, D and Edmunds, D (1997) 'Women, men and trees: gender, power and property in forest and agrarian landscapes'. *World Development* 25(8): 1351–1371

Sarin, M (1995) 'Regenerating India's forests – reconciling gender equity with joint forest management'. *IDS Bulletin* 26(1): 83–91

Sen, S and Nielsen, J R (1996) 'Fisheries co-management: a comparative analysis'. *Marine Policy* 20(5): 405–418

Sharpe, B (1998) '"First the forest": conservation, "community" and "participation" in south-west Cameroon'. *Africa* 68(1): 25–45

Sneddon, C (2002) 'Water conflicts and river basins: the contradictions of comanagement and scale in northeast Thailand'. *Society and Natural Resources* 15(8): 725–741

Songwar, A (1999) 'Community-based wildlife management in Tanzania: are the communities interested?' *World Development* 27(12): 2061–2079

Steins, N A and Edwards, V M (1999) 'Collective action in common-pool resource management: the contribution of a social constructivist perspective to existing theory'. *Society and Natural Resources* 12: 539 – 557

Sundar, N (2000) 'Unpacking the "joint" in joint forest management'. *Development and Change* 31(1): 255–279

Sunderlin, W D and Gorospe, M L G (1997) 'Fishers' organisations and modes of co-management: the case of San Miguel Bay, Philippines'. *Human Organisation* 56(3): 333–343

Swift, J (1991) 'Local customary institutions as the basis for natural resource management among Boran pastoralists in northern Kenya'. *IDS Bulletin* 22(4): 34–37

Tang, S Y (1992) *Institutions and Collective Action: Self-governance in Irrigation*, ICS Press, San Francisco

Taylor, M (1998) 'Governing natural resources'. *Society and Natural Resources* 11: 251–258

Thorburn, C (2000) 'Changing customary marine resources management practice and institutions: the case of Sasi Lola in the Kei Islands, Indonesia'. *World Development* 28(8): 1461–1479

Turner, M D (1999) 'Conflict, environment change, and social institutions in dryland Africa: limitations of the community resource management approach'. *Society and Natural Resources* 12: 643 –657

Twyman, C (1998) 'Rethinking community resource management: managing resources or managing people in western Botswana?' *Third World Quarterly* 19(4): 745–770

Twyman, C (2000) 'Livelihood opportunity and diversity in Kalahari wildlife management areas, Botswana: rethinking community resource management'. *Journal of Southern African Studies* 26(4): 783–805

Wainwright, C and Wehrmeyer, W (1998) 'Success in integrating conservation and development? A study from Zambia'. *World Development*, 26(6): 933–944

Western, D and Wright, R M (1994) *Natural Connections: Perspectives in Community-based Conservation*, Island Press, Washington DC

Wittayapak, C and Dearden, P (1999) 'Decision making arrangements in community-based watershed management in northern Thailand'. *Society and Natural Resources* 12: 673–691

6

Enchantment and Disenchantment: The Role of Community in Natural Resource Conservation

Arun Agrawal and Clark C. Gibson

Summary

The poor conservation outcomes that followed decades of intrusive resource management strategies and planned development have forced policy-makers and scholars to reconsider the role of community in resource use and conservation. In a break from previous work on development which considered communities a hindrance to progressive social change, current writings champion the role of community in bringing about decentralization, meaningful participation and conservation. But despite its recent popularity, the concept of community is rarely defined or carefully examined by those concerned with resource use and management. We seek to redress this omission by investigating 'community' in work concerning resource conservation and management. We explore the conceptual origins of the community, and the ways the term has been deployed in writings on resource use. We then analyse those aspects of community most important to advocates for community's role in resource management – community as a small spatial unit, as a homogeneous social structure, and as shared norms – and indicate the weaknesses of these approaches. Finally, we suggest a more political approach: community must be examined in the context of development and conservation by focusing on the multiple interests and actors within communities, on how these actors influence decision-making, and on the internal and external institutions that shape the decision-making process. A focus on institutions rather than 'community' is likely to be more fruitful for those interested in community-based natural resource management.

Reprinted from *World Development*, vol 27, Agrawal, A and Gibson, C C, 'Environment and Disenchantment: The Role of Community in Natural Resource Management', pp629–649, copyright © (1999), with permission from Elsevier.

Introduction

The poor conservation outcomes that followed decades of intrusive resource management strategies and planned development have forced policy-makers and scholars to reconsider the role of community in resource use and conservation. In a break from previous work on development which considered communities to hinder progressive social change, current writing champions the role of community in bringing about decentralization, meaningful participation, cultural autonomy and conservation (Chambers and McBeth, 1992; Chitere, 1994; Etzioni, 1996). But despite its recent popularity, the concept of community rarely receives the attention or analysis it needs from those concerned with resource use and management.

We seek to redress this omission by investigating 'community' in work concerning resource conservation and management.[1] We begin by exploring the conceptual origins of the community, especially as it relates to writings on resource use. The ensuing analysis reveals that three aspects of community are most important to those who advocate a positive role for communities in resource management – community as a small spatial unit, as a homogeneous social structure and as shared norms. We suggest a more political approach. Community, we argue, must be examined in the context of conservation by focusing on the multiple interests and actors within communities, on how these actors influence decision-making, and on the internal and external institutions that shape the decision-making process. A focus on institutions rather than 'community' is likely to be more fruitful for those interested in community-based natural resource management. We conclude by suggesting that research and policy move away from universalist claims either for or against community. Instead, community-based conservation initiatives must be founded on images of community that recognize their internal differences and processes, their relations with external actors, and the institutions that affect both.

Community in History

To understand the current widespread preoccupation with community requires an understanding of at least some history of the concept's use. Such a history shows the ways in which 'community' has moved in and out of fashion, and prompts caution in accepting community as a panacea to problems concerning the conservation of natural resources.

Current perceptions of community appear strongly linked to analyses of 19th and early 20th century scholars attempting to understand the portentous transformations that rocked their world.[2] The source of these changes was thought to lay in the economic sphere – industrialization, monetization and production to satisfy material needs. Sir Henry Maine, for example, saw the world moving from relationships based on status, kin networks, and joint property to one based on contract, territory and individual rights.[3] Maine's underlying image of societal evolution influenced Tonnies's formulation of *Gemeinschaft* and *Gesellschaft*, or community and society.[4] Tonnies's view of community as an organic whole continues to colour present conceptions to a significant degree, and accounts for some of the attraction community holds for many conservationists.

Most of these scholars of social change highlighted the disappearance of community and its replacement by other forms of social organization. Their theories of classification, in this sense, were also theories of evolution.[5] For Marx and Engels, Spencer and Comte, and even for Weber and Durkheim, society moved along an evolutionary path. Status, tradition, charisma and religion would increasingly give way to equality, modernity, rationality and a scientific temper. This theorization of social change automatically pits community against the market, since marketization and urbanization erode community.

Modernization theorists shared this evolutionary view. Under the strong influence of Parsonian structuralism, they characterized whole societies using the evolutionary labels of 'underdeveloped' 'developing' and 'developed'. The dichotomous pattern variables of Parsons were not only presumed to describe existing realities and directions of historical change, but also the desirability of movement in that direction.[6] Analytical categories representing discontinuous social states overshadowed the real processes of historical change.

While scholars of social change generally accepted the ongoing nature and irreversibility of change, they differed in their judgements regarding the benefits of progress and the desirability of traditional community. A strong correlation exists between those who view progress positively and community negatively: Marx, Spencer and the early Durkheim saw ongoing social changes as liberating humanity from the coercive and limiting world of the past, from the 'idiocy of rural life', that community, in part, embodied. The same is true of most modernization theorists.[7] Other scholars with less sanguine views about the benefits of progress did not abandon community altogether. Writers such as Tonnies, then later Durkheim and Dewey did not see any utopia at the end of the social changes they described. Instead of liberation from the tyranny of custom, they saw 'progress' dissolving the ties that anchor humans to their milieu, providing a sense of selfhood and belonging. Writers during this period and after made impossible searches for the community that they believe existed, fully formed, just prior to the disruptive set of social changes they experienced.

Community and Conservation

Like more general works on community, the history of community in conservation is also a history of revisionism. Images of pristine ecosystems and innocent primitives yielded over time to views of despoiling communities out of balance with nature, mostly due to the double-pronged intrusion of the state and market. A recuperative project on behalf of the indigenous and the local (community) has attempted to rescue community. But the rescue project has itself come under attack by new anthropological and historical research which suggests communities may not, after all, be as friendly to the environment. The practical and policy implications that accompany these changing images are immense.

The basic elements of earlier policy and scholarly writings about local communities and their residents are familiar. 'People' were an obstacle to efficient and 'rational' organization of resource use.[8] A convincing logic undergirded the belief that the goals of conservation and the interests of local communities were in opposition: Conservation required protection of threatened resources: wildlife, forests, pastures, fisheries, irrigation flows and drinking water. Members of local communities, however, rely on these resources for their fodder, fuelwood, water and food and thus exploit them without restraint. This schematic representation, popularized by Garrett Hardin and bolstered by several theoretical metaphors that served to (mis)guide policy, provided a persuasive explanation of how resource degradation and depletion took place.[9]

Empirical evidence about the context within which most rural communities are located helped prop up the view. The population of many rural areas in tropical countries has grown rapidly, even with outmigration to cities.[10] Demographic growth, it was argued, could only increase consumption pressures. Penetration by market forces, which linked local systems of resource use to a larger network of demand, further increased the pressure on natural resources.[11] At the same time, many believed that poorly articulated and enforced property rights arrangements provided disincentives for individuals to protect resources.

These factors implied that even if people had successfully managed resources in some harmonious past, that past was long gone. Instead, the way to effective conservation was through the heavy hand of the state or through the equally heavy, if less visible, hand of market and private property rights. Such ideas supported conservation policies that aimed to exclude locals. National parks and other protected areas are the most obvious result of this thinking. International conservation agencies backed many of these policies.[12]

While many of these beliefs persist,[13] most of the current ideas about the community's role in conservation have changed radically: communities are now the locus of conservationist thinking.[14] International agencies such as the World Bank, IDRC, SEDA, CIDA, Worldwide Fund for Nature Conservancy, The Ford Foundation, The MacArthur Foundation and USAID have all 'found' community. They direct enormous sums of money and effort toward community-based conservation and resource management programmes and policies. A flood of scholarly papers and policy-centric reports also feature community-based management (eg Perry and Dixon, 1986; Arnold, 1990; Dei, 1992; Douglass, 1992; Raju et al, 1993; Clugston and Rogers, 1995; Robinson, 1995). Exemplifying the swing toward community, a recent collection of essays on community-based conservation tells us, 'Communities down the millennia have developed elaborate rituals and practices to limit off take levels, restrict access to critical resources, and distribute harvests' (Western and Wright, 1994, p1).[15]

A host of other more specific factors have aided advocates of community-based conservation. The past several decades of planned development and top-down conservation practices have made one fact amply clear: the capacity of states to coerce their citizens into unpopular development and conservation programmes is limited. These limits are seen starkly when state actors attempt to discipline resource users.[16] Where resources such as fodder, fuelwood, fish and wildlife are intrinsic to everyday livelihood and household budgets, even well-funded coercive conservation generally fails. Faulty design, inefficient implementation and corrupt organizations have played an equally important role in the poor outcomes associated with state-centred policies. Combined with local intransigence and lack of livelihood alternatives, this mix of factors has pushed most enforced conservation projects into spectacular failures. In their review of 23 conservation and development programmes, Wells and Brandon (1992) argue that the weaknesses of state-centric policy means few options other than community-based conservation exist.[17]

Some contextual factors have also focused the attention of conservationists on community. With the spread of democratic political structures and the increasing insistence on participation,[18] unrepresentative development and conservation projects have become as unattractive as they are impractical. The increasing prominence of indigenous and ethnic claims about the stewardship role of native populations in relation to nature (Clay, 1988; Redford and Mansour, 1996) assists those who advocate a central role for community.[19] In addition, non-government organizations (NGOs) at different political levels have helped to amplify the voices of local, indigenous and community groups (Borda, 1985; Borghese, 1987; Bratton, 1989a).

The recognition of the limits of the state and the emphasis on popular participation have come roughly at the same time as new revisionist ecological research began to question the two other main planks of coercive conservation. The first was that pristine environments untouched by human hands existed until the very recent past. The second was the belief that indigenous and other local communities had been relatively isolated in the past (and therefore used their resources sustainably). Questioning these two beliefs has thrown the romantic image of the 'Ecologically Noble Savage' into disarray (Redford, 1990).[20]

Historical ecologists emphasize that environments have histories from which humans cannot be excluded. To categorize landscapes as natural or human-influenced is a false dichotomy since humans have modified ecosystems greatly for millennia. Many of the more recent studies that question the notion of 'virgin forests' received at least part of their inspiration from Darrell Posey's work on the forest islands of the Kayapo in Brazil (1984, 1985).[21] Denevan (1992) argues that most forests are, in fact, anthropogenic. An increasing number of scholars have marshalled evidence about how humans manipulate biodiversity and influence the species composition and structure of forests around them (Conklin, 1957; Alcorn, 1981; Hart and Hart, 1986; Posey and Balee, 1989; Roosevelt, 1989; Bailey and Headland, 1991; Balee, 1992, 1994; McDade, 1993; Brookfield and Padoch, 1994). The intentional clearing of central African forests for cultivation may have begun more than 5000 years ago (Clist, 1989; Phillipson, 1985). Traditional swidden agriculture, like small-scale disturbances in the forest, can enhance biodiversity (Bailey, 1990, 1996; Park, 1992; Sponsel, 1992; Yoon, 1993; Sponsel et al, 1996).[22]

Such studies undermine arguments that portray communities only as despoilers of natural resources. If humans have shaped and used their environments in sustainable ways for thousands of years, it may be possible to establish partnerships that accomplish the same results today. Indeed, as anthropologists begin to pay greater attention to the historical experiences of 'people without history' (Wolf, 1982), it has become increasingly obvious that if local communities in the past had used resources without destroying them, they had done so even as they remained in contact with other peoples. Such contacts contributed to survival and helped to conserve resources by allowing foragers, hunter-gatherers and pastoralists to get starches and other foods from farmers and traders.[23]

In addition to empirical and historical works that have helped resurrect community and local participation in conservation, a choice-theoretic foundation for the role of community in conservation has become available as well. Research from scholars of common property has shown communities to be successful and sustainable alternatives to state and private management of resources. Scholarships regarding the commons (Wade, 1987; Berkes, 1989; McCay and Acheson, 1989; Ostrom, 1990, 1992; Bromley, 1992; McKean, 1992; Peters, 1994) has highlighted the important time- and place-specific knowledge that members of local communities possess and the institutional arrangements they forge to achieve successful, local level resource management.

In light of the significant symbolic, theoretical and intellectual resources available to advocates of community, it is somewhat surprising that claims on behalf of community-based conservation often retain a rather simple quality. One such form such claims assume is that 'communities' have a long-term need for the renewable resources near which they live, and they possess more knowledge about these resources than other potential actors. They are, therefore, the best managers of resources.[24] Some refinements to this view can be found: if communities are not involved in the active management of their natural resources, they will use resources destructively (Western and Wright, 1994; Headland and Bailey, 1996; Sponsel et al, 1996). Still other work includes the notion of interests, in addition to that of needs: since it is in the interest of a community to protect its resources, it will.[25]

In its prescriptive form, this thesis of community-based conservation and resource management uses new beliefs about the suitability of communities to suggest policy recommendations. The implicit assumption behind these recommendations is that communities have incentives to use resources unsustainably when they are not involved in resource management. If communities are involved in conservation, the benefits they receive will create incentives for them to become good stewards of resources (if only the state and the market would get out of the way).[26]

This vision of community – as the centrepiece of conservation and resource management – is attractive. It permits the easy contestation of dominant narratives that favour state control or privatization of resources and their management (Li, 1996). Such positive, generalized representations of community make available 'points of leverage in ongoing processes of negotiation' (1996, pp505, 509).[27] But such representations of community ignore the critical interests and processes within communities, and between communities and other social actors. Ultimately, such representations can undermine their advocates' long-term goal of increasing the role of community in natural resource management.

What makes Community?

The vision of small, integrated communities using locally-evolved norms and rules to manage resources sustainably and equitably is powerful. But because it views community as a unified, organic whole, this vision fails to attend to differences within communities, and ignores how these differences affect resource management outcomes, local politics and strategic interactions within communities, as well as the possibility of layered alliances that can span multiple levels of politics. Attention to these details is critical if policy changes on behalf of community are to lead to outcomes that are sustainable and equitable.

Although current writings on community-based conservation assert that community is central to renewable resource management, they seldom devote much attention to analysing the concept of community, or explaining precisely how community affects outcomes.[28] Some authors refuse to elaborate on what it might mean, preferring to let readers infer its contours in the descriptions of specific cases (eg Western and Wright, 1994). Most studies in the conservation field, however, refer to a bundle of concepts related to space, size, composition, interactions, interests and objectives. Much of this literature sees community in three ways: as a spatial unit, as a social structure, and as a set of shared norms. It is on the basis of one or a combination of these three ideas that most of the advocacy for community rests. But these conceptions fail to explain the cause of these features or articulate their effect on natural resource use. They offer, therefore, a weak foundation upon which to base policy.

Community as a small spatial unit

Small size and territorial affiliation have been proxies for community since the very beginnings of writings on the subject. Tonnies, for example, saw *Gemeinschaft* as existing in villages, and characterized it by 'intimate, private, and exclusive living together' (cited in Bender, 1978, p17). Such closeness was impossible in large cities, and impractical if not impossible to achieve at a distance. Increased mobility and larger settlements that accompanied urbanization and industrialization, it was believed, weakened communal bonds naturally found in small villages. These two aspects of community – smallness (of both area and numbers of individuals) and territorial attachment – also mark many current writings on community-in-conservation. Instead of examining and drawing out the possible connections of shared space and small size with the political processes of local conservation, they tend to assume a link between the territorial conception of community and successful resource management.[29]

The popularity of this view of community can be traced, at least in part, to the fact that the renewable resources that communities use, manage and sometimes protect, are themselves usually located near territorially fixed homes and settlements. If top-down programmes to protect resources failed because of the inability of governments to exercise authority at a distance, the reasoning goes, then decentralization of authority to those social formations that are located near the resource might work better. There may be other contributing factors at work. Members of small groups, sharing the same geographical space, are more likely to interact with each other more often. Such regular, more frequent interactions can lower the costs of making collective decisions. These two aspects of community – fewer individuals and shared small spaces – may also contribute to group distinctiveness. Because of continuing interactions among members over time, territorially circumscribed communities might also be able to develop specific ways of managing the resources near which they are located. These advantages have led some policy-makers and analysts to define strictly the size of 'communities' that should be participating in community-based resource programmes.[30]

Because many small, territorially contained groups do not protect or manage resources well, and because some mobile, transitional groups manage them efficiently, important processes are at work that are not captured by spatial location alone (Agrawal, 1999). Indeed, the territorial attachment of small groups may make them *inappropriate* managers for particular resources because the geographical spread of the resource (large watersheds, forests, lakes, etc) could be larger than a small community could ever hope to control. Consequently, it becomes important to consider the negotiations and politics to which common spatial location and small size might contribute.

The bounded and stationary character of terrestrial resources such as forests and pastures does not imply a consequent ease in their allocation to particular spatial communities, eg a piece of forest or pasture for every community. Because more than one community (in the spatial sense) may be located near a given patch of forest or pasture, and because the members of each would have an interest in the resources nominally belonging to the other community, spatial bases for allocating resource management rights can prove untenable. For fugitive resources such as wildlife and fish, an added dimension of complexity might be introduced (Naughton-Treves and Sanderson, 1995). The literature on community-based conservation also often elides the thorny question of densities: does the success of a conservation practice depend on the density of individuals per hectare of land, per hectare of productive land, or per hectare of a certain natural resource (Matzke and Nabane, 1996)? Focusing on a community's shared space and small numbers alone, therefore, is necessarily incomplete and possibly misleading to analyse local level management of resources.

Community as a homogeneous social structure

Much of the rhetorical weight of community comes from papering over the differences that might prevail within actually existing communities. Indeed, the feature of community receiving the greatest attention in its construction as a social artifact is its homogeneous composition. Typically, observers assume communities to be groups of similarly endowed (in terms of assets and incomes), relatively homogeneous households who possess common characteristics in relation to ethnicity, religion, caste or language. The relationship proceeds both ways since ethnic, religious or linguistic homogeneity is often presumed to lead to community as well. Such homogeneity is assumed to further cooperative solutions, reduce hierarchical and conflictual interactions, and promote better resource management. Outside the community conflicts prevail; within, harmony reigns.[31]

The notion that a community is homogeneous meshes well with beliefs about its spatial boundaries. In the rural areas of poorer countries (the sites where most advocates of community-based resource management locate their analyses and projects) people living within the same location may indeed hold similar occupations, depend on the same resources, use the same language, and belong to the same ethnic or religious group. These similarities may facilitate regular interactions among group members.

Even if members of a group are similar in several respects, however, it is not clear at what point the label 'homogeneous' can be applied, nor is it clear that these shared characteristics are critical to conservation. Because all human groups are stratified to some extent or the other, it becomes important to analyse the degree of homogeneity and those dimensions of it that are important to resource conservation. Few studies, however, wrestle with the difficulty of operationalizing what social homogeneity might be.[32] Most studies, when they do focus on the social composition of a community rather than assume it to be homogeneous, indicate intentionally or unintentionally that within the same group (eg Masai, or pastoralist, or women), multiple axes of differentiation exist.[33] Recent studies of resource use at the local level have recognized the salience of intracommunity conflicts (Agrawal, 1994a; Gibson and Marks, 1995; Ilahaine, 1995; Madzudzo and Dzingirai, 1995; Moore, 1996a, 1996b). Yet even highly differentiated communities may be able to take steps to use local resources sustainably (eg Agrawal, 1994b). These studies show that there is no easy correspondence between social homogeneity and sustainable resource use.

Community as common interests and shared norms

The concept of community as shared norms and common interests depends strongly upon the perceptions of its members; in this sense all communities are imagined communities. This imagined sense of community attracts scholars of conservation to community. It is this notion of community that is supposed to grow out of common location, small size, homogeneous composition, and/or shared characteristics. As Ascher puts it, community exists among individuals who share '*common* interests and *common* identification ... growing out of shared characteristics' (1995, p83). Common and shared rather than individual and selfish is what makes successful resource management more likely. In a community, 'individuals give up some of their individuality to behave as a single entity to accomplish goals' (Kiss, 1990, p9).

Internalized norms of behaviour among members of communities can guide resource management outcomes in desired directions. Community as shared norms is itself an outcome of interactions and processes that take place within communities, often in relation to those perceived as outsiders. But community as shared norms also has an independent positive effect on resource use and conservation.

Shared community level norms can promote conservation in two different ways. First, norms may specifically prohibit some actions. In many villages in semi-arid western Rajasthan, for example, existing norms impede villagers from cutting *khejri* trees (*Prosopis cineraria*), especially when these trees are present in the local *oran*, a common area set aside for grazing, and often dedicated to a religious deity.[34] In the same region, the *Bishnois* have strong norms against the killing of wild animal species such as deer. Cook (1996, pp279–282) details how the Amung-me in Irian Jaya protect certain groves of trees as sacred, and a marsupial (*amat*) that plays a role in the propagation of the Pandanus trees. Mishra explains that women belonging to *Juang* and *Saora* tribal communities in Orissa follow strong norms about the timing and season for collecting non-timber forest products (1994). Other examples of 'conservationist' norms also exist.[35]

Second, it is possible that the existence of communal norms will promote cooperative decision-making within the community. If members of a community believe in shared identities and common experiences, they also may be willing to cooperate over more formal decisions to manage and conserve resources. The presence of community-level norms can facilitate resource management by preventing certain behaviours, or encouraging others (Coleman, 1990).

Although community as shared norms, especially when such norms are about the management of resources or conservation, may be the hope of conservationists, the extent to which norms aid conservation needs to be questioned.[36] At a minimum, current research indicates that conservationist norms cannot be equated with particular identities such as 'woman', or 'the indigenous'.[37] Norms, in fact, may be a significant part of the problem to a conservationist if a norm promotes exploitation (posing an enormous obstacle for those interested in community-based conservation).[38] For example, as a result of land laws in the early colonial periods of many countries in Latin America, there is a strong norm that land is only useful when cleared of trees and used for agriculture.[39] In many parts of Africa, wildlife is considered a threat to crops and human lives, not a resource to be conserved (Marks, 1984; Naughton-Treves, 1997). Further, norms cannot be taken as a set of beliefs that communities hold, never to give up. They come into being in relation to particular contextual factors, and even when codified and written do not remain static.[40] Just because some small social groups hold conservationist norms today, they will not necessarily hold them in the future.

Those who conceptualize community as shared norms may fail to recognize the difficulties this position poses for conservation. Unlike the factors of community size, composition, and links to a specific territorial space which can all be directly influenced through external intervention, community as shared understandings is probably the least amenable to such manipulation. Conservationist norms cannot be easily introduced into a community by external actors (although the current emphasis on participation and conservation by state actors means that at least the attempt is being made in many locations).[41] Indeed, we hardly know which strategies successfully alter the norms people hold about conservation, especially when the resources in question are a critical part of the family income.

Actors, Interactions and Institutions

To summarize, advocates of community-based conservation forward a conceptualization of communities as territorially fixed, small and homogeneous. These characteristics supposedly foster the interactions among members that promote desirable collective decisions. Figure 6.1 depicts the connections between different attributes of community and conservation outcomes indicated by the literature regarding community-based conservation. While certain types and levels of these characteristics might facilitate collective action, however, few studies demonstrate that this collective action is necessarily connected with conservation behaviour. Most important, few social scientists or policy makers have systematically tested these propositions in the field.

Figure 6.1 *A Conventional View of the Relationship Between Community and Conservation*

In fact, some community characteristics considered important to collective action may actually thwart conservation efforts. Small size groups may be unable to defend their resources in the face of strong external threats, or be unable to manage resources if they are spread over large areas. Strongly held norms may support exploitative behaviour, or be resistant to outside attempts at their modification.

To be more accurate in our efforts to depict communities and their relationship with their natural resources – and thus to be more relevant to policy-making – we argue greater attention be focused on three critical aspects of communities: the multiple actors with multiple interests that make up communities, the processes through which these actors interrelate, and, especially, the institutional arrangements that structure their interactions. These three proposed foci for the study of community-based conservation allow for a better understanding of the factors critical to the success or failure of efforts aimed at local-level conservation.

Multiple interests and actors

A growing number of studies that explore natural resource management at the local level do not find communities comprising just one group of individuals who possess similar endowments or goals. Instead, they find many subgroups; and within subgroups they find individuals with varying preferences for resource use and distribution. These authors bring to light the politics of the local: economic elites may vie with religious elites; chiefs may battle with their advisers; women may contest the rights of their husbands; the politically marginalized may dispute the acts of the politically dominant. Recognizing and working with the multiplicity of actors and interests is crucial for those advocating community-based programmes. Such recognition indicates that empowering local actors to use and manage their natural resources is more than the decentralization of authority over natural resources from the central government to 'a' community. The far more challenging task is to understand patterns of difference within communities.[42]

Recognizing that multiple actors exist at the local level is a useful step forward because it forces researchers to consider their different and dynamic interests.[43] A more acute understanding of community in conservation can be founded only by understanding that actors within communities seek their own interests in conservation programmes, and that these interests may change as new opportunities emerge.

Local-level processes

Within communities, individuals negotiate the use, management and conservation of resources. They attempt to implement the agreed-upon rules resulting from their negotiations. And they try to resolve disputes that arise in the processes of implementation of rules. These three types of local interactions are irreducibly influenced by the existing distribution of power and the structure of incentives within a given social group.[44] Because the exercise of power and incentive-oriented behaviour are variable over time and space, and because all groups have members who can be strategic in their behaviour, planned conservation efforts can never address all contingencies completely.

Analyses of only local-level phenomena are insufficient to explain interactions at the local level. All local interactions take place within the context of larger social forces. Attempts by governments to implement community-based conservation and specific projects of NGOs that seek to involve communities are examples of directed influence on local level conservation. Such initiatives bring into the local context those larger political forces that generated the programmes. Other pressures – changes in prices of different resources, development assistance, demographic shifts, technological innovations, institutional arrangements at different levels – also impinge on local interactions.[45]

Local interactions may also prompt responses from macro level actors. Local reactions to conservation programmes can lead to modifications in the shape of these programs. Thus, although it is convenient to talk about the community and the state, or about the local and the external, they are linked together in ways that it might be difficult to identify the precise line where local conservation begins and the external (that helps construct the local) ends.

Institutional arrangements

Institutions can be seen as sets of formal and informal rules and norms that shape interactions of humans with others and nature.[46] They constrain some activities and facilitate others; without them, social interactions would be impossible (Bates, 1989; North, 1990). Institutions promote stability of expectations *ex ante*, and consistency in actions, *ex post*. They contrast with uncertain political interactions among unequally placed actors, and unpredictable processes where performances of social actors do not follow any necessary script. Strategic actors may attempt to bypass the constraints of existing institutions, and create new institutions that match their interests. But institutions remain the primary mechanisms available to mediate, soften, attenuate, structure, mould, accentuate, and facilitate particular outcomes and actions (Ensminger, 1992; Agrawal, 1995b; Alston et al, 1996; Gibson, 1999). This holds whether change is radical, moderate or incremental.

When actors do not share goals for conserving resources and are unequally powerful, as is likely the case in most empirical situations, institutions are significant for two reasons. On the one hand, they denote some of the power relations (Foucault, 1983, pp 222, 224) that define the interactions among actors who created the institutions; on the other they also help to structure the interactions that take place around resources. Once formed, institutions exercise effects that are independent of the forces that constituted them. Institutions can change because of constant challenges to their form by the actions of individuals whose behaviour they are supposed to influence. No actual behaviour conforms precisely to a given institutional arrangement. Everyday performances of individuals around conservation goals possess the potential to reshape formal and informal institutions. Institutions can also change when explicitly renegotiated by actors. Institutions should be understood, therefore, as provisional agreements on how to accomplish tasks. Rather than setting the terms of interactions among parties with varying objectives, they help the behaviour of actors congeal along particular courses.

Authority to manage resources effectively at the local level requires the exercise of authority and control by local actors over three critical domains mentioned previously: (1) making rules about the use, management, and conservation of resources; (2) implementation of the rules that are created; and (3) resolution of disputes that arise during the interpretation and application of rules.[47]

The authority to make rules defines who has the rights to access, use and conserve resources and exclude others from carrying out these activities. It also includes the determination of the ability to transfer these above rights. The authority to implement implies the rights and the abilities to meter and monitor the use of the resource, and specify sanctions against those who violate existing rules. The authority to resolve disputes includes the rights and capacities to ensure that sanctions are followed, and adjudicate in the case of disputes.

The problem of analysing community-based conservation, thus, requires exploring a three-step process of institutional formation. At each step, two issues must be addressed: Who will exercise the authority to make the rules? and What will be the content of the rules? Typically, community-based conservation programmes devolve to local actors only the authority to implement rules created elsewhere. Government agencies generally reserve for themselves the right to create rules and to arbitrate disputes.

Institutions as Solutions

A focus on institutions, conceptualized as sets of rules describing and prescribing human actions in three related domains, leads to a substantially different focus for locally oriented conservation policies in comparison to policies that result from an acceptance of the 'mythic' community. Rather than feature the primacy of size, space or norms, an institutional approach focuses on the ability of communities to create and to enforce rules. Institutional analysis requires identifying the possibly multiple and overlapping rules, the groups and individuals affected by such rules, and the processes by which the particular sets of rules change in a given situation. In some cases, the homogeneity of a settlement's members or the norms they hold may be crucial to explaining the rules that people follow and the outcomes that their behaviour engenders. In other cases, formal and informal rules may have little to do with the conventional view of community, and an institutional analysis instead notices overlapping, multilevel and differentiated sets of rules that help explain resource outcomes.

There are substantial arguments in favor of recognizing that actors in the local space may be the more appropriate source of rule-making for a significant range of problems because of their specialized information about the local context and resources. Government agencies and bureaucracies are unlikely to be familiar with the specifics of local resource systems. Community actors and their representatives may possess far greater knowledge, as a raft of literature on 'indigenous knowledge' has begun to indicate.[48] But it is also important to ensure that local-level institutions for making rules about resource use have representatives from the multiple groups that are affected by the rules in question. Members of these groups should also have opportunities to exercise a right to remove their representatives if the performance of the representatives is unsatisfactory as deemed by those affected by rules (Ribot, 1996).

Further, vesting the authority to arbitrate disputes in distant government agencies can only increase the costs of dispute resolution. Arrangements to decide local disputes within the community by community representatives would be far more cost effective. Appeals against these decisions, and disputes involving individuals from multiple communities, could be settled in meetings attended by government officials and representatives from concerned communities in a far more cost-effective manner.

This does not eliminate the need for national or regional government involvement. Local communities often do not possess the material or political clout to fend off invasive actions by outsiders. Indeed, intracommunity conflicts themselves may need the arbitration or enforcement efforts of formal government agencies. In addition, there is almost always room for non-exploitative technical assistance from extension agents regarding management techniques.

To say that communities with assistance from state actors should possess the authority to make rules, to implement them and to resolve disputes, already specifies some of what the content of these rules should be: It should be what specific communities and their representatives decide. Such an answer to the question, one might argue, leaves very real concerns unresolved. What if communities are dominated by elites? What if they have scant interest in conservation?

To such concerns, one response may be that specifying the concrete content of rules at different stages goes against the very notion of community-based management. A second response is more realistic and more pointed. It is precisely because of the deficiencies of centralized, exclusionary policies ('Communities should protect wildlife, stop cutting trees, stop overgrazing, leave protected areas, etc') that we have now begun to talk about community-based management. The attempts to impose conservation have often failed. A focus on institutions does not necessarily lead to better outcomes (more biodiveristy, more biomass, sustainable stock levels, etc) but it does offer the tools for understanding local-level processes and outcomes better. It also offers more concrete points of intervention and design than a general reliance on community. It is important to recognize that not all local institutions can be changed in desired directions through an external intervention. Especially difficult to change would be deep-seated informal norms. Especially impotent in bringing about change would be policies that do not allow resources and authority for local-level management, enforcement and dispute resolution.

The plea to establish a partnership between the state and the community comes with two crucial qualifications. First, we must recognize that state officials and community representatives are located within asymmetric organizational structures. They enjoy access to very different levels of resources and power. For community actors to possess some leverage in their dealings with state officials, it would be imperative that they organize themselves into larger collectives or federations that can span the gap between the local and the national. Second, external forces, such as new state policies in relation to community-based conservation, can drastically change the shape of existing local institutions (eg Peluso, 1996; Agrawal and Yadama, 1997). On the other hand, introduced changes will themselves be contested in the local context, their limits tested, and their meanings transformed by the communities whose actions they are supposed to alter.

In light of the above discussion of multiple actors and interests, political processes, and institutional arrangements around conservation, a different conceptualization of the relationship between different aspects of community and resource management outcomes is possible. In contrast to Figure 6.1, the emphases of this review on multiple interests, processes, institutions, and outcomes are summarized in Figure 6.2. The figure does not present a theory of community-based conservation; rather, it summarizes

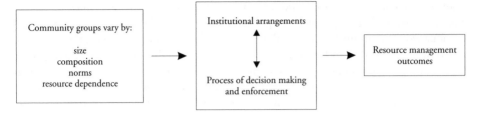

Figure 6.2 *An Alternative View of Community and Conservation*

the main thrust of this essay by indicating some of the directions in which we can seek insights about the devolution of power to actors in community-level institutions.

In Figure 6.2, community characteristics (eg size, composition, levels of dependence on the resource, prevailing norms, types of technology employed to use resources, etc) have an impact on resource management because they affect interactions of different actors around conservation. Their interactions are shaped by and simultaneously shape prevailing institutions. Viewed at any one point in time, institutions may be seen as constraints on political processes and the actions of individuals. Over time, however, they are under constant contestation and (re)formation through the performances and negotiations of actors.

Conclusion

To analyse community-based conservation, this essay began by casting a critical historical eye at the notion of community. Current works on community borrow extensively, if unconsciously, from past writings. Visions of community as an organic whole, as small and territorially fixed, as under siege and eroding, or as standing in opposition to markets and states, can be traced directly to writings from the 19th and the early 20th century. A longer-term perspective on community prompts caution before one embraces it as a general answer to conservation-related woes.

An analysis of the perceptions of community in the literature on conservation reveals strong oscillations over time in the recognition and value accorded to it. The current valorization of community should be viewed in the context of a general loss of faith in progress and future utopias. It also stems from the disillusionment of conservationists with two other gross concepts – the state and the market. In addition, revisionist historical ecological research and contributions from the scholars of the commons have also played a role in bringing community to the fore.

The celebration of community is a move in the right direction. But the implications of turning to it are little analysed in most writings on community-based conservation. The existing literature on community-based conservation reveals a widespread preoccupation with what might be called 'the mythic community': small, integrated groups using locally evolved norms to manage resources sustainably and equitably.

Such characteristics capture the realities of few, if any, existing communities. The vision of 'the mythic community' fails to attend to differences within communities. It ignores how differences affect processes around conservation, the differential access of actors within communities to various channels of influence, and the possibility of 'layered alliances' spanning multiple levels of politics. Small, territorially attached and relatively homogeneous communities, where they exist, might find it easy to make decisions collectively. They would still find it difficult, however, to withstand external threats (even from other community groups competing for access to the same resources), or manage resources that have a wide geographical spread. A focus on the shared norms of community is also incomplete because norms may not prevent overexploitation of resources, and they are scarcely amenable to change through external interventions.

We propose a shift in emphasis away from the usual assumptions about communities: small size, territorial fixity, group homogeneity and shared understandings and identities. Instead, we suggest a stronger focus on the divergent interests of multiple actors within communities, the interactions or politics through which these interests emerge and different actors interact with each other, and the institutions that influence the outcomes of political processes.

Our advocacy is for a changed emphasis for those of us who believe in locally-oriented management of resources and a move away from states and markets. Greater autonomy to local groups means that external actors would have to relinquish control over the rules and the outcomes of community-based conservation. In addition, the directions in which institutional outcomes in local spaces will unfold cannot be plotted precisely, they can only be roughly assessed. Demands for greater certainty suffer from the same utopian longings that identify 'community as shared norms' as the solution to problems of conservation.

We conclude our analysis by discussing four possible areas for new research. In the preceding text of the essay we have only hinted at each of these following four points. They require considerable more development. We state them here as issues for future work.

First, community-based conservation would more profitably be founded on principles of checks and balances among various parties – local groups, government actors, even NGOs and aid agencies – rather than faith in the regenerative capacities of any one of them. Unchecked authority for community-level decisions is likely to lead to perverse conservation outcomes.

Second, local groups are usually the least powerful among the different parties interested in conservation. Community-based conservation requires, therefore, that its advocates make more strenuous efforts to channel greater authority and power toward local groups. Only then can such groups form effective checks against arbitrary actions by governments and other actors. Critical to such attempts is the need to forge federated structures of community user groups that can negotiate with government officials and aid agencies on more equal terms than those prevailing today. Negotiations on terms of equality are foundational to hold government actors accountable.

Networked structures, bringing together the resources of several communities, are also important for other reasons. They may prove far more effective in resolving inter-community conflicts in comparison to distant, time-consuming legal mechanisms that are, in any case, biased against marginal groups. They may also be useful in addressing challenges from members of local elites to community-based conservation.

Third, those interested in community-based conservation should seek to implement reasonable processes of decision-making rather than focus upon guarantees about outcomes. 'Reasonable' implies that (1) different interests, especially those that are usually marginal, are represented in decision-making, (2) mechanisms exist to ensure that the outcomes of current decision processes are going to form part of the data on which future decisions will be based, and (3) the performance of those who make decisions is periodically reviewed by those affected by decisions. Local representatives of communities, and those elected as officials in federated structures of community groups must themselves be accountable to their constituents if a new understanding of community-based conservation is to have any teeth. Regular and open elections in which decision-makers submit to choices made by their constituents may be indispensable to ensure such accountability. Without mechanisms of accountability, federations of community groups may become yet another channel for centralizing tendencies.

Finally, effective institutionalization of community-based conservation requires that local groups have access to adequate funds for implementing the rules they create. The sources for these funds should also be local, raised through contributions of users rather than granted by central governments. Over time, this would mean that government agencies not just cede their authority to make rules about conservation, but that community groups also demand control over the resources themselves.

The points outlined above do not provide a blueprint for community-based conservation. Rather, they emphasize the importance of institutions, the ubiquity of political processes, the need to institute checks to contain arbitrary exercise of power, and the impossibility of escape from an uncertain future.

Acknowledgements

We would like to thank the following individuals for their patient and thoughtful comments on various drafts and earlier versions of this essay: Charla Britt, Walter Coward, Sabine Engel, Julie Greenberg, Michael McGinnis, Donald Moore, Nancy Peluso, Kimberly Pfeifer, Jesse Ribot, Steven Sanderson, Suzana Sawyer, Marianne Schmink, James Scott, K. Sivaramakrishnan, and James Walker. We also wish to acknowledge insightful conversations with Elinor and Vincent Ostrom in the course of writing this paper. Presentations to audiences at the Workshop in Political Theory and Policy Analysis at Indiana University and in the department of Political Science and the School of Forestry at Yale University have helped improve the quality of arguments. Responses from members of the board of the Conservation and Development Forum also prompted rethinking on several parts of the paper. An earlier draft of this paper was written by the first author as a report for and supported by the Conservation and Development Forum, University of Florida.

References

Abrams, E, Freter, A, Rue, D and Wingard, J (1996) 'The role of deforestation in the collapse of the late classic Copan Maya state', in L E Sponsel, T N Headland and R C Bailey (eds) *Tropical Deforestation: The Human Dimension*, Columbia University Press, New York, pp55–75.

Agrawal, A (1994a) 'Rules, rule-making and rule-breaking: examining the fit between rule systems and resource use', in E Ostrom, R Gardner and J Walker (eds), *Rules, Games and Common-Pool Resources*, University of Michigan Press, Ann Arbor, pp267–282

Agrawal, A (1994b) 'I don't need it but you can't have it: politics on the commons'. *Pastoral Development Network* **36**(July), 36–55

Agrawal, A (1995a) 'Dismantling the divide between indigenous and scientific knowledge'. *Development and Change* **26**, 413–439

Agrawal, A (1995b) 'Institutions for disadvantaged groups'. Paper prepared for the Department of Policy Coordination and Sustainable Development, United Nations, New York

Agrawal, A (1996) 'The community vs the market and the state'. *Journal of Agricultural and Environmental Ethics* **9**(1): 1–15

Agrawal, A (1999) *Greener Pastures: Politics, Markets, and Community among a Migrant Pastoral People*, Duke University Press, Durham, NC

Agrawal, A and Yadama, O (1997) 'How do local institutions mediate market and population pressures on resources? Forest Panchayats in Kumaon, India'. *Development and Change* **28**(3): 435–465

Agrawal, A and Goyal, S (1998) 'Group size and collective action: forest councils of Kumaon, India'. Mimeo, Department of Political Science, Yale University, New Haven

Alcorn, J (1981) 'Huastec noncrop resource management: implications for prehistoric rain forest management'. *Human Ecology* **9**: 395–417

Alcorn, J (1993) Indigenous peoples and conservation. *Conservation Biology* **7**(2): 424–426

Almond, G A and Verba, S (1963) *The Civic Culture: Political Attitudes and Democracy in Five Nations*, Princeton University Press, Princeton

Alston, L J, Eggertsson, T and North, D C (eds) (1996) *Empirical Studies in Institutional Change*, Cambridge University Press, Cambridge, UK

Alvard, M S (1993) 'Testing the "ecologically noble savage" hypothesis: interspecific prey choice by Piro hunters of Amazonian Peru'. *Human Ecology* **21**: 355–387

Anderson, A and Posey, D (1989) 'Management of a tropical scrub savanna by the Gorotire Kayapo of Brazil'. *Advances in Economic Botany* **7**: 159–173

Anderson, D and Grove, R (eds) (1989) *Conservation in Africa: People, Policies and Practice*, Cambridge University Press, Cambridge

Arizpe, L, Stone, M P and Major, D (eds) (1994) *Population and Environment: Rethinking the Debate*, Westview, Boulder, CO

Arnold, J E M (1990) 'Social forestry and communal management in India', Social Forestry Network Paper 11b, Overseas Development Institute, London

Ascher, W (1995) *Communities and Sustainable Forestry in Developing Countries*, ICS Press, San Francisco

Bailey, R C (1990) 'Exciting opportunities in tropical rain forest: a reply to Townsend'. *American Anthropologist* **92**(3): 747–748

Bailey, R C (1996) 'Promoting biodiversity and empowering local people in central African forests', in E Sponsel, T N Headland and R C Bailey (eds) *Tropical Deforestation: The Human Dimension*, Columbia University Press, New York, pp316–341

Bailey, R C et al (1989) 'Hunting and gathering in the tropical rain forest: Is it possible?' *American Anthropologist* **91**: 59–82

Bailey, R and Headland, T (1991) 'The tropical rain forest: is it a productive environment for human foragers?' *Human Ecology* **19**(2): 261–285

Baines, G (1991) Asserting traditional rights: community conservation in the Solomon Islands. *Cultural Survival Quarterly* **15**(2): 49–51

Balee, W (1992) 'People of the fallow: a historical ecology of foraging in lowland South America', in K Redford and C Padoch *Conservation of Neotropical Forests*, Columbia University Press, New York, pp35–57

Balee, W (1994) *Footprints in the Forest: Ka'apor Ethnobotany – The Historical Ecology of Plant Utilization by an Amazonian People*, Columbia University Press, New York

Bates, R H (1983) *Essays in the Political Economy of Tropical Africa*, University of California Press, Berkeley

Bates, R H (1989) *Beyond the Miracle of the Market*, Cambridge University Press, Cambridge

Baviskar, A (1995) *In the Belly of the River: Tribal Conflicts over Development in the Narmada Valley*, Oxford University Press, Delhi

Bender, T (1978) *Community and Social Change in America*, Johns Hopkins University Press, Baltimore

Berkes, F (ed) (1989) *Common Property Resources: Ecology and Community-Based Sustainable Development*, Belhaven Press, London

Bhatt, C P (1990) 'The Chipko Andolan: forest conservation based on people's power'. *Environment and Urbanization* 2: 7–18

Black, C (1967) *The Dynamics of Modernization*, Harper, New York

Booth, J W (1994) 'On the idea of the moral economy'. *American Political Science Review* 88: 653–667

Borda, F (ed) (1985) *The Challenge of Social Change*, Sage, London

Borghese, E (1987) *Third World Development: The Role of Non-governmental Organizations*, The OECD Observer, No 145

Bratton, M (1989a) 'The Politics of government–NGO relations in Africa'. *World Development* 17(4): 569–587

Bratton, M (1989b) 'Beyond the state: civil society and associational life in Africa'. *World Politics* 41(3): 407–430

Bromley, D et al (ed) (1992) *Making the Commons Work: Theory, Practice and Policy*, Institute for Contemporary Studies, San Francisco

Brookfield, H and Padoch, C (1994) 'Appreciating agrodiversity: a look at the dynamism and diversity of indigenous farming practices'. *Environment* 36(5): 6–11, 37–45

Chambers, R (1979) 'Rural development: whose knowledge counts?' *IDS Bulletin* 10(2)

Chambers, R E and McBeth, M K (1992) 'Community encouragement: returning to the basis for community development'. *Journal of the Community Development Society* 23(2): 20–38

Chitere, O P (ed) (1994) *Community Development: Its Conceptions and Practice with Emphasis on Africa*, Gideon S Were Press, Nairobi

Clark, J (1991) *Democratizing Development: The Role of Voluntary Organizations*, Kumarian Press, West Hartford, CT

Clay, J (ed) (1988) 'Indigenous peoples and tropical forests: models of land use and management from Latin America', Report no 27, *Cultural Survival*, Cambridge, MA

Clist, N (1989) 'Archaeology in Gabon, 1886–1988'. *African Archaeological Review* 7: 59–95

Clugston, R M and Rogers T J (1995) 'Sustainable livelihoods in North America'. *Development* 3 (Sept): 60–63

Coleman, J S (1990) *Foundations of Social Theory*, Harvard University Press, Cambridge, MA

Conklin, H (1957) *Hanunoo Agriculture*, United Nations, Rome

Cook, C (1996) 'The divided island of New Guinea: people, development and deforestation', in L E Sponsel, T N Headland and R C Bailey (eds) *Tropical Deforestation: The Human Dimension*, Columbia University Press, New York, pp253–271.

Cowen, M and Shenton R (1995) 'The invention of development', in J Crush (ed) *Powers of Development*, Routledge, New York, pp27–43

Dahlman, C (1980) *The Open Field System and Beyond: A Property Rights Analysis of an Economic Institution*, Cambridge University Press, Cambridge

Dei, G J S (1992) 'A forest beyond the trees: tree cutting in rural Ghana'. *Human Ecology* 20(1): 57–88

Denevan, W M (1992) 'The pristine myth: the landscape of the Americas in 1492'. *Annals of the Association of American Geographers* 82(3): 369–385

Deutsch, K (1961) 'Social mobilization and political development'. *American Political Science Review* 53(3): 493–514

Donovan, R (1994) 'BOSCOSA: Forest Conservation and Management through Local Institutions (Costa Rica)', in D Western and R M Wright (eds) *Natural Connection: Perspectives in Community-based Conservation*, Island Press, Washington, DC, pp215–233

Dorm-Adzobu, C and Veit P G (1991) *Religious Beliefs and Environmental Protection: The Malshegu Sacred Grove in Northern Ghana*, WRI Nairobi, Kenya

Douglass, M (1992) 'The political economy of urban poverty and environmental management in Asia: access, empowerment and community based alternatives'. *Environment and Urbanization* 4(2): 9–32

Dove, M (1982) 'The myth of the "communal" long-house in rural development', in C MacAndrews and L S Chin (eds) *Too Rapid Rural Development*, Ohio State University Press, Athens, pp14–48

Eckholm, E (1976) *Losing Ground: Environmental Stress and World Food Prospects*, WW Norton & Co, New York

Edgerton, R (1992) *Sick Societies: Challenging the Myth of Primitive Harmony*, Free Press, New York

Ensminger, J (1992) *Making a Market: The Institutional Transformation of an African Society*, Cambridge University Press, Cambridge

Etzioni, A (1996) 'Positive aspects of community and the dangers of fragmentation'. *Development and Change* 27: 301–314

Fairhead, J and Leach, M (1994) 'Contested forests: modern conservation and historical land use in Guinea's Ziama Reserve'. *African Affairs* 93: 481–512

Fairhead, J and Leach, M (1996) *Misreading the African Landscape: Society and Ecology in a Forest Savannah Mosaic*, Cambridge University Press, Cambridge

Fairservis, W Jr (1975) *The Roots of Ancient India*, University of Chicago Press, Chicago

Fernandes, A (1987) 'NGOs in South Asia: peoples participation and partnership'. *World Development* 15 (Supplement): 39–49

Foucault, M (1983) 'The subject and power', in H L Dreyfus and P Rabinow (eds) *Michel Foucault: Beyond Structuralism and Hermeneutics*, University of Chicago Press, Chicago, pp208–226

Fox, R (1969) '"Professional primitives": hunters and gatherers of nuclear South Asia'. *Man in India* 49: 139–160

Geertz, C (ed) (1963) *Old Societies and New States: The Quest for Modernity in Asia and Africa*, The Free Press of Glencoe, New York

Ghai, D (1993) 'Conservation, livelihood and democracy: social dynamics of environmental change in Africa'. *Osterreichische Zeitschrift fur Soziologie* 18: 56–75

Gibson, C (1999) *Politicians and Poachers: The Political Economy of Wildlife Policy in Africa*, Cambridge University Press, Cambridge

Gibson, C and Marks, S (1995) 'Transforming rural hunters into conservationists: an assessment of community-based wildlife management programs in Africa'. *World Development* 23: 941–957

Gurung, B (1992) 'Towards sustainable development: a case in the Eastern Himalayas'. *Futures* 24: 907–916

Gusfield, J R (1978) *Community: A Critical Response*, Harper and Row, New York

Hames, R (1991) 'Wildlife conservation in tribal societies', in M L Oldfield and J B Alcom (eds) *Biodiversity: Culture, Conservation and Ecodevelopment*, Westview, Boulder, CO, pp172–199

Hart, T and Hart, J (1986) 'The ecological basis of hunter-gatherer subsistence in African rain forests: The Mbuti of eastern Zaire'. *Human Ecology* 14(1): 29–56

Hayek, F (1937) 'Economics and knowledge'. *Economica*, February, 33–54

Hill, M A and Press, A J (1994) 'Kakadu National Park: an Australian experience in comanagement', in D Western and R M Wright (eds) *Natural Connections: Perspectives in Community-based Conservation*, Island Press, Washington, DC, pp135–160

Hoban, T J and Cook, M G (1988) 'Challenge of conservation'. *Forum for Applied Research and Public Policy* 3: 100–102

Hobsbawm, E and Ranger, T (1983) *The Invention of Tradition*, Cambridge University Press, Cambridge

Huntsinger, L and McCaffrey, A (1995) 'A forest for the trees: forest management and the Yurok environment'. *American Indian Culture and Research Journal* 19: 155–192

Ilahaine, H (1995) 'Common property, ethnicity, and social exploitation in the Ziz villey, southeast Morocco'. Paper presented at the IASCP conference

Ives, J D and Messerli, B (1989) *The Himalayan Dilemma: Reconciling Development and Conservation*, Routledge, London

Jagannathan, N V (1987) *Informal Markets in Developing Countries*, Oxford University Press, Oxford

Kiss, A (ed) (1990) *Living with Wildlife: Wildlife Resource Management with Local Participation in Africa*, The World Bank, Washington DC

Kothari, R (1984) 'Environment and alternative development'. *Alternatives* 5: 427–475

Lappé, F M and Shurman, R (1989) *Taking Population Seriously*, Earthscan, London

Lerner, D (1962) *The Passing of Traditional Society: Modernizing the Middle East*, The Free Press, Glencoe

Li, T M (1996) 'Images of community: discourse and strategy in property relations'. *Development and Change* 27(3): 501–528

Lowry, A and Donahue, T P (1994) 'Parks, politics, and pluralism: the demise of national parks in Togo'. *Society and Natural Resources* 7: 321–329

Lynch, O J and Talbott, K (1995) *Balancing Acts: Community-Based Forest Management and National Law in Asia and the Pacific*, World Resources Institute, Washington, DC

Madzudzo, E and Dzingirai, Y (1995) 'A comparative study of the implications of ethnicity on CAMPFIRE in Bulilimamangwe and Binga'. Centre for Applied Social Sciences Working Paper, University of Zimbabwe, Harare, Zimbabwe

Maine, H (1871) Village Communities in the East and the West

Maine, H (1905) *Ancient Law*, Murray, London

Marks, S (1984) *The Imperial Lion: Human Dimensions of Wildlife Management in Central Africa*, Westview Press, Boulder, CO

Matowanyika, J Z Z (1989) 'Cast out of Eden: peasants vs wildlife policy in savanna Africa'. *Alternatives* 16(1): 30–35

Matzke, G E and Nabane, N (1996) 'Outcomes of a community controlled wildlife program in a Zambezi valley community'. *Human Ecology* 24(1): 65–85

McCay, B J and Acheson, J (eds) (1989) *The Question of the Commons: The Culture and Ecology of Communal Resources*, University of Arizona Press, Tucson

McDade, L (ed) (1993) *La Selva: Ecology and Natural History of a Neotropical Rainforest*, University of Chicago Press, Chicago

McKean, M (1992) 'Success on the commons: a comparative examination of institutions for common property resource management'. *Journal of Theoretical Politics* 4(3): 247–282

McNeely, J A (1996) 'Foreword', in L Sponsel, T N Headland, and R C Bailey (eds) *Tropical Deforestation: The Human Dimension*, Columbia University Press, New York, ppxix–xxi

Meffe, G, Ehrlich, A and Ehrenfeld, D (1993) 'Human population control: the missing agenda'. *Conservation Biology* 7(1): 1–3

Meilleur, B A (1996) 'Forests and Polynesian adaptations', in L E Sponsel, T N Headland and R C Bailey (eds) *Tropical Deforestation: The Human Dimension*, Columbia University Press, New York, pp76–94

Meyer, W B and Turner II, B L (eds) (1994) *Changes in Land Use and Land Cover: A Global Perspective*, Cambridge University Press, Cambridge

Moore, D (1996a) 'A river runs through it: environmental history and the politics of community in Zimbabwe's eastern highlands'. Working paper series, Center for Applied Social Sciences, University of Zimbabwe, and Program for Land and Agrarian Studies, University of Western Cape, South Africa

Moore, D (1996b) 'Marxism, culture, and political ecology: environmental struggles in Zimbabwe's Eastern Highlands', in R Peet and M Watts (eds) *Liberation Ecologies: Environment, Development, Social Movements*, Routledge, New York

Morris, B (1977) 'Tappers, trappers and the hill Pandaram (South India)'. *Anthropos* 72: 225–241

Murphree, M W (1993) *Communities as Resource Management Institutions*, International Institute for Environment and Development, London

Myers, N (1991) 'The world's forests and human populations: the environmental interconnections', in K Davis and M Bernstam (eds) *Resources, Environment, and Population: Present Knowledge, Future Options*, Oxford University Press, New York, pp237–251

Naughton-Treves, L (1997) 'Wildlife versus farmers: vulnerable places and people around Kibale National Park, Uganda'. *Geographical Review* 87(1): 462–488

Naughton-Treves, L and Sanderson S (1995) 'Property, politics and wildlife conservation'. *World Development* 23(8): 1265–1275

Newmark, W D (1995) 'Extinction of mammal population in western North American national parks'. *Conservation Biology* 9(3): 512–526

Newmark, W D (1996) 'Insularization of Tanzanian parks and the local extinction of large mammals'. *Conservation Biology* 10(6): 1549–1556

Nikijuluw, V (1994) 'Indigenous fisheries resource management in the Maluku Islands'. *Indigenous Knowledge and Development Monitor* 2(2)

North, D (1990) *Institutions, Institutional Change, and Economic Performance*, Cambridge University Press, Cambridge

Ostrom, E (1990) *Governing the Commons: The Evolution of Institutions for Collective Action*, Cambridge University Press, Cambridge

Ostrom, E (1992) *Crafting Institutions for Self-Governing Irrigation Systems*, Institute for Contemporary Studies Press, San Francisco

Ostrom, E and Schlager, E (1995) 'The formation of property rights', in S Hanna, C Folke and K Maler (eds) *Rights to Nature*, Island Press, Washington, DC

Ostrom, E E, Schroeder, L and Wynne, S (1993) *Institutional Incentives and Sustainable Development: Infrastructure Policies in Perspective*, Westview Press, Boulder, CO

Park, C (1992) *Tropical Rainforests*, Routledge, New York

Parker, E (1993) 'Fact and fiction in Amazonia: the case of the Apete'. *American Anthropologist* 95: 715–723

Parker, H (1909) *Ancient Ceylon: An Account of the Aborigines and a Part of the Early Civilization*, Luzac, London

Parsons, T (1951) *The Social System*, The Free Press, New York

Parsons, T (1960) 'Pattern variables revisited: a response to Robert Dubin'. *American Sociological Review* 25: 467–483

Parsons, T (1966) *Societies: Evolutionary and Comparative Perspectives*, Prentice Hall, Englewood Cliffs, NJ

Parsons, T and Shils, E (1962) *Toward a General Theory of Action*, Harper, New York

Peluso, N (1996) 'Fruit trees and family trees in an anthropogenic forest: ethics of access, property zones and environmental change in Indonesia' *Comparative Studies in Society and History* 38: 510–548

Perry, J A and Dixon, R K (1986) 'An interdisciplinary approach to community resource management: preliminary field test in Thailand'. *Journal of Developing Areas* 21(1): 31–47

Peters, P (1994) *Dividing the Commons: Politics, Policy and Culture in Botswana*, University of Virginia Press, Charlottesville

Phillipson, D (1985) *African Archaeology*, Cambridge University Press, Cambridge

Poffenberger, M (ed) (1990) *Keepers of the Forest: Land Management Alternatives in Southeast Asia*, Kumarian, West Hartford, CT

Poffenberger, M (1994) 'The resurgence of community forest management in Eastern India', in D Western and R M Wright (eds) *Natural Connections: Perspectives in Community-based Conservation*, Island Press, Washington, DC, pp53–79

Posey, D and Balee, W (eds) (1989) *Resource Management in Amazonia: Indigenous and Folk Strategies*, New York Botanical Garden, Bronx, NY

Rae, D (1981) *Equalities*, Cambridge University Press, Cambridge

Rajasekaran, B and Warren, D M (1994) 'Socioeconomic development and biodiversity conservation: the Kolli hills'. *Indigenous Knowledge and Development Monitor* 2(2)

Raju, G, Vaghela, R and Raju, M S (1993) *Development of People's Institutions for Management of Forests*, Ahmedabad, India: Viksat, Nehru Foundation for Development

Rambo, T (1985) *Primitive Polluters: Semang Impact on the Malaysian Tropical Rain Forest Ecosystem*, University of Michigan, Museum of Anthropology, Ann Arbor

Redford, K (1990) 'The ecologically noble savage'. *Cultural Survival Quarterly* 15(1): 46–48

Redford, K and Stearman, A (1993) 'On common ground: Response to Alcorn'. *Conservation Biology* 7(2): 427–428

Redford, K and Mansour, J (eds) (1996) *Traditional Peoples and Biodiversity Conservation in Large Tropical Landscapes*, The Nature Conservancy, Latin America and Caribbean Division, Arlington VA

Repetto, R and Gillis, M (1988) *Public Policies and the Misuse of Forest Resources*, Cambridge University Press, Cambridge

Ribot, J (1996) 'Participation without representation: chiefs, councils, and forestry law in the West African Sahel'. *Cultural Survival Quarterly* 20(3): 40–44

Richards, P (1985) *Indigenous Agricultural Revolution: Ecology and Food Production in West Africa*, Westview Press, Boulder, CO

Riker, W (1980) 'Implications for the disequilibrium of majority rule for the study of institutions'. *American Political Science Review* 74: 432–447

Robbins, P (1996) 'Nomadization in western Rajasthan: an institutional and economic perspective'. Mimeo

Robinson, J G and Redford, K (eds) (1991) *Neotropical Wildlife Use and Conservation*, University of Chicago Press, Chicago

Robinson, M (1995) 'Towards a new paradigm of community development'. *Community Development Journal* 30(1): 21–30

Roosevelt, A (1989) 'Resource management in Amazonia before the conquest: beyond ethnographic projection'. *Advances in Economic Botany* 7: 30–62

Saberwal, V (1996) 'You can't grow timber and goats in the same patch of forest: grazing policy formulation in Himachal Pradesh, India, 1865–1960'. Prepared for presentation at the workshop on Agrarian Environments: Resources, Representations and Rule in India, Program in Agrarian Studies, New Haven Yale University, 2–4 May, 1997

Sanderson, S (1994) 'Political-economic institutions', in W B Meyer and B L Turner II (eds) *Changes in Land Use and Land Cover: A Global Perspective*, Cambridge University Press, Cambridge, pp329–356

Schlager, E and Ostrom, E (1992) 'Property rights regimes and natural resources: a conceptual analysis'. *Land Economics* **68**(3): 249–262

Sen, A (1992) *Inequality Reexamined*, Cambridge University Press, Cambridge

Shepsle, K (1989) 'Studying institutions: some lessons from the rational choice approach'. *Journal of Theoretical Politics* **1**: 131–149

Shils, E (1962) *Political Development in the New States*, Mouton, The Hague

Simon, J (1990) *Population Matters: People, Resources, Environment and Integration*, Transaction Publishers, New Brunswick

Singleton, S and Taylor, M (1992) 'Common property, collective action and community'. *Journal of Theoretical Politics* **4**(3): 309–324

Sivaramakrishnan, K (1995) 'Colonialism and forestry in India: imagining the past in present'. *Comparative Studies in Society and History* **37**(1): 3–40

Sivaramakrishnan, K (1996) 'Forests, politics and governance in Bengal, 1794–1994, Vols 1 and 2'. PhD thesis, Yale University, New Haven, CT

Sponsel, L (1992) 'The environmental history of Amazonia: natural and human disturbances and the ecological transition', in H Steen and R Tucker (eds) *Changing Tropical Forests*, Forest History Society, Durham, NC, pp233–251

Sponsel, L E, Headland, T N and Bailey R C (eds) (1996) *Tropical Deforestation: The Human Dimension*, Columbia University Press, New York

Steadman, D (1989) 'Extinction of birds in Eastern Polynesia: a review of the record, and comparison with other island groups'. *Journal of Archaeological Science* **16**: 175–205

Taylor, M (1982) *Community, Anarchy and Liberty*, Cambridge University Press, Cambridge

Tendler, J (1975) *Inside Foreign Aid*, Johns Hopkins University Press, Baltimore

Tully, J (1994) 'Aboriginal property and western theory: recovering middle ground'. *Social Philosophy and Policy* **11**(2): 153–180

Wade, R (1987) *Village Republics: Economic Conditions for Collective Action*, Cambridge University Press, Cambridge

Warren, M (1992) 'Democratic theory and self-transformation'. *American Political Science Review* **86**(1): 8–23

Watts, M (1995) 'A new deal in emotions: theory and practice and the crisis of development', in J Crush (ed) *Power of Development*, Routledge, London, pp44–62

Wells, M and Brandon, K (1992) *People and Parks: Linking Protected Area Management with Local Communities*, The World Bank, WWF, and USAID, Washington DC

Western, D (1994) 'Ecosystem conservation and rural development', in D Western and R M Wright (eds) *Natural Connections: Perspectives in Community-based Conservation*, Island Press, Washington, DC, pp15–52

Western, D and Wright, Michael R (eds) (1994) *Natural Connections: Perspectives in Community-based Conservation*, Island Press, Washington, DC

Wilmsen, E (1989) *Land Filled with Flies: A Political Economy of the Kalahari*, University of Chicago Press, Chicago

Wisner, B (1990) 'Harvest of sustainability: recent books on environmental management'. *Journal of Development Studies* **26**: 335–341

Wolf, E (1982) *Europe and the People Without History*, University of California Press, Berkeley

Yoon, C (1993) 'Rain forests seen as shaped by human hand'. *The New York Times*, 27 July, pp C1, C10

Zerner, C (1994) 'Through a green lens: the construction of customary environmental law and community in Indonesias Maluku Islands'. *Law and Society Review* 28(5): 1079–1122

Notes

1   Throughout the article we use the terms conservation, resource use and resource management interchangeably: renewable resources such as forests, pastures, wildlife, and fish have been, are being, and will always be used by people; those who wish to conserve must incorporate use and management in their strategies (Robinson and Redford, 1994, p3).

2   The quick review that follows pays little attention to the earliest scholars of community such as the Greek philosophers. For an introduction to these writings, see Booth (1994). The ensuing discussion on community is strongly influenced by Bender (1978) and Gusfield (1978).

3   Maine (1871, 1905) was focused primarily on issues of law and political economy, including a comparative study of property in village communities. But the distinctions he drew were equally influential in understanding social changes related to urbanization and modernization.

4   We note that community and society are not exact, but only close translations of *Gemeinschaft* and *Gesellschaft*.

5   For an introduction to how classical theories of cyclical change in Europe gave way to evolutionary beliefs in progress during the 19th century, see Cowen and Shenton (1995).

6   Parsons expanded the *Gemeinschaft/Gesellschaft* dichotomy into four parallel dimensions (Bender, 1978, p21; Parsons, 1951, 1960; Parsons and Shils, 1962). These comprised: affectivity versus affective neutrality; particularism versus universalism; ascription versus achievement; and diffuseness versus specificity. Initially, Parsons included a fifth, collectivity-orientation versus self-orientation. Parsons (1966) shows his interest in applying his pattern variables to social systems.

7   Writing to address concerns about the direction of change in the newly emerging nations of the so-called Third World, these theorists argued against particularistic affiliations of kinship, religion and ethnicity. These arguments were also explicit arguments against traditional community. Lerner (1962), perhaps, provides the classic statement of the apathy, fatalism, passivity and static nature of traditional communities. But he is certainly not alone. Almond and Verba (1963), Black (1967), Deutsch (1961), Geertz (1963), and Shils (1962) wrote influential studies of modernization, forming the viewing lens for an entire generation of scholars.

8   See, for example, Eckholm (1976). Ives and Messerli (1989) present a discussion of some of the literature, especially in the Himalayan context.

9   See Ostrom (1990) for a discussion of how the metaphors of the 'Prisoners Dilemma' and the 'Logic of Collective Action' have been important in shaping understandings about the (im)possibility of cooperation.

10   Given the large literature on the negative impact of population growth on resource conservation, it is perhaps unnecessary to refer to it at length. For some general

staements, see Meffe et al, (1993) and Myers (1991) and essays in the journal *Population and Environment*. Dissenting views are available in Lappé and Shurman (1989), and Simon (1990), Arizpe et al, (1994) provide a thoughtful summary.

11 For a critical review of some of the literature on over-population and market pressures, and an emphasis on institutions in the context of resource management, see Agrawal and Yadama (1997).

12 See Ascher (1995), Fairhead and Leach (1994), and Gibson and Marks (1995) for discussions of examples and brief reviews of the relevant literature.

13 Although new beliefs have entered the picture, not all who think about the role of community in resource use have begun to subscribe to new views. The result is a complex mosaic of notions about how villages or other non-urban groups may be connected to the resources upon which they depend. The ensuing lines on community in conservation attempt to pick on the most important beliefs that depart from earlier themes.

14 An enormous outpouring of literature bears witness. See Bhatt (1990), Ghai (1993), Gurung (1992), and Lowry and Donahue (1994). See also Wisner (1990) for a review.

15 Scholars in developed countries have also argued for the importance of community in resource management. See Huntsinger and McCaffrey (1995) for a study of the state against the Yurok in the US, and Hoban and Cook (1988) for a critique of the conservation provision of the US Farm Bill of 1985 for its inadequate involvement of local communities.

16 A number of works are available that point to the inadequacies of state-centric policy in general. See, for example, Bates (1989) and Repetto and Gillis (1988).

17 Ecologists have also underscored the limits of the state in protecting resources. Even if states had the power to enforce perfectly, some ecologists argue that protected areas are often too small to maintain valued biological diversity (Newmark, 1995, 1996)

18 A number of writings have focused on the importance of participation for sustainable democratization. Many of them have also highlighted the (potential) role of NGOs in the process (Kothari, 1984; Fernandes, 1987; Bratton, 1989b; Clark, 1991; Warren, 1992). The Fall 1996 special issue of *Cultural Survival Quarterly* edited by Pauline Peters (vol 20, no 3) contains a number of useful essays on the role of participation in conservation and development.

19 Agrawal (1995a) questions the possibility of separating indigenous forms of knowledge from western or scientific forms while stressing the political significance of claims on behalf of the indigenous.

20 On the subject of the 'Ecologically Noble Savage', see also Alvard (1993).

21 Anderson and Posey (1989) present a later work on the same group of Indians. For a strong critique of Posey's work, see Parker (1993).

22 A significant body of research argues against indigenous peoples being natural conservationists (Alcorn, 1993; Edgerton, 1992; Hames, 1991; Parker, 1993; Rambo, 1985; Robinson and Redford, 1991; Redford and Stearman, 1993). But as Sponsel et al conclude after an extensive survey, there is relatively widespread agreement that values, knowledge and skills of indigenous peoples and many local communities 'can be of considerable practical value' (1996, p23).

23 See Fox (1969), Morris (1977), and Parker (1909) for early arguments highlighting contacts between local groups and 'outsiders'. Bailey et al (1989), and Wilmsen (1989) present similar arguments more recently.

24 For two examples of this view, see Lynch and Talbott (1995) and Poffenberger (1990). Often the last part of the claim is probabilistically modified, Communities likely to prove the best managers.

25 McNeely (1996, pxvii). See also the various issues of the influential Indian news magazine *Down to Earth*, published by the Center for Science and Environment, New Delhi.

26 See the various chapters in Western and Wright (1994) for an elaboration of this perspective, and Gibson and Marks (1995) for a critique.

27 Zerner's, 1994 essay on *sasi*, a highly variable body of practices linked to religious beliefs and cultural beliefs about nature in Indonesia's Maluku islands, also makes the same point (cf. Zerner, 1994). Current images of *sasi* depict it as a body of customary environmental law promoting sustainable development. *Sasi* has, thus, emerged as a site and a resource for social activists to contest an oppressive, extractive political economy. In *sasi*, the rhetoric of local environmental management can be united with culturally distinctive communities. The result is an unusually potent political metaphor. See also, Baines (1991) for a similar argument in relation to assertions on the basis of traditional rights in the Solomon Islands.

28 One exception can be found in Singleton and Taylor (1992, p315). They conceive of community as implying a set of people with some shared beliefs, stable membership, who expect to interact in the future, and whose relations are direct (unmediated), and over multiple issues. Significantly, they do not include shared space, size or social composition, a concern of many other writers, in their discussion.

29 See, for example, Donovan (1994), Hill and Press (1994), and Poffenberger (1994). The point is not that links between group size and the emergence of community are non-existent. It is, rather, that such links, if present, require substantial attention and institutionalization if they are to become a foundation for community-based conservation.

30 For example, Murphree refers to the 'optimal' size for communities (around 90 families) for revenue-sharing schemes incorporated within the CAMPFIRE wildlife programme in Zimbabwe (Murphree, 1993). See also Agrawal and Goyal (1998) for a game theoretic argument about the relationship between group size and successful collective action in the context of resource management by village residents.

31 Such difficult-to-believe notions of community, in part, become possible owing to the conventional separation of market, state and community from each other, and the erosion of community that is presumed to proceed apace when external forces impinge upon it.

32 Taylor (1982) uses anthropological and historical sources to provide an extensive survey of hierarchy and stratification within even supposedly egalitarian communities. See also Rae (1981) and Sen (1992) for related arguments about the nature and existence of inequality.

33 See Western (1994) whose study of the Amboseli National Reserve shows, even though this is not a focus of the study, the differences within the putative community

of 'Masai'. Agrawal (1999) and Robbins (1996) point to stratification within *raika* pastoralist groups who see themselves as distinct from landowners within their villages.

34 For similar proscriptions on cutting particular tree species, see Dorm-Adzobu and Veit (1991) and Matowanyika (1989).

35 See for example, Nikijuluw (1994) for a discussion of *sasi* and *Petuanang* which influence harvests of fish; and Rajasekaran and Warren (1994) for a discussion of sacred forests among the *Malaiyala Gounder* in the *Kolli* hills in India.

36 Dove demonstrates how developers, planners, academics and bureaucrats working with the *Kantu* of Kalimantan incorporated their own desires, hopes and fears into the construction of a local 'community' (Dove, 1982).

37 The history of massive deforestation that occurred even prior to industrialization, and recent empirical literature that shows wasteful practices among indigenous groups shows that 'the indigenous' cannot be identified with a conservation ethic. See Abrams et al (1996) for a review of evidence in the case of the early Mayans: Fairservis (1975) for the Harappan civilization; and Meilleur (1996) and Stendman (1989) for Polynesia.

38 Western and Wright broach this idea in their first chapter (1994). See also the discussion in Wells and Brandon (1992) who point out that sometimes communities may not be as effective as state officials in protecting resources or ensuring conservation.

39 Tully (1994) presents a clear argument about how western theories of property, which provided the justification for taking over lands from native Americans, were founded on land being used for agricultural purposes.

40 For insightful discussions of how tradition may often be only recently created but change through politicized memory into a timeless, unchanging tradition, see Hobsbawm and Ranger (1983). Related work on how the past may be constituted in the present, or exert a strong influence to shape contemporary regimes of conservation, see Saberwal (1996) and Sivaramakrishnan (1995). In various forms these points are also being made in several recent writings on community, but rarely together. For some representative works, see Anderson and Grove (1989), Baviskar (1995), Fairhead and Leach (1996), and Sivaramakrishnan (1996).

41 For example, staff from the Game Department of Northern Rhodesia had a publicity van that travelled in rural areas trying to foment values for conservation in the early 1950s. Poaching rates remained unaffected.

42 Those who have worked with community-based projects in the field recognize this multi-actor reality, and are forced to deal with complex webs of interests on a daily basis. It is curious why this reality has not found its way into those papers and studies which advocate community-based conservation. Watts (1995, p60) approvingly cites Eagleton's concern (1990, p88) about the attention to difference, as if 'we have far too little variety, few social classes, that we should strive to generate "two or three new bourgeoisies and a fresh clutch of aristocracies"'. Eagleton's worry about too many different groups is explicable, perhaps, as the worry about not being able to carry out neat Marxist or rational choice analyses.

43 See for example Agrawal (1994b, 1995b).

44 The reverse also holds true. Power is visible only when it is put in action – its workings cannot be imagined or understood outside of the trace it leaves on processes. See Foucault (1983, pp219–220).

45 Indeed, the list of the possible political-economic factors that impact upon processes at the local level can be increased several times without redundancy. See Sanderson (1994) and the other essays in Meyer and Turner (1994) that examine land use and cover change more generally.

46 See Bates (1983), Riker (1980) and Shepsle (1989). We define institutions in keeping with the large literature on the subject. But we underline that institutions in the shape of informal norms are difficult if not impossible to change in desired directions through external intervention.

47 For this conceptualization of the different domains, we have drawn upon a number of different works, even if the manner in which we state them might differ from the works we have consulted. See, especially, Agrawal (1995b, 1996), Dahlman (1980), Ostrom (1990), Ostrom and Schlager (1995), and Schlager and Ostrom (1992).

48 The local knowledge of different members in a community, also often called 'time and place information' (Hayek, 1937; Ostrom et al, 1993), may be invaluable to the success of conservation projects. The entire corpus of writings on indigenous knowledge is based precisely on this premise (Chambers, 1979; Richards, 1985). For the significance of such information and the need to incorporate local expertise, see also Jagannathan (1987) and Tendler (1975).

Section III

Analytical Approaches in Environment and Development

Introduction – Section IIIA: Tools for Analysis

Grace Carswell and Samantha Jones

A multitude of analytical tools have emerged with which to analyse human–environment interactions in the developing world, and this introduction to Section IIIA outlines three different 'tools' for analysis, while the introduction to IIIB explores three theoretical approaches. It is tools and frameworks such as these highlighted here that have helped to generate findings that challenge received wisdoms about the environment and the causes of change that are discussed elsewhere. Other tools could have been discussed (such as the environmental entitlements approach – see Ahluwalia, 1997; Leach et al, 1997) but these three were included because (1) they continue to have a lasting influence; (2) they are particularly useful for understanding environment–people interactions and (in the case of Stakeholder Analysis) speaking to critiques of environment and development interventions highlighted in this text, such as insufficient attention to power relations and differentiated interests and (3) (in the case of Sustainable Livelihoods Approaches) because they are currently in vogue and enormously influential.

Participatory Methods

Concerns about the inadequacies of conventional approaches to research in development have fuelled the development of alternative, more participatory methodologies (Cornwall et al, 1994). Participatory methods are most closely associated with Robert Chambers (see Chambers, 1994a, 1994b, 1994c, 1995, 1997). He describes Participatory Rural Appraisal (PRA) as a 'family of approaches and methods that enable local people to share, enhance and analyze their knowledge' (1994a). He contrasts RRA Rapid Rural Appraisal (RRA), which developed and spread in the 1980s and is elicited and extracted by outsiders, with PRA, which gained ground in the 1990s. PRA has drawn on a number of research methods including RRA, farming systems research, agroecosystem analysis, applied anthropology and activist participatory research and Chambers explores these and traces the move to PRA. The increased use of PRA as a research tool is paralleled by the increased role given to 'participation' in development more broadly from the mid-1980s (see Section IIB).

Much of the critique of PRA revolves around the insufficient attention given to relations of power imbued in the PRA process and the role of social relations in the differentiation of interests and knowledge (see Cornwall et al, 1994; Mosse, 1994 and 1997;

Nelson and Wright, 1995; Pottier, 1997; Cooke and Kathari, 2001). This theme also emerged strongly in the previous section (IIC). Thus many of the critiques relate to how PRA is conducted and 'theorized' (particularly in Chambers' earlier work in 1994a, 1994b, 1994c) – rather than the tools themselves. It has been argued then that with PRA often being formal and public, dominant views will tend to dominate the PRA process, that participation 'may also be the means through which existing power relations are entrenched and reproduced' (White, 1996, p6) and it can be used as a way for people in authority to 'officialize' private interests by putting on record dominant views (Mosse, 1994, p509). As a consequence, certain groups' interests and knowledge may be marginalized or excluded (see Goebel, 1998) particularly gender interests though the under-valuing of the private sphere (Mosse, 1994; Mayoux, 1995; Guijat and Shah, 1998; Kapoor, 2002). Cornwall et al (1994) give particular attention to the social processes during and following the use of these methodologies and capture well the challenges that have been raised by other authors critiquing PRA.

PRA has tended to maintain the status quo as it refrains 'for the most part from ruffling feathers and entering the messy territory of politics' (Kapoor, 2002, p115). That successful PRA lies in the voluntaristic reversal of power between the powerful and the weak, the researchers and the researched (Chambers, 1994a, 1994b, 1994c) is a major challenge to the use of PRA methods (Kapoor, 2002). Despite these critiques, PRA continues to be hugely influential as a methodology.

Stakeholder Analysis (SA)

Stakeholder Analysis (SA) is an approach which places importance on disaggregating stakeholders and recognizing their competing interests and discourses and the power relations between various groups. This type of analysis is increasingly important in natural resource management as resource claims are so often contested and are arenas for struggle. SA facilitates an appreciation of the plural interests held by, and the relationships between, stakeholder groups. While it is consistent with analyses of discourse and power, it tends be conducted for more practical reasons. It is a relatively simple tool and is frequently employed to help to assess who would be the 'winners' and 'losers' of a given proposed project to help decide among alternative proposals – although its application is potentially much broader than this. First primary (those directly affected) and then secondary stakeholders are identified. The relative importance and influence of each stakeholder group is assessed. More importantly, the various interests of each group are considered and an assessment is made of the extent to which each stakeholder group is positively or negatively affected by a proposal. If a proposal can be identified that shows outcomes that are congruent with the interests of the intended beneficiaries then such a proposal may be supported. The methodology helps to draw attention to the fact that multiple and competing interests are always present and for any intervention there will always be losers. Grimble and Chan (1995) set out the principles of SA and provide guidelines for conducting SA in different situations. They understand that SA can get to the heart of natural resource problems, ensuring the interests of the less powerful groups are met, while taking into account 'the interests of the whole range of stakeholders who can influence or be influenced by the project or policy' (p115). They also discuss the relationship between SA and participatory methods. An example of SA is provided within Brown and Rosendo's contribution to this volume.

Sustainable Livelihoods Approach (SLA)

The third tool of analysis included in this section is that of the Sustainable Livelihoods Approach (SLA), the most recent of the tools outlined here. The term 'sustainable livelihoods' (SL) was first used by World Commission on Environment and Development in 1987, and later by Chambers and Conway (1992). The concept was taken up by a team at the IDS who note that:

> A livelihood comprises the capabilities, assets (including both material and social resources) and activities required for a means of living. A livelihood is sustainable when it can cope with and recover from stresses and shocks, maintain or enhance its capabilities and assets, while not undermining the natural resource base (Scoones, 1998, p5).

The IDS team developed a framework for use in the field (Scoones, 1998; Brock, 1999; Carswell et al, 2000), the object of which was to assist in the analysis of livelihoods: it provided a 'checklist' of factors to be considered, and was particularly useful in highlighting tradeoffs between these factors. Farrington et al (this volume) note that the framework is not intended to depict reality in any specific setting. Rather it is 'an analytical structure for coming to grips with the complexity of livelihoods, understanding influences on poverty and identifying where interventions can best be made'.

The framework has been further amended (Carney, 1998; Carney and Ashley, 1999) and the approach has been adopted by a wide range of institutions and policy-makers in the development field (for example, DFID, CARE, Oxfam and UNDP) as a way of thinking about the objectives, scope and priorities for development, in order to enhance progress in poverty elimination (see Carney et al, 1999). Whilst initially used in a rural setting (Brock, 1999; Ashley, 2000; Turton, 2000; Allison and Ellis, 2001; Orr and Mwale, 2001; Farrington et al, this volume) it has also been applied to an urban context (Rouse and Ali, 2001).

There are a number of advantages of SL approaches and the use of the SL framework. The approach starts with what people have (assets or capitals) and what they do (livelihood activities), so moving attention away from what they lack, and in doing so enables strengths to be strengthened. It thus shifts the focus from 'problems, constraints and needs to perceived strengths, opportunities, coping strategies, and local initiative' (Altarelli and Carloni, 2000). SL approaches rest on core principles that stress people-centred, responsive and multilevel approaches to development (Ashley and Carney, 1999). The approach highlights the trade-offs that people make between the different assets, livelihood activities and outcomes. Using the SL framework forces development agencies to 'focus on outcomes rather than outputs' and the 'focus on synergy between different types of capital' has also been noted as 'adding value' (Altarelli and Carloni, 2000). The framework helps to promote interdisciplinary teamwork, providing a common language (see Ashley and Carney, 1999; Altarelli and Carloni, 2000). It can thus be seen as a useful analytical tool, synthesizing the perspectives of different disciplines and encouraging effective multidisciplinary teamwork. It has an explicit focus on what matters to poor people, and ensures a 'focus [that] goes beyond economic and direct impacts' (Ashley, 2000, p28).

But there are also criticisms of the SL approach – related to both the application of the framework, and the framework itself. With regards to issues of application, using the SL framework has been found to be very time consuming and there may be some difficulty in sharing such a complex tool with partners (Ashley and Carney, 1999, p31–32). Here the very strength of the tool (that it seeks to understand the complexity of people's livelihoods) makes it difficult to use (because livelihoods *are* so complex). Furthermore, and perhaps most importantly from a policy point of view, even if poor people do not live in sectors, governments are still sectoral. Thus, as Conway et al have noted 'despite its cross-sectoral aspirations, for practical reasons a sectoral department or ministry will usually take the lead, and the resulting livelihoods analysis and programme of action will tend to reflect this sectoral perspective' (2002, p2).

The framework itself has also been critiqued. While the DFID version of the framework (as outlined in Farrington et al, this volume) has some significant improvements, it has also 'lost' some of the strengths of the earlier IDS version. First, it underestimates the significance of history, for example agrarian change and power relations (Ashley and Carney, 1999; Carswell et al, 2000; Longley and Maxwell, 2003). Second, aspects of it (such as the box 'transforming structures and processes') have been found by some to be 'too broad and all-encompassing to be useful' (Ashley and Carney, 1999, p20). In the light of this lack of clarity, this component is referred to as 'Policy, Institutions and Processes (PIPs) in later versions of the framework (see DFID, Sustainable Livelihoods Guidance Sheets, Glossary p6; Longley and Maxwell, 2003). Third, despite the use of the word 'sustainable' in SL, 'relatively little attention is paid to integrating sustainability with other concerns' and the importance of *environmental* sustainability within overall livelihood sustainability is not clear' (Ashley and Carney, 1999, pp33–34).

More fundamentally the SL framework has been criticized for paying insufficient attention to issues of power. Ashley and Carney have noted that the SL framework can 'convey a somewhat cleansed, neutral approach to power issues' observing that 'this contrasts starkly with the fundamental role that power imbalances play in causing poverty' (1999, p35). A stronger integration of politics and political economy analysis in SL has also been called for (Neefjes, 1999; Longley and Maxwell, 2003). Critically, while the framework might *highlight* the influence of power imbalances (or structural causes of poverty more broadly) it does not make them any easier to change (Ashley and Carney, 1999; Turton, 2000). Work by Turton in India showed that the SL approach gave new insights into the relationship of poverty to institutions and social structures, but she notes that 'there is little evidence … that donors can influence those underlying causes of poverty rooted in power structures' (2000, p25). To conclude therefore, the SL framework cannot, in itself, provide all the answers and solve all the problems. As Neefjes points out it is 'no more than a tool that can be used for good or bad objectives' (Neefjes, 1999, p16). While it may help us to better understand the poor, it does not necessarily help us to reach them (Altarelli and Carloni, 2000). Or in the words of Turton 'a better understanding does not make the reality any easier to change' (2000, p26).

References

Ahluwalia, M (1997) 'Representing communities: the case of a community-based watershed management project in Rajasthan, India'. *IDS Bulletin* **28**(4): 23–35

Allison, E H and Ellis, F (2001) 'The livelihoods approach and management of small-scale fisheries'. *Marine Policy* **25**: 377–88

Altarelli, V and Carloni, A (2000) *Inter-agency Experiences and Lessons.* From the Forum on operationalizing Sustainable Livelihoods Approaches, Pontignano (Siena) 7–11 March 2000, www.fao.org/docrep/x7749e/x7749e00.htm

Ashley, C and Carney, D (1999) *Sustainable Livelihoods: Lessons From Early Experience,* DFID, London

Ashley, C (2000) 'Applying livelihoods approaches to NRM initiatives: experiences in Namibia and Kenya', *ODI Working Paper* **134**

Brock, K (1999) 'Implementing a sustainable livelihoods framework for policy-directed research: reflections from practice in Mali'. *IDS Working Paper* **90**

Carney, D et al (1999) 'Livelihoods approaches compared. A brief comparison of the livelihoods approaches of the livelihoods approaches of the UK Department for International Development (DFID), CARE, Oxfam and the United Nations Development Programme (UNDP)', www.livelihoods.org

Carney, D (ed) (1998) *Sustainable Rural Livelihoods: What Contribution Can We Make?* The Department for International Development, London

Carswell, G et al (2000) 'Sustainable livelihoods in southern Ethiopia'. *IDS Research Report* **44**

Chambers, R (1994a) 'The origins and practice of participatory rural appraisal'. *World Development* **22**(7): 953–969

Chambers R (1994b) 'Participatory rural appraisal (PRA): analysis of experience'. *World Development* **22**(9): 1253–68

Chambers, R (1994c) 'Participatory rural appraisal (PRA): challenges potentials and paradigm'. *World Development* **22**(10): 1437–1454

Chambers, R (1995) 'Paradigm shifts and the practice of participatory research and development', in N Nelson and S Wright (eds) *Power and Participatory Development: Theory and Practice,* Intermediate Technology, London

Chambers, R (1997) *Whose Reality Counts? Putting the First Last',* Intermediate Technology, London

Chambers, R and Conway, G (1992) 'Sustainable rural livelihoods: practical concepts for the 21st century'. *IDS Discussion Paper* **296**, Brighton, IDS

Conway, T, Moser, C, Norton, A and Farrington, J (2002) 'Rights and livelihood approaches: Exploring policy dimensions'. *ODI Natural Resources Perspectives* **78**

Cooke, B and Kathari, U (eds) (2001) *Participation: The New Tyranny?,* Zed Books, London

Cornwall, A, Guijt, I and Welbourn, A (1994) 'Acknowledging process: methodological challenges for agricultural research and extension', in I Scoones and J Thompson (eds) *Beyond Farmer First: Rural People's Knowledge, Agricultural Research and Extension Practice*, IT Publications, London

DFID (n.d.). 'Sustainable rural livelihoods analysis: guidance sheets', DFID, London, www.livelihoods.org

Goebel, A (1998) 'Process, perception and power: notes from "participatory" research in a Zimbabwean resettlement area'. *Development and Change* **29**(2): 277–305

Grillo, R and Stirrat, R L (eds) (1997) *Discourses of Development*, Berg, Oxford

Grimble, R and Chan, M-K (1995) 'Stakeholder analysis for natural resource management in developing countries: some practical guidelines for making management more participatory and effective'. *Natural Resources Forum* **19**(2): 113–124

Guijt, I and Shah, M (1998) *Myth of Community: Gender Issues in Participatory Development*, Intermediate Technology, London

Kapoor, I (2002) 'The devil's in the theory: a critical assessment of Robert Chambers' work on participatory development'. *Third World Quarterly* **23**(1): 101–118

Leach, M, Mearns, R and Scoones, I (1997) 'Challenges to community-based sustainable development: dynamics, entitlements, institutions'. *IDS Bulletin* **28**(4): 4–14

Longley, C and Maxwell, D (2003) 'Livelihoods, chronic conflict and humanitarian response: a review of current approaches'. *ODI Natural Resources Perspectives* **89**

Mayoux, L (1995) 'Beyond naivety: women, gender inequality and participatory development'. *Development and Change* **26**(2): 235–258

Mosse, D (1994) 'Authority, gender and knowledge: theoretical reflections on the practice of participatory rural appraisal'. *Development and Change* **25**(3): 497–525

Mosse, D (1997) 'The ideology and politics of community participation: tank irrigation development in colonial and contemporary Tamil Nadu', in R Grillo and R L Stirrat (eds) *Discourses of Development,* Berg, Oxford

Neefjes, K (1999) 'Oxfam GB and sustainable livelihoods: lessons from learning'. Paper presented at 1999 DfID Natural Resource Advisers Conference

Nelson, N and Wright, S (1995) *Power and Participatory Development: Theory and Practice*, Intermediate Technology, London

Orr, A and Mwale B (2001) 'Adapting to adjustment: smallholder livelihood strategies in southern Malawi'. *World Development* **29**(8): 1325–1343

Pottier, J (1997) 'Towards an ethnography of participatory appraisal and research', in R Grillo and R L Stirrat (eds) *Discourses of Development,* Berg, Oxford

Rouse, J and Ali, M (2001) *Waste Pickers in Dhaka: Key Findings and Field Notes; Using the Sustainable Livelihoods Approach,* WEDC, Loughborough

Scoones, I (1998) 'Sustainable rural livelihoods: a framework for analysis'. *IDS Working Paper* **72**

Turton, C (2000) 'Sustainable livelihoods and project design in India'. *ODI Working Paper* **127**

White, S C (1996) 'Depoliticising development: the uses and abuses of participation'. *Development in Practice* **6**(1): 6–15

7

Sustainable Livelihoods In Practice: Early Applications Of Concepts In Rural Areas

John Farrington, Diana Carney, Caroline Ashley
and Cathryn Turton

Summary

What is poverty – and how it can best be addressed – are central questions at conceptual and practical levels in international development. Increased donor commitment to tackling poverty has made the search for answers more urgent. This paper outlines a new approach to poverty alleviation – sustainable livelihoods – setting out its basic concepts and drawing lessons from early experience. The approach is being pursued by, amongst others, the UK Department for International Development (DFID). Early experience in implementing a sustainable livelihoods approach suggests that it: helps to bring together different perspectives on poverty and integrate the contributions to eliminating that poverty different skills and sectors can make, in for instance designing projects and programmes, sector analysis and monitoring; makes explicit the choices and possible trade-offs in planning and executing different development activities; helps to identify the underlying contraints to improved livelihoods and the means of overcoming these; helps to link improved micro-level understanding of poverty into policy and institutional change processes. Practical difficulties remain in: understanding how conflict over access to resources impinges on livelihood choices, and what can be done to address this; developing cost effective modes of livelihood analysis that ensure that the needs of the poorest are prioritized; identifying appropriate in-country partners, and developing collaborative approaches to understanding the complexity of poverty and integrating that understanding into a common livelihoods frame; understanding how, in practice, to handle trade-offs, for instance between local pressures (eg for increased short-term income or better infrastructure) and wider concerns about resource sustainability and national-level policy considerations.

Reprinted from *Natural Resources Perspectives*, vol 42, Farrington, J, Carney, D, Ashley, C and Turton, C, 'Sustainable Livelihoods in Practice: Early Applications of Concepts in Rural Areas', copyright © (1999) with permission from ODI.

Concepts

Recent concepts addressing poverty

Poverty has most commonly been assessed against *income* or *consumption* criteria. In this interpretation, a person is poor only if his/her income level is below the defined poverty line, or if consumption falls below a stipulated minimum.

However, when the poor themselves are asked what poverty means to them, income is only one of a range of aspects which they highlight (Chambers, 1987). Others include: a sense of insecurity or vulnerability; lack of a sense of voice vis-à-vis other members of their household, community or government; and levels of health, literacy, education, and access to assets, many of which are influenced by the scope and quality of service delivery.

Dissatisfaction with the income/consumption model gave rise to *basic needs perspectives* which go far beyond income, and include the need for basic health and education, clean water and other services which are required to prevent people from falling into poverty. More recently, poverty has been defined in terms of the absence of *basic capabilities* to meet these physical needs, but also to achieve goals of participating in the life of the community and influencing decision-taking.

A sustainable livelihoods (SL) approach draws on this improved understanding of poverty, but also on other streams of analysis, relating for instance to households, gender, governance and farming systems, bringing together relevant concepts to allow poverty to be understood more holistically.

The DFID sustainable livelihoods approach[1]

The 1997 UK Government *White Paper on International Development* committed the UK to the International Development Target of reducing by one-half the proportion of people living in extreme poverty by 2015. As one measure towards achieving this, DFID consulted widely in order to increase its understanding of the nature of poverty and how it might be addressed. One of the outcomes of this consultation was a sustainable livelihoods framework (Figure 7.1).

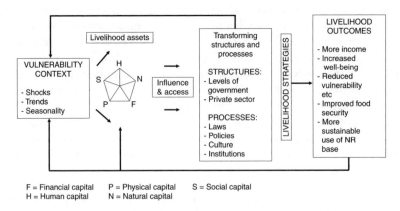

Figure 7.1 *The DFID Sustainable Livelihoods Framework*

The framework is an analytical device for improved understanding of livelihoods and poverty. The SL approach based on this framework supports poverty eradication by making enhancement of poor people's livelihoods a central goal of development efforts. In this context, a livelihood '… comprises the capabilities, assets (including both material and social resources) and activities required for a means of living. A livelihood is sustainable when it can cope with and recover from stresses and shocks, and maintain or enhance its capabilities and assets both now and in the future, while not undermining the natural resource base' (adapted from Scoones, 1998).

This paper reviews early experience in using an SL approach in practical settings. Much, but not all, of this discussion relates to DFID supported projects and programmes.

The SL framework

The livelihoods framework (Figure 7.1) is not intended to depict reality in any specific setting. It is, rather, intended as an analytical structure for coming to grips with the complexity of livelihoods, understanding influences on poverty and identifying where interventions can best be made. The assumption is that people pursue a range of livelihood outcomes (health, income, reduced vulnerability, etc) by drawing on a range of assets to pursue a variety of activities. The activities they adopt and the way they reinvest in asset-building are driven in part by their own preferences and priorities. However, they are also influenced by the types of vulnerability, including shocks (such as drought), overall trends (in, for instance, resource stocks) and seasonal variations. Options are also determined by the structures (such as the roles of government or of the private sector) and processes (such as institutional, policy and cultural factors) which people face. In aggregate, these conditions determine their access to assets and livelihood opportunities, and the way in which these can be converted into outcomes. In this way, poverty, and the opportunities to escape from it, depend on all of the above.

The framework identifies five types of capital asset which people can build up and/ or draw upon: human, natural, financial, social and physical. These assets constitute livelihood building blocks. To a limited extent they can be substituted for each other. Thus, the poor may draw on social capital such as family or neighbourhood security mechanisms at times when financial capital is in short supply.

Within this context, people are likely to pursue multiple activities and outcomes. They may, for instance, depend on their own farming, on selling their labour locally, or on migration, all within the same year. Outcomes will not be simply monetary, nor even tangible in all cases. They may include, for instance, a sense of being empowered to make wider, or clearer, choices. Generic types of livelihood outcome are given in the right-hand box of Figure 7.1.

In reality, the processes described here are not so neatly 'cut and dried': just as poverty is a dynamic process, with largely unpredictable changes in context, constraints and opportunities, so also are household strategies and activities. For instance, a household's long-term strategy may be to reduce its vulnerability to drought, and reducing rainwater run-off from farmland may be one set of activities within this strategy. However, some of the necessary labour may be diverted in response to new migration opportunities, or some of the capital needed may be diverted to respond to a medical crisis. In practice, an SL approach is therefore essentially concerned with the dynamic and, at times, iterative nature of livelihood strategies. Simple 'snapshots' of activities can be illuminating, but only against this more complex reality.

Core concepts

SL concepts are necessarily flexible in application, but are based on certain core principles, including:

A focus on people

A livelihoods approach puts people at the centre of development. This is equally important at macro-levels (eg in relation to economic reform) as it is at the micro or community level (where it may already be well embedded). This means that practical applications of SL concepts:

- start with an analysis of people's livelihoods and how these have been changing over time;
- fully involve people and support them in achieving their own livelihood goals;
- focus on the impact of different policy and institutional arrangements on people's livelihoods; and,
- seek to influence these arrangements so they promote the agenda of the poor.

Holism

SL concepts allow the identification of livelihood-related opportunities and constraints regardless of where these occur:

- it is non-sectoral and applicable across social groups;
- it recognizes multiple influences on people, and seeks to understand the relationships between these influences;
- it recognizes multiple actors (from the private sector to national ministries, from community-based organizations to newly emerging decentralized government bodies);
- it acknowledges the multiple livelihood strategies that people adopt to secure their livelihoods;
- it seeks to achieve multiple livelihood outcomes, to be determined and negotiated by people themselves.

As with Integrated Rural Development Programmes of the 1960s and 1970s, ideas on where external interventions can best be made are formed holistically. But by contrast, the *implementation* of these need not be multisectoral: SL approaches recognise that support can best be initiated in response to particular opportunities or needs, even within sub-sectors or within small areas, and then gradually expanded. Examples in the section headed 'Recent experience' highlight the importance of sequencing, but this does not imply that expansion must be linear.

Macro–micro links

People's assets and aspirations form one pillar of an SL approach, and efforts to gather information on these – for instance, through participatory poverty assessments – are necessarily micro in orientation. However, many factors that affect livelihoods have distinctly macro-characteristics.

For instance, natural capital may be threatened by flash-flooding, which will be influenced by the design and implementation of policies to prevent deforestation further upstream; access to financial capital will be influenced by policies towards credit and the rural banking sector more generally; vulnerability may increase or decrease depending on, for instance, on how well emergency feeding and employment schemes are designed and implemented. A thorough SL analysis seeks to understand what such policies are, why they operate well or poorly in practice, and then to identify how the structures and processes through which they function can be improved.

Sustainability and trade-offs

There is a long tradition of considering sustainability narrowly within the context of natural resource management. This is reflected in the International Development Targets, which maintain that preservation or replenishment of natural resources should be the aim. A wider view is that sustainability is achieved when overall stocks of physical capital (in whatever combination) are maintained. This can allow, for instance, for losses in biodiversity as modern crop varieties are introduced.

In a yet broader view, sustainability relates not just to natural resources, nor to stocks of physical capital. For specific activities to be maintained, the institutions underpinning them – whether traditional, governmental or commercial – need to be sustained. This would imply, for instance, that state subsidies or any other intervention in response to market failure should be sustainable. But even this does not fully capture 'sustainability' for, as we have argued, portfolios of activities shift in response to people's capacity to generate new activities in response to needs and opportunities. This *capacity* depends on the vulnerability, assets, structures and processes in Figure 7.1. Individually, these will wax and wane, but the platform that they provide *in combination* must be stable or rising if people's capacity to generate new activities is to be sustainable.

As people develop their capacity to switch among activities, they may, as argued above, substitute one type of capital for another. The feasibility or acceptability of interchanging types of capital will depend on the context in which people live (e.g. the types of shocks and trends that they are likely to face, the reliability of markets and institutions, etc). They may also face wider tensions, including those between:

- maximizing short-term income or guarding against vulnerability, and responding to concerns about longer-term environmental sustainability; and between
- the achievement of individual, household or community livelihood objectives and the desirability of not compromising livelihood opportunities open to others.

The SL approach recognizes these trade-offs, but does not yet suggest how they might be resolved. In any event, solutions will be context-specific and much more practical experience is required before general guidelines can be defined.

Recent Experience[2]

This section does not claim to present a comprehensive overview of the numerous SL-based initiatives currently under way. Nor can it claim to cover the full range of potential strengths and weaknesses of an SL approach. Nevertheless, the examples provide insights into the different ways SL approaches can be used, and the strengths and difficulties of using it in practice. We have grouped them into five types, mainly by their use in the project/programme cycle (Box 7.1).

Box 7.1 *Recent experiences in implementing SL approaches*

Project design In western Orissa, an SL approach was used in re-thinking and broadening earlier DFLD project ideas.

Programme design In Pakistan and Zambia, DFLD used an SL approach to define the broad parameters of rural development programmes and identify appropriate entry points.

Project review and impact assessment The Africa Wildlife Foundation assessed the economic and livelihood impacts of wildlife enterprises in Kenya. This moved beyond financial analysis, and sought to understand long-term developmental impact.

Programme review A review of community-based natural resource management (CBNRM) in Namibia sought to synthesize information on livelihood strategies, how they affect people's participation in CBNRM and how CBNRM can best 'fit' with livelihoods.

Assessment of sectors – tourism and wildlife A review of varying impacts of tourism on rural livelihoods in Namibia compared people, enterprises and provinces, to identify how livelihood impacts could be enhanced. In a different project, similar analysis was conducted for wildlife enterprises.

Use in project design

As in several other cases, resource conflict was found to limit the livelihood options immediately available to the poor in the western Orissa Rural Livelihoods Project (Box 7.2). The livelihoods were less dependent on natural resources (NR) than expected, partly because the poor had such limited access to these resources. An SL approach helped to identify how to empower the poor to break existing cycles of impoverishment, by strengthening their access to capital assets, and by working at policy and institutional levels to strengthen the capacity of the public sector, local government and NGOs jointly to design and implement poverty-focused programmes. It also indicated how interventions should be sequenced.

Box 7.2 *Resource conflict: Sequencing interventions*

An early and important insight obtained via SL perspectives in Orissa was that the focus districts had moderately good natural resource (NR) endowments, and yet had levels of per capita income among the lowest in the country. This prompted assessment of the role of local moneylenders and merchants in controlling access to NR. They also controlled input and output markets, and monopolized access to external resources such as opportunities for seasonal migratory employment.

This imbalance in access opportunities made it likely that the better-off would capture the lion's share of benefits generated by any NR-based intervention, such as micro-watershed rehabilitation. An early decision in project preparation, therefore, was to prioritize opportunities to strengthen the livelihoods of the poor in areas less likely to be contested, and so enhance their capability to assert their requirements and rights in relation to the more contested areas that might subsequently be supported.

In the Orissa context, this resulted in decisions to postpone major land-based investments (which had been the initial focus of the project) and prioritise instead support for the rehabilitation of domestic water supplies, backyard vegetable production and seasonal migration.

Use in programme design

In both Pakistan and Zambia, DFID used SL approaches to design new programmes. The aim was to develop these around the central concept of rural poverty, but promote links with individual sector initiatives, as well as with wider macro-economic and social processes. In northern Zambia, a series of field visits constituted the major effort. These followed largely from an earlier proposal for a feeder road project which had been found inappropriate. Poverty assessments identified food security and access to health care as major concerns of the poor. Major constraints to alleviating poverty lay in elite domination of access to resources and in limited access by the poor to public services.

In the Pakistan case, a review of existing documents helped to identify major constraints, again rooted in power relations and the marginalization of the poor from access to virtually all capital resources, but especially land. It also provided the preliminary strategic dimensions of a programme (including support for activities outside the traditional arenas of conflict) and helped identify entry points (geographical, institutional and thematic). A subsequent scoping mission took forward these early ideas. The strengths and weaknesses of using an SL approach in programme design are summarized in Box 7.3.

It is important to recognize that design teams rarely start with a blank sheet of paper. There are generally important initiatives already on the ground; these should not be ignored. In any case, SL approaches should not be seen as an effort to fill in every part of a blank sheet. But they do encourage explicit identification of how issues not tackled within a given programme will be addressed, and by whom (an individual donor can, after all, only focus on a limited number of entry points).

Box 7.3 *Programme design in Pakistan and Zambia*

On the positive side, the SL approach:

- provided a basis for a coherent poverty-focused programme;
- helped in setting up a platform for policy linkages;
- drew in the findings of a wide range of experience from development projects and from policy (and other) research;
- provided a common goal for technical specialists to work towards in place of sectoral or disciplinary interests.

Remaining difficulties included:

- the lack of any obvious institutional partner willing to champion anti-poverty programmes;
- the pervasiveness of discrimination against the poor, making it likely that – without high-level political commitment – initiatives, even in apparently uncontested arenas, will be challenged or dominated by the better-off;
- potential tensions with those (including politicians and some aid administrators) whose preference is for discrete, new projects that have high public relations value.

Project review and impact assessment

The SL approach has been used in a Kenyan NGO project on wildlife enterprises for *monitoring and evaluation*, as distinct from *design*. This has helped to highlight less tangible livelihood issues, and identify necessary course-corrections (Box 7.4).

Many impacts on livelihoods were unquantifiable, and dependent on the subjective assessments of the individuals concerned. Nevertheless, the reviews allowed assessment of:

- the main types of positive and negative impacts – including those (eg on access to assets) that are difficult to quantify;
- how well interventions 'fit' with livelihoods and how they can be modified to fit better;
- how and why participation worked (or did not work), and why the poor at times found it difficult to participate.

Review of a programme

In Namibia, appraisals in the early 1990s of the potential for a Community-Based Natural Resource Management Programme (CBNRM) focused mainly on institution-building and the legal rights required for cash incomes to be generated. By 1997, field staff had gained insights into livelihood issues affecting, and affected by CBNRM, while agricultural staff had accumulated complementary information on agricultural strategies, through Farming Systems Research and surveys. Their insights were then drawn together to identify:

- how CBNRM activities affected the livelihoods of different stakeholders;
- how and why their interest and participation differed;

Box 7.4 *Using SL concepts for project reviews: A livelihood analysis of butterfly farming in Kenya*

An internal review of a Kenyan butterfly-farming project in 1997 asked farmers how much they earned from butterflies and from agriculture. The former was a high percentage of the latter, and the positive impacts of butterfly-farming seemed incontrovertible. The analysis of livelihood impacts in 1998 was much more finely textured, identifying improvements in income and support to household strategies of diversification, but less improvement in *security* because earnings were unpredictable and the activity is risky (more so than other local activities because the nature of risk and variation are less understood by farmers). The high level of risk explains low participation among poorer farmers. Project impacts were assessed in relation to all elements of the livelihood framework. This highlighted positive and negative affects on assets, and two other advantages: the low trade-off with other activities, and increased access of butterfly farmers to external institutions, such as the Forest Department.

- how CBNRM activities could be made more effective in supporting SL, particularly those of the poor.

For the more secure households, the main issues were how CBNRM affected their livestock herds (via predation, exclusion from grazing, and/or enhanced common property resource management) and whether they had access to new tourism jobs. For poorer households, access to small amounts of income, elephant damage to crops, and continued access to wildlife/tourism areas for harvesting plant resources were the critical issues. A large minority faced a considerable seasonal cash shortage, so even small amounts of CBNRM income (eg from a bed-night levy) could help meet food needs or school bills if timed correctly. The analysis highlighted that *minimizing* costs to livelihoods was as important as maximizing benefits.

Assessing sectors: tourism and wildlife

In Namibia, SL analysis has been used to assess the tourism sector. The approach recognizes that tourism impacts on many aspects of livelihoods, and puts these as the priority concern. By contrast, conventional analyses of tourism tend to focus on macro-economic benefits, or environmental impacts, or negative social consequences.

Fieldwork with communities combined with financial analysis led to identification of a vast array of positive and negative impacts. SL perspectives were used for pulling the results together. The findings indicate that:

- livelihood concerns vary between people and places, but go well beyond cash income, so donor/NGO strategies of maximizing local revenue through tourism are inadequate; coping with drought, access to grazing and veld foods, and maintaining local control were key issues;
- different types of tourism enterprise have quite different livelihood impacts;
- much can be done to enhance livelihood impacts of tourism; given the chance, people will adapt tourism to meet their livelihood concerns, so the important principle is

to ensure local participation in planning; for the poor an expansion of informal sales and casual labour opportunities is more important than formal sector employment;

• livelihoods approaches can be informative at the international level, where tourism analysis has been dominated by macro-economic and conservation perspectives.

Also in Namibia, the Wildlife Integration for Livelihood Diversification (WILD) project used a wide range of participatory techniques to assess how different project options affected, or were affected by people's livelihood choices.

Some Emerging Issues

Integrating SL and other approaches and methods

The SL framework cannot be used in isolation as a tool to design projects. It is essentially an integrating device, helping to form and bring together the perspectives which contribute to a people-centred SL approach. As we have argued, this approach relies on certain principles, but is in part opportunistic and context-specific, relying on integration with other approaches and methods, and with other development initiatives, as the context requires. Considerable time and skill are needed to use SL perspectives in this way. One facet of the SL framework is that it helps to indicate where existing methods and techniques should be focused, and to draw out from these the implications for the livelihoods of the poor.

In these ways, the SL framework does not replace other approaches but builds on them. Experience has demonstrated the need to use other tools. For instance, stakeholder analysis is particularly important as, in principle, livelihood analysis can apply to anyone, whether poor or not.

The review referred to in Box 7.4 drew together several techniques. Commercial analysis showed that the enterprise was not viable in the long term, but that local incomes were significant. Stakeholder analysis identified the characteristics of those included and excluded, while several participatory rural appraisal (PRA) tools and a previous household survey were used for the analysis of impacts on livelihoods.

In certain contexts, rights-based and SL perspectives are complementary. It is often relatively easy to compile a picture of issues relating to economic, political, cultural, social and civil rights and the linkages between public institutions and civil society at the central level. It is less easy to identify the specific constraints that prevent the realization of people's rights at the local level and undermine their livelihood strategies. A clear example is provided by weak rights to NR assets in the India, Pakistan and Zambia cases.

Identifying partners, and cross-sectoral work

An SL approach requires holistic, people-centred perspectives as a basis for understanding the complexity and diversity characterising the livelihood strategies of the poor. Many potential users of SL approaches come from specific disciplines and sectors. This does not make it impossible to implement SL approaches, but it does place a strong premium on the ability of multidisciplinary teams to work together. Some (usually informal) 'partnership analysis' is generally needed. The choice of partner organization or department will often depend as much on the enthusiasm and orientation of individuals as on specific mandate. In some countries, departments (such as rural development) having an appropriately broad mandate are weaker than those (such as agriculture) which are narrowly sector-based.

One of the main strengths of an SL approach identified by practitioners so far is that it facilitates cross-sectoral collaboration by providing a common framework. Several principles of the SL approach are not 'new' – as argued in the section on 'Concepts', they are lessons that have been learnt in different sectors over recent decades. The SL approach does not seek to invent these anew, but has the potential to integrate and share them across sectors.

Learning processes and working with partners

Learning processes are important to promote on at least two levels: first, the teams using the approach need an initial familiarization and learning period, where necessary devising simplified versions of the framework for local presentation. This can usefully be followed by periodic opportunities to 'take stock', examining the scope and direction of findings against the framework.

Second, funding approval marks the end of formal project preparation and, often, some slackening in the pace of learning. Inevitably, however, a 'process' approach implies that project details need to be filled in as more evidence becomes available. In the same way, changes over time in the opportunities and constraints influencing the livelihood options of the poor need to be mapped and course corrections incorporated. Concern to support district-level authorities' responsiveness to people's needs in the Zambia case led to a proposal to establish multidisciplinary Listening Teams. In the Orissa case, concerns to identify the livelihood needs of the most vulnerable, initiate social organization and capacity building, and facilitate negotiation of their resource rights led to the establishment of Livelihood Support Teams, comprising government and NGO staff, and individuals from Orissa and beyond.

Iterative approaches to project design and implementation of this kind can only work if funding agencies can cope with the demands of greater flexibility. These include potential incompatibilities with budget cycle management and logframes, and a need for largely qualitative performance indicators. Much progress is still needed in these areas.

Managing micro–macro links

Poverty elimination is not only a matter of supporting local-level initiatives in response to needs and opportunities which the poor perceive. Many facets of their situation which they may perceive as 'fixed' (such as, for instance, weak provision of health and education services) may, in fact, be amenable to change. In principle, the holistic nature of SL analysis lends itself to identification of priority areas for policy intervention or improvement. In practice, however, windows of opportunity for influencing policy may be transient, and will vary substantially from one setting to another. Those wishing to exploit opportunities for policy leverage will, therefore, have to develop location-specific tactics for doing so, informed in part by examples of success or failure from elsewhere, and by a small number of general principles (Box 7.5).

Box 7.5 *SL and policy dialogue – illustrations from India*

Policy dialogue implies a productive debate sustained over a period of time, based on a shared view of what the role of the state should ideally be, what it should be in specific contexts of market failure, and what overall priority it should attach to poverty elimination. In parallel with its support for rural livelihoods projects in India, DFID has been engaging in policy dialogue with government agencies at national, state and local levels. At central level, for instance, DFID has supported a review of the implementation of new watershed guidelines and the design of a field manual intended to strengthen a range of procedures, including monitoring and evaluation. In Orissa, a number of changes to state-level legislation concerning access to, and sale of, minor forest products are being considered. Yet other crucial areas of policy, such as that relating to NR access, remain difficult to change.

Creating change through empowerment?

A critical conclusion from those using SL approaches in India was that SL approaches may help in understanding problems, such as power relations, but they do not necessarily make them any easier to change. In other words, aspects of the intellectual coherence which the SL approach enjoys in the abstract are challenged in the real world, not least by the pervasive political marginalization of the poor and the distorted power relations which restrict their access to capital assets. The need to cope with the contested nature of resource access reinforced the perception in almost all cases that livelihoods analysis and the design of interventions needs to be part of a process of learning, reflection and course correction. For some, it raises the question of whether the needs of the poor might be met more quickly and more fully through political struggle than through dealings with the bureaucracy.

From an incrementalist perspective, it is clear that progress achievable by the poor under inegalitarian structures and processes will be severely constrained unless there is high-level commitment to increase the capacity of the poor to determine their own future, and there are procedures in place to guarantee these. Improvements of this kind have to be embedded in the fabric of society – the poor themselves need a kind of 'political capital' in order to achieve their cause. The opportunities for external agents such as donors to increase this capital may be limited. Nevertheless, even slender opportunities can bring some advantage, and the need for empowerment must underpin donors' thinking if these opportunities are not to be missed.

Measuring results

Interventions that aim to support the livelihoods of the poor are likely to be multi-faceted and in some respects geared to qualitative change. This poses particular difficulties for performance assessment.

How will we know whether livelihoods have been improved, particularly given the qualitative, subjective and often transient nature of some aspects of livelihoods? For instance, it is difficult to assess levels of, or changes in, social capital or vulnerability. The difficulty is compounded by the fact that livelihood security is a matter of *perception*, which can change easily without any change in tangible outcomes. Yet the pressures in development agencies are towards quantifiable evidence of progress – particularly in the light of the widely accepted international poverty eradication targets. Experience so far suggests that a range of PRA-type and conventional tools are needed for assessing changes in livelihoods, but that the trade-off will remain: SL approaches are more realistic in the complexity they depict, but less amenable to quantification than, for example, money-based approaches to poverty.

Conclusions

To its potential critics, an SL approach may appear excessively micro-focused, time-consuming and complex, with only limited value-adding. It does not obviate the need for existing methods and tools, and yet requires investment of time and resources to implement wider perspectives and achieve a degree of synergy among existing initiatives. It can be regarded as useful in the abstract but difficult in practice because of: the complexity of conducting livelihood analysis; the difficulty of sharing a complex tool with partners; the reality that even if poor people do not live in sectors, professional partners do, particularly those in government; the long time-frame needed to make a difference to livelihoods; and the fact that qualitative results will be very difficult to assess.

Experience reviewed here suggests that some of these are indeed limitations of the approach: compromises are needed in working with single sector partners, trade-offs between responsiveness to the needs of the poor and quantifiability of impact will remain. However, ways are being sought to: share the approach with partners, using simplified versions at the outset; to explore how to integrate SL approaches with other tools; and develop indicators. There are certainly no complete answers to these challenges yet.

However, experience to date also highlights several strengths of an SL approach. Perhaps the most positive lesson is the unanimous view from the evidence here that an SL approach does provide a useful framework for understanding the nature of poverty and how interventions can be better tailored to enhance livelihoods. Experience shows that it can be used at all stages in the planning cycle and applied to projects, programmes and sectors. It can improve the design of interventions in several ways: by identifying what information is needed for making sound decisions; identifying different livelihood interests between stakeholders (particularly poor groups) that need to be taken into account; emphasizing links between the local and policy levels; and enhancing cross-sectoral coordination.

Those long experienced in poverty analysis may argue – no doubt correctly – that, used sensitively, existing skills are adequate to achieve these benefits, since an SL approach builds on lessons already learned in other sectors. But this argument misses the point: most of those concerned with project design are accustomed to using a particular resource or sector as the point of departure, not to putting people and the issues of most concern to them at the centre of analysis, nor to drawing on best practice in other sectors. In this sense, the SL approach provides all with a common framework and reduces the prospect that any one discipline or sector will dominate. So long as it is regarded only as an 'approach' and not a panacea, it has the potential to enhance the search for poverty-focused solutions across the sectors.

References

Carney, D (ed) (1998) *Sustainable Rural Livelihoods: What Contribution Can We Make?*, DFID, London

Chambers, R (1987) 'Sustainable livelihoods, environment and development: Putting poor rural people first'. IDS Discussion Paper No 240, IDS, Brighton

Scoones, I (1998) 'Sustainable rural livelihoods: a framework for analysis'. *Working Paper 72*, IDS, Brighton

DFID (1997) *The UK White Paper on International Development – And Beyond*, DFID, London

Notes

1   This section draws on Carney, D. (ed) (1998) and DFID Sustainable Livelihoods Guidance Sheets. See www.ids.ac.uk/livelihoods.

2   This section draws on the seven cases (see Box 7.1) discussed at the ODI Workshop on 15 February 1999. For details of the presentations, see www.odi.org.uk/

Introduction – Section IIIB: Conceptual Frameworks in Environment and Development

Samantha Jones and Grace Carswell

Theoretical approaches assist in understandings of environment and development. This section concentrates on the dominant theoretical and conceptual frameworks to have informed research on environment and development, notably political ecology and poststructural political ecology. While arguably these perspectives borrow as much from the social sciences as the political sciences, it is suggested here that other theoretical frameworks in the social sciences have much to offer in this field and are as yet under-utilized. Structuration theory is discussed below and mention is made briefly of social capital (it is beyond the scope of this text to cover this in any detail but refer to Harriss and DeRenzio, 1997; Fine, 2001; Harriss, 2001 for excellent overviews and critiques). These frameworks are capable of taking on board, and indeed drawing attention to, some of the themes that have emerged throughout this text: attention to the mediating role of institutions, an analysis of power and mindfulness of social differentiation.

Political Ecology

Peet and Watts (1996, p4) describe political ecology as 'perhaps the most important line of recent social scientific thinking about environment and development'. It has certainly emerged as a dominant framework of analysis in the field since the late 1980s (see, for example, Atkinson, 1991; Bryant, 1992, 1997, 1998; Blaikie, 1995; Bryant and Bailey, 1997; Keil et al, 1998; Low and Gleeson, 1998; Escobar, 1999; Vayda and Walters, 1999; Stott and Sullivan, 2000; Forsyth, 2003). Its specific applications have been have been numerous and include global environmental problems (Adger et al, 2001); water resources (Swynegedouw, 1997); tourism (Stonich, 1998); feminism and gender relations (Schroeder, 1993; Rocheleau et al, 1996); biodiversity and forest conservation (Brown, 1998; Bates and Rudel, 2000; Armitage, 2002); agriculture and agricultural change (Park, 1993; Anderson, 1994; Jansen, 1998; Steinberg, 1998; Stonich, 1998; Neuburger, 2000; Awanyo, 2001); livelihoods (Batterbury, 2001); resource conflicts (Bassett, 1988; Moore, 1993, 1998; Gezon, 1997, 1999; Le Billon, 2000), soil conservation and environmental management (Bell and Roberts, 1991; Hershkovitz, 1993; Grossman, 1997; Warren et al, 2001).

Political ecology is regarded to have been developed in response to the more narrow perspective offered by cultural ecologists, particularly the lack of attention given to the political and social contexts of environmental change, the overemphasis on homeostatic human–environment relations and Malthusian explanations for environmental problems (Bryant, 1992, 1998). Its roots lie in radical development geography and it is an approach heavily informed by neo-Marxism. Political ecology is characterized by attention to the diversity of ecological environments; a sensitivity to the role of the state and the wider global economy in fashioning environmental change; contextual analysis of multiple scales of influence; emphasis on the diverse responses of decision-makers; and affirmation of the centrality of poverty as a cause of ecological deterioration (Bassett, 1988; Bell and Roberts, 1991; Moore, 1993; Peet and Watts, 1996). Thus the emergence of political ecology has facilitated a significant deepening of the analysis of environmental problems in the developing world, not least by combining attention to local specificity with an appreciation of the importance of the wider political and economic context in shaping decision-makers' behaviour (see Bryant, 1998, for a fuller discussion).

However, since its development in the latter part of the 1980s, it has been the target of some criticism.

- First, it has been noted that there has been no serious attempt at analysing the means by which control of and access to resources are defined, negotiated and contested within the political arenas of household, the workplace and the state (Peet and Watts, 1996).
- Second, while Blaikie and Brookfield, the pioneers of political ecology, actually defined it as encompassing 'the constantly shifting dialectic between society and land-based resources' (1987, p17), the 'Chain of Explanation' which forms a cornerstone framework in the approach, has been described as overly deterministic (Peet and Watts, 1993).
- Third, insufficient attention has been given to the underlying processes effecting change or how 'factors become causes' (Whitesell, 1994; Peet and Watts, 1996).

These points will be returned to in the following sections.

Poststructural political ecology

Poststructural political ecology is propelling political ecology in new and fruitful directions and addresses the first of these concerns, in particular, very well. Given the label of 'liberation ecology' by Peet and Watts (1996), poststructural political ecology, emphasizes power and knowledge in studies of environment and development. Two key new directions may be identified. First is the attention to 'politics of resistance' (this includes overt and covert forms of resistance, formal (NGOs) and informal institutions (new social movement and household/gender struggles)). This has been precipitated in part by the explosive growth of organizations and civic movements with an implicit critique (and alternative vision) of 'development' (Peet and Watts, 1996). This area of poststructural political ecology has been addressed in section IIB of this text.

The second new direction involves a questioning of the positivist and realist epistemologies that have governed ideas about the generation of knowledge, particularly through the practice of science. Poststructural perspectives do not uphold the view that people, even through the practice of science, are able to know nature exactly as it is. Knowledge is not regarded to mirror nature but is considered to consist of socially produced discourses, constructed through economic, political and cultural processes. A discourse refers 'not only to observable linguistic activities, but also to the world of human signs, symbols, activities, texts, etc which together comprise a particular worldview' (Macnaghten, 1993, p54). Discourses are often competing among those with differing interests and as such there exists a plurality of perceptions and definitions about environmental problems and resource management among different stakeholders. Poststructuralists tend to employ discourse analysis and deconstruction as their primary analytical tools. Attention is given, in discourse analysis, to how claims are made, contested and negotiated and how one discourse comes to prevail over others through the exercise of power, using conscious and unconscious strategies of exclusion and repression. It may also involve an exploration of the consequences of these constructions (Macnaghten, 1993). Deconstruction is a technique for analysing texts to tease out the incoherencies, limits and unintentioned effects, unspoken or unformulated presuppositions, gaps and supplements and subtle internal self-contradictions (Cloke et al, 1992 citing Poole, 1988). In recent political ecology writings a notable shift is evident towards deconstructing environmental narratives and/or examining power relations and resource struggles (Stonich, 1998; Adger et al, 2001; Awanyo, 2001; Armitage, 2002).

In the field of environment and development, colonial and scientific discourses have been a key target for poststructural analyses. Studies have attempted to destabilize dominant (hegemonic) discourses by uncovering erroneous assumptions and recovering the alternative discourses of protest and resistance or the voices of colonized peoples. Concepts of ecology, processes of land degradation and scientific forest management practices have come under particular scrutiny, as conventional wisdoms are challenged (see Section I of this text and Zimmerer, 1991, 1994; Pouchepadass, 1995; Jones, 1996; Jeffery, 1998; Robbins, 1998; Sioh, 1998). In this area of literature an intersection with the sociology of scientific knowledge and social constructionism (in particular the social construction of nature) is apparent (eg Robbins, 1998). It is a common perception that taking on board a social constructionist perspective creates potential problems for asserting remedial environmental action as the 'reality' of the environment and/or environmental problems is questioned. This however is known as the 'epistemic fallacy' (see Jones, 2000a for further explanation). As Escobar (this volume) and Macnaghten (1993) note, suggesting that the environment, or environmental problems, are socially constructed is entirely different from suggesting that 'there is no real nature out there' or that environmental problems are not real. Jones (2002a) discusses this further with respect to different levels of social constructionism and a philosophical stance is suggested which is not incompatible with calls for remedial action. Less obvious epistemological tensions exist around the deconstruction of western discursive formations of development as they are based on claims that are normative ('what should be') rather than positive ('what is').

Understanding the social construction of environment and development does not merely reveal how interests and worldviews shape discourses, it also can show how discourses shape reality. Escobar (this volume) connects the making and evolution of discourses through which nature is known, with the making and evolution of nature itself, noting that discourse is the process through which social reality inevitably comes into being. For some, he notes, there is no materiality unmediated by discourse. Through the discourses of 'sustainable development' and 'biodiversity conservation', Escobar explores the shift from the expansionist (exploitative) drive of capital *onto* nature (nature as a raw material for economic growth activities) to a deeper, more pervasive incorporation of nature *as* capital (in the form of genes of living species being a basis for profit). This latter form of capital relies on the symbolic conquest of nature (in terms of 'biodiversity reserves') and local communities (as 'stewards' of nature); it also requires the semiotic conquest of local knowledges, to the extent that 'saving nature' demands the valuation of local knowledges of sustaining nature (Escobar, this volume).

Sociological concepts, approaches and frameworks

The emergence of liberation ecology has certainly pushed forward the frontiers of political ecology, and in particular has helped to address the first critique of political ecology noted above (relating to the production and contestation of knowledges about the physical environment). However, other potentially valuable avenues from the social sciences could be better utilized to address the other two key critiques of political ecology (relating to the understanding of human–environment interactions).

One such concept is 'social capital', which relates to the 'features of social organization such as networks, norms and trust that facilitate coordination and cooperation for mutual benefit' (Putnam, 1993). It has generated much interest recently in the field of development, being considered by some as the 'missing link' in development (Grootaert, 1997 cited in Harriss, 2001, p2). As it is regarded as underpinning collective action, it has relevance to the governance of non-privately held resources, playing a role in avoiding the negative consequences of excessive exploitation or under-maintenance of assets (Narayan and Pritchett, 1999) and has been linked in the literature to common property management (Ostrom, 1994; Katz, 2000; Anderson et al, 2002). There is considerable scope for its further application in the field of environment and development (see Bebbington and Perreault, 1999 and Pretty and Ward, 2001), such as exploration of its role and significance in action to conserve or protect the environment and rural livelihoods; in the emergence of new social movements; or in community-based natural resource management projects. However, the concept shares with political ecology the critique that insufficient attention has been given to the role of power (see in particular Fine, 2001; Harriss, 2001). Perhaps a more significant concern is that it is a concept, which in trying to encompass too much, is at risk of explaining nothing (Grootaert and van Bastelaer, 2001).

Structuration theory and its operationalized actor-oriented approach also have much to offer in terms of understanding the dynamic and intricate interplay between people and their environment (Jones, this volume). In so doing, they help to highlight the inter-linkages between decision-makers and environmental and social change, and 'how factors become causes'. The environment is part of external structure that (differentially) affects actors and is continuously mediated and reshaped by internal (institutional) variables as people act as conscious agents to intervene in the world around them (Long, 1992). While debates in development sociology have drawn upon the actor-oriented approach (Long and Long, 1992), its application in the field of environment and development is still relatively undeveloped (see Biggs and Matsaert, 1999; Jones, this volume, 1997, 2002b; Cleaver, 2000 for applications in contrasting settings). The approach can provide a valuable framework for dealing with the call made by a number of contributors to this volume (Mazzucato and Niemeijer, and Agrawal and Gibson for example) for a greater emphasis to be placed on exploring the role of institutions (including the role of new social movements) in mediating human–environment interactions by linking structure and agency.

References

Adger, W M (2001) 'Advancing a political ecology of global environmental discourses'. *Development and Change* 32(4): 681–715

Anderson, C L, Locker, L and Nugent, R (2002) 'Microcredit, social capital and common pool resources'. *World Development* 30(1): 95–105

Armitage, D (2002) 'Socio-institutional dynamics and the political ecology of mangrove forest conservation in Central Sulawesi, Indonesia'. *Global Environmental Change* 12(3): 203–217

Anderson, L (1994) *The Political Ecology of the Modern Peasant – Calculation and Community*, Johns Hopkins University Press, London

Atkinson, A (1991) *Principles of Political Ecology*, Belhaven Press, London

Awanyo, L (2001) 'Labor, ecology and a failed agenda of market incentives: the political ecology of agrarian reforms in Ghana'. *Annals of the Association of American Geographers* 91(1): 92–121

Bassett, T J (1988) 'The political ecology of peasant-herder conflicts in the northern Ivory Coast'. *Annals of the Association of American Geographers* 78(3): 453–472

Bates, D and Rudel, T K (2000) 'The political ecology of conserving tropical rain forests: a cross-national analysis'. *Society and Natural Resources* 13(7): 619–634

Batterbury, S (2001) 'Landscapes of diversity: a local political ecology of livelihood diversification in SW Niger'. *Ecumene* 8(4): 437–464

Bebbington, A and Perreault, T (1999) 'Social capital, development and access to resources in highland Ecuador'. *Economic Geography* 74(4): 395–418

Bell, M and Roberts, N (1991) 'The political ecology of dambo soil and water resources in Zimbabwe'. *Transactions of the Institute of British Geographers* 16: 301–318

Biggs, S and Matsaert, H (1999) 'An actor-oriented approach for strengthening research and development in natural resource systems'. *Public Administration and Development* 19(3): 231–262

Blaikie, P (1995) 'Changing environments or changing views? A political ecology for developing countries'. *Geography* 80(3): 203–214

Blaikie, P and Brookfield, H (1987) *Land Degradation and Society*, Methuen and Co Ltd, London and NY

Brown, K (1998) 'The political ecology of biodiversity, conservation and development in Nepal's Terai: confused meanings, means and ends'. *Ecological Economics* 24(1): 73–87

Bryant, R (1992) 'Political ecology: an emerging research agenda in Third World studies'. *Political Geography* 11(1): 12–36

Bryant, R L (1997) *The Political Ecology of Forestry in Burma, 1824–1994*, Hurst, London

Bryant, R (1998) 'Power, knowledge and political ecology in the third world: a review'. *Progress in Physical Geography* 22(1): 79–94

Bryant, R and Bailey, S (1997) *Third World Political Ecology*, Routledge, London

Cleaver, F (2000) 'Moral ecological rationality, institutions and the management of common property resources'. *Development and Change* 31(2): 361–383

Cloke, P, Philo, C and Sadler, D (1991) *Approaching Human Geography: An introduction to contemporary theoretical debates*, Paul Chapman Publishing Ltd, London

Escobar, A (1999) 'Steps to an anti-essentialist political ecology'. *Current Anthropology* 40(1): 1–30

Fine, B (2001) *Social Capital vs Social Theory: Political Economy and Social Science at the Turn of the Millennium,* Routledge, London

Forsyth, T (2003) *Critical Political Ecology: The Politics of Environmental Science*, Routledge, London

Gezon, L L (1997) 'Political ecology and conflict in Ankarana, Madagascar'. *Ethnology* 36(2): 85–100

Gezon, L L (1999) 'Of shrimps and spirit possession: toward a political ecology of resource management in northern Madagascar'. *American Anthropologist* 101(1): 58–67

Grootaert, C and van Bastelaer, T (2001) 'Understanding and measuring social capital: a synthesis of findings and recommendations from the Social Capital Initiative'. *Social Capital Initiative Working Paper No 24*, World Bank, Washington DC

Grossman, L S (1997) 'Soil conservation, political ecology and technological change on St Vincent'. *Geographical Review* 87(3): 353–374

Harriss, J (2001) *Depoliticizing Development: The World Bank and Social Capital,* Left Word, New Delhi

Harriss, J and De Renzio, P (1997) "Missing link' or analytically missing?: the concept of social capital. An introductory bibliographic essay'. *Journal of International Development* 9(7): 919–937

Hershkovitz, L (1993) 'Political ecology and environmental management in the Loess Plateau, China'. *Human Ecology* 21(4): 327–353

Jansen, K (1998) *Political Ecology, Mountain Agriculture and Knowledge in Honduras*, Thela Publishers, Amsterdam

Jeffery, R (ed) (1998) *The Social Construction of India's Forests*, Centre for South Asian Studies and Manohar Publishers, Edinburgh

Jones, S J (1996) 'Degradation discourses in the Uluguru Mountains, Tanzania: evolution and influences'. *Journal of Rural Studies* 12(2): 187–199

Jones, S J (1997) 'An actor-level analysis of the constraints on sustainable land management in northern Thailand: a study from Chiang Dao District'. *South East Asia Research* 5(3): 243–267

Jones, S J (2002a) 'Social constructionism and the environment: through the quagmire'. *Global Environmental Change-Human and Policy Dimensions* 12(4): 247–251

Jones, S J (2002b) 'A framework for understanding on-farm environmental degradation and constraints to the adoption of soil conservation measures: case studies from highland Tanzania and Thailand'. *World Development* 30(9): 1607–1620

Katz, E G (2000) 'Social capital and natural capital: a comparative analysis of land tenure and natural resource management in Guatemala'. *Land Economics* 76(1): 114–132

Keil, R, Bell, D Penz, P and Fawcett, L (eds) (1998) *Political Ecology: Global and Local*, Routledge, London

Le Billon, P (2000) 'The political ecology of transition in Cambodia 1989–1999: war, peace and forest exploration'. *Development and Change* 31: 785–805

Long, N (1992) 'An actor-oriented paradigm', in N Long and A Long (eds) *Battlefields of Knowledge,* Routledge, London

Long, N and Long, A (1992) *Battlefields of Knowledge*, Routledge, London

Low, N and Gleeson, B (1998) *Justice, Society and Nature: An Exploration of Political Ecology,* Routledge, London

Macnaghten, P (1993) 'Discourses of nature: argumentation and power', in Burman E and Parker, I (eds) *Discourse Analytic Research. Repertoires and Readings of Texts in Action*, Routledge, London, pp53–71

Moore, D S (1993) 'Contesting terrain in Zimbabwe's eastern highlands: political ecology, ethnography, and peasant resource struggles'. *Economic Geography* **69**(4): 380–401

Moore, D S (1998) 'Clear waters and muddied histories: environmental history and the politics of community in Zimbabwe's eastern highlands'. *Journal of Southern African Studies* **24**(2): 377–403

Narayan, D and Pritchett, L (1999) 'Cents and sociability – household income and social capital in rural Tanzania'. *Economic Development and Cultural Change* **47**(4): 871–97

Neuburger, M (2000) 'The vulnerability of smallholders in degraded areas: the political ecology of frontier processes in Brazil'. *Geographische Zeitschrift* **88**(1): 21–35

Ostrom, E (1994) 'Constituting social capital and collective action'. *Journal of Theoretical Politics* **6**(4): 527–562

Park, T K (ed) (1993) *Risk and Tenure in Arid Lands: The Political Ecology of Development in the Senegal River Basin*, University of Arizona Press, Tuscon

Peet, R and Watts, M (1993) 'Development theory and environment in an age of market triumphalism – Introduction'. *Economic Geography* **69**(3): 227–253

Peet, R. and Watts, M. (1996) *Liberation Ecologies: Environment, Development, Social Movements*, Routledge, London

Pouchepadass, J (1995) 'Colonialism and environment in India: comparative perspective'. *Economic and Political Weekly*, 19 Aug, 2059–2067

Pretty, J and Ward, H (2001) 'Social capital and the environment'. *World Development* **29**(2): 209–27

Robbins, P (1998) 'Paper forests: imagining and deploying exogenous ecologies in arid India'. *Geoforum* **29**(1): 69–86

Rocheleau, D, Thomas-Slater, B and Wangari, E (1996) *Feminist Political Ecology*, Routledge, London

Schroeder, R A (1993) 'Shady practice: gender and the political ecology of resource stabilisation in Gambian gardens/orchards'. *Economic Geography* **69**(4): 349–365

Stott, P and Sullivan, S (2000) *Political Ecology: Science, Myth and Power*, Arnold, London

Sioh, M (1998) 'Authorizing the Malaysian rainforest: configuring space, contesting claims and conquering imaginaries'. *Ecumene* **5**(2):144–166

Steinberg, M K (1998) 'Political ecology and cultural change: impacts on swidden-fallow agroforestry among the Mopan Maya in southern Belize'. *Professional Geographer* **50**(4): 407–417

Stonich, S C (1993) *I am Destroying the Land: The Political Ecology of Poverty and Environmental Destruction in Honduras*, Westview Press, Boulder, CO.

Stonich, S C (1998) 'Political ecology of tourism'. *Annals of Tourism Research* **25**(1): 25–54

Swyngedouw, E (1997) 'Power, nature and the city: the conquest of water and the political ecology of urbanisation in Guayaquil, Ecuador: 1880–1990'. *Environment and Planning A* **29**(2): 311–332

Vayda, A P and Walters, B B (1999) 'Against political ecology'. *Human Ecology* **27**(1): 167–179

Warren A, Batterbury, S and Osbahr H (2001) 'Soil erosion in the West African Sahel: a review and an application of a "local political ecology" approach in south west Niger'. *Global Environmental Change* **11**(1): 79–95

Whitesell, T (1994) 'Some thoughts on the unresolved epistemological dilemmas confronting political ecology'. *Proceedings from the Political Ecology Workshop*, MSU, April 1994

Zimmerer, K S (1991) 'Wetland production and smallholder persistence: agricultural change in a highland Peruvian region'. *Annals of the Association of American Geographers* **81**(3): 443–463

Zimmerer, K S (1994) 'Human geography and the "new ecology" – the prospect and promise of integration'. *Annals of the Association of American Geographers* **84**(1): 108–125

8

Construction Nature: Elements for a Post-Structuralist Political Ecology

Arturo Escobar

Summary

This paper argues for the development of a poststructuralist political ecology. While political ecology studies the relationships between society and nature in contexts of power – particularly from the perspective of political economy – this study, it is proposed, must include a consideration of the discourses and practices through which nature is historically produced and known. The paper examines the complex cultural and discursive articulations between natural and social systems established by capital and technoscience, particularly through discourses of sustainable development and biodiversity conservation. The paper concludes with the implications of the analysis for imagining alternative productive rationalities in conjunction with social movements.

Introduction

This article argues for the development of a poststructuralist political ecology. This need reflects not only the growing belief that nature is socially constructed (entirely different from saying 'there is no real nature out there'); it takes a step further in insisting that the constructs of political economy and ecology – as specifically modern forms of knowledge – as well as their objects of study must be analysed discursively. It is necessary to reiterate the connection between the making and evolution of nature and the making and evolution of the discourses and practices through which nature is historically produced and known. The relationship between nature and capital has been articulated historically by different discursive regimes, including in recent times – as we see below – the discourses of sustainable development and biodiversity conservation. The argument developed here is thus a reflection on the discourses of nature from the vantage point of recent theory on the nature of discourse.

Reprinted from *Futures*, vol 28, Escobar A, 'Constructive Nature: Elements for a Post-Structuralist Political Ecology', pp 325–343, copyright © (1996), with permission from Elsevier.

From a certain poststructuralist perspective (Foucaultian and Deleuzian, in particular), there cannot be a materialist analysis which is not at the same time a discursive analysis. The poststructuralist analysis of discourse is not only a linguistic theory; it is a social theory, a theory of the production of social reality which includes the analysis of representations as social facts, inseparable from what is commonly thought of as 'material reality'. Poststructuralism focuses on the role of language in the construction of social reality; it treats language not as the reflection of 'reality' but as constitutive of it. That was the whole point, for instance, of Said's *Orientalism*. For some, there is no materiality unmediated by discourse, as there is no discourse which is unrelated to materialities.[1] Discourse, as used in this paper, is the articulation of knowledge and power, of statements and visibilities, of the visible and the expressible. Discourse is the process through which social reality inevitably comes into being.

Anthropologists have recently incorporated these insights in their analyses of systems of production and systems of signification, systems of meanings of nature and systems of use of resources, as inextricably bound.[2] This is a fruitful trend that political ecologists are beginning to emulate. Space, poverty and nature – among others – begin to be seen through the lens of a discursive materialism 'where ideas, matter, discourse, and power are intertwined in ways that virtually defy dissection'.[3] The insistence that we look at the way local cultures process the conditions of global capital and modernity[4] is another important step in this direction.

In this article, I also take as a point of departure a recent claim in political economy; this is the suggestion that capital is undergoing a significant change in form, and is entering an 'ecological phase'. No longer is nature defined and treated as an external, exploitable domain; through a new process of capitalization, effected primarily by a shift in representation, previously 'uncapitalized' aspects of nature and society become internal to capital. 'Correspondingly, the primary dynamic of capitalism changes form, from accumulation and growth feeding on an external domain, to ostensible self-management and conservation of the system of capitalized nature closed back upon itself'.[5] This transformation is perhaps most visible in discussions of rainforest biodiversity: the key to the survival of the rainforest is seen as lying in the genes of the species, the usefulness of which could be released for profit through genetic engineering and biotechnology in the production of commercially valuable products, such as pharmaceuticals. Capital thus develops a conservationist tendency, significantly different from its usual reckless, destructive form.

This proposal is a significant qualification of recent views of the dialectic of nature and capital. As has been argued, capitalist restructuring today takes place at the expense of production conditions, such as nature, the body and space. Driven by competition and cost-shifting among individual capitals/capitalists, this restructuring signifies a deepening of the encroachment of capital on nature and labour, an aggravation of the ecological crisis, and an impairment of capital's own conditions of reproduction – what James O'Connor has called 'the second contradiction'.[6] For M O'Connor, the expansionist drive of capital on to external nature implied by the second contradiction is only a tendency. A second entails a more pervasive discursive incorporation of nature as capital. This calls not for exploitative accumulation – with the concomitant impairment of production conditions – but, on the contrary, the sustainable management of the system of capitalized nature. In this view, although the two forms may coexist, the first is the prelude to the second, which appears when brute appropriation is contested by social movements. To the extent that the second entails deeper cultural domination – even the genes of live species are seen in terms of production and profitability – we are led to conclude that this second form will continue to achieve dominance in the strategies of both capital and social movements.

The present article is a contribution to the understanding of the articulations established by capital between natural and social systems. It argues that: both forms of capital – exploitative and conservationist, modern and postmodern, let us say – are necessary to capital given current conditions in the Third and First Worlds; that both – not only the second form – require complex cultural and discursive articulations; both take on different but increasingly overlapping characteristics in the Third and First Worlds, and must be studied simultaneously; both can be studied by appealing to a post-structuralist political ecology; social movements and communities are increasingly faced with the double task of building alternative productive rationalities and strategies, on the one hand, and of resisting culturally the inroads of new forms of capital and technology into the fabric of nature and culture.

This article develops a nuanced reading of the discourse of sustainable development, in order to show the mediation between nature and capital effected by this discourse, particularly in the Third World. The second part elaborates on the two forms of ecological capital; a brief example from the Pacific Coast region of Colombia is presented to show the respective rationalities and modes of operation of the two forms of capital. The article then analyses the discourses of technoscience and biotechnology through which a veritable reinvention of nature is being effected, most clearly in the most industrialized countries, but increasingly in the Third World as well. Then follows discussion of the implications of the analysis for social practice; it focuses on the possibility of building alternative productive rationalities by social movements faced with the two logics of ecological capital. The conclusion restates the case for the development of a post-structuralist political ecology as a means to ascertaining the types of knowledge that might be conducive to eco-socialist strategies.

'Sustainable Development': Death of Nature, Rise of Environment

By starting with the contemporary discourse that most forcefully seeks to articulate our relation to nature, we can 'unpack' dominant assumptions about society and nature, and the political economy that makes such assumptions possible: the discourse of 'sustainable development', launched globally in 1987 with the report of the World Commission on Environment and Development convened by the United Nations under the chair (wo)manship of Norway's former prime minister, Gro Harlem Bruntland. That report, published under the title *Our Common Future*, begins as follows:

> In the middle of the 20th century, we saw our planet from space for the first time. Historians may eventually find that this vision had a greater impact on thought than did the Copernican revolution of the 16th century, which upset the human self-image by revealing that the earth is not the center of the universe. From space, we saw a small

and fragile ball dominated not by human activity and edifice, but by a pattern of clouds, oceans, greenery, and soils. Humanity's inability to fit its doings into that pattern is changing planetary systems, fundamentally. Many such changes are accompanied by life-threatening hazards. This new reality, from which there is no escape, must be recognized – and managed.[7]

The category 'global problems', to which *Our Common Future* belongs, is of recent invention. It derives its main impetus from the ecological fervour fostered by the Club of Rome reports of the 1970s, which provided a distinctive vision of the world as a global system where all parts are inter-related, thus demanding management of planetary proportions.[8] That nature and the earth can be 'managed' is a historically novel assertion. Like the earlier scientific management of labour, the management of nature entails its capitalization, its treatment as commodity. Moreover, the sustainable development discourse purports to reconcile two old enemies – economic growth and the preservation of the environment – without any significant adjustments in the market system. This reconciliation is the result of complex discursive operations involving capital, representations of nature, management and science. In the sustainable development discourse nature is reinvented as environment so that capital, not nature and culture, may be sustained.

Seeing the earth from space was not as great a revolution as has been claimed. This vision only re-enacted the scientific gaze as it was established in clinical medicine at the end of the 18th century. The representation of the globe from space is but another chapter of the alliance which, two centuries ago, 'was forged between words and things, enabling one *to see* and *to say*'.[9] Twentieth-century space exploration belongs to the paradigm defined by the spatialization and verbalization of the pathological, effected by the scientific gaze of the 19th-century clinician. As with the gaze of the clinician at an earlier time, environmental sciences today challenge the earth to reveal its secrets to the positive gaze of scientists. This operation only ensures, however, that the degradation of the earth be redistributed, and dispersed, through the professional discourses of environmentalists, economists, geographers and politicians. The globe and its 'problems' have finally entered rational discourse. Disease is housed in nature in a new manner. In a similar vein, as the medicine of the pathological led to a medicine of the social space (the healthy biological space was also the social space dreamt of by the French revolution), so will the 'medicine of the earth' result in new constructions of the social that allows some version of nature's health to be preserved.

In the Bruntland Report, we find a reinforcing effect between epistemology and the technologies of vision. 'The instruments of visualization in multinationalist, postmodernist culture have compounded [the] meanings of disembodiment. The visualizing technologies are without apparent limit... Vision in this technological feast becomes unregulated gluttony; all seems not just mythical about the god trick of seeing everything from nowhere, but to have put the myth into ordinary practice'.[10] The Report has thus inaugurated a period of unprecedented gluttony in the history of vision and knowledge with the concomitant rise of a global ecocracy. This might sound too harsh a judgement; we should construct the argument step by step. To begin with, management is the sibling of gluttonous vision, particularly now when the world is theorized in terms of global systems. The narrative of management is linked to the visualization of the earth as a 'fragile ball'. Carrying the baton from Bruntland, *Scientific American's* September 1989 special issue on 'Managing Planet Earth' reveals the essence of the managerial attitude. At stake for these scientists (all either male academics or businessmen) is the continuation of the models of growth and development through appropriate management strategies. 'What kind of planet do we want? What kind of planet can we get?' – asks the opening article.[11] 'We' have the responsibility for managing the human use of planet earth. 'We' 'need to move peoples and nations towards sustainability' by effecting a change in values and institutions that parallel the agricultural or industrial revolutions of the past.

The question in this discourse is what new manipulations can we invent to make the most out of nature and 'resources'. But who is this 'we' who knows what is best for the world as a whole? Once again, we find the familiar figure of the (white male) western scientist-turned-manager. A full-page picture of a young Nepalese woman 'planting a tree as part of a reforestation project' is exemplary of the mindset of this 'we'. Not portrayed are the women of the Chipko movement in India, with their militancy, their radically different forms of knowledge and practice of forestry, defending their trees politically and not through carefully managed 'reforestation' projects. Instead there is a picture of an a-historical young dark woman, whose control by masculinist and colonialist sciences, as Shiva[12] has shown, is assured in the very act of representation. This regime of representation assumes that it is up to the benevolent hand of the west to save the earth; it is the fathers of the World Bank, mediated by Gro Harlem Bruntland, the matriarch-scientist and the few cosmopolitan Third Worlders who made it to the World Commission, who will reconcile 'humankind' with 'nature'. It is still the western scientist that speaks for the earth.

But can reality be 'managed'? The concepts of planning and management embody the belief that social change can be engineered and directed, produced at will. The idea that poor countries could more or less smoothly move along the path of progress through planning has always been held as an indubitable truth by development experts. Perhaps no other concept has been so insidious, no other idea gone so unchallenged, as modern planning. The narratives of planning and management, always presented as 'rational' and 'objective', are essential to developers.[13] A blindness to the role of planning in the normalization and control of the social world is also present in environmental managerialism. As they are incorporated into the world capitalist economy, even the most remote communities in the Third World are torn from their local context, redefined as 'resources' to be planned for and managed.

The rise of sustainable development is related to complex historical processes, including modifications in various practices (of assessing the viability and impact of development projects, obtaining knowledge at the local level, development assistance by NGOs); new social situations (the failure of top-down development projects, new social and ecological problems associated with that failure, new forms of protest, deficiencies that have become accentuated); and international economic and technological factors (new international divisions of labour with the concomitant globalization of ecological degradation, coupled with novel technologies that measure such degradation). What needs to be explained, however, is precisely why the response to this set of conditions has taken the form of 'sustainable development', and what important problems might be associated with it. Four aspects are involved in answering this question.

First, the emergence of the concept of 'sustainable development' is part of a broader process of the problematization of global survival, a process which induces a reworking of the relationship between nature and society. This problematization has appeared as a response to the destructive character of development, on the one hand, and the rise of environmental movements in both the north and the south, on the other, resulting in a complex process of internationalization of the environment.[14] What is problematized is not the sustainability of local cultures and realities, but rather that of the global ecosystem, the 'global' being defined according to a perception of the world shared by those who rule it. Ecosystems professionals tend to see ecological problems as the result of complex processes that transcend cultural and local contexts. The slogan 'think globally, act locally' assumes not only that problems can be defined at a global level, but also that they are equally compelling for all communities. They believe that since all people are passengers of spaceship earth, all are responsible for environmental degradation. They do not always see, in short, that there are great differences and inequities in resource problems between countries, regions, communities and classes.

Second, the sustainable development discourse is regulated by a peculiar economy of visibilities. Over the years, ecosystems analysts have discovered the 'degrading' activities of the poor, but seldom recognized that such problems were rooted in development processes that displaced indigenous communities, disrupted peoples' habitats and occupations, and forced many rural societies to increase their pressure on the environment. Now the poor are admonished not for their lack of industriousness but for their 'irrationality' and lack of environmental consciousness. Popular and scholarly texts alike come to be populated with representations of dark and poor peasant masses destroying forests and mountain sides with axes and machetes, thus shifting visibility and blame away from the large industrial polluters in north and south and the predatory way of life fostered by capitalism and development to poor peasants and 'backward' practices such as slash-and-burn agriculture.

Third, the eco-developmentalist vision expressed in the mainstream versions of sustainable development reproduces the central aspects of economism and developmentalism. The sustainable development discourse redistributes in new fields many of the concerns of classical development: basic needs, population, resources, technology, institutional cooperation, food security and industrialism are found reconfigured and reshuffled in the sustainable development discourse. The discourse upholds ecological concerns, although with a slightly altered logic. By adopting the concept of 'sustainable development', two old enemies, growth and the environment, are reconciled,[15] unfolding a new field of social intervention and control. Given the present visibility of ecological degradation, today this process necessitates an epistemological and political reconciliation of ecology and economy.

This reconciliation of economy and ecology is intended to create the impression that only minor corrections to the market system are needed to launch an era of environmentally sound development, hiding the fact that the economic framework itself cannot hope to accommodate environmental concerns without substantial reform.[16] The sustainable development strategy, after all, focuses not so much on the negative consequences of economic growth on the environment, as on the effects of environmental degradation on growth and potential for growth. It is growth (ie capitalist market expansion), and not the environment, that has to be sustained. Since poverty is believed to be a cause, as well as an effect, of environmental problems, growth is needed with the purpose of eliminating poverty and with the purpose, in turn, of protecting the environment. Unlike the discourse of the 1970s which focused on 'the limits to growth', the discourse of the 1980s became fixated on 'growth of the limits'.[17]

Fourth, the reconciliation of growth and environment is facilitated exactly by the new concept of the 'environment', the importance of which, in ecological discourse, has grown steadily in the post-World War II period. The development of ecological consciousness that accompanied the rapid growth of industrial civilization also effected the transformation of 'nature' into 'environment'.[18] No longer does nature denote an entity with its own agency, a source of life and discourse, as was the case in many traditional societies, with European Romantic literature and art of the 19th century. For those committed to the world as resource, the 'environment' becomes an indispensable construct. As the term is used today, environment includes a view of nature according to the urban-industrial system. Everything that is relevant to the functioning of this system becomes part of the environment. The active principle of this conceptualization is the human agent and his/her creations, while nature is confined to an ever more passive role. What circulates are raw materials, industrial products, toxic wastes, 'resources'; nature is reduced to stasis, a mere appendage to the environment. Along with the physical deterioration of nature, we are witnessing its symbolic death. That which moves, creates, inspires – that is, the organizing principle of life – now resides in the environment.

The danger of accepting uncritically the sustainable development discourse is highlighted by a group of environmental activists from Canada:

> A genuine belief that the Bruntland Report is a big step forward for the environmental/green movement... amounts to a selective reading, where the data on environmental degradation and poverty are emphasized, and the growth economics and 'resource' orientation of the Report are ignored or downplayed. This point of view says that given the Bruntland's Report endorsement of sustainable development, activists can now point out some particular environmental atrocity and say, 'This is not sustainable development'. However, environmentalists are thereby accepting a 'development' framework for discussion.[19]

Becoming a new client of the development apparatus by adopting the sustainable development discourse means accepting the scarcity of natural resources as a given fact; this leads environmental managers into emphasizing the need to find the most efficient forms of using resources without threatening the survival of nature and people. As the Bruntland report put it, the goal should be to 'produce more with less'.[20] The World Commission is not alone in this endeavour. Year after year, this dictum is reawakened by The Worldwatch Institute in its *State of the World* reports, one of the chief sources for ecodevelopers. Ecology, as Wolfgang Sachs[21] perceptively says, is reduced in these reports to a higher form of efficiency.

Although ecologists and eco-developmentalists recognize environmental limits to production, a large proportion does not seem to perceive the cultural character of the commercialization of nature and life integral to the western economy, nor do they seriously account for the cultural limits which many societies have posed to unchecked production. It is not surprising that their policies are restricted to promoting the 'rational' management of resources. As long as environmentalists accept this presupposition, they also accept the imperatives for capital accumulation, material growth, and the disciplining of labour and nature, since in doing so they are extrapolating the occidental economic culture to the entire universe. Even the call for a people-centred economy runs the risk of perpetuating the basic assumptions of scarcity and productivism which underlie the dominant economic vision. In sum, by rationalizing the defence of nature in economic terms, advocates of sustainable development contribute to extending the economization of life and history.

This effect is most visible in the World Bank approach to sustainable development, an approach based on the belief that, as the President of the World Bank put it shortly after the publication of the Bruntland Report, 'sound ecology is good economics'.[22] The establishment in 1987 of a top level Environment Department, and the 'Global Environmental Facility' (read: the earth as a giant market/utility company under Group of Seven and World Bank control) created in 1992, reinforce the managerial attitude towards nature: 'Environmental planning' – said Conable[23] in the same address – 'can make the most of nature's resources so that human resourcefulness can make the most of the future'.

Again this is about the further capitalization of nature, the propagation of certain views of nature and society in terms of production and efficiency, not of respect and the common good. This is why Visvanathan calls the world of Bruntland and the World Bank 'a disenchanted cosmos'. The Bruntland Report, and much of the sustainable development discourse, is a tale that a disenchanted (modern) world tells itself about its sad condition. As a renewal of the contract between the modern nation-state and modern science, sustainable development seeks not so much to caricature the past, as with early development theory, as to control a future whose vision is highly impoverished. Visvanathan is also concerned with the ascendancy of the sustainable development discourse among ecologists and activists. It is fitting to end this section with his call for resistance to cooptation:

> Bruntland seeks a cooptation of the very groups that are creating a new dance of politics, where democracy is not merely order and discipline, where earth is a magic cosmos, where life is still a mystery to be celebrated... The experts of the global state would love to coopt them, turning them into a secondary, second-rate bunch of consultants, a lower order of nurses and paramedics still assisting the expert as surgeon and physician. It is this that we seek to resist by creating an explosion of imaginations that this club of experts seeks to destroy with its cries of lack and excess. The world of official science and the nation-state is not only destroying soils and silting up lakes, it is freezing the imagination... We have to see the Bruntland report as a form of published illiteracy and say a prayer for the energy depleted and the forests lost in publishing the report. And finally, a little prayer, an apology to the tree that supplied the paper for this document. Thank you, tree.[24]

Capitalization of Nature: Modern and Postmodern Forms

The sustainable development strategy is the main way of bringing nature into discourse in what still is known as the Third World. The continuous reinvention of nature requires not only bringing nature into new domains of discourse but also bringing it into capital in novel ways. This process takes two general forms, both entailing discursive construction of different kinds. Let us call these forms the modern and postmodern forms of capital in its ecological phase.

The modern form of capital

The first form that capital takes in its ecological phase tends to operate according to the logic of the modern capitalist culture and rationality; it is theorized in terms of what J. O'Connor[25] calls 'the second contradiction' of capitalism. Let it be recalled that the starting point of Marxist crisis theory is the contradiction between capitalist productive forces and production relations, or between the production and realization of value and surplus value. This first contradiction is well known to political economists. Important to emphasize from the perspective of traditional Marxist theory is that capitalism restructures itself through realization crises.

But there is a second contradiction of capitalism that has become pressing with the aggravation of the ecological crisis and the social forms of protest this crisis generates. This theorization shows that we need to refocus our attention on the role played by the *conditions of production* in capital accumulation and capitalist restructuring, insufficiently theorized by Marx but placed at the centre of inquiry by Polanyi's[26] critique of the self-regulating market. Why? Because it has become clear that capitalist restructuring increasingly takes place at the expense of these conditions. A 'condition of production' is defined as everything that is treated as if it were a commodity, even if it is not produced as a commodity, that is according to the laws of value and the market: labour power, land, nature, urban space, fit this definition. Recall that Polanyi called 'land' (that is, nature) and 'labour' (that is, human life), 'fictitious commodities'. The history of modernity and the history of capitalism must be seen as the progressive capitalization of production conditions. Trees produced capitalistically on plantations, privatized land and water rights, genetically altered species sold in the market, and the entire training and professionalization of labour – from its crudest form in slavery to today's PhDs – are all examples of the 'capitalization' of nature and human life.

This process is mediated by the state; indeed, the state must be seen as an interface between capital and nature, including human beings and space. As far as human beings are concerned, the disciplining and normalization of labour, the management of poverty and the rise of the social[27] marked the beginning of the capitalization of life within the modern era, while urban planning normalized and accelerated the capitalization of space.[28] This type of capitalization has been central to capitalism ever since the beginning of the primitive accumulation process and the enclosure of the commons. The instrumental tendency of science has also been crucial in this regard, as discussed by philosophers, feminists and ecologists.[29]

In fact, one of the defining features of modernity is the increasing appropriation of 'traditional' or pre-modern cultural contents by scientific knowledges, and the subsequent subjection of vast areas of life to regulation by administrative apparatuses based on expert knowledge.[30] The history of capital is thus not only the history of exploitation of production conditions; it is also the history of the advance of the scientific discourses of modernity in areas such as health, planning, the family, education, the economy and the like, through what Habermas[31] refers to as the colonization of the lifeworld and Foucault[32] as the advance of bio-power. The accumulation of capital, in other words, required the accumulation of normalized individuals and the accumulation of knowledge about the processes of capital and populations. This is the primary lesson of what might be called the anthropology of modernity of western societies since the end of the 18th century. With this observation we wish to emphasize that the modern form of capital is inevitably mediated by the expert discourses of modernity.

Capital's threatening of its own conditions of production elicits manifold and contradictory attempts to restructure those conditions in order to reduce costs or defend profits. Conversely, social struggles generated around the defence of production conditions must face two objectives: to defend life and production conditions against capital's excesses; and to seek control over the policies to restructure production conditions, usually via further privatization. In other words, social movements have to face simultaneously the destruction of life, the body, nature and space, and the crisis-induced restructuring of these conditions.[33] These struggles often set the poor against the rich as both cultural and economic actors; there is an 'environmentalism of the poor'[34] which is a type of class struggle and, at the same time, a cultural struggle to the extent that the poor try to defend their natural environments from material and cultural reconversion by the market. These struggles are often gender struggles in that many aspects of the destruction of production conditions affect women particularly and contribute to restructure class and gender relations.[35]

The postmodern form of ecological capital

In the Third World, the continued existence of conventional forms of capitalist exploitation of people and the environment is organized according to the rules of the dominant development discourse of the past 40 years, for which nature exists as raw material for economic growth activities.[36] While there are areas which are 'sold' to the sustainable development discourse, others remain under the firm grasp of crude and reckless developmentalism that has characterized most of the post-World War II period. As we see in our example from Colombia, both forms may coexist schizophrenically in the same geographical and cultural region.

M O'Connor is right, however, in pointing to a qualitative change in the form which capital tends to take today. If with modernity one can speak of a progressive semiotic conquest of social life by expert discourses and economistic conceptions, today this conquest is being extended to the very heart of nature and life. This new conquest takes for granted the normalization already achieved by the modern discourses of science and its administrative apparatuses; not only does it move on to new territories, it also develops new modes of operation, which O'Connor understands particularly in the Baudrillardian sense of the pre-eminence of the sign. Once modernity is consolidated, once 'the economy' becomes a seemingly ineluctable reality (a true descriptor of reality for most), capital and the struggles around it must broach the question of the domestication of all remaining social and symbolic relations in terms of the code of political economy, that of production. It is no longer capital and labour that are at stake *per se,* but the reproduction of the code. Social reality becomes, to borrow Baudrillard's phrase,[37] 'the mirror of production'.

This second form of capital relies not only on the symbolic conquest of nature (in terms of 'biodiversity reserves') and local communities (as 'stewards' of nature); it also requires the semiotic conquest of local knowledges, to the extent that 'saving nature' demands the valuation of local knowledges of sustaining nature. Local, 'indigenous' and 'traditional' knowledge systems are found to be useful complements to modern biology. However, in these discourses, knowledge is seen as something existing in the 'minds' of individual persons (shamans or elders) about external 'objects' ('plants', 'species'), the medical or economic 'utility' of which their bearers are supposed to transmit to us. Local knowledge is seen not as a complex cultural construction, involving movements and events profoundly historical and relational. Moreover, these forms of knowledge usually have entirely different modes of operation and relations to social and cultural fields.[38] By bringing them into the politics of science, more often than not they end up being recodified by modern science in utilitarian ways.

This triple cultural re-coversion of nature, people and knowledge represent a novel internalization of production conditions. Nature and local people themselves are seen as the source and creators of value – not merely as labour or raw material. The discourse of biodiversity in particular achieves this effect. Species of micro-organisms, flora and fauna are valuable not so much as 'resources', but as reservoirs of value – this value residing in their very genes – that scientific research, along with biotechnology, can release for capital and communities. This is one of the reasons why communities – particularly ethnic and peasant communities in the tropical rainforest areas of the world – are finally recognized as the owners of their territories (or what is left of them), but only to the extent that they accept viewing and treating territory and themselves as reservoirs of capital. Communities in various parts of the world are then enticed by biodiversity projects to become 'stewards of the social and natural "capitals" whose sustainable management is, henceforth, both their responsibility and the business of the world economy'.[39] Once the semiotic conquest of nature is completed, the sustainable and rational use of the environment becomes an imperative. It is here that the fundamental logic of the discourses of sustainable development and biodiversity must be found.

'Biodiversity conservation' in Colombia

A brief example will illustrate the differences between forms of capital. The Pacific coast region of Colombia has one of the highest degrees of biological diversity in the world. Covering about 5.4 million hectares of tropical rainforest, it is populated by about 800,000 African-Colombians and 40,000 indigenous people belonging to various ethnic groups, particular Emberas and Waunanas. Since the early 1980s the national and regional governments have increased their development activities in the region, culminating in the elaboration of ambitious development plans.[40] The 1992 'Sustainable Development Plan' is a conventional strategy intended to foster the development of capitalism in the region. Since the early 1980s, capital has flowed to various parts of the region, particularly in the form of investments in sectors such as African palm plantations, large-scale shrimp cultivation, gold mining, timber and tourism. These investments operate, for the most part, in the mode of the first form of capital. All the activities of this type of capital tend to contribute to ecological degradation, the displacement and proletarianization of local people – who can no longer subsist as farmers and have to find precarious jobs in the palm oil plantations and the shrimp-packing plants.

Parallel to this, the government has launched a more modest, but symbolically ambitious, project for the protection of the region's almost legendary biodiversity, in peril of being destroyed by activities mediated by the development plan. The Biodiversity Project,[41] conceived under the directives of the Global Biodiversity Strategy[42] and within the scope of the World Bank's Global Environmental Facility (GEF), purports to effect an alternative strategy for the sustainable and culturally appropriate development of the area. The project is organized along four different axes: 'to know' (to gather and systematize modern and traditional knowledge of the region's biodiversity); 'to valorize' (to design ecologically sound strategies to create economic value out of biodiversity); 'to mobilize' (to foster the organization of the black and indigenous communities so that they can take charge of the sustainable development of their environments); and 'to formulate and implement' (to modify institutional structures so that they can serve as support for community-oriented sustainable development strategies).

The Biodiversity Project obeys the global logic of the second form of ecological capital. The project became possible not only because of international trends, but also out of the pressure exerted on the state by black and indigenous communities in the context of the new territorial and cultural rights accorded to them by the reform of the national constitution of 1991. The project designers had to take into account the views of local communities, and had to accept as important interlocutors the representatives of the black movement that has grown in the context of the developmentalist onslaught and the reform of the constitution. A few progressive professionals associated with the black movement have been able to insert themselves in the national and regional staff of the project. While these professionals seem aware of the risks involved in their participation in a government project of this kind, they also believe that the project presents a space of struggle that they cannot afford to ignore.

Along with new forms of biotechnology, the discourse of biodiversity conservation produced mostly by northern NGOs and international organizations in the 1990s, in sum, achieves an important transformation in our consciousness and practices of nature. As far as the world rainforests are concerned, this discourse constructs an equation between 'knowing' (classifying species), 'saving' (protecting from total destruction), and 'using' (through the development of commercial applications based on the genetic properties of species). Biodiversity prospectors would roam the rainforest in search of potential uses of rainforest species, and the biotechnological developments that would allegedly ensue from this task would provide the key to rainforest preservation – if appropriately protected, of course, by intellectual property rights so that prospectors and investors have the need incentive to invest in the epic enterprise of saving nature.[43] Both capitalism and nature would not only survive but thrive under the new scheme dreamed of by scientists, planners, multinational corporations, and genetic and molecular biology laboratories, among others. Social movements confront a greening of economics, knowledge and communities more pervasive than ever before.

Making Nature: From (Modern) Death to (Postmodern) Reinvention

It should be clear by now that sustainable development and biodiversity strategies play a crucial role in the discursive production of production conditions. Production conditions are not just transformed by 'capital': they have to be transformed in/through discourse. The Bruntland Report, indeed the entire sustainable development movement, is an attempt at resignifying nature, resources, the earth, human life itself, at a scale perhaps not witnessed since the rise of empirical sciences and their reconstruction of nature – since nature's 'death', to use Carolyn Merchant's expression.[44] Sustainable development is the last attempt to articulate nature, modernity and capitalism before the advent of cyberculture.

The reconversion of nature effected by the discourses of biodiversity and sustainable development may be placed in the broader context of what Donna Haraway[45] calls 'the reinvention of nature'. This reinvention is being fostered by sciences such as molecular biology and genetics, research strategies such as the Human Genome Project, and biotechnology. For Haraway, however, this process of reinvention started with the languages of systems analysis developed since the early post-World War II period, and is marking the final disappearance of our organic notions of nature. The logic and technologies of command-control have become more central in recent years, particularly with the development of immunological discourses[46] and projects such as the mapping of the human genome. The language of this discourse is decidedly post-modern and is not inimical to the post-Fordist regime of accumulation,[47] with its new cultural order of 'flexible labour', which might also be read symbolically as an attempt to keep dark invaders at a distance or quickly isolate them if they come close enough or become numerous enough to pose a threat of contagion and disorder.

Haraway reads in these developments the de-naturalization of the notions of organism' and 'individual,' so dear to pre-World War II science. She sees the emergence of a new entity, the cyborg, which arises to fill in the vacuum[48] Cyborgs are hybrid creatures, composed of organism and machine, 'special kinds of machines and special kinds of organisms appropriate to the late twentieth century'.[49] Cyborgs are not organic wholes but strategic assemblages of organic, textual, and technical components. In the language of sustainable development one would say that cyborgs do not belong in/to nature; they belong in/to the environment, and the environment belongs in/to systems.

Haraway concludes that we need to develop a different way of thinking about nature and ourselves in relation to nature. Taking Simone de Beauvoir's declaration that 'one is not born a woman' into the postmodern domain of late 20th-century biology, Haraway adds that 'one is not born an organism. Organisms are made; they are constructs of a world-changing kind'.[50] To be more precise, organisms make themselves and are also made by history. This deeply historicized account of life is difficult to accept if one remains within the modern traditions of realism, rationalism and organic nature. The historicized view assumes that what counts as nature and what counts as culture in the west ceaselessly change according to complex historical factors. Since at least the end of the 18th century, 'the themes of race, sexuality, gender, nation, family and class have been written into the body of nature in western life sciences', even if in every case nature 'remains a crucially important and deeply contested myth and real-ity'.[51] Nature as such (unconstructed) has ceased to exist, if indeed it ever existed.

Nature, bodies and organisms must thus be seen as 'material-semiotic' actors, rather than as mere objects of science preexisting in purity. Nature and organisms thus emerge from a discursive processes involving complex apparatuses of science, capital and culture. This implies that the boundaries between the organic, the technoeconomic, and the textual (or, broadly, cultural) are permeable. While nature, bodies and organ-isms certainly have an organic basis, they are increasingly produced in conjunction with machines, and this production is always mediated by scientific and cultural narratives. Haraway emphasizes that nature is a co-construction among humans and non-humans. Nature has a certain agency, an 'artefactuality' of sorts. We thus have the possibility of engaging in new conversations with/around nature, involving humans and non-humans together in the reconstruction of nature as public culture. Even more, 'there are great riches for feminists [and others] in explicitly embracing the possibilities inherent in the breakdown of clean distinctions between organism and machine and similar distinc-tions structuring the western self'.[52]

Haraway's work reflects and seeks to engage with the profound transformation being brought about by new computer technologies and biotechnology that is just begin-ning but quickly advancing in the centre countries of the capitalist system. The advent of the new era – which we can perhaps call cyberculture, as a truly post-industrial and postmodern society[53] – entails a certain cultural promise for more just social configura-tions. We should have no doubts by now that a fundamental social and cultural transformation is under way, which promises to reshape biological and social life, and which involves both dangers and possibilities. A new regime of bio-sociality is upon us, implying that 'nature will be modeled on culture understood as practice. Nature will be known and remade through technique and will finally become artificial, just as culture becomes natural'.[54] This might bring the dissolution of modern society and of the nature/culture split, marking also the end of the ideologies of naturalism – of an organic nature existing outside of history – and even the possibility that the organic might be improved on by artificial means.

What all this means for the Third World is yet to be examined. This examination has to start with inventing a new language to speak of these issues from Third World perspectives, a language of transformative self-affirmation that allows the Third World to reposition itself in the global conversations and processes that are reshaping the world, without submitting passively to the rules of the game created by them. Sustaina-ble development will not do. Biodiversity, on the contrary, is becoming inextricably linked to other discourses, such as biotechnology, genetics and intellectual property rights.[55] But the implications for the Third World communities placed as 'stewards' of organic nature are by no means well understood. The issues are crucial for the commu-nities, as the African-Colombian activists of the Pacific coast have discovered. Not in vain are corporations developing aggressive policies of privatizing nature and life. Com-munities in various parts of the Third World will have to conduct a dialogue with each other in order to face the internationalization of ecological capital. Ecological solidarity (south–south and north–south) must travel this perilous terrain, and perhaps entertain the idea of strategic alliances between the organic and the artificial (in terms of biotechnology applications of rainforests' biodiversity, for instance) against the most destructive forms of capital.

Semiotic Resistance and Alternative Productive Rationality

The role of discourse and culture in organizing and mediating 'nature' and 'production conditions' is still undeveloped in both the eco-socialist and eco-feminist conceptions. For the most part, the economistic culture of modernity is taken as the norm. Behind this question lie the relationships between natural and historical processes. Haraway's work provides valuable elements for examining this relation particularly in the context of raising technoculture. The Mexican ecologist, Enrique Leff, has made a general case for theorizing the mutual inscription of nature, culture and history in terms useful for thinking about Third World situations. As the ecological becomes part of the accumulation process, Leff argues, the natural is absorbed into history and can thus be studied by historical materialism. Yet he insists that culture remains an important mediating instance. The transformation of nature and ecosystems by capital depends on the cultural practices of specific societies and the processes of cultural transformations that are taking place.[56]

Leff's[57] conceptual effort is linked specifically to the articulation of an alternative, ecologically sustainable productive rationality from an integrated perspective of ecology, culture, and production. For Leff, ecological, technological and cultural productivity must be woven together in order to theorize a new view of rationality that generates processes that are equitable and sustainable. 'The environment should be regarded as the articulation of cultural, ecological, technological and economic processes that come together to generate a complex, balanced, and sustained productive system open to a variety of options and development styles.'[58]

On the cultural level, cultural practices should be seen as a principle of productivity for the sustainable use of natural resources. Most clearly in the case of indigenous and ethnic groups, every social group possesses an 'ecological culture' that must be seen as forming part of the social relations and forces of production. At the level of production, Leff advocates for the development of 'a productive paradigm that is not economistic yet pertains to political economy'.[59] The result would be an alternative production paradigm that relates technological innovation, cultural processes and ecological productivity. Less clear in Leff's work is how concepts such as 'production' and 'rationality' can be theorized from the perspective of different cultural orders.

Based on his reformed view of the environment, Leff calls on ecology activists and theorists to think in terms of 'ecological conditions of production' and a 'positive theory of production', in which nature is not only seen as a production condition, but actively incorporated into a new productive rationality along with labour and technology. This call parallels J O'Connor's redefinition of production conditions from the

standpoint of the second contradiction, particularly through the action of social movements. Leff's formulation brings into sharper focus the real need that social movements
and communities have to articulate their own views of alternative development and
alternative productive schemes specifically from the perspective of ecology. The pressure on social movements and community activists in many parts of the world to engage
in this constructive task is mounting, as the case of the black and indigenous activists in
the Colombian Pacific coast shows. Leff's ongoing effort at conceptualizing an alternative productive rationality is helpful in this regard.

The creation of a new productive rationality would entail forms of environmental
democracy, economic decentralization and cultural and political pluralism. The creation of spaces in which to foster local alternative productive projects is one concrete
way to advance the strategy. In sum, Leff seeks to redefine and radicalize three basic
constructs: production, away from economistic cultural constructions and pure market
mechanisms; rationality, away from the dominant reductionistic and utilitarian views;
and management, away from its bureaucratized practice and towards a participatory
approach. A strategy such as this, one might add, implies cultural resistance to the
symbolic reconversion of nature; socio-economic proposals with concrete alternative
strategies; and political organizing to ensure a minimum of local control over the entire
process. In the landscape of Latin American hybrid cultures,[60] strategies that combine
modern and non-modern, capitalist and non-capitalist forms and practices seem to be
required.

One thing is clear in this debate: social movements and communities in the Third
World need to articulate alternative productive strategies that are ecologically sustainable, lest they be swept away by a new round of conventional development. The fact that
these alternatives must also be culturally defined – from the perspectives of cultures
which, although hybrid, nevertheless retain a socially significant difference *vis à vis*
western modernity – necessarily entails that a certain semiotic resistance will take place.
The worst would be for communities to opt for conventional development styles. To
accede to an era of post-development – in which the hegemonic effect of the constructs
of modernity might be held in check[61] – communities will need to simultaneously practise experimentation with alternative productive strategies and cultural resistance to
capital's and modernity's material and symbolic restructuring of nature. Communities
will need to prevent conventional development, green redevelopment via sustainable
development discourses, and the greening of communities and local knowledge via discourses of biodiversity.

Is it really possible to imagine an alternative ecological economy based on a different cultural (not only social) order? If one accepts that this has become an essential
political task today, how could analysts investigate the concrete cultural practices that
might serve as a basis for it? What are macro-economic conditions and political processes
that could make its implementation and survival possible? How should this alternative
social reality engage with dominant market-dominated forces? The importance of these
questions will grow as researchers come to realize the increasing complexity of the cultural politics of nature under way in the wake of new forms of capital, technoscience
and globalization.

Conclusion: Towards a Poststructuralist Political Ecology

The two socially necessary forms of capital – modern and postmodern – maintain an uneasy articulation that depends on local, regional and transnational conditions. Both forms are mediated by discourse: conventional discourses of development, plus the scientific discourses of modernity, in the case of the first form of ecological capital; discourses of biodiversity and sustainable development (particularly in the Third World), and molecular biology, biotechnology and cyberculture in the First (and increasingly the Third) Worlds, in the case of the second form of ecological capital. The regimes of sustainable development in the south, and of biosociality and cyberculture in the north show a certain degree of geographical unevenness; yet the connections among them are becoming clearer. While some regions in the Third World are joining the ranks of cyberculture, poor communities in the First World are affected by the logic of reckless capital and the paradoxes of sustainability. The division between First and Third World is undergoing a fundamental mutation in the wake of post-Fordism, cyberculture and the ecological phase of capital.

The discursive nature of capital is evident in the case of the production of 'production conditions'. The resignification of nature as environment; the reinscription of the earth into capital via the gaze of science; the reinterpretation of poverty as an effect of destroyed environments; the destruction of vernacular gender and the concomitant proletarianization and rearticulation of women's subordination under modern principles; and the new lease on management and planning as arbiters between people and nature, all these are effects of the discursive construction of sustainable development. As more and more professionals and activists adopt the grammar of sustainable development, the reinvention of production conditions effected by this discourse will be more effective. Institutions will continue to re/produce the world as seen by those who rule it.

Although everybody today seems to be aware that nature is 'socially constructed', many continue to assume a relatively unproblematic rendition of nature. Central to this rendition is the assumption that 'nature' exists out there, beyond our constructions. Nature, however, is neither unconstructed nor unconnected. Nature's constructions are effected by history, economics, technology, science and myths of all kinds as part of the 'traffic between nature and culture'.[62] Leff[63] emphasizes a similar point in his own way. Capital accumulation, he says, requires the articulation of the sciences to the production process, so that the truths they produce become, themselves, productive forces in the economic process. Thus the sustainable development discourse must be seen as part of the creation of knowledge linked to capital, to the extent that the concepts produced participate in reinscribing nature into the law of value. Although the process of transdisciplinarity involved in the sciences of ecology is hopeful, Leff[64] believes, the lack of epistemological vigilance has resulted in a certain disciplining of environmental themes which has precluded the creation of concepts useful for the formulation of alternative ecological rationalities. The analysis of discourses can serve as a basis to elaborate practical concepts useful to reorient strategies concerning development and the environment.

If nature and other life forms must now be understood as articulations of organic, technoeconomic and cultural elements, does this not imply that we need to theorize this mixture as the appropriate object of biology and ecology, perhaps at the same time

– and dialectically – that these sciences seek to theorize the 'laws of nature' in and of themselves? As Leff (personal communication) rightly says, one must be cautious in this endeavour, and raise the question of 'to what extent by manipulating nature as reality you manipulate the scientific object of biology. By manipulating evolution and genetics, to what extent do we also manipulate and reconstruct the object and the internal laws of biology and genetics?' Perhaps what is needed is a new epistemology of biology, such as the one being proposed by the phenomenological biology of Humberto Maturana and Francisco Varela.[65] Works of this type, that attempt to step outside the traditional space of science by taking seriously the continuity between cognizant self and world, between knowledge and the social practices that make that knowledge possible, might have important elements to contribute to a new biology and ecology. The question of the epistemology of the natural sciences is being broached from post-structuralist perspectives, and from a reformed phenomenology in Maturana and Varela's case. Should it not be broached as well from that of political ecology?

The worldwide spread of value seems to privilege the new biotechnologies. These further capitalize nature by planting value into it through scientific R&D. Even human genes become conditions of production, an important arena for capitalist restructuring and, so, for contestation. The reinvention of nature currently under way, effected by/within webs of meaning and production that link the discourses of science and capital, should be incorporated into a political ecology appropriate to that new age whose dawn we are witnessing. What will count as 'organisms' and even 'human' for biology, ecology, geography and biological anthropology will be intimately mediated by these processes.

Nature is now modelled as culture; sooner or later, 'nature' will be produced to order. If the production of trees in plantations constituted an important step in the capitalization of nature, for example, the production of genetically produced trees (or the 'perfect' tomatoes produced at the University of California at Davis) takes this process to new levels; it takes the tree a step further away from 'organic nature'. The implications of this are unclear. This is why the raising regime of biosociality must find its place at the basis of a political ecology and biology as forms of knowledge about material-semiotic objects – organisms and communities – that are historically constituted.

This is to say we need new narratives of life and culture. These narratives are likely to be hybrids of sorts; they will arise out of the mediations that local cultures are able to effect on the discourses and practices of nature, capital and modernity. This is a collective task that perhaps only social movements are in a position to advance. The task entails the construction of collective identities, as well as struggles over the redefinition of the boundaries between nature and culture. These boundaries will be reimagined to the extent that the practice of social movement succeeds in reconnecting life and thought by fostering a plural political ecology of knowledge. As the analysis of concrete practices of thinking and doing, discursive approaches have much to contribute to this reimagining. Materialist approaches do not need to exclude this type of analysis.

Notes and References

1   Ernesto Laclau and Chantal Mouffe, *Hegemony and Socialist Strategy* (London, Verso, 1985).

2   Jean and John Comaroff, *Of Revelation and Revolution* (Chicago, IL, University of Chicago Press, 1991); Stephen Gudeman and Alberto Rivera, *Conversations in Colombia* (Cambridge, Cambridge University Press, 1990); Soren Hvalkoff, 'The nature of development: native and settlers' views in Gran Pajonal, Peruvian Amazons', *Folk, 31,* 1989; pp125–150.

3   Lakshman Yapa, 'Can postmodern discourse theory help alleviate poverty? Yes!', presented at Annual Meeting of the American Association of Geography, Chicago, 17 March 1995, p1.

4   Alan Pred and Michael Watts, *Reworking Moderity* (New Brunswick, NJ, Rutgers University Press, 1992).

5   Martin O'Connor, 'On the misadventures of capitalist nature', *Capitalism, Nature, Socialism,* 4(3), 1993, pp7–40 at p8.

6   James O'Connor, *Conference Papers* (Santa Cruz, CES/CNS), 1991, pamphlet 1.

7   World Commission on Environment and Development, *Our Common Future* (Oxford, Oxford University Press, 1987), p1.

8   Wolfgang Sachs, 'The gospel of global efficiency', *IDFA Dossier,* No 68, 1988, pp33–39.

9   Michael Focault, *The Birth of the Clinic* (New York, Vintage Books), pxii.

10 Donna Harraway, 'Situated knowledges: the science question in feminism and the privilege of partial perspective', *Feminist Studies,* 14(3), 1988, pp575–599 at p581.

11 William Clark, 'Managing planet earth', *Scientific American,* 261(3), 1989, pp46–57 at p48.

12 Vandana Shiva, *Staying Alive. Women, Ecology and Development* (London, Zed Books, 1989).

13 Arturo Escobar, 'Planning', in *The Development Dictionary* (London, Zed Books, 1992), pp132–145.

14 Fredrick Buttel, A Hawkins and G Power, 'From limits to growth to global change: contrasts and contradictions in the evolution of environmental science and ideology', *Global Environmental Change,* 7(1), 1990, pp57–66.

15 Michael Redclift, *Sustainable Development: Exploring the Contradictions* (London, Routledge, 1987).

16 Richard Norgaard, *Sustainability as Intergenerational Equity* (Washington, DC, World Bank Internal Discussions Paper No IDP 97, 1991); 'Sustainability: the pragmatic challenge to agricultural economies', presented at the 21st Conference of the International Association of Agricultural Economists, Tokyo, 22–29 August 1991.

17 Sachs, *op cit,* reference 8.

18 Wolfgang Sachs (ed), *The Development Dictionary. A Guide to Knowledge as Power* (London, Zed Books, 1992).

19 Green Web, 'Sustainable development: expanded environmental destruction', *Green Web Bulletin,* No 16, p6.

20 World Commission on Environment and Development, *op cit,* reference 7, p15.

21 Sachs, *op cit,* reference 8.

22 Barber Conable, 'Address to the World Resources Institute' (Washington, DC, The World Bank, 1987), p6.

23 *Ibid,* p3.

24 Shiv Visvanathan, 'Mrs Bruntland's disenchanted cosmos', *Alternatives*, 16(3), 1991, pp 377–384 at p384.

25 James O'Connor, 'Capitalism, nature, socialism: a theoretical introduction', *Capitalism, Nature, Socialism*, 7(1), 1988, pp11–38; 'Political economy of ecology of socialism an capitalism', *Capitalism, Nature, Socialism*, 1(3), 1989, pp93–108; *Conference Papers op cit*, reference 6.

26 Karl Polanyi, *The Great Transformation* (Boston, MA, Beacon Press, 1957).

27 Michael Foucault, Discipline and Punish (New York, Vintage Books, 1979); *The History of Sexuality. Volume 1. An Introduction* (New York, Vintage Books, 1980); Giovanna Procacci, 'Social economy and the government of poverty', *The Foucault Effect*, Graham Burchell, Colin Gordon, and Peter Millers (eds), (Chicago, IL, University of Chicago Press, 1991), pp 151–168; Jacques Donzelot, *The Policing of Families* (New York, Pantheon Books, 1979); 'The promotion of the social', *Economy and Society*, 17(3), 1988, pp 217–234.

28 Paun Rabinow, French Modern: Norms and Forms of the Social Environment (Cambridge, MA, MIT Press, 1989).

29 Carolyn Merchant, *The Death of Nature* (New York, Harper and Row, 1980); Vandana Shiva, *Staying Alive. Women, Ecology and Development* (London, Zed Books, 1989).

30 Jurgen Harbermas, *Legitimation Crisis* (Boston, MA, Beacon Press, 1975); Michael Foucault, *Discipline and Punish* (New York, Vintage Books, 1979); Anthony Giddens, *The Consequences of Modernity* (Stanford, CA, Stanford University Press, 1990).

31 Jurgen Habermas, *The Philosophical Discourse of Modernity* (Boston, MA, Beacon Press, 1987).

32 Foucault, *The History of Sexuality, op cit*, reference 27.

33 O'Connor, 'Capitalism, nature, socialism', *op cit*, reference 25; *Conference Papers, op cit*, reference 6.

34 Ramachandra Guha, 'The environmentalism of the poor', presented at the Conference, 'Dissent and Direct Action in the Late Twentieth Century', Otavalo, Ecuador, June 1994; Juan Martinez-Alier, *Ecología y Pobreza* (Barcelona, Centre Cultural Bancaixa, 1992).

35 Brinda Rao, 'Struggling for production conditions and producing conditions of emancipation: women and water in rural Maharashtra', *Capitalism, Nature, Socialism*, 1(2), 1989, pp65–82; Mary Mellor, *Breaking the Boundaries: Towards a Feminist Green Socialism* (London, Virago, 1992).

36 Auturo Escobar, *Encountering Development: The Making and Unmaking of the Third World Princeton*, NJ, (Princeton University Press, 1995).

37 Jean Baudrillard, *The Mirror of Production* (St Louis, MO, Telos Press, 1975).

38 Gilles Deleuze, and Felix Guattari, *A Thousand Plateaus* (Minneapolis, MN, University of Minnesota Press, 1987).

39 O'Connor, *op cit*, reference 5, p8.

40 DNP (Departamento Nacional de Planeación de Colombia), *Plan de Desarrollo Integral para la Costa Pacífica (Cali, DNP/CVC, 1983): DNP (Departamento Nacional de Planeación de Colombia), Plan Pacífico. Una Estrategia de Desarrollo Sostenible para la Costa Pacífica Colombiana* (Bogotá, DNP, 1992).

41 GEF-PNUD (Global Environmental Facility-Programa de las Naciones Unidas para el Desarrollo), *Conservación de la Biodiversidad del Chocó Biogeográfico. Proyecto Biopacífico* (Bogotá, DNP/Biopacífico, 1993).

42 World Resources Institute (WRI), World Conservation Union, and United Nations Environment Program, *Global Biodiversity Strategy* (Washington, DC, WRI, 1992).

43 *Ibid;* World Resources Institute, *Biodiversity Prospecting* (Washington, DC, WRI, 1993)

44 Merchant, *op cit,* reference 29.

45 Donna Haraway, *Simians, Cyborgs, and Women. The Reinvention of Nature* (New York, Routledge, 1991).

46 Emily Martin, *Flexible Bodies* (Boston, MA, Beacon Press, 1994).

47 David Harvey, *The Condition of Postmodernity* (Oxford, Basil Blackwell, 1989).

48 Donna Haraway, 'Manifesto for cyborgs: science, technology, and socialist feminism in the 1980's', *Socialist Review,* No 80, 1985, pp65–107; 'The biopolitics of postmodern bodies: determination of self in immune system discourse', *Differences,* 1(1), 1989, pp 3–43; *Simians, Cyborgs, and Women. The Reinvention of Nature* (New York, Routledge, 1991).

49 Donna Haraway, *Simians, Cyborgs, and Women. The Reinvention of Nature* (New York, Routledge, 1991), p1.

50 Haraway, 'The biopolitics of postmodern bodies', *op cit,* reference 48, p10.

51 Donna Haraway, *Primate Visions* (New York, Routledge, 1989), p1.

52 Haraway, 'Manifesto for cyborgs', *op cit,* reference 48, p92.

53 Arturo Escobar, 'Welcome to cyberia: notes on the anthropology of cyberculture', *Current Anthropology,* 35(3), 1994, pp211–231.

54 Paul Rainbow, 'Artificiality and enlightenment: from sociobiology to biosociality', in Jonathan Crary and Sanford Kwinter (editors), *Incorporations* (New York, Zone Books, 1992), p241.

55 Vandana Shiva. 'The seed and the earth: women, ecology and biotechnology', *The Ecologist,* 22(1), 1992, pp4–8.

56 Enrique Leff, *Green Production: Toward an Environmental Rationality* (New York, Guildford Press, 1995); Maurice Godelier, *The Mental and the Material* (London, Verso, 1986).

57 Enrique Leff, 'Ambiente y articulación de ciencias', in Enrique Leff (editor), *Los Problemas del Conocimiento y la Perspectiva Ambiental del Desarrollo* (México, DF, Siglo XXI, 1986), pp72–125; 'La dimensión cultural y el manejo sustentable de los recursos naturales', in Enrique Leff and J Carabias (editors) *Cultura y Manejo Sustentable de los Recursos Naturales* (México, DF, CIIH/UNAM, 1992); 'Marxism and the environmental question: from critical theory of production to an environmental rationality for sustainable development', *Capitalism, Nature, Socialism,* 4(1), 1993, pp44–66; *Green Production: Toward an Environmental Rationality* (New York, Guildford Press, 1995).

58 Leff, 'Marxism and the environmental question', *op cit,* reference 57; *Green Production, op cit,* reference 57, p60.

59 *Ibid,* p 50: Leff, 'Marxism and the environmental question', *op cit,* reference 57.

60 Néstor García Canclini, *Culturas Híbridas: Estrategias para Entrar y Salir de la Modernidad* (México, DF, Grijalbo, 1990).
61 Arturo Escobar, *Encountering Development: The Making and Unmaking of the Third World* (Princeton, N), Princeton University Press, 1995).
62 Haraway, *op cit,* reference 51.
63 Leff, 'Ambiente y articulacion de ciencias', *op cit,* reference 57; *Green Production, op cit,* reference 57.
64 Leff, 'Ambiente y articulacion de ciencias', *op cit,* reference 57.
65 Humberto Maturana and Francisco Varela, *Autopoiesis and Cognition: The Realization of the Living* (Boston, MA, D Reidel Publishing Company, 1980); *The Tree of Knowledge: The Biological Roots of Human Understanding* (Boston, MA, New Science Library/Shambhala, 1987); Francisco Varela, Evan Thompson and Elanor Rosch, *The Embodied Mind: Cognitive Science and Human Experience* (Cambridge, MA, The MIT Press, 1991).

9

From Meta–Narratives to Flexible Frameworks: An Actor Level Analysis of Land Degradation in Highland Tanzania

Samantha Jones

Summary

This paper first highlights some of the problems that exist with studies that try to explain the causes of environmental degradation, in particular land degradation. Based on this critique it provides a framework, set in the context of an actor-oriented approach, that helps to attain a clearer understanding of the social causes of the physical changes that are interpreted as degradation. The framework is illustrated with reference to a case study from a mountainous area of central-eastern Tanzania.

Introduction

Many studies attempting to uncover the human causes of environmental degradation are simplistic and deterministic in their analysis (Barraclough and Ghimire, 1996; Scoones, 1997). The dynamic and intricate interplay between people and their environment is often ignored and insufficient attention has been given to the way that people act as conscious agents to intervene in the world around them (Long, 1992; Leach et al, 1997). This paper provides a framework that highlights the inter-linkages between decision-makers and environmental change to improve understandings of how and why people transform their environment. For illustrative purposes, the framework is applied to a case study in highland Tanzania. First, the limitations of existing approaches to the study of causes of land degradation are highlighted.

Reprinted from *Global Environment Change*, vol 9, Jones, S, 'From Meta-narratives to flexible Frameworks: An Actor Level Analysis of Land Degradation in Highland Tanzania', pp 211–219, copyright © (1999) with permission from Elsevier.

Problems with Existing Studies of the Causes of Degradation

Two types of study attempting to assess the causes of degradation may be identified and problems exist with each. First, research has most often concentrated on identification and quantification of external causal variables without adequate attention to *how* 'factors become causes' (Whitesell, 1994), that is, the specific links and mechanisms between social variables and land degradation. Barrow (1991), for example, presents nine categories of factors causing degradation, including political instability, marginalization and economic factors (itself divided into various components) as a 'shopping list' of causes (Mortimore, 1989, p199). As Tolba et al (1992, p132) note, land degradation is, in fact, 'the result of complex interactions between physical, chemical, biological and socio-economic and political issues of local, national and global nature'.

Second are those studies that have greater explanatory depth yet tend to view the causes of environmental degradation from a particular lens or theoretical perspective. The postmodernist would label these 'meta-narratives' (or grand narratives), that is, overarching explanatory theoretical frameworks. A narrative is a 'story' (Roe, 1991) with a beginning, middle and end.[1] Each of the theoretical stances highlighted below contains these in the form of cause, effect and solution. This type of study is critiqued below after the most dominant of these meta-narratives in the environmental arena are briefly outlined.

- *Neo-Malthusian*: Demographic pressure is regarded as the cause of degradation. As the ceiling to production or carrying capacity of the land is exceeded, resources are mined to support growing populations.
- *Paternalist/Technocratic*: The land user is seen as irrational and inefficient (environmentally unaware, ignorant, apathetic or lazy) and mismanagement is regarded as the cause of land degradation. Environmental problems have technical solutions that should be adopted.
- *Populist*: Land degradation is imperfectly understood and there has been a lack of appreciation of the dynamic and adaptive nature of indigenous systems of cultivation, technology and institutions. Western interventions, in contrast, have often been environmentally inappropriate.
- *Neo-Marxist/Dependency*: Environmental problems are an indirect consequence of the capitalist world economy. Poverty, caused by exploitative relations of production, has forced people to mine their environment in order to survive.
- *Economic/Neo-liberal*: Policy failure through inappropriate or excessive government intervention (eg price distortions from subsidies, quotas and misvalued exchange rates), and market failure (eg externalities, inadequate property rights and inability to properly value the future) are considered to be the underlying causes of degradation. (Adapted from Stonich, 1989; Biot et al, 1995; Jones, 1995.)

Studies adopting these perspectives are often implicitly theory-led and as such, specific data may be collected to the exclusion of other potentially relevant data, to test or refute the perspective. Therefore these studies present only a partial picture.[2] Because land degradation is often attributed to more distant explanatory levels (such as the exploitative nature of the world economy) uncertainty is rife and although shifts in thinking are evident, lack of 'proof' allows competing theories to exist simultaneously.

A further problem regarding attempts to explain land degradation is of a more philosophical nature and is a problem for explanation in the social sciences at large. The social sciences can conveniently be divided into naturalist (positivist) or humanist (anti-naturalist or interpretive) approaches. Briefly, the naturalist maintains that the approach of social science should mimic the natural sciences and focus on causal mechanisms. Positivism denies the subjective aspects of human experience and the power of human consciousness and action to redirect the course of events (Jackson and Smith, 1984) and 'rides roughshod over the specificities of culture and context' (Long and van der Ploeg, 1994, p65). Thus in contrast, the humanist believes that social phenomena should be approached from the point of view of the meaningful behaviour of the social agent, as people do not act in determined ways. They attempt to understand reasons and meanings, rather than try to explain human action. However, Little (1991) understands there to be substantial areas of human action in which structural variables rather than meanings play the central influential role.

The perspectives on the causes of land degradation most often fall into the positivist approach. For example, in the neo-Malthusian perspective, notions of carrying capacity imply an unchangeable external environment within which humans respond in a determined manner. In the neo-Marxist perspective, poverty is a deterministic consequence of capitalism. In contrast, the populist perspective fits more into the humanist approach as it recognizes the validity of local knowledge and capacity of people to process their experience and 'make a difference' to a pre-existing state of affairs or flow of events (Giddens, 1984).

A methodological challenge thus exists, because while aspects of the two approaches are valuable, they represent an ontological dichotomy between the 'active' view of human agency implicit in humanism and the 'passive' view adopted in structural analyses (Jackson and Smith, 1984). This is reflected in Siddle and Swindell's (1990, p1) comment that '[T]he difficulty in coming to grips with African rural society is one of reconciling individual actions and perceptions with the larger structural forces of society and the state'.

Despite this apparent dichotomy, there is nothing preventing reasons (of humanist inquiry) from figuring in causal explanations (Fay and Moon, 1994). Interpretive social science can provide accounts of the social mechanisms that underlie social causation (Little, 1991). Giddens, in his theory of structuration, marries these two approaches recognizing that neither the experience of the individual actor nor any form of societal totality are the basic domain of study, but social practices ordered across space and time (Giddens, 1984). Through recursive practices, social (and environmental) systems are reproduced and transformed and form the medium of subsequent practices. The structuration perspective, hitherto primarily used to understand social situations, has considerable potential for aiding the understanding of human–environment interactions.[3]

Norman Long and his colleagues have operationalized structuration theory into a workable approach, termed the actor-oriented approach. Long and van der Ploeg (1994, p64) write that one begins with an interest in explaining differential responses to similar structural circumstances (eg the economy and the environment). Forms of external intervention are mediated and transformed as they enter the existing lifeworlds of individuals and social groups as people act in intended ways, rather than merely respond to external forces (Long, 1992). Thus 'the interplay and mutual determination of "internal" and "external" factors and relationships which recognises the central role played by human action and consciousness' are explored (Long, 1992, p20). However restricted their choices, actors always face some alternative ways of formulating their objectives, deploying specific modes of action and giving reasons for their action (Long, 1992). In addition, Long (1992, p277) notes, the actor-oriented approach requires the analysis of social forms that result from a mix of intended and unintended actions (eg social norms and routines) and consequences of actions (such as slope failure or incremental fertility decline). The environment is part of external structure that (differentially) affects actors and is continuously affected by them, but it must also be recognized that it is socially constructed. The actor-oriented approach facilitates the unpacking of such local meanings and culturally specific perceptions and behaviour. As Blaikie (1994) notes the environment 'is constantly in a state of being conceived of, learnt about, acted upon, created and recreated and modified'.

The Framework

The level of analysis for the framework below, then, is the everyday lives and 'situated contexts' of actors and their decision-making environment. This micro-level focus reduces the uncertainty from distant variables and the influence of explicit or pre-attentive theories. It copes with a wide range of potential causes of land degradation and can simultaneously highlight mechanisms of local particularity, such as heterogeneity within a culture, and the more abstract structural influences on people's actions. The framework is utilized in conjunction with the concept of limiting factors used by ecologists. After deriving a list of variables affecting an organism, ecologists use the idea of limiting factors to identify the different circumstances in which a certain factor or synergistic interaction of a few factors takes precedence over all others in determining outcomes (Whitesell, 1994). Whitesell suggests that 'in the effort to derive a theory of environmental degradation and conservation with at least minimal predictive capabilities, the construction of a similar theory of limiting factors within political ecology may allow us to explain how "factors become causes"' (1994 p4). In the framework outlined below, if any of the four criteria listed are limiting and below a certain threshold they are identified as the reason for the detrimental action that causes degradation. In this way the framework provides a deeper insight into the cause of degradation. Thus decision-makers will maintain and improve the land if the following criteria are fulfilled:

They have a perception of a problem of degradation

Unless soil improvement is an unintended consequence of other action, or an unconscious routine activity, a perception of there being a problem of degradation is one of the prerequisites for action being taken to prevent degradation. While farmers are often proficient at perceiving subtle changes in the soil, some aspects of change are very difficult to detect as processes are slow and plant productivity may not be affected until a critical threshold level is reached (Kinlund, 1991; Blaikie and Brookfield, 1987). It is important to obtain an understanding not only of how soil is perceived to be changing but also of how concepts relating to the soil are culturally constructed. This is an important factor mediating responses to structural forces and may account for farmers not acting in predictable (determined) ways. Measuring perception in terms of western meanings may lead to misinterpretation as an example in the case study below shows.

They hold the knowledge of how to remedy the problem

This term is used here to refer specifically to knowledge of ways to improve the land. Boserup (1965, p22) identifies knowledge as a critical factor affecting intensification. She writes '[I]t has no doubt happened in many cases that a population, faced with a critically increasing density was without knowledge of any types of fertilisation techniques. They might shorten the period of fallow without any other changes in methods. This constellation would typically lead to a decline in crop yields and sometimes to an exhaustion of land resources.' Often though, soil and water conservation is the principle underlying indigenous farming methods (Pawluk et al., 1992). The actor-oriented approach stresses the mutual determination of internal and external variables and this is relevant to the knowledge of soil improvement techniques. Long and van der Ploeg (1994, p83) note for example, that farmers' knowledge includes both indigenous experience and introduced techniques, as outside ideas and technology are absorbed and reworked. In addition, knowledge should not be seen as a stock that is easily definable and ready for extraction and incorporation, but as multiple, partial, fragmented and socially and politically differentiated. As with perception, an analysis that allows an exploration of multiple constructions of rural peoples' knowledge is required (Scoones and Thompson, 1992).

They have the incentive to remedy the problem

Individuals need to have the incentive or motivation to maintain the productive capacity of the land and a lack of incentive is therefore a potential cause of degradation. Neo-liberal economists have regarded incentives in soil and water conservation projects as important and schemes have frequently been established providing monetary incentives to encourage the adoption of promoted measures. That these have rarely yielded the desired effects illustrates that incentives should not be regarded purely as 'external'. The term should be used in its widest sense and is particularly culture-bound. There is usually sufficient incentive to invest in the land, for example, where land users have control over their own resources and lives. Most notable factors affecting incentive might be the security of tenure and prices for produce but other factors are important such as the relative priority accorded to land productivity maintenance (over, for example, off-farm activities that may yield higher returns to labour). Disincentives may include feelings of exploitation such as through extraction of surplus and fluctuating prices, and powerlessness, such as may result from imposed conservation measures.

It is also important to recognize the way in which external incentives are internally mediated. Land quality (an initial 'external' environmental condition), for example, is an important factor affecting incentive to improve land (with better land tending to receive more investment) but this factor constantly changes as the recursive practices of social agents alter land quality in intended and unintended ways.

They have the capability to remedy the problem

Capability can be seen as a function of available resources (conservation or land improvement often require additional land, labour or capital) and the social relations determining access and control (institutional/community and household). For example, the capability to manage common property resources without degradation implies an effective system of social organization where mutually agreed upon rules or policies are developed and adhered to. At an individual or household level, capability implies the power to make decisions and effect action. The concept of 'environmental entitlements' is similar to capability in this context. Environmental entitlements, Mearns explains, are the 'combined outcome of both (a) the environmental resource bundles that people have command over as a result of their ownership, their own production or their membership of a particular social or economic group; and (b) their ability to make effective use of those resource bundles' (Mearns, 1995, p8). Given the complexity of these entitlements it is clear that changes to external factors affecting capability (such as removal of subsidies on artificial fertilizers with structural adjustment programmes) will not be responded to in determined ways.

All aspects of this analytical framework are recognized by other authors and discussed frequently in the literature in relation to land degradation, but have not been used together as an all-encompassing framework for understanding farmer rationale and the links with wider structural forces. The four criteria listed here are not independent of each other. Knowledge and power, for example, are intimately related and therefore knowledge and capability may be positively correlated. Or, if the incentive to improve land is great enough, resources may be mobilized to increase the capability to improve land and as such the distinction between capability and incentive may become blurred. The thresholds are socially determined and they are constantly changing through the recursive experience of the decision-makers.

A parallel may be drawn between this analytical framework and the different perspectives on the causes of land degradation previously outlined. This is not surprising, given that these categories refer to factors that, if limiting, are identified in the various meta-narratives as the reason behind the action causing degradation. The paternalist perspective identifies land degradation as an environmental problem that has technical solutions and blames ignorant farmers for environmental damage, thus focusing on lack of *knowledge* and *perception* as the cause of the problem. The economic perspective attributes price and property regimes providing inappropriate *incentives* as the cause of environmental problems. The populist and neo-Marxist perspectives consider the cause to be a lack of access to resources and poverty through exploitation or imposition of inappropriate technical knowledge, believing that people have both sufficient knowledge and incentive to prevent land degradation if they are able to. Thus these perspectives recognize the need to understand the *capability* constraints that cause degrading land use practices. The neo-Malthusian perspective also indicates reduced capability due to declining *per capita* access to resources. Thus the framework has explanatory value without the use of a priori explanations.

Blaikie and Brookfield (1987, p240) note that 'ignorance of the consequences of actions on the land, the reckless quest for profit, poverty and deprivation leading to "desperate ecocide", pressure of population on resources (PPR) – on which we remain somewhat ambivalent – and population decline all emerge as underlying causal agents of degradation'. Ignorance of the consequences, relates to lack of perception of the problem, reckless quest for profit results from insufficient incentive to maintain the land and rapid population growth and poverty reduce the capability to maintain land. Whitesell (1994, p2) criticises Blaikie and Brookfield's conclusions as resorting to 'conditional and multiple hypotheses' instead of integrating their case studies into a set of theoretical concepts. The causes of degradation are so wide ranging that the possibility or value of an overarching theory may be questioned. The analytical framework proposed in this research, does however, provide a universal 'model' for explanation while allowing for complex and diverse reasons spanning the external to the cultural. It avoids determinism by accommodating recursive practices and the mutually affecting relations between people and their environment. Understanding the reasons for actions affecting the environment helps to reveal the underlying processes or 'how factors become causes'.[4]

Case Study: Tanzania

The Uluguru Mountains lie approximately 200km directly west of Dar-es-Salaam. The mountains rise to an altitude of 2600m and are composed of steeply dissected slopes. Colonial administrators in the 1940s believed the area to be suffering from land degradation as a result of population pressure (see Jones, 1996a for a more detailed discussion). However, since the failed attempts to implement bench terraces in the early 1950s, little research has been undertaken in the area and population densities continue to rise (currently standing at about 160 persons/km^2). The Luguru have maintained a strong system of matriliny despite highly commercialized vegetable production and social mechanisms mitigate against the development of proletarianization (see Jones, 1996b).

The Luguru almost universally grow maize and beans as their primary staple crops during the rainy season. A system of ladder terracing has developed which incorporates crop residues back into the system and minimizes erosion and landsliding. However, this method involves pulling down soil from upslope to bury the residues and therefore is gradually resulting in shallow and less fertile soils on the upper slopes (Jones, 1995). Temperate vegetables are grown during the dry season on wider flatter terraces with access to irrigation water. These are reverted to ladder terraces for rainy season cultivation. Although on the surface there appears to be little differentiation of practices and all farmers face the same structural conditions as determined by the wider economy (for example, the costs of fertilizer, maize bran, pesticides, seeds and prices for livestock and crops), a wide variety of livelihood strategies emerge with differing implications for the way land is managed.

The criteria need to be examined with relation to the power individuals have to influence land management outcomes. In Mgeta, men and women work the same hours on the same tasks on the same fields, (although women undertake 80% of domestic tasks in addition, Mtenga, 1993). This relative absence of agricultural division of labour leads to rather undifferentiated interests, knowledges and perceptions, and most constraints and incentives affect men and women equally. The results from chi square tests revealed no significant difference in men's and women's knowledge and perceptions (Jones, 1995).

Perception

Before considering the extent to which the Luguru consider degradation to be a problem, it was first necessary to explore local concepts relating to the soil. Soil *fertility* was fairly consistently conceptualized as the capability of soils to produce crop yields (the greater the yield the more fertile the soil). Soil *erosion*, on the other hand, appeared initially to mean different things to different people until one Mluguru eloquently explained why: 'Soil erosion occurs during heavy rains. A large portion of soil may be broken off and washed away by rapidly flowing water. Everything in its path is destroyed; crops, terraces, even trees and houses. This is "large soil erosion"; it is like an earthquake, a natural catastrophe and nothing can stop it. This is what most people regard as soil erosion. But in Mgeta there is another type of erosion "small soil erosion" where soil moves only a short distance. Most of us do not regard this as erosion because it is not harmful to the land.'

It has been widely assumed by outsiders that the Luguru do not consider erosion to be a problem because they resisted the measures promoted by the colonial administrators. However, erosion is almost universally considered a problem, primarily because it is defined in terms of landsliding. 'Small erosion', or sheetwash and rilling, was not considered a serious problem and it is likely that the ladder terraces are effective in curbing it (Temple and Murray-Rust, 1972). However, one unintended consequence of the ladder terracing system is gradual soil movement downslope. People agree that as part of the practice, they pull the soil downslope but do not believe that this is causing a reduction in soil depth on the upper slopes. This might lend one towards thinking that the Luguru are irrational or wrong. However, given the deeply weathered nature of the subsoil and the continual re-incorporation of crop residues (resulting in yields still being obtained from these upper slopes) this view can be better understood.

It was widely perceived that the maize fields, particularly on sloping land, were becoming exhausted and it was often reported that 'the land is tired'. All those interviewed (N = 40) regarded the forest soils to be different from the cultivated soils and 62.5 per cent thought fertility was the main difference with forest soils more fertile. In terms of yields, 47.5 per cent felt that they were declining and 95 per cent of these people attributed the decline to erosion and exhaustion. Only 2.5 per cent of people felt yields were increasing (solely because of increased artificial fertilizer use) and 45 per cent of people felt yields varied annually depending on rainfall and fertilizer inputs primarily.[5]

Given the widespread perception that land degradation is a problem in this area, this criterion cannot be considered to be operating as a limiting factor to the improvement of soil. As further evidence for this point, interviewing revealed that those who felt that the measures were insufficient to retain fertility and reduce erosion practised on average 1.9 techniques that they considered to reduce fertility and 1.1 techniques to reduce erosion, whereas those who felt the measures were sufficient practised 2.9 and 2.7, respectively.[6] Thus, those areas likely to be experiencing a greater level of land degradation because fewer measures are taken to prevent it are perceived by their land managers to be degrading.

Knowledge

When asked, farmers knew on average 3.7 methods to improve soil fertility and 2.2 methods to reduce erosion. These included a wide range of techniques for improving the land. Many were not mentioned yet people considered them to be beneficial when asked specifically and as such this figure under-represents knowledge of soil fertility improvement techniques. The practice of ladder terracing, for example, is very much an unconscious action and a social norm, predominantly routinely rather than consciously practised. While it was unanimously explained that residues are buried to improve the fertility of the soil (a universal practice in Mgeta), when asked what methods individuals used to improve soil fertility, 30 per cent of people failed to mention it.[7] Pig manure and artificial fertilizer were identified as most beneficial for fertility improvement. These both represent a net import of nutrients into the area (pigs need to be fed on maize bran to be profitable and this has to be brought into the area). The remaining techniques such as mulching, burning, intercropping, agroforestry and fallowing primarily represent maximizing nutrient recycling within the system. Trees were most preferred for erosion reduction as their roots reduced the incidence of landsliding. Few techniques were 'known' to reduce 'large soil erosion' but this reflects the way it is defined in terms of mass movements, rather than limited knowledge.

It is of much significance that people employed on average 1.5 fewer fertility improving measures and 0.4 fewer erosion prevention measures than they knew about and thus a lack of knowledge of techniques cannot be a limiting factor contributing to soil improvement. All farmers said that they would keep pigs and manure their fields if they were financially able to do so.

Incentive

Because of the strong ideology of self-reliance which places food crop production at the fore and a system of inheritance that ensures security of tenure, incentives to improve land are strong. Private ownership of land is considered by most economists as a prerequisite for investment in conservation measures. However, Noronha and Lethem (1983) explain that the key is 'rights to possession'. Long-term tenurial land rights in Mgeta are secure and lack of legal titles for land or the absence of a significant market for land do not act as a disincentive to improve land (out of 173 fields only 6 were purchased and 1 leased, although seasonal renting is more common). Furthermore, it is a social norm that the land manager, whether she or he be a tenant or owner, has a duty to maintain land productivity.

Returns to labour affect incentives significantly and in this area greater returns may be obtained from off-farm employment than investment in conservation. Thus, seasonal and semi-permanent out-migration is an important livelihood strategy, reflected in the sex ratios for the 15–44 age group of 0.78 in 1988.[8] However, this factor is strongly mediated by the fact that the Luguru are very attached to the mountains, as their ancestral home, for the cool climate and low incidence of malaria (Brain, 1980). Were it not for this, migration might be expected to be higher. Thus, it is mostly men who do not have secure access to land in this matrilineal society (ie single males or married men from poor clans with low fall-back positions). They have lower incentives to invest in the land and tend to migrate and seek off-farm employment.

Land quality is a very important 'external' variable affecting incentives in this area and therefore investment levels. Barbier (1990, p53) notes that 'the more productive or profitable the land use the more farmers will be willing to maintain and invest in better land management and erosion control practices'. In Mgeta, greater returns to labour and investment can be obtained on the relatively flat, irrigable land suitable for vegetable production, therefore there is a greater incentive to invest in this type of land and it receives much more attention than steeply sloping fields. Here the reflexive relations between people and their environment are particularly evident. Higher productivity irrigable land has been improved over time creating nutrient rich hot-spots (Scoones, 1997), which further increases its value for commercial production. Most maize fields in contrast, benefit only from nutrient recycling, with infrequent additions of artificial fertilizer, as explained below.

Maximizing yields takes a higher priority locally than maximizing soil fertility. These objectives are usually mutually complementary, with the possible exception of artificial fertilizers application. Artificial fertilizer is favoured over pig manure on maize fields that are some distance from the homesteads (homesteads are usually built nearer the flat, better quality irrigable land) because pig manure is heavy to transport. Artificial fertilizer provides a more concentrated source of nutrients than pig manure and so its relative transport costs are cheaper. While it may help to maintain the yields (and therefore provide protective vegetation cover and residues for reincorporation), it is a poor substitute for organic matter, which releases nutrients more slowly and helps to bind the soil together. Artificial fertilizer is reported by local people to harden the soil and make it more difficult to work and causes the crops to 'burn' (due to acidification). The recursive practices of farmers then, due to the different structures of incentives on different land types have accentuated differences in land quality (Jones, 1995).

Some wealthy farmers invest less than they could afford to in improving the productivity of their maize fields. This is because maize can be purchased more cheaply on the market than it costs to cultivate. Returns to investment therefore rarely warrant the use of pig manure or optimal artificial fertilizer applications, so wealthy people direct investment elsewhere (commercial vegetable production, trade and house improvement). While poorer households prefer to grow maize because of low access to cash incomes that would enable them to buy it, the persistence of a strong self-sufficiency ideology in this area means that wealthier households continue to grow maize without making investments in the land that they could afford.

Thus, low access to land, poor quality land, distance from homesteads and low returns for maize production all generate relatively low incentives to the improvement of land in some areas, despite secure tenure. Incentives to invest in land suitable for vegetable production are strong.

Capability

Land: Land shortage was the main reason cited for people being unable to implement erosion prevention methods (43 per cent) as trees both absorb land and shade crops. It was also cited as a constraint to improving fertility by 26 per cent of people (referring to the desire for longer and more frequent fallows). Thus, population pressure could be regarded as a factor contributing to degradation in Mgeta but other factors discussed here mediate this factor, affecting whether the outcome is intensification and soil improvment or degradation.

Labour: Local people will not convert their ladder terraces into more permanent terraces because they say they would be too labour intensive to maintain (it would involve digging residues into the soil twice annually rather than pulling soil downslope to bury them). With significant rates of out-migration, labour can hardly be said to be a constraining variable to land improvement – thus returns to labour, as outlined above, must be regarded as more significant.

Capital: Poverty is reported to be increasing in the area as the removal of the subsidy on artificial fertilizers combined with increased competition for vegetable produce is causing a 'reproductive squeeze' (Blaikie, 1985). Whilst it has been noted that there is relatively little wealth differentiation in Mgeta due to 'internal' (cultural) redistribution mechanisms (Jones, 1996b), that which does exist clearly indicates the role of poverty in causing land degradation. A financial constraint was the main reason cited for not being able to improve the fertility of the land (noted by 67 per cent of people). Pigs and artificial fertilizer, ranked most highly in terms of their capacity to improve the soil are also the most expensive measures. However, it does not follow that it is the poorest who degrade the land most (or that it is the wealthiest who invest most in the land, as shown in the previous section). What actually happens in Mgeta is that the poorest are often eager to sell their labour, as they are desperate for cash income to buy necessities. In so doing they are rarely able to cultivate all their own fields and so these fields benefit from more regular fallowing than those belonging to wealthier people. Furthermore, poorer households sometimes have access to land suitable for vegetable cultivation. Vegetable production requires much investment to be profitable (eg pig manure), which can rarely be afforded. Therefore, this land is frequently rented to wealthier farmers and benefits from the additional nutrients.

The priority given to pig manure application over manure from other livestock (the nutrients from which are more concentrated and take longer to become available to plants) and burying residues over mulching (which has a relatively slower rate of decomposition due to lower moisture) is evidence of nutrient and land shortage. It reflects farmers' 'inability' to practice other methods that may require a short-term sacrifice in yields for a long-term increase in productivity (such as alley-cropping).

Concluding Comments

The use of this framework in an actor-oriented context has illustrated how it is possible to avoid a 'shopping list' of causes by examining the webs of interactions between different variables. The diversity of outcomes in terms of land management and soil quality can be explained by grounding concepts of land management in the everyday lives of men and women. A complex picture emerges as the various responses to the same structural conditions are explored. A financial constraint (poverty) emerges as a primary cause of land degradation on the more productive soils, although poorer peoples' strategies include renting out fields, hiring labour, and growing less demanding crops (such as cassava) help to avoid land degradation. On the low fertility land, poor returns and distance from homesteads are primary reasons for lack of investment. Here the reflexive relationship between structure ('external') and action ('internal') is evident. As less is invested in the more distant soils, the poorer quality they become and the less incentive there is to invest in them. This may be responded to by a change in action to: (1) fallowing, although this is made difficult by higher population densities, (2) increased inputs, which is difficult due to increasing poverty, (3) out-migration, which is not a preferred option but is practised by many single, landless males or those from poor clans with low access to land or (4) land exhaustion, which is an outcome on many farmers' sloping maize fields.

Local people perceived soil erosion primarily in terms of landsliding, which in Mgeta has swept away terraces and trees. If the social construction of erosion had not been understood, it would have been logical to assume that the lack of knowledge of methods to prevent it was an important causal factor in land degradation, supporting the paternalist perspective. Also, many people in the area are so poor that economists would see it as irrational for them not to sell their land and/or migrate and sell their labour. Cultural reasons, such as strong ancestral bonds, supportive family networks and the ideology of matrilineal inheritance account for their apparent irrationality. Thus, structural factors or external forces enter the existing lifeworlds of groups and individuals and are clearly mediated and transformed internally (Long, 1992). The value of determinism is undermined.

This paper has presented a framework to show how factors affecting degradation become causes. It focused on the decision-making context of the land user as a medium for explanation rather than a grand-theoretical perspective. Such a focus may be of value in explaining other forms of environmental degradation such as deforestation. Other authors (eg Barraclough and Ghimire, 1996; Scoones, 1997) have called for a move away from simplistic and deterministic explanations of environmental degradation. It is hoped that this paper offers an approach capable of explaining spatial heterogeneity, and generating embedded and context-specific studies, to deepen understandings and enable the formulation of more appropriate policy.

References

Barraclough, S L, Ghimire, K B (1996) 'Deforestation in Tanzania: beyond simplistic generalisations'. *The Ecologist* **26**(3): 104–109

Barrow, C J (1991) *Land Degradation: Development and Breakdowns of Terrestrial Environments*, Cambridge University Press, Cambridge

Barbier, E (1990) 'Natural resource degradation: policy, economics and management', in J T Winpenny (ed) *Development Research: The Environmental Challenge*, ODI, London

Biot, Y, Blaikie, P M, Jackson, C, Palmer-Jones, R (1995) 'Rethinking research on land degradation in developing countries'. World Bank Discussion Paper No 289, World Bank, Washington DC

Blaikie, P M (1985) *The Political Economy of Soil Erosion in Developing Countries*, Longman Scientific and Technical, Harlow, Essex

Blaikie, P, Brookfield, H (1987) *Land Degradation and Society*, Methuen, London

Blaikie, P (1994) 'Political ecology in the 1990s: an evolving view of nature and society'. Proceedings from the Political Ecology Workshop, MSU, April

Boserup, E (1965) *The Conditions of Agricultural Growth*, Allen and Unwin, London

Brain, J L (1980) 'The Uluguru land usage scheme: success and failure'. *Journal of Developing Areas* **14**: 175–190

Fay, B, Moon, J D (1994) 'What would an adequate philosophy of social science look like?' in M Martin, L C McIntyre (eds) *Readings in the Philosophy of Social Science*, MIT Press, Cambridge, MA, pp21–35

Giddens, A (1984) *The Constitution of Society: Outline of the Theory of Structuration*, Polity Press, Cambridge

Jackson, P, Smith, S J (1984) *Exploring Social Geography*, Allen and Unwin, London

Jones, S (1995) 'Deconstructing the degradation debate: a study of land degradation in the Uluguru mountains, Tanzania'. PhD thesis, School of Development Studies, University of East Anglia, Norwich

Jones, S J (1996a) 'Degradation discourses in the Uluguru mountains, Tanzania: evolution and influences'. *Journal of Rural Studies* **12**(2): 187–199

Jones, S J (1996b) 'Farming systems and nutrient flows: a study from the Uluguru mountains, Tanzania'. *Geography* **353**(81, 4): 289–300

Kinlund, P (1991) *Does Land Degradation Matter? The case of Land Degradation and its Consequences in NE Botswana*, Stockholm University, School of Geography Working Paper

Leach, M, Mearns, R, Scoones, I (1997) 'Challenges to community-based sustainable development: dynamics, institutions, entitlements'. IDS Bulletin **28**(4): 4–14

Little, D (1991) *Varieties of Social Explanation: An Introduction to the Philosophy of Social Science*, Westview Press, Oxford

Long, N (1992) 'An actor-oriented paradigm, Part 1', in: N Long and A Long (eds) *Battlefields of Knowledge*, Routledge, London, pp3–467

Long, N, van der Ploeg, J D (1994) 'Heterogeneity, actor and structure: towards a reconstitution of the concept of structure'. in D Booth (ed) *Rethinking Social Development: Theory, Research and Practice*, Longman Scientific and Technical, Harlow, Essex

Mearns, R (1995) 'Environmental entitlements: an outline framework for analysis and a Mongolian case study'. IDS Working Paper 15, University of Sussex, Brighton

Mortimore, M (1989) *Adapting to Drought*, Cambridge University Press, Cambridge

Mtenga, N A (1993) 'Gender roles in the domestic and farming systems of the Tchenzema Ward, Morogoro district, Tanzania'. MSc Dissertation, Sokoine University of Agriculture, Morogoro, Tanzania

Noronha, R, Lethem, F J (1983) 'Traditional land tenures and land use systems in the design of agricultural projects'. World Bank Staff Working Paper No 561

Pawluk, R R, Sandor, J A, Tabor, J A (1992) 'The role of indigenous soil knowledge in agricultural development'. *Journal of Soil and Water Conservation*, 298–302

Roe, E (1991) 'Development narratives, or making the best of blueprint development'. *World Development* **19**(4): 287–300

Rosenau, P M (1992) *Post-modernism and the Social Sciences: Insights, Inroads and Intrusions*, Princeton University Press, New Jersey

Scoones, I (1997) 'The dynamics of soil fertility change: historical perspectives on environmental transformation from Zimbabwe'. *The Geographical Journal* **163**(2): 161–169

Scoones, I, Thompson, J (1994) 'Knowledge, power and agriculture: towards a theoretical understanding'. in I Scoones, J Thompson (eds) *Beyond Farmer First*, Intermediate Technology Publications Ltd, IIED, London, pp16–31

Siddle, D, Swindell, K (1990) *Rural Change in Tropical Africa*, Basil Blackwell, Oxford

Stonich, S (1989) 'The dynamics of social processes and environmental destruction: a Central American case study'. *Population and Development Review* **15**(2): 269–296

Swift, J (1996) 'Desertification: narratives, winners and losers'. in M Leach, R Mearns (eds) *The Lie of the Land: Challenging Received Wisdom on the African Environment*, James Currey, Oxford and Heinemann, Portsmouth, pp54–72

Temple, PH, Murray–Rust, DH (1972) 'Sheet wash measurements on erosion plots at Mfumbwe, Eastern Uluguru mountains, Tanzania'. *Geografiska Annaler* **54A**(3–4): 195–202

Tolba, M K, El-Kholy, O A et al (1992) *The World Environment 1972–1992: Two Decades of Challenges*, UNEP/Chapman & Hall, London

Watmore, S, Boucher, S (1993) 'Bargaining with nature: the discourse and practice of "environmental planning gain"'. Transactions of the Institute of British Geographers N.S. 18, 166–178

Whitesell, T (1994) 'Some thoughts on the unresolved epistemological dilemmas confronting political ecology'. Proceedings from the Political Ecology Workshop, MSU, April 1994

Yapa, L (1996) 'What causes poverty? A postmodern view'. *Annals of the Association of American Geographers* **86**(4): 707–728

Notes

1   Such postmodern stances are being more frequently adopted and reference is being made increasingly to narratives in the development and environment literature (see, for example, Roe, 1991; Watmore and Boucher, 1993; Swift, 1996; Yapa, 1996). While the postmodern approach may be valuable in uncovering implicit and frequently erroneous assumptions, and for understanding the dominance of one view over another, it offers little in the way of alternate methods of understanding causes of change and formulating action. Rosenau (1992), however, suggests that there are two types of postmodernist, the sceptic and the affirmative. While the sceptic argues that neither truth nor reality exists, the affirmative believes in grounded local and multiple truths. Thus, the approach adopted in this paper is consistent with the affirmative perspective – by providing a more situated and non-deterministic approach it avoids the pitfalls of the meta-narrative without resorting to relativism.

2   It is not suggested here that it is possible to present a whole or an objective picture but the framework presented here goes some way towards removing some of the biases.

3   Leach et al (1997) provide a valuable framework, applied in an environmental context and set, like this study, in the context of an actor-oriented approach. However, their framework, derived from Sen's entitlements approach, is geared towards understanding how people (and institutions) effect command over their resources and is of minimal value in explaining the social causes of environmental degradation.

4   The framework presented above cannot claim to aspire to the same depth or consider all the components of the type of actor-oriented approach used by Long (1992). For example, an exploration of life-worlds is quite central to the actor-oriented approach, while the analytical framework used here focuses on specific components of the lifeworld relevant to understanding the causes of land degradation. It explores meanings primarily in the form of soil erosion and fertility. It examines aspects of lifeworlds to understand the multiple objectives and realities of land users so that the opportunities, interests and constraints individuals have in preventing land degradation can be identified.

5   The remaining 5 per cent of people did not know.

6   This says nothing of the extent to which these measures are practised. In addition, the actual techniques practised may be greater as some are pre-attentive.

7   This is evidence of the importance of unconscious and routine activities highlighted by Giddens (1984). It also demonstrates the need, in using the framework, to observe what people do in addition to what they say.

8   The sex ratio for Tanzania as a whole in the 15–64 age group, by comparison, was 0.94 in the same year.

Index